THE LAW OF CORPORATIONS

IN A NUTSHELL

Fourth Edition

By

ROBERT W. HAMILTON

Minerva House Drysdale Regents Chair in Law
The University of Texas at Austin

ST. PAUL, MINN.
WEST PUBLISHING CO.
1996

Nutshell Series, In a Nutshell, the Nutshell Logo and the WP symbol are registered trademarks of West Publishing Co. Registered in the U.S. Patent and Trademark Office.

Library of Congress Cataloging-in-Publication Data

Hamilton, Robert W., 1931–
    The law of corporations in a nutshell / by Robert W. Hamilton. —
4th ed.
        p.   cm. — (Nutshell series)
    Includes index.
    ISBN 0–314–09874–7
    1. Corporation law—United States.   I. Title.   II. Series.
KF1414.3.H35   1996
346.73 ' 066—dc20
[347.30666]
                                            96–8960
                                            CIP

ISBN 0–314–09874–7

OUTLINE

OUTLINE

OUTLINE

*

TABLE OF CASES

References are to Pages

---

*

THE LAW OF CORPORATIONS

IN A NUTSHELL

Fourth Edition

*

CHAPTER ONE

THE CORPORATION IN PERSPECTIVE

§ 1.1 What Is a Corporation? The Concept of an Artificial Entity

A corporation may be formed simply by filing an appropriate document with a state official, usually the secretary of state, and paying the appropriate fee. (Some states, however, require additional steps; see § 3.3 of this Nutshell.) Assuming that the necessary steps have been followed, what has been created?

The simplest and usually the most useful way of viewing a corporation is to consider it an *artificial person* or *artificial entity* independent of the owners or investors. This artificial person may conduct a business or businesses in its own name much in the same way that a "real" person could. Business is done, assets acquired, contracts entered into, and liabilities incurred, all in the name of the corporation rather than in the name of any individual. This artificial person has most of the legal rights of a "real" person: It may sue or be sued as though it were a "real" person, it must pay taxes, it may apply for business licenses in its own name, it may have its own bank account, it may hire employees, and so forth.

Conducting a business in this way often has advantages over conducting business in the name of one or more individuals. The most obvious advantage is that the corporation is unlimitedly liable for the debts and obligations of the business but the shareholders are not, since in theory all debts are the artificial entity's obligations, not the shareholders'. In effect, the shareholders risk what they

1

have invested but no more; in legal language the shareholders enjoy *limited liability*.

A corporation has other characteristics that distinguish it from other business forms:

(a) The existence of the corporation is not dependent on who the owners or investors are at any one time. If shareholders die, or decide to sell out, or what have you, the corporation continues to exist as a separate entity. In legal language, a corporation has *continuity of life*.

(b) The corporation does not have a limited life span. Rather it has *perpetual existence*. One should not be misled, however, about what "perpetual existence" means: It does not really mean that all corporations will continue until the end of time but rather that a corporation will continue indefinitely until the owners decide to dissolve it or merge it into another business.

(c) The management of the corporation is vested in a board of directors (which is elected by the shareholders) and not in the shareholders themselves. There is *centralized management* in a corporation. Indeed, the shareholders as such have no right at all to interfere with the operations of the corporation (except for very specific rights such as a limited right to inspect the books and records of the corporation).

(d) The ownership interests of the shareholders may be sold or transferred to third persons without the approval or consent of the corporation or other shareholders. There is free transferability of interest in a corporation.

These various characteristics of a corporation constitute the default form of corporation. A corporation that is formed without any specialized planning has each of these basic characteristics. However, there may be a great deal of contract-type planning that goes on within a specific corporate structure, and these basic characteristics may be modified significantly by agreement among the interested parties. The basic point is that the concept of a corporation greatly simplifies things by permitting a business to have a separate legal identity independent of the flesh-and-blood persons who own and operate it.

The artificial entity theory has been criticized as being unrealistic and formalistic. It is true that it is a reification, the personalization of an abstract concept. The starting point for this criticism is a fundamental truth about corporations: flesh-and-blood people underlie every corporation, and are essential to everything a corporation does. Some individual must decide what the corporation is to do; some individual must actually do the required act on behalf of the corporation, because manifestly an artificial entity has no arms, legs, mouth, or eyes. Some individual will ultimately reap the profits earned by the corporation, and some person must ultimately bear any loss. In realistic terms, a corporation is simply a device by which some individuals conduct a business and the same or different individuals share in the profit or loss. Professor Hohfeld summarized this view of the corporation when he said, "Strangely enough, it has not always been perceived with perfect clearness that transacting business under the forms, methods, and procedure pertaining to so-called corporations is simply another mode by which individuals or natural persons can enjoy their property and engage in business. Just as several individuals may transact business collectively as partners, so they may as members of a corporation—the corporation being nothing more than an association of such individuals * * *." He added, when "we speak of the corporation * * * contracting in the corporate name, * * * we are merely employing a short and convenient mode of describing the complex and peculiar process by which the benefits and burdens of the corporate members are worked out * * *." Hohfeld, Fundamental Legal Conceptions 197 (1923). Hohfeld's analysis illustrates the fallacy of accepting uncritically the "artificial entity" theory. A corporation is treated as an entity for most purposes but it need not be treated as an entity for all purposes. At some point the reality which Hohfeld describes may control over the formalistic argument being relied on. For this reason, arguments grounded solely on the artificial entity theory and not supported by considerations of fairness, justice, or policy have sometimes not prevailed.

Most provisions of modern corporation statutes are consistent with the theory that a corporation is a separate legal entity. As a "short and convenient mode" of describing most of the powers of a corporation and the legal relationships surrounding it, therefore, the artificial entity concept is extremely useful. It should be emphasized, however, that a corporation possesses these statutory attributes not because it is an artificial entity but because the statute so provides. And it does not follow that because a corporation possesses many entity attributes under the statutes, it necessarily possesses other entity attributes as well.

§ 1.2 What Is a Corporation? Other Theories

The artificial entity theory is the most useful one in the context of most modern problems, particularly in the case of a newly formed corporation just starting out. However, there have been other attempts to describe the theoretical concept of a corporation. These other formulations often arise in situations involving the power of states to regulate corporations or the rights or duties of participants in a corporation among themselves. They include:

(a) The corporation may be viewed as a "privilege," "concession," "franchise," or "grant" from the state which allows the owners and investors to conduct business as a corporation. Conceptually, when documents are filed with the secretary of state, that officer's issuance of a "charter" or "certificate of incorporation" can be viewed as a grant by the state of a franchise to conduct business in corporate form. This conception had greater importance in an earlier day when significant limitations or conditions were imposed on the privilege of incorporating. Indeed, in an earlier age, charters were granted individually by the state legislature and not through a simple filing process; when a charter was obtained by legislative enactment, the concept of franchise or grant had considerable meaning. Today, incorporation involves only routine or ministerial acts. However, the concession theory is still sometimes referred to in the literature in connection with the social policy debate about the appropriate role of large corporations in modern society (see § 1.9 of this Nutshell.) Further, the notion that a corporation receives a "franchise" from the state of incorporation apparently establishes that the business must be taxed as a corporation under the federal Internal Revenue Code. States also may impose special "franchise taxes" solely on businesses conducted in the corporate form.

(b) The corporate charter may also be viewed as a "compact" or "contract." Depending on the circumstances, the parties to this contract may be:

(i) The shareholders themselves; or

(ii) The shareholders and the corporation; or

(iii) The corporation and the state.

For example, the contract theory often appears in situations where disputes have arisen between classes or members. In a dispute between preferred and common shareholders, for example, it is not uncommon to refer to the provisions of the charter that describes the rights of preferred shareholders as "the preferred shareholders' contract" which, many cases state, constitutes the full and exclusive description of the rights of that class of share-holders as against the common shareholders.

In the famous decision in Dartmouth College v. Wood-ward (S.Ct.1819), the Court considered the charter of Dartmouth College to be a contract between the corporation and the state which was protected against unilateral impairment by the state under the contracts clause of the United States Constitution. This case is of historic interest today since all states have adopted constitutional provisions or incorporation statutes that specifically require every charter granted by that state to be subject to later amendments by the state. An example of such a statute is section 1.02 of the Model Business Corporation Act (1984).

The theories of corporateness discussed in these first two sections—the "artificial entity" theory, the "realistic" theory, the "concession" theory, the "franchise" theory, and the "contract" theory—are the traditional explanations of what a corporation "really" is. All help to explain the modern concept of a corporation. None is totally correct, none is totally wrong, and each has its place in defining the concept of corporateness.

§ 1.3   The "Nexus of Contracts" Theory

An entirely different and quite novel contract theory of the corporation has recently been developed by law and economics theorists. This theory is likely to be discussed early in every corporation law course. Usually known as the "nexus of contracts," this theory develops a model of the corporation as a bundle of contracts entered into by the managers of the enterprise with providers of labor, services, raw materials, capital, and contractual commitments of various types. In this model, the managers are viewed as the essential glue that fits together all the various contributors to the firm in the most efficient way.

The shareholders are viewed as contractual suppliers of residual capital, the group whose contract entitles them to the residual profits of the business and requires them to assume the primary risk of loss since all other providers to the corporation have priority in payment over them. Shareholders are not viewed as "owners" of the corporation. Rather, shareholders are only one of several contractual suppliers of debt capital, labor, and services to the corporation. A corporation is viewed entirely as a set of consensual relationships established by the managers of that corporation to best fit (i.e. to make most profitable and efficient) that particular business.

In this model there is no room for mandatory legal rules defining intra-corporate relationships; all such relationships are created by contract, either express or implicit, and these contractual relationships establish the most efficient enterprise. The role of corporation statutes therefore becomes very limited; at best, they provide an "off the rack" standard set of intra-corporate relationships that many individual corporations may find to be efficient, but every corporation must be free to modify this set of intra-corporate relationships by contract as they think appropriate. Since many corporations will find that their nexus of contracts are quite consistent with this "off the rack" standard form, the corporation statute avoids the costs involved if many different corporations were to "reinvent the wheel" and develop similar intra-corporate relationships from scratch.

The one clear implication of this theory is that no provision of the corporation statute should ever be mandatory.

What is one to make of this theory? Is it a "true" picture of the modern corporation? The correct answer to this question is that it is an economic model, a theoretical construct of the corporation, and not necessarily a description of the reality of what a corporation is. Models are of two basic types. A "normative" model is one that does not necessarily describe what reality is but what it ought to be. A "descriptive" model is one that describes what reality is; with the use of such a model, one can discover internal relationships that may not be visible in the real world. Professor McChesney has neatly encapsulated this distinction when he distinguishes "positive economics"—attempts to understand the world the way it is—from "normative economics"—a study of the way the world ought to be. McChesney, Positive Economics and All That—A Review of the Economic Structure of Corporate Law by Frank H. Easterbrook and Daniel R. Fischel, 61 Geo. Wash. L.Rev. 272 (1992). Initially, it is not clear in which category the nexus of contracts theory fits. Indeed, there is some dispute among law and economics scholars as to whether the nexus of contracts should be viewed as essentially normative, or as descriptive, or as both.

It seems clear that the nexus of contracts is not entirely descriptive of today's real world, even though many corporate relationships are clearly based on contract concepts. For example, a contract analysis seems entirely plausible for a corporation in which there are a relatively few shareholders who negotiate and hammer out the details of their relationship in advance. On the other hand, many corporate relationships appear not to be created by contract at all. This is particularly true of corporations whose shares are publicly traded on the securities markets. For example, it is difficult to say that a person who buys 100 shares of General Motors Corporation through a broker on the New York Stock Exchange has entered into a contract with General Motors. It is true, of course, that a purchaser of GM shares obtains certain rights. If GM declares a dividend, the shareholder is entitled to receive a payment. But the shareholder has not paid General Motors anything or agreed to do anything with or for General Motors. One might equally well argue that a farmer has entered into a contract with his land when he plants a crop.

The person who buys shares on the open market and becomes a GM shareholder is certainly bound to accept the judgment of a majority of the shareholders even if he is in the minority. Did the shareholder ever into a contract agreeing to this? Similarly, a corporation may make mid-course corrections in its financial plans without the consent of any of its shareholders. Where did the shareholder agree to such a provision? It seems that many corporate relationships with shareholders are in fact not contractual, at least in the sense that lawyers are accustomed to use the word "contracts." As a positive description of what the world "really" is, the nexus of contracts model appears deficient. If the artificial entity or franchise theories described in the previous section are criticized for codifying a fiction, the nexus of contracts approach may equally be criticized for finding contractual relationships in many situations where in fact no contract exists.

It is also simply not true that modern corporation statutes today provide "off the rack" models which participants in the corporation are completely free to amend or modify as they wish. Modern corporation statutes, while permitting corporations considerable freedom to establish internal rules as they see fit, also contain a large number of mandatory requirements that corporations have no power to waive or modify. An even larger number of mandatory rules appear in the federal and state securities laws that affect capital-raising by corporations.

While it may seem obvious to lawyers or law students that a person who buys one hundred shares of GM stock on the New York Stock Exchange does not thereby enter into a contract with GM in any meaningful sense, the defenders of the nexus of contracts theory argue that in such a situation an "implicit" contract nevertheless exists between GM and the new shareholder. To a lawyer, such statements do not make much sense. To a lawyer, an "implicit" contract suggests (to the extent the phrase means anything at all) a quasi-contract or implied-in-fact contract that the law constructs in the absence of actual agreement between the parties in order to do basic justice in the particular situation. Those concepts seem to have nothing to do with the investor who buys one hundred shares of General Motors.

When used by economists, the terms "contracts" or "implicit contracts" sometimes are used in a much broader sense than when the same words are used by lawyers. To a lawyer, the word "contract" means a real agreement that the legal system will enforce if one party tries to welsh. However, "to an economist, an implied contract is one that is enforced through marketplace mechanisms such as reputation effects rather than in a court, a means of enforcement that may not bring relief to the aggrieved party but will over time penalize parties who welsh." Gordon, The Mandatory Structure of Corporate Law, 89 Colum. L.Rev. 1549, 1550 (1989). In other words, to an economist, a "contract" may mean something quite different than what it means to a lawyer.

Another alternative explanation that also builds on the notion that a fundamental ambiguity exists as to what the word "contract" means is the suggestion that the economist views "implicit" contracts to be arrangements that do not involve actual consensual exchanges:

> Voluntary arrangements are contracts. Some may be negotiated over a bargaining table. Some may be a set of terms that are dictated by managers or investors and accepted or not; only the price is negotiated. Some may be fixed and must be accepted at the "going price" (as when people buy investment instruments traded in the market). Some may be implied by courts or legislatures trying to supply the terms that would have been negotiated had people addressed the problem explicitly. Even

terms that are invariant—such as the requirement that the board of directors act only by a majority of a quorum—are contractual to the extent that they produce offsetting voluntary arrangements. The result of all of these voluntary arrangements will be contractual. Easterbrook and Fischel, The Corporate Contract, 89 Colum. L.Rev. 1416, 1428 (1989).

It is probably difficult for most lawyers to accept the propositions that an arrangement created by a court "trying to supply the terms that would have been negotiated had people addressed the problem explicitly" is a contract, or that when parties "produce offsetting voluntary arrangements" they are entering into a contract that includes the rule that is being offset. If the economists' understanding of what "contract" means is accepted, the nexus of contracts theory virtually becomes a tautology.

The "nexus of contracts" may also be viewed as a normative model, incorporating what "ought to be" rather than "what is." It is this issue which has made the "nexus of contracts" theory so controversial. If the nexus of contracts is a normative model, corporation statutes should be changed to grant all corporations the freedom to adapt whatever contractual relationships they see fit, including the right to "opt out" of all mandatory legal requirements when their nexus of contracts suggests that that is efficient to do so. Normative arguments are more difficult to address than descriptive arguments. The principal argument against accepting the nexus of contracts approach used by economists as the normative model for statutory revisions is that it is based on certain fundamental assumptions that all persons have adequate knowledge about transactions and that they act rationally to maximize their wealth. Many persons, of course, act rationally and insist on being informed before a decision is made. Unfortunately, in the real world, there are people who do not meet the economic ideal. There is never perfect information on the part of all participants; many persons are unsophisticated and easy "marks" for the knowledgeable and unscrupulous; individuals sometimes act irrationally or perversely and may not seek to maximize their individual wealth in a rational manner; and unscrupulous individuals may act in opportunistic ways even though the reputational affects in the long run may cause a greater loss of wealth than gained by the opportunistic conduct. Further, there appears to be a never ending supply of such situations. The old adage that "there is a sucker born every minute," seems true in the sense that as one person in the market learns a bitter lesson, another unsophisticated person is entering it. Scoundrels who fleece the unsophisticated of their worldly goods may go to prison if they are caught. However, the markets in which scoundrels operate do not appear to be self-correcting as the basic premises on which the nexus of contracts model is based would seem to suggest. Thus, the assumptions about human behavior on which the nexus of contracts theory as a normative model rests are, at best, only partially correct.

Having criticized the "nexus of contracts" theory, it should be added that many law and economics scholars, including many teachers of corporation law, accept it as a valid normative model.

§ 1.4 The Development of Corporation Law in the United States

While the concept of a corporation was clearly developed by the time of Blackstone and can be traced much earlier, the modern law of corporations is largely a product of developments in the latter part of the nineteenth and the early part of the twentieth centuries. In the early part of the nineteenth century, business in the United States tended to be local in nature and of primary concern to individual states (though there were some exceptions such as the national bank). Corporations during this period were usually created for public or near public purposes—e.g. to build canals, bridges, or toll roads—and often enjoyed some monopoly privileges. However, intensive industrial development began in about 1825. The corporation proved to be an ideal instrument for this development since it could raise large amounts of capital from numerous investors and yet provide centralized direction of large industrial concerns. Even though many corporations rapidly became national in scope during the nineteenth century, they were and remained the descendants of local state-related enterprises, and received their charters from states rather than from the Federal Government.

Originally, state legislatures approved each individual corporate charter. Approval of a charter was a political issue, involving lobbying, campaign contributions, and worse. The first general incorporation statutes permitting businesses to incorporate for any lawful purpose by action of an administrative agency without specific legislative approval were adopted beginning in about 1840. However, throughout the nineteenth century, corporations in many states were subject to restrictions in terms of size, capital invested, and permissible purposes or powers. These artificial restrictions have gradually been removed in most states, though traces of them still remain in a few states.

Beginning roughly at the turn of the century, several states systematically began to seek to attract corporations to incorporate or reincorporate in their states. Statutes were amended to simplify procedures and make the applicable rules more attractive, particularly for large corporations doing business in most or all of the states. The uncrowned winner of this "race" in the early years of this century was the state of New Jersey. However, that state lost its position to its sister state of Delaware when New

Jersey decided to adopt a stronger regulatory stance toward corporations under Governor Woodrow Wilson. Today, near the end of the twentieth century, it is clear that the winner is Delaware. Over one-third of all the corporations listed on the New York Stock Exchange are incorporated in that single state even though most of these corporations have their home office and principal business operations elsewhere.

This competition among states for incorporation business was initially viewed as being rather unseemly, if not totally inappropriate. It was vividly described in Mr. Justice Brandeis's dissent in Liggett Co. v. Lee (S.Ct.1933) as being a race "not of diligence but of laxity." Thirty years later it was described by Professor Cary as a "race for the bottom". Cary, Federalism and Corporate Law: Reflections Upon Delaware, 83 Yale L.J. 663, 670 (1974). This "race" was viewed by critics basically as involving the systematic elimination of regulatory controls on the corporation, and the adoption of a "pro-management" stance whenever conflicts arose between managers and shareholders.

§ 1.5　Economic Analysis of the "Race for the Bottom"

Delaware, according to the "race for the bottom" theory, has been successful because it has permitted management excessive freedom to use and manipulate corporate assets as they wish, to the detriment of innocent and defenseless shareholders. Modern economic analysis tends to view this question in a very different light.

The underlying premise of modern economic analysis of corporations is that there is a fundamental conflict of interest between the managers of a publicly held corporation and the widely scattered owners of the enterprise. Managers that have an insignificant interest in the ownership of the corporation will make decisions that benefit their own personal interests rather than the interests of the owners as a whole. The "race for the bottom" advocates recognize this basic fact, but they also assume that the corporate agents can freely select the state of incorporation that is most favorable to them, and the shareholders can do nothing about that decision.

Judge Winter in a well known book [R. Winter, Government and the Corporation (1978)] pointed out that Cary's thesis was flawed because it overlooked the existence of an efficient and broad market for corporate securities. If Delaware in fact permits management to profit at the expense of shareholders (and other states do not, or do not as much), then earnings of Delaware corporations that are allocable to shareholders must be less than earnings of comparable corporations that are subject to more rigorous control elsewhere. The result must be that shares of Delaware corporations will trade at lower prices than shares of equivalent corporations incorporated elsewhere. Thus, if the "race to the bottom" theory is correct, corporations formed in Delaware will be at a disadvantage in raising capital and ultimately this disadvantage should cause publicly held corporations to incorporate elsewhere.

There are a couple of ways in which these inconsistent hypotheses may be tested. One is simply to examine the Delaware corporation statute and Delaware judicial decisions and compare them to other state statutes and judicial decisions in an effort to determine whether the differences are material and whether the differences favor management over shareholders. Admittedly, this is impressionistic rather than scientific since there are numerous variations from state to state and it is often unclear which provisions help management and which do not. However, an attempt to actually make such a comparison will yield the conclusion that one cannot find a significant number of points of Delaware law that are more favorable to management than the laws of other states.

While the Delaware statute is rather wordy, its substance is really not very different from the Model Business Corporation Act discussed in section 1.7 and the statutes of other states.

A second method is by using sophisticated statistical techniques to determine whether the reincorporation of corporations in Delaware from another state results in a decline in the share price of those corporations. If so, this would support Professor Cary's thesis. Several different statistical studies have been made to test the hypothesis; they tend to show that reincorporation in Delaware more often leads to an *increase* in share prices than a decrease; thus, they generally support Judge Winter's thesis and tend to disprove Professor Cary's. Unfortunately, share prices may be affected by other possible factors interacting at the time of a reincorporation decision, and it is not possible to say with certainty that Delaware law is the sole, or even the principal, cause of the favorable price movement. However, the fact that no one has found significant price decreases in any of these studies is itself an indication that Professor Cary's thesis as to the reason for the success of Delaware is not likely to be correct.

§ 1.6   What Explains Delaware's Success in Attracting Corporations?

If the "race to the bottom" thesis is not accepted, some explanation must be put forth to explain why Delaware has been so successful in the incorporation business. This also has been the subject of considerable discussion and commentary.

It is useful to first consider the reasons corporation attorneys in states other than Delaware give as to why they use Delaware as their preferred state of incorporation. Their responses generally fall into the following categories: (1) We use Delaware because it has been a leading state of incorporation for many years, and there are answers to most questions of corporation law in the Delaware statute or the Delaware case law. If there are answers to questions we can work around them; what we cannot deal with is uncertainty, and the law in all other states, including heavily populated states such as California, New York, and Texas, has many areas of uncertainty. (2) We use Delaware because the corporation lawyers in our firm are familiar with Delaware law, and it is cheaper and more efficient for our clients if we create Delaware corporations rather than corporations in other states. As evidence of this, we customarily give opinions with respect to Delaware corporation law even though our offices are located in New York City (or Chicago, Los Angeles, Denver, or wherever). (3) We use Delaware law because if a problem arises we will be dealing with state officials who are sophisticated in corporation law, and we will get useful advice and assistance from them. (4) We use Delaware law because if we have to litigate, we will be before sophisticated judges well versed in corporation law and we will have the assistance of well trained Delaware corporation lawyers. (5) We use Delaware law because we know that that state will respond promptly if unexpected problems arise by amending its corporation law. Delaware is usually years' ahead of most states in this regard. (6) We use Delaware law because it is stable. It is unlikely that major policy changes will be made in Delaware without the most careful consideration by corporate specialists.

These statements have a convincing air about them, and probably do in fact explain why Delaware is where it is today. It is not because it is more permissive than other states. Rather, it is because Delaware is reaping the benefits of its many years of experience with corporation law, the familiarity of corporation lawyers around the country with its statute, and the stability and responsiveness this small state has shown in addressing corporation law issues. In addition, an important factor is that the Delaware Court of Chancery is predominantly a "business law" court and its judges have wide experience in such disputes. Other states have attempted to create similar specialized courts, but the efforts have not been very successful.

From the standpoint of Delaware's selfish interests, there is no secret as to why it wishes to retain this incorporation business. More than 15 percent of the state's total budget comes from franchise taxes paid by corporations. Mandatory local filings by corporations provide the backbone of support for the three county courthouses in the state. The major law firms in Wilmington would doubtless be a small fraction of their present size if their foreign corporation business disappeared. Several large firms with principal offices in New York, Chicago, or other large cities maintain offices in Wilmington, Delaware. Insurance firms and corporation service companies are similarly dependent on foreign corporations for much of their business. Indeed, from a financial standpoint, the Delaware corporation business is the envy of all other states, large and small.

§ 1.7   The Model Business Corporation Act

In addition to Delaware, a second major influence on modern corporation law has been the Model Business Corporation Act, developed and maintained by a committee of the American Bar Association. The original MBCA, as it is usually referred to, was first published in 1950 and was influential in the development of state incorporation statutes in some thirty states. In 1984, a new version of the Model Act, originally referred to as the Revised Model Business Corporation Act, but now called the "Model Business Corporation Act (1984)" or "MBCA (1984)" was published and has received a favorable reception in numerous states since its introduction. MBCA (1984) largely builds on the provisions of the older MBCA, but adopts innovative provisions in a number of areas and effects a considerable simplification of language in many provisions. All references in this book are to MBCA (1984). (Candor also requires disclosure that the author of this Nutshell served as the reporter for MBCA (1984)).

MBCA (1984) is in the tradition of most modern corporation statutes: it is primarily an enabling statute rather than a regulatory statute. Whether or not it (or the Delaware statute, for that matter) is too flexible or too permissive depends to a large extent on the social views of the observer.

§ 1.8   The Federal Securities Laws

Finally, mention should be made of developments at the federal level. In the early 1930s, Congress enacted two statutes relating to corporate matters. The Securities Act of 1933 and the Securities Exchange Act of 1934 have formed the springboard for considerable federal regulation of the internal affairs of publicly held corporations; at one stage a trend appeared to be developing toward an inclusive "federal law of corporations" based on these two statutes. While this development has been stopped in its tracks by the modern trend toward deregulation and by a series of narrow and restrictive holdings by the federal courts, federal regulation is still of great importance in corporation law.

The Securities Act of 1933 regulates raising of capital by corporations from members of the public. It is supplemented by state statutes, called "blue sky laws" that regulate capital raising within each specific state.

The Securities Exchange Act of 1934 primarily affects corporation law through its regulation of the disclosure policies of publicly held corporations. This statute also provides the basis for the regulation of securities exchanges and securities brokers and dealers.

§ 1.9 The Debate Over Social Responsibility and the Publicly Held Corporation

There has been a long debate over the social responsibility of large publicly held corporations in modern society. Such corporations unquestionably wield immense economic power when they make decisions. A decision where to locate a plant, what environmental equipment to install, what products to manufacture, what to charge for them, what safety devices to build into them, and so forth, are all decisions that may fairly be described as "social" as well as "economic" since they have dramatic consequences for individuals, communities, and entire states. These decisions, furthermore, are usually made by corporate management without public input or the approval of voters, investors, shareholders, or anyone else. The concentration of power in such corporations has been decried by some commentators and defended by others. This debate goes back to before the New Deal era.

The social responsibility debate has several different levels. At the most basic level the issue can be phrased in terms of whether corporate management should explicitly take social considerations into account when they make important decisions or whether they should make the decision on the basis of the "bottom line" of what produces the best profit for the corporation. While these two positions may at first seem polar opposites, in fact they are not. Profit-maximizing decisions are not made in the abstract but in the broader societal context of possible governmental intervention, and the like. Further, since the accepted aim of corporate governance is to maximize long run rather than short run profits, these social factors may quite legitimately be taken into account in the overall profit calculation. A decision to raise prices to monopoly levels (assuming that that is feasible), for example, may maximize short run profits but have devastating long run consequences in terms of adverse publicity, the entry of new competitors in the industry, and governmental intervention. Rational profit maximizers take these long run consequences into account.

Another branch of the social responsibility debate considers whether the interests represented in the governing body of large publicly held corporations—the board of directors—should be broadened. Suggestions typically include adding one or more representatives of government, labor, suppliers, consumers, creditors, etc. to the board. While there has been limited experimentation with this idea, it has never really caught on, and, where it has been tried, it is difficult to find tangible evidence that the representational directors have made any significant difference.

In the middle nineteen-seventies the debate over social responsibility received new impetus from the disclosure by hundreds of publicly held corporations that they had paid domestic or foreign bribes, made illegal payments overseas to obtain business, or had made illegal campaign contributions in the United States. These disclosures led not only to new calls for greater social responsibility of corporations but also focused on the role of the board of directors and the need for better control mechanisms to insure that corporate management conform with legal and moral principles of conduct. The takeover movement of the 1980s also focused attention on the decisions by boards of directors faced with unwanted bids from outside interests to purchase a majority or more of the outstanding shares. Many public corporations made important changes in their methods of internal governance as a result of these pressures. See Chapter 13.

As this is written in the mid–1990s, it seems that the social responsibility debate has ended. Laissez faire and the goal of profit maximization appear to have carried the day.

§ 1.10 "Closely Held" and "Publicly Held" Corporations

Throughout the cases and literature dealing with the law of corporations appear references to "publicly held" corporations and "closely held" corporations. There are many similar references scattered throughout this book. This section explores what is meant by these terms.

It is simplest to begin with a definition of a publicly held corporation. "Publicly held" means "held by members of the general public" and has nothing to do with governmental ownership. A "publicly held" corporation may be defined as a corporation with a sufficiently large number of shareholders that an established market has developed for its shares. The largest and best known securities market is the New York Stock Exchange, but several other important securities markets exist. The importance of such a market is that it permits any investor to become a shareholder, and any shareholder who is dissatisfied with his investment to exit by selling his shares into the public market.

Another factor that is usually (but not invariably) present in a publicly held corporation is that the business is managed by professional managers who do not own, in the aggregate, a significant percentage of the ownership interests of the business. Some publicly held corporations are managed by the founders or principal shareholders. Microsoft Corporation is a good example. However, such corporations are relatively uncommon among the publicly held corporations.

A business that does not have an active trading market for its shares may be defined as a "closely held" corporation. The typical "closely held" corporation has relatively few shareholders—probably less than ten. Such a corporation is often referred to as an "incorporated partnership." In such a corporation all or most of the shareholders participate in management. In addition, in such a corporation the shareholders will have modified the default form of corporation (see section 1.1) at least by entering into agreements restricting the transferability of shares. This ensures that outsiders cannot become shareholders without the consent of the existing shareholders and may provide a device by which existing shareholders may have their shares purchased when they die or decide to leave the corporation. See sections 9.17 through 9.25. A small number of shareholders and the presence of restrictions on share transfer are often viewed as hallmarks of a closely held corporation.

In one sense the suggested line between "publicly held" and "closely held" corporations is unrealistic because there is a substantial group of "in between" corporations that may have a substantial number of shareholders but no organized trading market for shares exists. A corporation with 300 shareholders, for example, may be quite substantial in terms of size and assets, have professional management, and yet only a sporadic or "thin" market for shares exists. The existence of such corporations, however, does not destroy the basic validity of the distinction.

The corporate model that appears in state corporation statutes and the MBCA (1984) is an idealized model that is not tailored specifically either for the close corporation or for the publicly held corporation. It is a model that is sufficiently broad and generalized that large portions of it are appropriate for both the very large and the very small. Many states have supplemented their general corporation statutes by adopting special statutes to provide relaxed rules for closely held corporations that elect to take advantage of their provisions. See section 12.13 of this Nutshell. Sections 7.32 and 14.34 of MBCA (1984) provide an alternative set of provisions designed specifically for closely held corporations.

[For unfamiliar terms see the Glossary]

CHAPTER TWO

UNINCORPORATED BUSINESS FORMS

§ 2.1   Unincorporated Business Forms In General

A new venture must adopt a business form in which it is to operate. Historically, the basic choices were (a) a partnership (or proprietorship if there is only one owner), (b) a limited partnership, or (c) a corporation. Today, a whole stable of new unincorporated business forms have been created, many dating back less than ten years. Of these new business forms, the limited liability company (usually referred to as an "LLC"), has been authorized in virtually all states, and has become an important alternative business form to the corporation. Because of this proliferation, the future of business forms is more clouded today than it has been anytime during the twentieth century.

If a new business venture is simply launched without a conscious selection of business form being made, the partnership or proprietorship form has been chosen, for better or for worse.

§ 2.2   A Dictionary of Unincorporated Business Forms

A *partnership* is the simplest form of organization involving more than one person. It is formed merely by agreement of the partners, who share the right to manage and the right to participate in the profits. Profit participation may be allocated by agreement; in the absence of agreement each partner shares equally in profits. Each partner is also personally liable on partnership obli-

25

gations; losses are shared by the partners, and if the losses exceed the accumulated profits, each partner must make a further contribution to the partnership on dissolution to cover the losses, including capital losses of other partners. In the absence of agreement, each partner shares equally in the losses. Each partner is also an agent of the partnership for purposes of its business and has a voice in management. In the absence of a specific agreement, all partners share equally in management decisions. The partners may agree among themselves as to how profits and losses are to be allocated and how the partnership business is to be managed; the partnership agreement is sometimes referred to as the "law" for that partnership. It is binding on the partners but not binding on persons who are not parties to the agreement. Because of the agency and profit sharing relationships within a partnership, broad fiduciary duties exist among the partners. A partnership is a fragile form of business: it is dissolved automatically when a partner dies or leaves the partnership; it may also be dissolved by any partner by his express will at any time. Upon dissolution, the withdrawing partners are entitled to receive the value of their partnership interest from the partnership, which may either be wound up and terminated, or continued by the remaining partners and possibly new partners as well.

The major drawbacks of the partnership form of business are the unlimited sharing of losses and the personal liability of partners for partnership obligations, considering the modern litigious society in which we live.

A partnership is sometimes referred to as a "general partnership" and the partners as "general partners," to distinguish them from the limited partnership and its limited partners, described below.

The partnership is a flexible business form. For example, the partnership agreement may create classes of partners, with different rights and responsibilities. Many law firms have created two classes of partners: "equity partners," who share in the profits of the business and who must contribute toward losses, and "income partners," who receive a more limited stipend, and who are indemnified by the partnership against losses. Creditors, however, may hold both classes of partners personally liable on partnership obligations.

A *proprietorship* is a business owned by a single person who has the sole right to manage, is solely entitled to the profits, and is unlimitedly responsible for the debts of the business. A proprietorship is essentially a one person partnership.

A *limited partnership* is a partnership in which there are one or more general partners unlimitedly liable for the debts of the business with general powers of management and one or more limited partners who have no personal liability for the debts of the business (except to the extent of their capital contributions) and who have only limited rights to participate in the management. A limited partnership is created by the filing of a certificate with an appropriate state official and the payment of a fee. Limited partners are generally passive investors with limited powers of management; limited partners who participate in the control of the business may lose their shield of limited liability. However, modern limited partnership statutes permit limited partners to participate in management in limited circumstances without becoming personally responsible for its debts.

The modern limited partnership typically has a corporation as its sole general partner. This combination of forms largely eliminates liability concerns in the limited partnership if the corporate general partner is reasonably financed, considering the nature of the business. Limited partners may generally participate in the management of the general partner without fear of personal liability.

A *limited liability company* (an LLC) may be roughly analogized to a limited partnership composed only of limited partners. However, its internal structure may closely resemble that of a corporation. It is created by filing a document with a state officer called "articles of organization," that is patterned after corporate articles of incorporation. An LLC may also adopt "regulations" or an "operating agreement" that is patterned after traditional corporate bylaws. An LLC provides limited liability for all of its members. In addition, unlike a limited partnership, members of an LLC may freely participate in the management of the business without incurring personal liability for the obligations of the business. LLC statutes permit the internal management structure to be modeled either after a corporation or after a general partnership. LLC statutes permit each LLC to elect whether to be *member managed* or *manager managed*. A member managed LLC is governed in a manner similar to a partnership while a manager managed LLC is governed in a manner more analogous to a corporation. The attractiveness of the LLC as a form of business is that it combines (1) limited liability for all members, (2) flexibility of management structure, and (3) most importantly, as described in the following section, a desirable income tax treatment.

An LLC differs from a corporation in that it does not obtain a "charter" or "franchise" from the state. It may be objected that this is a distinction without a difference, since a filing is required for an LLC, and the two forms of business are superficially quite similar. However, this difference may be important for income tax classification purposes. Limited liability is provided to members of an LLC simply by a statutory provision that states that limited partners are not personally liable for the organization's debts in most circumstances.

Several variations of the above forms have been authorized:

A *professional limited partnership* is a limited partnership with general and limited partners that is engaged in the practice of a profession. This business form is currently recognized in only a handful of states.

A *limited liability partnership* (usually referred to as an LLP) is authorized in about twenty states. An LLP is a general partnership that has elected to provide innocent partners protection against malpractice or similar tort claims arising from actions of other partners. In some states, an LLP election also protects innocent partners against contract claims as well as tort claims. An LLP election is made by filing a certificate with a public official and paying a fee usually based on the number of partners; such an election is valid for one year in most states and must be renewed annually.

A *limited liability limited partnership* (usually referred to as an LLLP) is authorized in only a handful of states. It is a traditional limited partnership except that its general partners have elected LLP status as among themselves. In an LLLP, limited partners have the traditional protection of limited partners while innocent general partners have the limited protection against malpractice and tort claims provided by the LLP election.

Some states have also recently enacted statutes authorizing *business trusts, joint stock companies, limited partnership associations* and other variations of business forms. Some of these new forms of business are variations of long-standing but little-used business forms; others are novel.

The current menu of unincorporated business forms is unquestionably confusing and untidy. The business forms that are widely used in the United States today overlap in various ways; each has its own particularized history that leads to unique rules and limitations. Many of the differences among the traditional business forms—partnerships, limited partnerships, and corporations—can be explained by history and not by logic. These traditional forms can be traced back to medieval times for the limited partnership, and even earlier for the partnership and the corporation. The newer business forms have been created as a result of federal income tax considerations, and their life span is probably dependent on the continuation of the present tax rules.

Suggestions have been made to unify the various business forms into a single model that would permit the owners to select the characteristics most suitable for their specific business without regard to the traditional differences in the various business forms. It is unlikely that such unification will occur in the near future, if it ever occurs at all.

§ 2.3   Personal Liability and Taxes: The Most Important Factors in Selecting a Business Form

The selection of business forms today largely revolve around two core issues: limitation of personal liability of owners for the debts of the business and the proper classification of the business for purposes of the federal income tax law. Of these two factors, the tax classification issue is the more influential. The new business forms described in section 2.2 are attractive because they permit partnership tax treatment to be combined with limitation of personal liability. Twenty years ago, limited liability for owners could be assured only by incorporating, which meant that the firm would automatically be subject to corporate tax treatment. Today, the tax rules for unincorporated firms have been so relaxed that the tax treatment of such firms has become virtually elective.

The tax treatment of firms is usually more important than limited liability because the possibility that personal liability may be imposed on an owner in a business form in which there is no limitation on personal liability is only a possibility, a risk that may never mature into a liability that must be discharged by the payment of real dollars. Furthermore, insurance is available to protect owners against tort claims, the most feared type of liability. Most assuredly, all risks of personal liability should be avoided if possible: Affluent individuals, particularly, sleep better at night if they feel snug and secure behind a shield of limited liability. But the liabilities may never actually arise, and if they do, most firms are able to satisfy them out of their own assets or through liability insurance without calling on the owners to contribute toward their payment. Taxation on the other hand is quite a different matter; it is not a possibility but something that every business has to face almost constantly. It involves real dollars that must be paid every year.

Emphasis on limited liability and taxation should not hide the fact that other factors also enter into the selection of an appropriate business form. These factors include:

1.   Considerations of internal efficiency, operational cost, and organizational convenience given the nature of the business, the number of owners, and their relationships with each other.

2.   The husbanding of scarce capital and resources during the period before the business becomes established.

3.   Considerations relating to the ease of raising capital in the future.

Certainly one basic rule for newly formed businesses is to keep matters simple at the outset. Small, marginal businesses with limited capital usually benefit by limiting organizational expenses and devoting capital to operations and inventory rather than to lawyers. Simplicity also means that the owners may concentrate on business matters and not be saddled with unessential organizational details. Certainly, it may not be sensible to invest limited capital resources in creating a complex corporate or limited liability company structure when the money might be better used by being directly invested in the business.

These factors generally favor unincorporated business forms over incorporation.

§ 2.4   An Introduction to Federal Taxation of Business Forms

For many students, the role of federal income taxation in the selection of the business form is difficult to understand. They may not be familiar with the broad structure of the federal income tax which, of course, is the subject of a separate law school course. Indeed, in many corporations courses, the role of federal income taxes is not covered for just this reason. However, it is not possible to appreciate the issues arising around the selection of business forms without some knowledge of the basic principles of modern federal income taxation.

In general terms, partnerships and "associations taxable as partnerships" are not separate taxable units. Rather, the various tax consequences of their activities are passed through to the owners of the enterprise. The partnership files an information return calculating its business income or loss and then allocates the pro rata share of gains, losses, income, deductions, and so forth, to each individual partner who must include those items in his or her individual income tax return. This method of taxation is usually described as "conduit," "pass through," "partnership-type" taxation.

In contrast, to the pass-through tax treatment of unincorporated business forms, the starting point for corporate taxation is that a corporation that receives a charter or franchise from a state must be taxed as a corporation. Further, the corporation is a separate taxable entity independent of its shareholders. I.R.C. § 11(a) imposes a separate tax on the income of corporations while § 301 in effect imposes a tax on shareholders on distributions to them of property from corporations out of its earnings or profits. Thus, the earnings of a corporation may be subject to federal income taxation at two different levels: at the corporate level on the corporation's "taxable income" and a second time, at the shareholders' level when the corporation distributes assets to the shareholders (up to an amount equal to the earnings and profits of the corporation).

It should be emphasized that as an abstract matter neither system of taxation is inherently superior to the other. It all depends on relative tax rates and the detailed rules as to what deductions and credits are available to shareholders at the shareholder level.

For many years during and after World War II individual tax rates for wealthy individuals were much higher than the corporate tax rate, which was capped at 52 percent of income. Furthermore, the tax rate on long term capital gains was capped at 25 percent. Given this structure of rates, partnership type taxation for a profitable business was to be avoided at all costs, since it subjected all the business' income to the very high individual tax rates. Shareholders were much better off if the corporation made no distributions at all, paying tax on its income at a maximum rate of 52 percent, and accumulating its income. Shareholders might then sell their shares to a third person in order to indirectly capture this increase in value. The gain from such a sale was taxed as a "long term capital gain" at a maximum 25 percent rate. The strategy of allowing earnings to accumulate in the corporation and then selling the shares was so common that it became known as the "accumulate and bail-out strategy." An even better tax result was obtained if a shareholder died owning shares of stock, since a special tax rule permits the appreciation in value of the stock to escape tax entirely.

The accumulate and bail out strategy was usually supplemented by another tax-oriented device. It is usually possible to structure the contractual relationships between the corporation and the shareholders in such a way that most of the distribution to the shareholder is deductible by the corporation as salary, rent, interest, or other deductible payment, rather than as a distribution that is a non-deductible dividend. This not only reduces the "double tax" bite by eliminating the tax at the corporate level but also permits at least some shareholders to receive substantial amounts of income from the corporation. If payments to shareholders are "ordinary and necessary" expenses of the corporation, they are deductible by it and are not income taxable to the shareholder.

In the 1980s, the structure of income tax rates were dramatically changed. In 1986, individual tax rates were reduced sharply to a maximum rate of 28 percent while corporate tax rates were reduced to a maximum rate of 34 percent. Further, the special tax treatment of long term capital gains was entirely eliminated. Suddenly, the rules of the tax avoidance game changed abruptly, as partnership-type taxation suddenly became extremely attractive. Partnership tax treatment involves a pure conduit or pass through tax treatment; this permitted business income to be taxed only once, at 28 percent, in the hands of the owners. Accumulation within a corporation at 34 percent was obviously less attractive, and doubly so when the tax on distributions at the shareholder level was added in.

Rate changes since 1986 have reduced the advantages of partnership type taxation, though these advantages have not been eliminated. As a result, the extent of the penalty caused by the corporate double tax has been reduced but the penalty still exists.

The double taxation problem is of concern primarily for shareholders who are individuals. Shareholders which are themselves corporations may claim a dividend received deduction based on their percentage of ownership. This deduction ranges from a 100 percent deduction for dividends paid to an affiliated corporation that owns 80 percent or more of the voting power and value of the payer's stock to a 70 percent deduction for dividends paid to corporations owning less than 20 percent of the payer's stock.

§ 2.5   Taxation of "C" and "S" Corporations

The comparison of partnership and corporate taxation is complicated because in 1957 Congress created a special tax election for certain closely held corporations, the so-called S corporation election. This election permits most corporations with less than 35 shareholders to elect to be taxed in a manner that generally permits income to be passed through the corporation and be taxed directly to shareholders. Subchapter S tax treatment is similar to (but in some respects significantly different from) the conduit tax treatment applicable to partnerships and other unincorporated entities.

A corporation that has elected to be taxed under subchapter S is called, not surprisingly, an "S corporation." A corporation that is ineligible for, or has not elected to be, an S corporation is called a "C corporation." These names are derived from the subchapters of the Internal Revenue Code which deal with the treatment of electing and non-electing corporations.

S corporation tax treatment is not as attractive as partnership type tax treatment. For one thing, the technical eligibility requirements for the S corporation election make many corporations with less than 35 shareholders ineligible for S corporation treatment. Further, there are a number of technical differences between partnership-type taxation and S corporation taxation, and these differences make the partnership type taxation more attractive than the S corporation. Hence most businesses with a relatively few owners today are better off, tax-wise, if they can elect partnership-type taxation rather than S corporation taxation.

The S corporation election is sometimes loosely referred to as a corporation being "taxed as a partnership" or "electing partnership taxation." However, that is not really accurate; S corporation election is different from true partnership type taxation in several respects.

To be eligible for subchapter S, a corporation must meet the following conditions on the date of election:

(a) It must be a domestic corporation;

(b) It must not be part of an affiliated group of corporations;

(c) It must have no more than 35 shareholders;

(d) Each shareholder must be an individual, a decedent's estate, or certain types of trusts; no shareholder may be a nonresident alien; and

(e) It may have only one class of stock outstanding, except that classes of common stock differing only in voting rights do not result in the loss of the election.

An S corporation is a true corporation with all attributes of a corporation other than the peculiar tax treatment. Thus, an S corporation has the normal corporate characteristics of limited liability, centralization of management, perpetual existence, and free transferability of interest.

Disadvantages of the S corporation election include the limitation on the number of shareholders, the types of shareholders, the prohibition against having multiple classes of stock, and the prohibition against having subsidiaries or corporate shareholders.

§ 2.6 Combining Partnership Tax Treatment and Limited Liability

For many years it was accepted wisdom that partnership tax treatment was available only in a business form that provided for unlimited liability of the owners. The Internal Revenue Service gradually abandoned this position and adopted more flexible standards, generally known as the "Kintner regulations." Under these regulations, today, many unincorporated business forms may provide limited liability for some or all of the owners and yet remain eligible for partnership type taxation.

The determination whether an unincorporated business entity is eligible for partnership type taxation under the Kintner regulations turns on the question whether the entity has a predominance of "non-corporate" characteristics. The "Kintner" regulations list four "corporate" characteristics that are to be considered in determining whether an entity should be classified as an association taxable as a corporation—continuity of life, centralization of management, limited liability, and free transferability of interests. An unincorporated business that has three or more of these characteristics will be taxed as a corporation; an entity with less than three of these characteristics will be taxed as a partnership. These four factors are weighted equally in this calculation. Thus, limited liability is only one of the characteristics to be taken into account in determining the proper tax classification of an unincorporated business entity.

A traditional corporation of course possesses all four of these characteristics: It has continuity of life because a death of a shareholder or change in membership in the organization does not cause its termination. It has centralization of management because it must have a board of directors selected by the shareholders with full power of management. It has limited liability because shareholders are not personally liable for the debts of the business. And, it has free transferability of interests because shares may be sold by a shareholder to an outsider without the consent or approval of the corporation or the other shareholders. In contrast, a traditional general partnership created under the default rules of partnership law has none of these four corporate characteristics. It does not have continuity of life because the death of a partner dissolves the partnership. It does not have centralization of management because the partners collectively have the power to manage the business of the partnership. It does not have limited liability because each partner is liable on the partnership's debts. And, it does not have free transferability of interest because no person can become a partner without the consent of the other partners.

In some instances a general partnership agreement may structure the enterprise so that it lacks one or more of these characteristics. If it lacks three of these four characteristics, it will be taxed as a corporation. Because conduit type taxation is now preferable to corporate taxation, it is unlikely that a partnership would intentionally do this today. The issue of tax classification is obviously much more difficult in the case of limited partnerships with a corporation as the sole general partner and limited liability companies where most or all of the participants are not personally liable for the obligations of the business. Detailed regulations have been promulgated by the Internal Revenue Service defining when each of these corporate characteristics exist in connection with LPs and LLCs.

An LLP and similar kinds of unincorporated entities are likely to have little difficulty qualifying for partnership type tax treatment under these regulations.

It is possible that a corporation may lack three of the corporate characteristics by careful planning. However, the IRS takes the position that such a corporation is not eligible for partnership type tax treatment. A corporation receives a charter from the state and therefore is subject to either C or S corporate taxation.

There are two major exceptions to the pass through tax treatment of unincorporated business forms. First, any unincorporated business that has sufficient members or owners that a public trading market exists for ownership interests in the business is taxed as a corporation, no matter what the business form actually adopted. Second, any unincorporated business that wishes for some reason to be taxed as a corporation may structure its internal affairs so that it will be taxed as a corporation. One minor additional exception might be mentioned. Because of some rather quirky rules in the tax laws, a limited liability company composed of a single member may conceivably be taxed as a corporation. Such an entity, of course, may be eligible for S corporation tax treatment.

§ 2.7 Economic Effects of the Double Tax Regime

From an economic standpoint, the double tax structure applicable to C corporations has serious economic costs. For example, it encourages indirect distributions that are claimed as tax deductions by the corporation. It is common practice for closely held corporations to provide automobiles, country club memberships, and the like, for shareholder/employees. The corporate tax treatment also imposes tax at the corporate level without regard to shareholder characteristics, arguably overtaxing low bracket or tax exempt shareholders. It encourages the excessive use of debt since corporations prefer debt financing rather than equity financing because interest payments are tax deductible while dividend payments are not. It leads corporations to adopt a policy of retaining excess earnings within the corporation rather than distributing them promptly to shareholders who may reinvest them. It therefore may encourage over-investment at the corporate level and a misallocation of limited capital resources. Reinvestment of earnings also limits oversight by the capital markets that would be present if capital was raised directly from publicly available sources. Finally, it deters the use of the corporate form of business for closely held businesses and encourages the development of new business forms whose principal advantage is tax savings. The issue of who actually bears the cost of the double taxation imposed on corporations is a difficult one, but there is general agreement among economists that the double taxation environment does not lead to optimal results.

Most industrialized nations do not impose a double tax burden on corporate distributions; the United States appears to be unique in this respect. As a result, there have been numerous proposals to amend the tax structure in some way in order to eliminate the double tax.

The double taxation problem might be eliminated by the outright repeal of the corporate income tax or by permitting corporations to deduct dividend payments the way they now deduct interest payments. Shareholders might be permitted to exclude all or a substantial portion of dividend distributions from their adjusted gross income or to treat corporate tax payments as a credit against their own tax bill in much the same way as employer withholding from income for the payment of income taxes by employees creates credits for individual taxpayers. Plans to eliminate the double tax are generally referred to as "integration proposals."

Enactment of an integration proposal requires recognition of certain political realities and numerous conflicting claims of equity. The simple fact is that the present law has developed a morass of tax preferences, rules of deductibility, and special tax rates for certain types of receipts, e.g. capital gains, or for certain types of taxpayers. Integration is difficult because it reopens many controversial and difficult issues over which figurative blood has been shed in the past.

While amendments to the Internal Revenue Code eliminating the double taxation of dividends is possible, as this is written it does not appear to have very high priority. In part, this may be because the development of the limited liability company permits businesses with relatively few owners to obtain the desired benefits of incorporation combined with true conduit or pass through taxation.

There are also pending in 1996 several proposals to change radically the federal tax structure. Such suggestions include a "flat tax," a national sales tax, a value added tax, and so forth. Adoption of any of these more radical proposals would render moot the integration proposals discussed above.

[For unfamiliar terms see the Glossary]

CHAPTER THREE

FORMATION OF CORPORATIONS

§ 3.1 In General

The process of corporate formation is essentially a very simple one, and much (though not all) of it may be performed by a competent legal secretary. Indeed, one of the great modern innovations in corporate formation is the microcomputer word processor which permits the mass production of corporate documents with only special name and other minor changes. Many readers have doubtless seen advertisements in legal journals for "kits" for the creation of corporations; they are also based on mass produced, standard-form incorporation documents. There are two significant pitfalls in the routine use of such forms. The first is the danger that no one with a broad perspective on the law of corporations will bring that perspective to bear on the potentially unique problems of the particular venture. The second is the universal danger in the use of "boiler-plate" forms: they may contain some provision that was suitable for the last corporation but is egregiously inappropriate for the next one. Overall, however, the process by which a corporation is formed is simple and routine and not in any way mysterious.

§ 3.2 Selection of the State of Incorporation

A large, publicly held corporation that transacts business in every state may theoretically choose its state of incorporation from among any of the fifty states. As a practical matter, however, most such corporations have selected

Delaware as their state of incorporation. The small corporation doing business in only a single state or locality has the same theoretical freedom as the publicly held corporation in this regard, since it is possible to incorporate in any state and qualify to transact business as a foreign corporation in any other state. However, practical considerations usually dictate that the small corporation be formed in the jurisdiction in which it is solely or principally doing business. There are real costs if any foreign state is selected: the corporation will have to qualify as a foreign corporation in its "home state;" it will be subject to two taxing authorities; and it may be subject to suit in a distant state. If there is some reason not to incorporate in the local jurisdiction despite these costs, the alternative usually is Delaware, with its popular statute. As other states have modernized their corporation statutes, the advantages of Delaware as a state of incorporation for small businesses active in other jurisdictions have lessened, and most local businesses today are incorporated in the state in which they primarily conduct business.

§ 3.3   Mechanics of Creating a Corporation

The mechanics of creating a corporation vary from state to state, and the specific statute must be consulted for details.

Every state requires the filing of a document with a state official, usually the secretary of state, together with the payment of a filing fee. Depending on the state, the document may be called the "articles of incorporation," the "certificate of incorporation," the "charter" or some other name. In this Nutshell, this document is described as the "articles of incorporation."

The traditional manner of filing articles of incorporation is to mail them in, deliver them by overnight mail service, or deliver them by messenger or courier to the secretary of state. Many state filing offices now also permit electronic filing, setting up a fax machine and fax number for that purpose. This development usually required special legislation since the language of corporation statutes often required submission of an "executed" original as well as a conformed copy, and telefaxed communications did not comply with these requirements. With further improvements in technology, an electronic filing directly into the computer system maintained by the secretary of state may become authorized.

In every state, the filing is reviewed by the secretary of state, which commonly means by a professional staff member within that office. If the document meets the statutory requirements, the corporate existence is usually deemed to relate back to the date and time the document was originally received, any post-filing delays being ignored. In the case of a traditional document, this is the date evidenced by a time stamp placed on the document when it was received or on its envelope. The secretary of state reflects its approval of the filing by an action, traditionally the issuance of a formal "charter" or "certificate of incorporation" which is attached to a duplicate original or copy of the original filing. Increasingly the approval of the filing is evidenced merely by the issuance of a receipt for the filing fee. The original document is retained by the secretary of state in most states, and the same information may also be kept in computer-readable form.

Some states have additional filing requirements. Delaware, for example, requires local filing in the county in which the corporation's registered office is located (as well as filing in a state office) [Del. Code Ann. Tit. 8, § 103(c)(5)]. Arizona requires that evidence that the statutory agent has accepted his appointment be submitted and that the articles of incorporation be published in a newspaper of general circulation in the county in which the corporation's known place of business is located three consecutive times within 60 days after the articles are filed [Ariz. Rev.Stat.Ann. § 10–055]. A handful of states still require recording in every county in which the corporation transacts business. It is generally believed that these additional requirements serve little or no practical benefit; they are retained usually because of the political power of county clerks or newspaper publishers who have come to rely on the fees or charges generated by those requirements.

Local filing or advertising requirements may also create legal problems as to when the corporate existence begins if some, but not all of them, are complied with. A few states have statutes that deal with this question. Delaware, for example, provides that corporate existence begins with the acceptance of the filing by the secretary of state, and the failure to file locally within the specified period increases the filing fee but does not affect the existence of the corporation [Del. Code Ann. Tit. 8, § 103(d)]. Some states, however, condition the existence of the corporation on the completion of all filing and advertising requirements.

§ 3.4 Incorporators

The person or persons who execute the articles of incorporation are called "incorporators." Traditionally, three incorporators were required; all but a handful of states today require only a single incorporator. A few states still have residency or age requirements for incorporators, but most states now permit an individual to act as incorporator if he or she is of legal age without regard to residency or later participation in the corporation. Many states now permit artificial entities such as corporations or trusts also to serve as incorporators.

The relaxation of the requirements relating to incorporators reflects the minor role they play in the formation of a modern corporation. Depending on the state, incorporators may serve one or more of the following roles:

(1) They execute and deliver the articles of incorporation to the secretary of state;

(2) They, or their representatives, receive the charter or certificate of incorporation back from the secretary of state;

(3) They either (i) meet to complete the organization of the corporation or (ii) call the first meeting of the initial board of directors (named in the articles of incorporation) at which the organization of the corporation is completed;

(4) They may voluntarily dissolve the corporation if the corporation has not commenced business and has not issued any shares; and

(5) They may amend the articles of incorporation by unanimous consent if the corporation has not commenced business and has not issued any shares.

Traditionally the incorporators met to complete the organization of the corporation. The original Model Business Corporation Act changed this pattern by providing that initial directors should be named in the articles of incorporation, and the initial directors meet to complete the organization of the corporation on the call of the incorporators. Many states today follow this pattern. In these states, the role of incorporators is basically limited to the ceremonial function of signing the articles of incorporation. Sections 2.02(b)(1) and 2.05(a) of the Model Business Corporation Act give each new corporation the option either of having the incorporators complete the formation of the corporation or of naming initial directors in the articles of incorporation and having them complete the organization of the corporation. As discussed below, (see section 3.16 of this Nutshell) this flexibility was added to permit corporations in diverse situations to complete their formation with a minimum number of meetings and a minimum of expense.

It is generally believed that there is no risk of liability for actions taken while acting as incorporator of a corporation. Indeed, many attorneys or their secretaries or other law office employees routinely serve as incorporators. The same may not always be true of acting as a director or an initial director. Many attorneys decline to serve as a director of small corporations they form, or do so only reluctantly.

An "incorporator" must be sharply distinguished from a "subscriber." The latter agrees to buy shares in the corporation; in other words, a subscriber is an investor and participant in the venture. An "incorporator" on the other hand serves the largely ceremonial or ministerial functions described in this section. At one time many states required that an incorporator also be a subscriber of shares; however, such requirements appear to have disappeared in all states.

§ 3.5 Articles of Incorporation: In General

The document filed with the secretary of state must contain certain mandatory information. While the requirements vary from state to state, the following modest list (drawn from § 54 of the old Model Business Corporation Act) is typical:

(a) The name of the corporation;

(b) The period of duration which may be perpetual;

(c) The purpose or purposes of the corporation, which may be generally described as "for any lawful business purpose;"

(d) The number of shares authorized to be issued, including information about the rights and preferences of such shares;

(e) The address of its registered office and the name of its registered agent at that office;

(f) The number of directors and the names and addresses of the members of the initial board of directors; and

(g) The names and addresses of each incorporator.

When the committee drafting the 1984 Model Business Corporation Act considered the analogous section, MBCA (1984) § 2.02, it was recognized that virtually all modern corporations elected perpetual duration and a purpose of engaging in any lawful business. In order to simplify the articles of incorporation even further, the MBCA (1984) simply provides that every corporation has these attributes unless a shorter duration or narrower purpose is set forth in the articles of incorporation. Further, if the corporation has only a single class of shares and elects to be created and organized by a single incorporator rather than by initial directors, item (f) is eliminated and item (d) is responded to in a single sentence; the resulting minimum form of articles of incorporation fits conveniently on a post card!

In addition, state statutes provide that a corporation may elect to be governed by certain statutory provisions, the election of which must be reflected by an appropriate provision in the articles of incorporation. For example, many statutes provide that a majority in interest of the shareholders shall constitute a quorum of shareholders except that the quorum may be reduced by specific provision in the articles of incorporation to a number smaller than a majority (MBCA (1984), § 7.25). Many statutes provide that shareholders shall have a preemptive right to acquire new shares (see § 7.18 of this Nutshell) or to vote shares cumulatively (see § 9.6 of this Nutshell) unless these rights are specifically negated by appropriate provisions in the articles of incorporation. Sections 6.30 and

7.28(b) of MBCA (1984) instead provide "opt in" provisions for these rights—i.e., a corporation's shareholders do not have preemptive rights or the right to vote cumulatively unless the articles of incorporation specifically provide for them. The statute of each specific state must be consulted to determine the pattern adopted by that state in connection with these rights.

Finally, corporations may elect to place optional provisions relating to internal governance in the articles of incorporation in order to make them more permanent, more difficult to amend, and, hopefully, binding on persons who may not have actual knowledge of them. Such provisions usually may also be placed in the corporation's bylaws. However, many lawyers and judges expect important provisions, or unusual provisions denying customary rights to shareholders or others, to appear in the articles of incorporation. Such provisions are often repeated in the bylaws.

§ 3.6 Articles of Incorporation: The Corporate Name

Most statutes set up minimum requirements with respect to the corporate name. Typical provisions include:

(1) The name must contain a word indicating corporateness, such as "corporation," "company," or "incorporated," or an abbreviation of one or more such words.

(2) The name may not contain any word or phrase which indicates that it is organized for a purpose that it is not permitted to engage in. As a practical matter, with the development of very general purposes clauses, the principal impact of this restriction is to preclude the use of names which suggest a purpose for which corporations may not be organized under the state business corporation act. Thus, in many states, "bank," "bank and trust," "certificate of deposit," "title guaranty," and "insurance" may not appear in corporate names since there are special

regulatory requirements in statutes relating to formation of corporations for such purposes. These limitations are being gradually relaxed as a result of the development of bank holding companies and other corporations involved in some aspects of banking and insurance.

(3) The name may not resemble too closely the name of any other corporation formed or qualified to transact business in the state. The precise statutory test varies. The old Model Business Corporation Act prohibited a name that was the "same or deceptively similar" to any other corporate name, and most state statutes embody this test. Section 4.01 of MBCA (1984) substitutes the test that the name be "distinguishable upon the records of the secretary of state" from any other corporate name. This language was basically taken from the Delaware statute. The primary purpose of this requirement, however it is phrased, is to make sure that each corporation has a unique name. States that adopt the "same or deceptively similar" standard involve the secretary of state in making decisions in part on the basis of unfair competition, a policy which (for reasons discussed below) the secretary of state may not be well equipped to enforce.

(4) Some states add another layer to the name availability rules. Texas, for example, provides that if the name is "similar" (as contrasted with the "same or deceptively similar") to any other corporate name, it may be used only if a "letter of consent" is obtained from the owner of the similar name which expressly permits the name to be used. The purpose of this requirement appears clearly to be the prevention of unfair competition.

Secretaries of state usually maintain lists of corporate names that are in use and therefore not currently available, and check proposed new names against that list. This list is usually stored on a computer to provide instant access. This list is usually the sole standard applied by the secretary of state who typically has neither the staff nor the resources to make an independent investigation of whether the use of the proposed name may constitute unfair competition. It was for this reason that the Model Business Corporation Act rephrases the test of name availability as "distinguishable upon the records of the secretary of state." However, it is important to recognize that the decision as to name availability (whether the test is that the name is "the same," "distinguishable," or "deceptively similar") involves questions of judgment; some secretaries of state have developed "rules of thumb" or "house rules" to guide their discretion on judgments as to name availability. As a practical matter, the issue whether or not a specific name is available is seldom litigated. Even if an attorney strongly disagrees with the secretary of state as to the availability of a name, it is much simpler and cheaper to select another name than to litigate over name availability. However, when two corporations or businesses have used similar names in the past, the right to the continued use of such name may be so valuable as to lead to bitter litigation over whether the use of the name constitutes unfair competition. Secretaries of state are usually directed by statute to accept the results of such litigation in establishing name availability.

The discussion so far deals only with "official names," that is the name of the corporation that appears in its articles of incorporation and in the records of the secretary of state. A corporation, like an individual, may do business under an assumed name so long as the purpose is not fraudulent and does not constitute unfair competition. Many states have assumed name statutes that require a person, whether an individual or a corporation, that is conducting a business under an assumed name to file a statement (usually at the county level) disclosing who is conducting business under that assumed name. The possible use of an assumed name by a corporation reduces significantly the importance of the name availability determination by the secretary of state. A corporation named ABC Corporation, for example, may do business under the name XYZ Corporation upon complying with the assumed name statute, if the state has one. If there happens to be another corporation that has the official name XYZ Corporation, it can enjoin ABC Corporation from using that name as an assumed name only if there is unfair competition, typically name confusion. If the two corporations are not competing against each other because they are in different geographic locations or in totally different businesses, there is probably nothing that the "real" XYZ Corporation can do about it. The secretary of state typically does not know what assumed name a corporation is using or plans to use or in what area of the state the corporation is operating, or even what the nature of the business of the corporation is; as a result the secretary of state is usually not in a position to make reliable judgments about questions of unfair competition.

Because official corporate names are handled on a first-come first-serve basis, many state statutes permit the reservation of a proposed corporate name for a limited time for a nominal fee while corporate papers are prepared. See MBCA (1984) § 4.02. This *reservation* of a corporate name should be contrasted with the *registration* of a name by a foreign corporation permitted in some states. See MBCA (1984) § 4.03. A registration of a corporate name allows a foreign corporation with long-term plans to expand into the state to reserve the exclusive use of its name and prevent a local corporation from using the same name as an "official name." A reservation of a name is for a brief period, usually three months, and in most states is not renewable (though once a reservation period has expired, anyone, including the holder of the original reserved name, may thereafter reserve the name again); a registration is for a year or more and may be renewed indefinitely without any break in continuity of protection.

It is unclear what effect, if any, should be given to a registered name in a suit for unfair competition.

§ 3.7   Articles of Incorporation: Period of Duration

All business corporation acts now permit a corporation to have perpetual existence. In the past some statutes limited corporations to a fifty year or some other specified life span. These provisions are now obsolete. As noted earlier, the old Model Act requires a statement of the duration of the corporation; the practice of stating the duration to be perpetual was so common that the Model Business Corporation Act (1984) omitted this requirement unless a limited period of duration is desired. It is probably unwise ever to take advantage of this option and designate a term less than perpetual even if it is contemplated that the corporation will exist only for a limited period: such provisions are apt to create more problems than benefits in the long run since expiration of the term before the business of the corporation is completed may result in the corporation having uncertain status. If this occurs, it is always possible to amend the articles to extend the term (or make the term perpetual), but why create a corporate structure that requires someone to remember to do this?

§ 3.8   Articles of Incorporation: Purposes and Powers

All state statutes now provide that a corporation may be formed for any lawful purpose. Many state statutes still require that the articles of incorporation specify what the corporation's purpose or purposes are, but permit a general statement such as the corporation is formed "for general business purposes" or "to engage in any lawful business." The use of such clauses has become so common that the Model Business Corporation Act (1984)

§ 3.01 provides that all corporations have the "purpose of engaging in any lawful business unless a more limited purpose is set forth in the articles of incorporation."

The historical development of purposes clauses is interesting and is typical of basic trends in state corporation law. In the nineteenth century, corporations could only be formed for specific purposes, and under many statutes could only list a single purpose. These provisions were viewed as providing a significant regulatory component: corporations were viewed with mistrust and permission to do business in corporate form was given only grudgingly. Application of these limiting principles often raised problems of ultra vires (discussed in § 4.1 of this Nutshell; literally, ultra vires means beyond the purposes or powers of the corporation) and led to a large amount of litigation construing purposes clauses. The first major innovation was a superficially simple one: it permitted a corporation to state multiple purposes while preserving the rule that the corporation was organized only for the limited purposes set forth in the articles of incorporation. This, however, opened the proverbial flood gates since there was no limitation on the number of purposes for which a single corporation may be formed. It was theoretically possible for a corporation's purposes clause to list every conceivable business in which a corporation may engage, including mining diamonds on the moon. Purposes clauses therefore had a tendency to become increasingly prolix, increasingly unreadable, and often completely uninformative as to what business the corporation actually planned to engage in. The next step, permitting a corporation to use a very simple and general clause, e.g., "this corporation may engage in any lawful business," was a natural and sensible innovation. Since practically all corporations elected to take advantage of this innovation, the requirement of a purposes clause has been reduced to a formality, and the final step taken in the MBCA (1984) also seems to be natural and sensible.

Despite the modern freedom to use "any lawful business" clauses (or to omit the purpose clause entirely), articles of incorporation are sometimes filed with a narrow purposes clause as part of internal corporate planning. Like the limited duration clause, such a provision is apt to create more problems than benefits since, as discussed in the section on ultra vires (§ 4.2 of this Nutshell), a limited purposes clause does not effectively limit the scope of the corporation's activities.

Some attorneys use purposes clauses that specify the principal business or activity of the corporation, but couple it with language such as, "and to engage in any other lawful business." This provides the reader of the articles of incorporation some information as to the nature of the corporation's business without restricting the freedom of the corporation to engage in new businesses. It also may be important to use narrow purposes clauses in corporations that are to engage in businesses subject to specific state or federal regulation that require regulated corporations to have specified purposes.

Corporate "purposes" should be distinguished from corporate "powers." Every state business corporation act contains a list of corporate powers that every corporation organized under that act automatically possesses. In most states this list is broad and not exclusive. Section 3.02 of the Model Business Corporation Act (1984) is based on the long tradition of powers clauses in state statutes, but it contains additional language in the introductory clause, "and has the same powers as an individual to do all things necessary or convenient to carry out its business and affairs," that is designed to eliminate any historical remnant of doctrines of limited or enumerated powers. Section 3.02 is also broader than many state statutes in specific areas, such as section 3.02(15), authorizing the making of payments or donations or doing of other acts "not inconsistent with law, that furthers the business and affairs of the corporation." This language is independent of the power to make charitable donations [section 3.02(13)], and includes payments for political purposes or to influence elections.

A corporation with a narrow purposes clause may nevertheless possess broad powers under section 3.02 of the MBCA (1984) or similar state statutes, the broad powers to be exercised in furtherance of the narrow purpose.

Where a state statute contains a modern and broad list of powers, it is generally undesirable to include powers clauses in articles of incorporation since the inclusion of certain powers may be construed as negating the existence of non-enumerated ones. Because of peculiar historical problems in some states, however, it may be desirable to refer to certain specific powers in the articles. Where this is felt necessary, the drafting should make clear that the clause relates to powers rather than purposes. A clause that permits a corporation, for example, "to enter into partnerships or joint ventures" states a "power" and not a "purpose." The corporation is utilizing the "power" of entering into a partnership to achieve a "purpose," e.g., a purpose of buying, selling, and trading in real estate. The partnership power clause in this example, incidentally, changes the common law rule that a corporation could not be a general partner in a partnership, and therefore may be appropriate in a state which does not recognize expressly in its business corporation statute that a corporation may act as a general partner in a partnership.

§ 3.9 Articles of Incorporation: Capitalization

Articles of incorporation must include information about the types or kinds of securities the corporation is authorized to issue. A separate chapter of this Nutshell is devoted to corporate securities, and the disclosure requirements applicable to articles of incorporation are discussed there. (See Chapter Seven of this Nutshell, particularly § 7.2.)

The required information about types or kinds of securities in articles of incorporation relates to securities the corporation is authorized to issue rather than the securities the corporation actually plans to issue. However, the statutes of several states require disclosure of what securities will actually be issued, either as a part of a tax return or a general information filing available to the public generally.

Minimum capital requirements in state statutes were practically universal twenty-five years ago. These statutes prohibited the corporation from commencing business unless it had received a specified minimum amount of capital and usually imposed personal liability on the directors if they permitted a corporation to commence business without the minimum capital. The most popular amount was $1,000, but some statutes required $500 or some other amount, and some required some specified percentage of authorized capital. Today all but a handful of states have eliminated such requirements on the theory that any minimum amount of capitalization is arbitrary and does not provide meaningful protection to creditors. The major problem with these minimum capital provisions was that they took no account of the specific capital needs of the particular business. It made no difference whether a corporation needed $1,000,000 or $100 to start up the contemplated business; both needed an initial capitalization of $1,000 under these minimum capital requirements. Also, the requirement of $1,000, while perhaps meaningful in the 1950's and 1960's, had become the victim of inflation and was much less significant by the 1980's. The old Model Business Corporation Act eliminated its minimum capitalization requirement in 1969, and the trend is definitely in the direction of eliminating all such requirements. Thus, in most states today it is theoretically possible (as it is under the Model Business Corporation Act (1984)) to form a corporation with a capitalization of one cent.

In states with a minimum capital requirement, the principal enforcement mechanism is to make directors who assent to the corporation commencing business before it had received the required capital liable jointly and severally for such part of the capital as had not been received. Usually this liability terminates when the required consideration was received. At one time, a few states had *in terrorem* statutes that made the directors personally liable for all corporate obligations incurred before the minimum capital was paid in, even if the shortfall of capital was small and the liabilities incurred were large. None of the remaining states with minimum capital requirements appear to fall within this category.

§ 3.10 Articles of Incorporation: Registered Office and Registered Agent

Every corporation must maintain a registered office and a registered agent at that office. Some states describe the agent as the "statutory agent." The registered office may but need not be the corporation's business office. The primary purpose of a registered office and registered agent is to provide an agent for service of process. The underlying idea is that it should be possible at all times to find a corporation and to have a person upon whom, and a place at which, any notice or process required or permitted by law may be served. A second purpose is to have an office to which tax notices and other official communications from the state may be sent. The original registered office and registered agent must usually be specified in the articles of incorporation; if either is changed thereafter a statement describing the change must be filed with the Secretary of State.

Often a corporation designates its principal business office to be its registered office. In such a case, the registered agent usually is a corporate officer or employee. The principal disadvantage of this is the possibility that summons, legal documents, or other communications may be mixed in with routine business mail and not receive the attention they deserve. For this reason, many attorneys suggest that they be designated as the registered agent and their office be designated as the registered office.

Corporation service companies provide registered offices and registered agents for a modest fee. Corporations that are incorporated in a state in which they do not have a business office—Delaware is the most prominent example—often utilize this service provided by corporations service companies.

§ 3.11 Articles of Incorporation: Initial Board of Directors

The initial board of directors of the corporation must be named in the articles of incorporation in states in which the initial directors are to complete the formation of the contract. In states where the incorporators perform this function there is usually no requirement that initial directors be named in the articles of incorporation.

In states in which the initial board of directors is named in the articles of incorporation, there is no requirement that subsequent changes in membership be reflected by amendments to the articles of incorporation or in later filings with the secretary of state. Unlike the registered office and registered agent, the records maintained by the secretary of state do not indicate who the current directors of a corporation are.

Where the initial board of directors is named in the articles, it serves as the board only until the first annual meeting of shareholders or until the directors' successors are elected and qualify. The first annual meeting of shareholders may be set immediately after the organizational meeting of the initial board of directors so that elected directors take office almost immediately. It is possible in these states to name in the articles of incorporation persons who are nominal directors (that is, directors who have no continuing interest in the business and cease to serve as directors immediately after the organizational meeting). In this way all disclosure of the identity of the permanent board of directors in the articles of incorporation may be avoided. Whether or not this is desirable depends on the wishes of the clients.

Unlike incorporators, directors may sometimes incur liabilities by virtue of their office. Hence, it may be unwise for an attorney or his or her employees to serve as directors, nominal or otherwise, though the risk may be slight as a practical matter if the directorship is for a short period.

§ 3.12   Articles of Incorporation: Limitation of Directoral Liability

As a result of concern about the liability imposed on directors in the famous case of Smith v. Van Gorkom, 488 A.2d 858 (Del.1985), the corporation statutes of many states have been amended to permit the shareholders to limit the personal liability of directors for monetary damages for violations of the duty of due care. See § 14.6 of this Nutshell. In 1994, corporations were also authorized to grant obligatory indemnification of directors (see Chapter 15 of this Nutshell) with respect to all actions taken by a director except liability for "(A) receipt of a financial benefit to which he is not entitled, (B) an intentional infliction of harm on the corporation by its shareholders," or (C) an intentional violation of criminal law or statutory personal liability for making illegal distributions to shareholders [MBCA (1984) § 8.33].

§ 3.13 Completion of the Organization of the Corporation: In General

In addition to preparing and filing the articles of incorporation, the attorney usually handles a number of other routine details in connection with the formation of a corporation. He may:

(1) Prepare the corporate bylaws;

(2) Prepare the call of meeting of the initial board of directors or the incorporators, minutes of this meeting, and waivers of notice or consents if necessary;

(3) Obtain a corporate seal and minute book for the corporation;

(4) Obtain blank certificates for the shares of stock, arrange for their printing or typing, and ensure that they are properly issued;

(5) Arrange for the opening of the corporate bank account;

(6) Prepare the call of meeting of the shareholders, minutes of this meeting and waivers of notice, if necessary;

(7) Prepare employment contracts, voting trusts, pooling agreements, share transfer restrictions, and other special arrangements which are to be entered into with respect to the corporation and its shares;

(8) Obtain taxpayer and employer identification numbers from the Internal Revenue Service and from appropriate state agencies; and

(9) Ensure that the manner in which capital is proposed to be raised is in compliance with the requirements of the federal Securities Act of 1933 and the applicable state blue sky laws.

§ 3.14   Nature and Purpose of Bylaws

The bylaws of a corporation are a set of rules for governing the internal affairs of the corporation. They are adopted by the corporation and technically are binding only on intra-corporate matters. They are often viewed as a contract between the corporation and its officers, directors and shareholders, and among those individuals themselves.

Bylaws are generally not filed with the secretary of state, and are not a matter of public record. They usually may be amended with considerable more facility than the articles of incorporation. In case of conflict between the articles of incorporation and the bylaws, the former, of course, control.

As indicated earlier, it is often optional whether a specific provision is included in the articles of incorporation or in the bylaws. If the provision is unusual or important, maximum legal efficacy is obtained by placing the provision on public record in the articles. On the other hand, corporate officers are much more likely to be conversant with the provisions of the bylaws. For this reason, procedural matters and mandatory provisions that appear in the articles of incorporation and even in the statute should be repeated in the bylaws. The bylaws should set out what amounts to an operating manual of basic rules for ordinary transactions, sufficiently complete to be relied upon by the directors and officers of the corporation as a checklist in administering the affairs of the corporation.

See § 8.9 of this Nutshell for a discussion of the power to amend bylaws.

§ 3.15 The Corporate Seal

In most states a formal corporate seal is no longer necessary. A handwritten facsimile seal has the same legal effect as a metal die, and some states have attempted to dispehse entirely with the requirement of a seal. See MBCA (1984) § 3.02(2). Nevertheless, a seal is probably desirable since it helps to delineate corporate transactions from individual transactions. Also, title and abstract companies and attorneys in real estate work are accustomed to corporate conveyances being under seal, and it may be easier to satisfy them if a formal seal is available. No one need fight city hall unnecessarily.

The corporate seal is usually affixed to share certificates, bonds, debentures, evidences of indebtedness, corporate conveyances of land, certified excerpts from minutes of meetings, and important corporate contracts.

§ 3.16 Organizational Meetings

Most of the miscellaneous matters relating to the launching of a new corporation are accomplished at a meeting of the initial directors, or in some states, the incorporators. Under most statutes today these matters may be handled by written unanimous consent if there is no dispute or controversy, thereby dispensing with the requirement of a formal meeting.

Typical actions include the acceptance of share subscriptions or contracts; the issuance of shares and the establishment of the consideration for them (see Chapter 7 of this Nutshell); the selection and election of officers; the approval of contracts, loans, leases and other business-related matters; approval of the bylaws and the seal; the approval of the payment of the expenses of incorporation (see § 5.8 of this Nutshell); the adoption of a resolution opening a bank account and the designation of the officers authorized to sign checks; and numerous other possible business-related matters. As a practical matter, the attorney normally drafts the written consent or the minutes of this meeting before any meeting takes place. Also, in some circumstances it may be necessary to have a meeting of the shareholders to elect permanent directors; a written unanimous consent may be used instead of a formal meeting. The attorney normally also drafts the minutes of this meeting or the written consent before any meeting takes place. If meetings are actually held, it may be necessary to have a formal waiver of the notice of the meeting; where required, the attorney also prepares this document.

When preparing the documents for the organization of the corporation—whether in the form of written consent or minutes of meetings, the attorney must be careful that the documents reflect compliance with the statutory requirements as well as the wishes of the participants. In states that require the organizational meeting to be held by initial directors named in the articles of incorporation, attorneys sometimes find it necessary, where the permanent parties in interest do not want their names to appear in the records of the secretary of state, to use nominal initial directors, hold a "meeting" of these initial directors to organize the corporation and issue stock, followed immediately by a "meeting" of shareholders to elect permanent directors, followed immediately by another "meeting" of the permanent directors to conduct other necessary business transactions. It might be somewhat more efficient in this scenario to have incorporators organize the corporation since they could issue stock and name the permanent board of directors at a single "meeting": two meetings rather than three would therefore complete the organization of the corporation. On the other hand, if the permanent directors are willing to serve as the initial directors and be named as such in the articles of incorporation, it is simpler for the permanent directors to be named as initial directors, since only a single "meeting" would suffice to complete the formation of the corporation. It was because of scenarios such as these that the draftsmen of the Model Business Corporation Act (1984) decided to give each new corporation an option whether to have organizational meetings conducted by incorporators or by initial directors named in the articles of incorporation. As a practical matter, of course, this is made by the attorney forming the corporation as he or she contemplates the desires of the client and the steps needed to complete the formation of the corporation.

Where the unanimous written consent procedure is not available (as may be the case, for example, where one director is absent), the question sometimes arises as to whether it is necessary to actually hold meetings to reflect what the minutes describe. If the corporation is closely held and there is no disagreement about what is to be done, it seems to be a waste of time and silly play-acting to assemble several persons in a single room and actually hold a meeting at which the already-prepared minutes serve as a script. However, it is generally desirable to actually hold an informal meeting at which the actions referred to in the minutes are quickly approved. Such meetings do have a play-acting atmosphere but the validity of actions taken without a meeting may be questioned otherwise. Such a meeting may take only a minute or so if there is consensus as to what should be done.

[For unfamiliar terms see the Glossary]

CHAPTER FOUR

THE LIMITED ROLE OF ULTRA VIRES

§ 4.1   The Common Law Doctrine of Ultra Vires

The doctrine of ultra vires (literally beyond the scope of the purposes or powers of a corporation) is now largely obsolete in modern corporation law. In an earlier day, however, the doctrine had considerable practical importance and was given major attention. Before turning to the vestigial remnants of the doctrine in modern law, a brief description of the scope of the doctrine at common law should be given.

An ultra vires act was one beyond the purposes or powers of a corporation. The earliest view of the matter was that such acts were totally void. A corporation was formed only for limited purposes, the argument ran, and it could do nothing more than it was authorized to do. This early view, however, was unworkable and unrealistic. Carried to its logical conclusion it would permit a corporation to accept the benefits of a contract and then refuse to perform its obligations on the ground that the contract was ultra vires. (Indeed that may have been the view taken early by the English courts.) It would also impair the security of title to property in fully executed transactions in which a corporation participated. As a result, even though dicta supporting the view that ultra vires acts were totally void appeared in many cases, most courts actually adopted the view that such acts were voidable rather than void. The doctrine continued to be firmly grounded on the notion that a corporation possessed only limited power, but a rather elaborate body of principles developed defining when the defense of ultra vires might be asserted. Basic principles included the following:

(a) An ultra vires transaction might be ratified by all the shareholders. Ratification could be express or implied, e.g., by the receipt of benefits without objection. Ratification, however, had to be by unanimous consent.

(b) The doctrine of estoppel usually precluded reliance on the defense of ultra vires where the transaction was fully performed by one party. In some cases, however, the corporation was held not to be estopped even where the other party had performed fully because the corporation had not received a "direct" benefit from the transaction. When benefits were classed as "direct" or "indirect" appeared to be erratic.

(c) A fortiori, a transaction which was fully performed by both parties could not be attacked. This principle was generally applied to assure security of land titles in transactions that had been closed.

(d) If the contract was fully executory, the defense of ultra vires might be raised by either party.

(e) If the contract was partially performed, and the performance was held to be insufficient to bring the doctrine of estoppel into play, a suit in quasi-contract for recovery of benefits conferred was available.

(f) If an agent of the corporation committed a tort within the scope of his or her employment, the corporation could not defend on the ground the act was ultra vires. This conclusion was reached because of the overriding necessity of protecting innocent third parties from corporate abuses over which they had no means of control.

These principles somewhat tamed the doctrine of ultra vires. That doctrine, however, continued to defeat legitimate expectations where the contract was still executory and possessed an unfortunate capacity to be applied in an erratic fashion in other situations as well. As a result, the modern trend has been to eliminate this doctrine from the law of corporations, or at least to sharply restrict its availability.

§ 4.2   The Modern Role of Ultra Vires

Several modern developments relating to corporate formation have limited the probability that ultra vires acts will occur. Thus, the development of multiple purposes clauses and general clauses permitting corporations to "engage in any lawful business" indirectly limits the role of the doctrine. Further, it is now very simple to amend purposes clauses to broaden them to cover new activities if an ultra vires issue is presented. However, despite these factors, cases involving narrowly drawn purposes clauses still occasionally arise. In order to eliminate the complicated and arbitrary ultra vires rules in these cases, virtually all states have adopted statutes patterned on the following 1950 Model Act provision:

> No act of a corporation and no conveyance or transfer of real or personal property to or by a corporation shall be invalid by reason of the fact that the corporation was without capacity or power to do such act or to make or receive such conveyance or transfer. (§ 7.)

The Model Business Corporation Act (1984) says exactly the same thing in somewhat more elegant language: "The validity of corporate action may not be challenged on the ground that the corporation lacks or lacked power to act." [MBCA (1984) § 3.04(a)] However, both statutes permit the lack of capacity or power to be asserted in the following types of proceedings:

(1) In a proceeding by the corporation (or by a shareholder in a representative capacity) against the incumbent

or former officers or directors of the corporation for exceeding their authority;

(2) In a proceeding by the Attorney General to dissolve the corporation, or to enjoin it from the transaction of unauthorized business; or

(3) In a proceeding by a shareholder against the corporation to enjoin the commission of an ultra vires act or the ultra vires transfer of real or personal property if all parties are before the court and circumstances make such an action equitable.

A limited purposes clause may be included because one or more of the participants desire to restrict the freedom of a corporation to go into new or different ventures (see § 3.8 of this Nutshell). The possibility of enjoining a corporation from violating such a limited clause is recognized in clause (3) "if the circumstances make such an action equitable." However, the Official Comment to section 3.04 points out that rights of third persons who may be unaware of the restrictions must be taken into account in assessing equity; in view of the routine and pro forma nature of the modern incorporation process it is unlikely that a third person would be held subject to a limited purposes clause unless he or she was actually aware of it. The notion that a filing in a public office creates "constructive notice," whatever its merits in other contexts, probably should not extend to unusual provisions in articles of incorporation and, given the modern practice of virtual universal use of general purposes clauses, certainly should not extend to limited purposes clauses.

§ 4.3 Ultra Vires Problems in Connection With Corporate Powers

The concept of ultra vires may arise in one other modern context. As described in § 3.8 of this Nutshell, modern corporation statutes contain a list of powers that every corporation formed under the statute automatically possesses. A corporation may do some act that is beyond its powers as set forth in this list. The language of the Model Business Corporation Act (1984) is so broad, however, that it is unlikely that any action of a corporation formed under that statute would be beyond its powers, and therefore ultra vires. However, the language of powers clauses vary and in some states corporations may not be specifically authorized to engage in certain actions even though they appear to be in furtherance of the stated purposes of the corporation. This problem is also declining in importance as the language of statutes are modernized, but the following kinds of activities may create ultra vires problems in some states.

(1) *Charitable or Political Contributions.* Under early decisions corporations did not have implied power to make donations to charitable, religious, or civic organizations. Most states now generally authorize such contributions though doubt may exist whether power exists to make gifts that are large in comparison to the income or assets of the corporation. A leading Delaware case, Theodora Holding Corp. v. Henderson (Del.Ch.1969), upholds such gifts so long as they are reasonable in amount given the corporate assets and do not exceed the maximum deduction allowed under the federal income tax law. Also a distinction may be drawn between gifts to established charities such as universities, hospitals, or the Red Cross and gifts to organizations or foundations chartered by a controlling shareholder or director. Arguments may also be made that many charitable gifts directly further the corporation's purpose and should be viewed as business rather than eleemosynary transactions.

Direct political contributions by corporations are unlawful and subject to severe civil and criminal sanctions in many states. In First National Bank v. Bellotti (S.Ct.1978), however, the United States Supreme Court held unconstitutional a Massachusetts criminal statute that prohibited corporations from making contributions or expenditures to influence a state referendum. In Austin v. Michigan Chamber of Commerce (S.Ct.1990), the Court recognized that "narrowly drawn" limitations on corporate political speech were constitutionally permissible. In establishing First Amendment rights for corporations, the Supreme Court appears to be concerned with the rights of the hearer of the speech more than its source.

Sections 3.02(13) and 3.02(15) of the Model Business Corporation Act (1984) codify the power of corporations to make charitable contributions and other payments or donations in furtherance of the corporation's business and affairs.

(2) *Pensions, Bonuses, Stock Option Plans, Job Severance Payments, and Other Fringe Benefits.* These arrangements obviously serve legitimate business purposes, and it is clear that a corporation in an appropriate case may award these benefits without express statutory authority.

Most doubts about the propriety of these financial arrangements arise in either of two contexts: where the compensation appears to be excessive or based on self-dealing (discussed in § 14.12 of this Nutshell), or where arguably there is an absence of consideration. For example, consideration may be lacking where, as a humanitarian gesture, a corporation supplements the modest pension of a retired employee. Or a bonus may be paid to an employee at the end of the year without a prior agreement that a bonus would be paid. Or a voluntary payment may be made to the spouse of a deceased employee. Technically, the argument about lack of consideration is not based on lack of corporate power but on substantive contract law. In most cases consideration may be found if the court is willing to look for it. For example, a bonus in one year may lead to an inference that a bonus will be paid the following year; a promise to remain in the corporation's employment may be implied; or the payment of an apparently gratuitous pension may yield contemplated benefits to the corporation in the form of improved employee morale and a happier labor force. In the absence of excessive compensation or blatant self-dealing, courts generally strive to uphold rather than strike down compensation arrangements.

Section 3.02(12) of the Model Business Corporation Act (1984) expressly addresses the power of corporations to provide pension and similar benefits to present or former employees.

(3) *The Power to Enter Into a Partnership*. The statement that it is ultra vires for corporations to enter into partnerships appears in numerous cases. The concern is that the fiduciary duties owed to other partners may conflict with the directors' duties to the shareholders. Because of the prominence of these statements the Model Business Corporation Act (1984) specifically authorizes every corporation "to be a promoter, partner, member, associate, or manager of any partnership, joint venture, trust or other enterprise." [MBCA (1984) § 3.02(9)] The same language appears in the 1969 Model Act. Under such a statute there seems to be no doubt that a corporation has the power to become a partner. All but a handful of states have adopted such a provision.

The major case dealing with the duties that directors of a corporation that is a general partner in a limited partnership has toward the limited partners is In re USACafes (Del.1990).

(4) *The Power to Acquire Shares of Other Corporations*. The power of corporations at common law to acquire shares of other corporations was sharply restricted on the theory that a general power to invest in shares of another corporation constituted an indirect way for corporations to avoid limitations in their own purposes clauses. These

restrictions are obsolete; corporations today generally have power to purchase, sell, and hold shares or other interests in, or obligations of, other domestic or foreign corporations. This power is now codified in section 3.02(6) of the Model Business Corporation Act (1984); virtually identical language appeared in earlier versions of the Model Act.

(5) *Guaranty of Indebtedness of Another.* At common law, it was ultra vires for a general business corporation to guarantee the indebtedness of another person, e.g., a potential customer (an exception was made for corporations who were formed for the specific purpose of writing surety bonds for a fee). This principle, which has little to commend it as an abstract matter, gave rise to a considerable amount of injustice since third persons might readily rely on a corporate guarantee. Fortunately, it has been reversed by statutory provision or judicial decision; section 3.02(7) of the Model Business Corporation Act (1984), for example, authorizes corporations "to make contracts and guarantees [and] incur liabilities;" virtually identical language appeared in earlier versions of the Model Act.

(6) *Loans to Officers or Directors.* Section 3.02(11) of the Model Business Corporation Act (1984) provides that a corporation may elect directors, appoint officers, employees, and agents "and lend them money and credit." The MBCA (1984) recognizes that loans to officers or directors may be beneficial to the corporation, and imposes no special restraints or limitations on them. It was not always so, and it is not so in most states today.

The 1969 and earlier versions of the Model Business Corporation Act contained an unqualified prohibition against such loans: they simply stated that "no loans shall be made by a corporation to its officers or directors." In one form or another, restrictions on loans to officers or directors appear in the statutes of many states; most of these restrictions are not total prohibitions (as in the 1969 Model Act) but permit loans, for example, that are approved by the shareholders or loans that are for the express purpose of permitting the individual to purchase shares of the corporation. Generally these restrictions have been construed as a "limitation on a specific power granted, not a positive prohibition." In other words, loans that violate these restrictions are ultra vires but not illegal. The 1969 version of the Model Act and the statutes of many states also provide that directors who vote for or assent to the making of an improper loan to an officer or director are jointly and severally liable for the amount of the loan until it is repaid. It may be argued that this specific provision constitutes the sole remedy for a violation of this restriction on the general powers of a corporation.

As originally approved, section 8.32 of the MBCA (1984) dealt specifically with loans by a corporation to a director. This section built off the more liberal state statutes, and permitted loans to directors that were (1) approved by a majority of the voting shareholders, (2) approved by the board of directors after a finding that the loan benefits the corporation, or (3) made pursuant to a general plan authorizing loans that was approved by the board of directors after a finding that the plan benefits the corporation. In 1988, however, the Committee on Corporate Laws adopted a new Model Act provision that dealt systematically with conflict of interest transactions between directors and their corporations. Viewing loans to directors as only a special case of conflict of interest transactions that did not require special treatment, the Committee repealed section 8.32. There is therefore now no special provision in the MBCA (1984) dealing with loans to directors.

Restrictions on loans to officers and directors are based on fear that loans to corporate decision-makers are peculiarly subject to abuse; in effect statutes like the 1969

Model Act address this fear by making ultra vires all loans to officers or directors whether or not they are in fact abusive. MBCA (1984) rejects this per se rule and treats such loans as merely one type of conflict of interest transaction. (See § 14.9 of this Nutshell for a discussion of the new MBCA (1984) provisions dealing with conflict of interest transactions.)

The early statutes prohibiting loans to officers or directors sometimes also included a general prohibition (which appears in the 1969 version of the Model Act) against loans "secured by shares of stock of a corporation." Apparently this provision was included to emphasize that from the standpoint of the corporation such a loan was in fact unsecured. (See § 7.8 of this Nutshell, discussing the role of treasury shares.) However, the desirability of including such a limitation on powers seems questionable and the clause was eliminated from the Model Act in 1969; it also has been eliminated from the statutes of all but a handful of states.

[For unfamiliar terms see the Glossary]

CHAPTER FIVE

PREINCORPORATION TRANSACTIONS

§ 5.1 Introduction

The formation of a new corporation is often not a clean birth. Transactions on behalf of the corporation, or in the corporate name, may occur before the articles of incorporation are filed and the corporate existence begins. Such transactions may be entered into with full knowledge that the corporation is not yet formed (such as subscription agreements or contracts by promoters to ensure that the necessary business assets are available), or inadvertently, resulting from unexpected delays in the formation of the corporation. Preliminary transactions are usually classified under several different headings: promoters' transactions, de facto corporations, and so forth. They are, however, all closely related and often factual situations may be classified under more than one of these headings.

§ 5.2 Subscriptions for Shares

A "subscription" is simply an offer to purchase and pay for a specified number of theretofore unissued shares of a corporation. Subscriptions may be divided into "pre-incorporation subscriptions," that is, subscriptions for shares of a corporation that has not yet been formed, and "post-incorporation subscriptions," that is, subscriptions for unissued shares of an already existing corporation.

(a) Pre-incorporation subscriptions. Older texts devote a great deal of attention to pre-incorporation subscrip-

tions as a device by which a new venture may be assured of adequate capitalization before it is launched. Typically, potential investors would be approached individually to determine whether they would be willing to purchase a specified number of shares; those that agreed to purchase shares signed a simple statement that they had subscribed for a specified number of shares. At common law, uncertainty existed whether a subscriber might withdraw from his subscription before the corporation came into existence and accepted it. The reason for this uncertainty was that pre-incorporation subscriptions were obtained individually and were usually viewed as independent offers running from each subscriber to the corporation rather than as a contract among subscribers with the promise of each subscriber supporting the promises of other subscribers. There was no contract in this situation since one "party"—the corporation—was not in existence and could not be bound so that the other party—the subscriber—was not bound either.

This problem has largely faded away. Corporation statutes make pre-incorporation subscriptions irrevocable for a limited period (six months in section 6.20(a) of the Model Business Corporation Act (1984)) during which the formation of the corporation may be completed and the subscriptions accepted without regard to technical questions of consideration; until that period has expired, the statute makes the pre-incorporation subscription irrevocable by the subscriber. This six month period is itself a matter of negotiation between promoter and subscriber, and a longer or shorter period of irrevocability may be agreed upon. Also, without regard to the period of irrevocability, all the subscribers to shares of a not-yet-formed corporation may agree to the revocation of a subscription by one or more specific subscribers.

A subscription may be conditioned on the occurrence of certain events, such as obtaining a specified amount of capital, or a specified loan, or a specified lease. The fulfillment of such conditions is a condition precedent to the obligation of the subscribers. The common law developed a rather confusing distinction between conditional subscriptions and "subscriptions on special terms" which constituted a type of condition subsequent. There was little practical difference, however, because failure of the corporation to comply with a "special term" also permitted the subscriber to rescind or withdraw from his or her subscription. A subscription induced by fraud may be rescinded as any other contract. The fraud may be committed by an agent of the corporation or a promoter of the corporation.

When the corporation is formed, its board of directors may call upon the subscribers to make payment on their subscriptions. See MBCA § 6.20(b). The board of directors may determine the payment terms of pre-incorporation subscriptions, but calls for payment must be uniform among all subscribers of the same class of shares, as far as practicable.

Modern distribution techniques for securities permit the meeting of all capital needs of publicly held corporations without resort to subscriptions. Indeed, the use of subscriptions is unattractive as a practical matter under the Federal Securities Act of 1933 and state "blue sky laws," because the subscriptions themselves constitute securities and must be registered as provided by those acts. Since the underlying securities themselves also must be registered, the use of subscriptions results in two expensive registrations.

In closely held corporations where it is contemplated that there will be only a few shareholders, a contractual agreement among the contemplated shareholders to form a corporation and purchase specified shares is a binding agreement whether or not it is described as a "subscription agreement." Pre-incorporation agreements have largely supplanted the common law subscription, though the wording in such agreements is usually that each investor "agrees to purchase *and subscribe* for * * *" the securities he or she agreed to purchase. Pre-incorporation agreements are enforceable as multilateral contracts among the subscribers without reference to the special statutory provision relating to pre-incorporation subscriptions described above (which applies when each subscriber commits to a subscription individually and not in consideration of other subscribers' similar commitments).

A person who subscribes or agrees to purchase shares does not become a shareholder until the subscription price has been fully paid, though some states permit shares to be issued for promissory notes for the unpaid portion of the purchase price.

(b) Post-incorporation subscriptions. An existing corporation may also seek to raise capital by obtaining commitments from potential investors to purchase shares. Subscriptions of this nature are normally cast in the form of a contract between the corporation and the investor, and are enforceable as any other contract by the corporation or the subscriber. See MBCA (1984) § 6.20(e).

§ 5.3   Agreements to Form Corporation

A so-called pre-incorporation agreement is a contract between proposed shareholders to develop a business to be conducted in the form of a corporation. The contribution of each participant and the number of shares each is to receive are important aspects of this contract, which is a substitute for the common law pre-incorporation subscriptions discussed in section 5.2. Because it is a contract among the participants, it is enforceable in the same manner as any other contract.

A pre-incorporation agreement may be a summary memorandum outlining the main points of an oral agreement, or a complete formal document describing all the details of the understanding. In a formal document, all aspects of the agreement between shareholders may be stated, as may understandings as to employment, capitalization, voting power, share transfer restrictions, or any other matter which is the subject of preliminary agreement. Copies of proposed articles of incorporation, bylaws, and even minutes of meetings may be attached as exhibits.

One important issue with a pre-incorporation agreement is whether it will be fully executed by the formation of a corporation as provided in the agreement or whether specific provisions will survive the creation of the corporation. If it is desired to have certain provisions of the agreement survive and continue to bind the parties, the agreement should specifically so state, since otherwise a court may easily infer that only the provisions actually included in the articles of incorporation, bylaws, and minutes were intended to survive. If the agreement is to survive it should usually be specifically assumed by the corporation after its formation. If the state in question has enacted § 7.32 of MBCA (1984)[discussed in § 12.14 of this Nutshell], the pre-incorporation agreement may also serve as a shareholders' agreement if it is appropriately described and executed by all of the shareholders of the corporation.

An agreement to form a corporation usually places the parties to the agreement in the relationship of joint venturers, the object of the venture being the formation of the corporation and the establishment of its business. If the agreement survives, there may be a conceptual difficulty since after the corporation is formed the parties are simultaneously being treated as having the rights of shareholders in the corporation and the rights of joint venturers in an underlying arrangement to form the corporation. To avoid possible conflicts, some courts have taken the position that when the parties adopt the corporate form, with the corporate shield to protect them, they necessarily "cease to be partners and have only the rights, duties and obligations of stockholders." Other courts however, have taken the position that the joint venture may continue after the formation of the corporation, at least where the parties' intention to this effect is clear. The question appears to be one of "intention" since there appears to be no reason why both relationships cannot exist simultaneously if that is what the parties desire.

§ 5.4 Promoters in General

A promoter is a person who takes the initiative in developing and organizing a new business venture. A promoter may act either alone or with co-promoters. The term "promoter" is not one of opprobrium; indeed, the promoter is often an aggressive, imaginative entrepreneur who fulfills the essential economic function of taking an idea and creating a profitable business to capitalize on the idea.

The activities of promoters fall into three principal areas. (1) The promoter must arrange for the necessary capital for the corporation. He or she may invest only personal funds, or use personal funds plus loans from banks to obtain the necessary capital. Outside capital may be obtained from a small number of investors, who may be friends or neighbors. If so, the promoter must negotiate with the outside investors to determine their share in the forthcoming enterprise, and arrange either by contract or subscription to ensure that the capital will be forthcoming when needed. If a public offering is to be made (which is rare for a newly-commenced business) the promoter must secure compliance with the Federal Securities Act of 1933 and state "blue sky" laws as well as arranging for the distribution and sale of the securities, often through an underwriter. (2) The promoter must obtain the necessary

assets and personnel so that the corporation may function. He or she may obtain a lease or an option to
purchase needed land, or may enter into a contract to
purchase with a view of assigning the contract to the
corporation. He or she may negotiate construction contracts to build or remodel the necessary buildings. Arrangements must be made to secure the necessary employees which usually will include the promoter as an
officer of the new enterprise. The necessary machinery,
equipment, or fixtures must be secured; customers must
be contacted; arrangements made for advertising; and so
forth. Obviously, in this area, the kinds of activities promoters engage in are numerous and varied, depending on
the nature of the business being promoted. (3) The promoter must arrange for the formation of the corporation
itself. As described in chapter 3 of this Nutshell, he or she
must arrange for the filing of the articles of incorporation,
the preparation of the necessary papers, the issuance of
shares, and the like.

If the promoter first forms the corporation, subsequent
contractual problems are usually minimized since all the
necessary steps may thereafter be conducted in the name
of the corporation, and there is little chance of confusion
between the promoter's individual liability and the corporate liability on the arrangements being negotiated. Thus,
actions may be taken in the corporate name and not in
the name of the promoter individual. Of course, if a third
person requests the personal liability of the promoter as
well as the corporation, as may be the case with banks, the
promoter may execute an obligation individually or separately guaranteeing its performance.

Often, however, the formation of the corporation turns
out to be one of the last steps in the promotional process.
The promoter may begin investigation of the profitability
of the proposed business, determine that the prospects of
success are good, and proceed at once with business

negotiations in the areas of capital formation, obtaining business assets, and entering into contracts without actually forming the corporation. In this situation there is great likelihood of confusion and uncertainty, and most contractual litigation involving promoters arises in connection with not-yet-formed corporations.

§ 5.5   Promoters' Contracts

Let us assume that before the corporation is formed the promoter enters into a contract to purchase machinery for the new business being promoted, and consider whether the promoter is personally liable on that contract. No single, simple answer is possible. In some circumstances personal liability will exist, in other circumstances it will not. There are at least three different situations:

(a) Contracts Executed in the Name of the Promoter. If the promoter enters into a contract in his or her own name without referring to the corporation with the thought of subsequently assigning the contract to the corporation, personal liability on the part of the promoter clearly exists. The subsequent assignment of the contract to the corporation does not relieve the promoter of personal liability unless the creditor agrees, explicitly or implicitly, to release the promoter and look only to the corporation for performance. The release of a party to a contract when it is assumed by another is called a *novation.*

(1) *Contracts Entered in the Name of the Corporation.* The promoter may execute a contract in the corporate name when in fact the corporation has not yet been formed. Many cases say that such a promoter is personally liable on the theory that a person acting as agent represents that a principal exists, and the promoter is liable because of a misrepresentation. Other cases rely on the agency principle that a person who purports to act as

agent for a nonexistent principal thereby automatically becomes liable for the action. The latter theory is based on contract and the former on tort, though in most cases they should lead to the same result.

These cases often give the third person a windfall because presumably that person is not relying on the promoter's credit when entering into a contract in which a corporation is named as the other party; rather he or she is relying on the corporation's credit or, more likely, on the possibility that the corporation will do well and be able to pay off the obligations. However, virtually all courts in this situation hold the promoter personally liable despite the potential windfall.

If the corporation is thereafter formed and adopts the contract, the promoter may argue that the subsequent formation of the corporation corrected any misrepresentation or deception that may have occurred. Or he may argue that the manner of execution of the agreement indicates that the third person was content to accept the liability of the corporation, and that therefore the adoption of the contract by the corporation should release the promoter—in other words, that the transaction should be construed as a novation. Depending on the specific circumstances, other arguments may also be available to the promoter, but their probability of success is not very good.

To summarize: if the promoter enters into a contract with a third person in the name of the corporation without disclosing that it is not in existence, the promoter is personally liable on the contract. If the corporation is thereafter created and takes over the contract, the promoter has a chance of being relieved of liability but there is a substantial chance that a court will conclude that no novation was intended and the promoter remains liable.

(3) *Contracts Referring to the Fact the Corporation Is Not Yet Formed.* In this class of case the contract is executed by the promoter and the third party when both are aware that the corporation has not been formed. The contract itself usually reveals this fact, as for example when it is executed in a name such as "ABC Corporation, a corporation to be formed." Or the promoter may advise the third person that the corporation has not yet been formed when the contract is executed in the corporate name. It may be noted that this situation differs from situation (2) in that both parties are aware that the corporation is not yet in existence and there is no possible misrepresentation as to that fact.

This pattern may be analyzed in several different ways with widely divergent consequences. For example, it may be analyzed as an offer to the corporation which is revocable by either party and will result in a contract only if the corporation is thereafter formed and accepts the offer before it is withdrawn. Or it may be analyzed as an irrevocable option running to the corporation, with the consideration being a promise, express or implied, by the promoter to form the corporation and use best efforts to cause the corporation to adopt the contract. Or, it may be analyzed as a present contract between the third person and the promoter by which the promoter is bound, with the understanding that if the contract is adopted by the corporation the promoter will be released from liability under the contract. It is also possible that a court may conclude that the mere formation of the corporation did not constitute a novation.

Which of these various alternatives is the proper one in any specific situation depends on the elusive "intention of the parties." If an attorney is called upon to draft a pre-incorporation agreement it is relatively simple to ascertain the parties' intention and describe it in a written agreement in terms so precise that there can be no cause for misunderstanding. If the promoter is to be bound until the corporation adopts the contract, and then is to be released from liability, a contract that specifically so provides should avoid later disputes.

Litigation in this area generally involves agreements in which the intention is not clearly spelled out. The contract may have been negotiated by the parties without legal assistance, or the language chosen may not illuminate the specific problem one way or the other. Or the parties may have been unable to agree on their respective rights in the event of some remote contingency. Rather than forego a lucrative transaction, the parties use language such as "ABC Corporation, a corporation to be formed," hoping that the question of the liability of the promoter will not arise. In such situations, the search for intent is truly hopeless, though the courts must resolve the dispute one way or another.

Generalizations about tests which courts use to find "intention" are hazardous. Probably most courts feel that it is likely that the third person intended for *someone* to be liable. Hence, there is a strong probability that the promoter will initially be held liable, especially where the corporation is never formed. Indeed, many cases state without qualification that the promoter is personally liable in this situation unless there is specific agreement to the contrary. If the third person is to receive payments or partial performance before the corporation is formed, an intention to hold the promoter personally responsible may readily be inferred; presumably the promoter intends to make those payments or render the performance personally until the corporation is formed.

Professor Williston suggested that most persons assume that even if the promoter is initially liable, he or she is nevertheless to be released if the corporation is later formed and adopts the contract. In other words, there is to be a novation. The testimony of the plaintiff in Brad-

mere corporate existence is in effect a use of the benefits of the contract by the corporation. Arguably, therefore, by its mere existence the corporation has agreed to pay whatever fee was negotiated by the promoter. The majority view, however, rejects this reasoning and holds that the corporation is not automatically bound. Rather the corporation—since it cannot refuse the services—can only be compelled to pay a reasonable fee under the circumstances.

Many states have statutes that permit the payment of reasonable charges and expenses of organization of a corporation out of the capital received by it in payment for its shares without impairing capital or rendering such shares not fully paid and non-assessable. See MBCA (1984) § 6.28. It is not clear whether such a provision is necessary in modern corporation statutes; it was retained by the draftsmen of the Model Business Corporation Act (1984) essentially because it could do no harm and might do some good.

The promoter or the attorney may suggest that the attorney take shares in the corporation for organizational expenses and services. There is nothing inherently wrong with this practice: indeed, it somewhat resembles a contingent fee which is based on the success of the business rather than on the outcome of litigation. The value of shares received by an attorney or promoter for services is, of course, taxable income to him or her and may be deducted by the corporation as an expense over a 60 month period.

Promoters naturally expect to be compensated for their efforts, and in view of the nature of their innovative efforts, they may legitimately expect compensation which would be considered generous by a salaried person. A promoter may form a corporation with nominal capital, and then seek outside financial support to make the promotion a success. The subsequent investors will usually purchase shares in the corporation at a higher price than the shares previously issued to the promoter. The investors' interest is thereby diluted and the promoters' interest increased in value. In a sense this increase in value represents partial compensation to the promoter; it is often a subject of negotiation between promoters and investors. However, both hope that the major portion of the promoter's compensation will result from the fact that the business does well so that the value of everyone's shares will be enhanced.

§ 5.9 Premature Commencement of Business and the De Facto Doctrine

The procedure to form a corporation under most corporation statutes is basically a very simple one. As a matter of fact, it is so simple and routine that attorneys may become careless and fail to comply with all the requirements that do exist. Mistakes may range from the trivial, such as using an incorrect address, to the more serious, where the attorney becomes so careless that he or she prepares but fails to file the articles of incorporation at all (this has actually happened). Delays in filing are not uncommon. Perhaps the secretary of state declines to accept the first filing because of some minor defect which the attorney subsequently corrects. In the mean time, the "corporation" has commenced business. What is the liability of shareholders for the interim debts in such situations?

At common law, these problems were usually handled under the "de facto corporation" doctrine, though occasionally they appeared as promoters contracts; today many courts still apply this common law concept though it has been largely superseded by a statutory analysis. A "de facto corporation" according to the common law was not a fully formed corporation (a "de jure corporation"), but was nearly as good since it was sufficiently formed to be immune from attack by everyone but the state. The usual test for de facto existence was threefold: there must be a statute under which incorporation was permitted, there must have been a "good faith" or "colorable" attempt to comply with the statute, and there must have been actual user of the corporate privilege. However, the cases arising under this doctrine were confusing, particularly with regard to the second requirement and legal commentators convincingly proved that the traditional tests provide little guidance for the decisions of concrete cases. After examining more than 200 de facto corporation cases arising prior to 1950, for example, the late Professor Frey concluded that the de facto doctrine was "legal conceptualism at its worst." In a later study, considering cases arising between 1950 and 1989, Professor Bradley reaches a similar conclusion.

At common law a "de jure corporation" might exist even though there were some minor defects in its formation. The common law drew a distinction between "mandatory" and "directory" requirements; failure to comply with the latter did not prevent the creation of a de jure corporation. An example of a "directory" requirement was the listing of addresses of directors or incorporators.

These problems today are usually resolved by reference to the specific language of the state's incorporation statute. Every state has a statute that provides in substance that the corporate existence begins either upon the filing of the articles of incorporation or the issuance of the certificate of incorporation. See MBCA (1984) § 2.03(a). Most statutes add that acceptance of the articles (or the issuance of the certificate of incorporation) is "conclusive proof" that all conditions precedent to incorporation have been complied with except in suits brought by the State. See MBCA (1984) § 2.03(b). Thus, if the Secretary of State accepts a filing (or issues a certificate of incorporation), a de jure corporation is in existence despite mistakes or omissions in the articles of incorporation. Professor Bradley criticizes these statutes on the ground they often lead to results "which are contrary to the intent of the parties and thus provides one party with a windfall" since by hypothesis both parties intended only for the (unformed) corporation to be personally liable.

Another problem that arises under section 2.03(b) and similar statutes is whether a negative inference should be drawn that the corporate existence has *not* begun before the articles are filed or the certificate is issued, so that personal liability exists for all pre-filing transactions. A few states have addressed this issue by adopting an additional statute that deals specifically with transactions that occur during the pre-filing period. Many of these statutes are based on section 146 of the 1969 Model Act, which states that "all persons who assume to act as a corporation without authority so to do shall be jointly and severally liable" for all debts and liabilities. However, even in states in which this statute is in effect, some courts have refused to hold participants personally liable on pre-incorporation transactions. One court construed the phrase "all persons who assume to act" as referring only to active participants in the venture, thereby immunizing inactive participants from liability. Timberline Equipment Co., Inc. v. Davenport (Or.1973). All in all, the predictability of result under this statute was not much greater than under the de facto-de jure tests of common law.

The committee creating the Model Business Corporation Act (1984) took a fresh look at the standard to be applied to shareholder liability for pre-formation transactions, and came up with a somewhat different standard. Section 2.04 of MBCA (1984) provides that "all persons purporting to act as or on behalf of a corporation, *knowing there was no incorporation under this Act*, are jointly and severally liable for all liabilities created while so acting."

The basic problem with a simple rule conditioning the existence or nonexistence of a corporation on the acceptance of a filing (or the issuance of a certificate by the secretary of state) is that it has a substantial capacity for unfairness. Under such a rule, if the secretary of state has not accepted the articles (or issued the certificate), the shareholders and promoters may be liable as partners for the pre-incorporation debts of the business. The result is that negligence in filing on the part of A may cause crushing liabilities to be imposed on B who may have bought "shares" in the honest belief that the corporation's articles had been properly filed. Of course, B might first check with the secretary of state's office, but most investors would not normally think to do so. The standard of section 2.04 of MBCA (1984), "knowing there was no incorporation under this Act," provides protection to B in this situation.

§ 5.10   Corporations by Estoppel

Problems of the type discussed in the last section have sometimes been handled in the absence of statute under the phrase "corporation by estoppel." This phrase is not meaningful in and of itself. It is necessary to ask who is "estopped," under what circumstances, and for what reason. The classic requirements for equitable estoppel (or "estoppel in pais") are (1) there be a false representation to or concealment of a fact from a person ignorant of the truth (2) with the intention by the person making the representation of causing reliance, and (3) actual reliance by the innocent party on the basis of the false representation. "Corporations by estoppel" do not involve these principles. For example, consider the situation where a third person deals with a "corporation" as such relying only on its credit and then discovers that a certificate of incorporation was never obtained. She seeks to hold the

promoters and shareholders personally liable as partners.
The defendants who were unaware that no filing had been
made in turn may argue that the plaintiff is "estopped" by
his or her prior dealings on a corporate basis from holding them personally liable. Some courts have accepted this
argument. This is certainly not equitable estoppel in the
classic sense, since the third person who is being "estopped" never made any representation of any kind which
was relied on by any other party. Rather, the person who
herself relied is the one being estopped. In effect, courts
are applying the label "corporation by estoppel" to reach
a desirable result: used in this way "estoppel" is a conclusion, not an explanation. Nevertheless, there may be
strong equitable grounds for limiting the third person's
claim to the business assets and the personal assets of the
participants who conducted business knowing that no
articles had been filed. The third person receives a windfall if, after dealing and relying solely on the "corporation," he or she is permitted to hold the promoters or
shareholders personally liable. Further, it may be harsh to
hold investors personally liable because of the negligence
or neglect of some other person, particularly where the
investors honestly and reasonably believed that the articles
of incorporation had been filed. For these various reasons,
some courts have held that the third person is "estopped"
from suing the promoters or shareholders, or that there is
a "corporation by estoppel."

It should be noted that this reasoning apparently results
in the recognition of limited liability for some participants
despite the fact that the promoters may have failed to
comply with the most important statutory requirements
for obtaining this privilege. Indeed, if an estoppel principle were universally recognized one might consider saving
the filing fee by not filing anything and simply conducting
business in the corporate name. As a result, not all courts
agree that "estoppel" should be applied in this type of

situation (though the variations in decisions possibly may be explained by factual variations and variations in statutory wording). There is much to be said for the proposition that a "shareholder" should not be personally liable where (a) the plaintiff dealt with the "corporation" as such, and (b) the defendant believed that the articles of incorporation had been properly filed and was not personally negligent in failing to make sure that the filing actually occurred. This position—which of course should also be reached under § 2.04 of the Model Business Corporation Act—appears to do justice to all parties and does not seriously undermine the statutory policy requiring filing of articles of incorporation, since persons knowing that the articles have not been filed would have unlimited liability under all circumstances. It is believed that the results of the pre-statutory case law are basically consistent with this view, which is incorporated in the Model Business Corporation Act (1984).

[For unfamiliar terms see the Glossary]

CHAPTER SIX

"PIERCING THE CORPORATE VEIL" AND RELATED PROBLEMS

§ 6.1 "Piercing the Corporate Veil" In Context

Assume for a moment that a corporation has been properly and fully created in accordance with state law so that a "de jure corporation" has been created in the fullest sense of that phrase. The basic question discussed in this Chapter is whether and to what extent the separate existence of that corporation should be ignored in order to do basic justice or avoid the frustration of some clearly articulated public policy. At first blush, the basic concept that a corporation is a fictitious person or separate legal entity seems to dictate the answer that the separate existence of such a duly formed corporation should never be ignored. The law has not taken this extreme position, however, and the courts in a large number of cases have refused to recognize the separate existence of a duly formed corporation. To put the matter into perspective, it should be added that in an even larger number of cases courts have respected the separate existence of corporations despite arguments that they should not do so. The corporate fiction is a basic assumption that underlies commercial transactions; there must be compelling reasons before a court will ignore such a basic assumption.

When the separate existence of the corporation is ignored, courts often use the colorful metaphor of "piercing the corporate veil." They also use phrases such as "alter ego" or "mere instrumentality" that shed little light on why the corporate existence is being ignored.

§ 6.2 Shareholder Responsibility for Corporate Indebtedness: Introduction

A shareholder may become liable for corporate indebtedness in a variety of ways. She may voluntarily guarantee the performance of the corporation's obligation. She also may become personally liable by executing a document, such as a promissory note, in a way that makes it appear that she is acting as a co-obligor rather than as an agent of the corporation. She may also incur personal liability by failing to describe accurately the name of the corporation when dealing on behalf of the corporation, though case law tends to be generous to shareholders in these cases. For example, in one case a Mr. Pinson executed a lease in the name "Pinson Air Freight, Inc." when in fact his corporation's name was "Pinson Air Freight of Chattanooga, Inc." The court held the corporation and not Mr. Pinson liable on the lease. Pinson v. Hartsfield Int'l Comm. Ctr., Ltd. (Ga.App.1989). These are not true "piercing the corporate veil" cases.

In considering cases involving shareholder responsibility for corporate indebtedness, there should also be put aside cases where liability is imposed upon shareholders under conventional theories of agency or tort law. In other words, if individual A is personally liable for something individual B did under principles of agency, the same result should be reached if B is a corporation rather than an individual. To argue that the corporate veil is "pierced" in such cases is both unnecessary and confusing. Where the shareholder is actually acting as a principal in his or her own name, there is clearly liability on the obligation under accepted principles of agency. Similarly, if the shareholder is personally involved in the commission of a tort while acting as an agent for his or her corporation, she is personally liable for the tort because of her own actions and again it is unnecessary to discuss piercing the corporate veil.

The balance of this chapter assumes that liability is sought to be imposed on shareholders because of their ownership interest in the corporation and not because of their own conduct or the conduct of their agents.

§ 6.3   The Standard Rhetoric of Piercing the Corporate Veil

The question of the status of a corporation usually arises in situations where a liability has clearly been incurred in the name of a corporation, but the corporation has become insolvent. The creditor, seeking to find a solvent defendant, may sue some or all of the shareholders, arguing that for some reason the corporate veil should be pierced and they should be called upon to pay the corporation's debts. [Indeed, such a creditor may also sue directors, officers, and anyone else in any way connected with the corporation. The possible liabilities of directors, officers, or employees are discussed in later chapters (see particularly Chapters 11 and 14 of this Nutshell); this Chapter is limited to the possible liability of shareholders.] When the corporation is insolvent and recovery is sought from shareholders, the court is faced with the basic issue of most piercing the corporate veil cases: should a loss be imposed on third persons or on the shareholders; there is a loss and someone must pay. A blind application of the "artificial entity" approach would mean that the creditor always suffers the loss; certainly that result is often reasonable but it is not inevitable.

Most opinions by courts shed little light on the considerations governing how this issue should be resolved. The traditional statement of the piercing corporate veil doctrine, taken from the leading case of Bartle v. Home Owners Cooperative (N.Y.1955), is that:

The law permits the incorporation of a business for the very purpose of escaping personal liability. Generally speaking, the doctrine of "piercing the corporate veil" is invoked "to prevent fraud or to achieve equity." But in the instant case there has been neither fraud, misrepresentation nor illegality.

Such statements essentially restate the issue by using terms of uncertain content—equity, misrepresentation, fraud, or illegality. Other tests also have some support in the cases: for example, that the question is whether the corporation is the "instrumentality" of the shareholder [i.e. the shareholder has exercised excessive control and there is wrongful or inequitable conduct]; or whether the corporation is the "alter ego" of the shareholder [i.e. such unity of ownership and interest exists that the separate existence of the corporation has ceased and recognition of the separate entity might lead to an inequitable result]. Still other cases utilize a variety of different metaphors [e.g., "shell," "dummy," or "fiction"] rather than analysis; all of this name-calling asserts a conclusion without giving any clue as to the reasons underlying it. As early as 1926, Justice Cardozo complained that the whole problem "is still enveloped in the mists of metaphor" and that the appropriate tests should be "honesty and justice." Berkey v. Third Avenue R. Co. (1926).

§ 6.4 Piercing the Corporate Veil in Contract and Tort Cases

In the great bulk of piercing cases a major consideration in determining whether the shareholder should be liable for losses or injuries suffered by a third party is whether the third party dealt voluntarily with the corporation or whether he or she is an involuntary creditor, typically a tort claimant. The standards should be quite different in these two types of cases.

In a contract case, the third party has usually dealt in some way with the corporation and should be aware that the corporation lacks substance. In the absence of some sort of deception, the creditor thus more or less assumed the risk of loss; if the creditor was concerned that the corporation might not be able to pay the obligation, he should insist that some solvent third person guarantee the performance by the corporation. If such a guarantee is requested and refused, the creditor may either simply forego the transaction or consciously assume the risk that the corporation may not be able to discharge its obligation. Where a request for a personal guarantee is made and refused, the parties have in effect agreed upon the allocation of risk (at least in the absence of deception) and the court should not interfere with that allocation. Much the same analysis is true when no request for a guarantee is made, but the creditor simply enters into the transaction without investigation. In effect, he is assuming a risk when he enters into the transaction. Thus, in contracts cases, the loss should usually be placed on the third person—the result actually reached in the great bulk of the contract cases by not "piercing the corporate veil."

In tort cases, on the other hand, there is usually no element of voluntary dealing, and the question is whether it is reasonable for owners of a business to transfer a risk of loss or injury to members of the general public through the device of a corporation. This logically should depend on whether the corporation was adequately financed to cover the reasonably foreseeable risks incident to the particular business the corporation is in. If the corporation was not adequately financed in this sense, there is objectionable risk shifting to members of the general public. In this regard, liability insurance should count as "capitalization" if the risk is an insurable one, since insurance makes funds available to injured tort victims just as much as equity capital does. The issues of public policy raised by tort claims thus bear little relationship to the issues raised by contract claims. This fundamental distinction, however, has not always been perceived by courts, which sometimes indiscriminately cite, and purport to apply, tort precedents in contract cases and vice versa.

These general policies do not explain all cases; the separate existence of a corporation may also be ignored even though it meets the requirements of the above paragraphs if its business is conducted in a way designed to cause injury to creditors. The most common example is when the shareholders make distributions of excess assets to themselves, thereby rendering the corporation virtually judgment proof. Since these cases involve shareholder enrichment at the expense of creditors, it is not surprising that judicial rhetoric in such cases is strong. Such transactions may be subject to attack as a fraudulent transfer or as fraud on creditors, but in close cases courts may prefer to analyze the situation in terms of the rather vague tests of piercing the corporate veil.

Another example of misconduct by shareholders is where the shareholder misleads a third person regarding the financial status of the corporation so that the third person believes the corporation has more capital than it actually has. The element of voluntary risk allocation disappears in this situation, and shareholder liability should be imposed. A similar principle may be applied if a shell corporation is substituted—without overt misrepresentation—at the last minute and the other party. is tricked into dealing with the shell corporation. Mere silence or even an oral promise by a shareholder to guarantee payment by the corporation's debt, which itself is unenforceable under the statute of frauds, normally is itself not a misrepresentation, though some courts have relied upon such a promise in piercing the corporate veil. Situations involving manifest unfairness arising from unequal bargaining power not reaching the level of unconscionability or other types of inequitable, unfair, or fraudulent conduct may also be envisioned that may be found to have been designed to injure creditors. These situations gradually shade over into those involving duress, coercion, or other independent grounds for setting aside a contract.

Opinions in many cases accept these basic principles and rely on "inadequate capitalization" in holding shareholders liable for corporate tort obligations while talking about "risk assumption" in contracts cases. Cases, furthermore, usually talk about piercing whenever recognition of the separate corporate existence will lead to "fraud" or an "unfair result" or cause harm. Many cases, however, are not entirely consistent with these principles. Many courts, for example, list "adequate capitalization" as a factor to be considered in contracts cases; courts may apply a laundry list of factors to all cases indiscriminately and may expressly disavow any distinction in the tests applicable to contract and tort cases. Perhaps the one common feature in piercing cases is that virtually all courts agree that piercing is appropriate only when recognition of the separate corporate existence will lead to injustice or an unfair or inequitable result.

There has been one empirical study of the actual outcomes of litigated piercing cases (Thompson, Piercing the Corporate Veil: An Empirical Study, 76 Cornell L.Rev. 1036 (1991)). This study indicates that the corporate veil was pierced in 42 percent of the contracts cases and 31 percent of the tort cases; undercapitalization was a factor in 19 percent of the contracts cases and 13 percent of the tort cases. In this study, the results in 779 contracts cases and 226 tort cases were examined.

§ 6.5 Inadequate Capitalization

As indicated above, inadequate capitalization should be relevant primarily in tort cases, though it is often referred to (and sometimes relied upon) in contracts cases as well. The phrase "inadequate capitalization" has more than one possible meaning. A few states require a corporation, before commencing business, to have received some minimum amount of capital, usually $1,000, for the issuance of shares. In a sense, a corporation in these states that begins business with less than $1,000 is inadequately capitalized, but that is not the usual meaning. In the "piercing" area, "inadequate capitalization" usually means a capitalization that is very small in relation to the nature of the risks the business of the corporation necessarily entails; in other words it is based on likely economic needs rather than legal requirements. Thus, while the corporation need not be capitalized so as to ensure that all conceivable liabilities will be discharged, a corporation should be reasonably capitalized in light of the nature and risks of the business. This argument was accepted in the leading California case of Minton v. Cavaney (Cal.1961), and traces of it appear in opinions in several other jurisdictions. Minton v. Cavaney, like many other cases in this area, also involved another factor: a failure to complete the formation of the corporation, and the court may have been partially influenced by that factor as well. Whether a corporation is under capitalized in the sense used here obviously presents a question of fact that turns on the nature of the business of the particular corporation.

Logically, in a tort case, liability insurance should "count" as equity capital, since it is available to compensate injured members of the general public. The leading case recognizing this principle is Radaszewski v. Telecom Corp. (8th Cir.1992).

There is a serious question as to when the adequacy of capital should be measured. Normally, it should be measured at the time of formation of the corporation or perhaps at the time an existing corporation goes into a new line of business. However, what about a corporation that was adequately capitalized originally, but as a result of economic losses is now undercapitalized? Assuming that an adequately capitalized corporation has suffered un-avoidable losses, the general rule should be that it should not be viewed as undercapitalized. It is not reasonable to inflict personal liability for a tort on shareholders who originally capitalized their corporation merely because the corporation suffered unavoidable economic losses. Many individuals continue in business even though their re-sources are depleted by losses, and corporations should be treated no differently.

A further powerful policy argument may be made in these cases if assets that might be used for the purchase of insurance or retained in the business to increase the creditor's cushion are siphoned off through dividends, salaries or similar payments. Corporate affairs obviously should not be conducted so as to minimize the assets available for tort claimants. The bounds of this rather appealing policy argument are totally undefined, and as a result it seldom appears in court opinions. Indeed, it was apparently rejected in the majority opinion in another leading New York case, Walkovszky v. Carlton (N.Y.1966). Its influence, however, should not be underestimated: courts are much more likely to "pierce the corporate veil" and hold shareholders liable in tort cases when the ele-ments of marginal capitalization and systematic dispersal of assets are combined. Conversely adequate capitalization and clear evidence that the corporation "did the best it could" are likely to protect shareholders against tort claims based on the corporation's acts.

The taxicab industry has been an important source of new cases concerning shareholder responsibility for tort liabilities of the corporation. Particularly in New York City the practice has developed of separately incorporating one or two taxicabs in a large fleet and establishing a separate corporation to operate the central garage, and perhaps yet another corporation to run the dispatching service. Each operating taxicab company has the minimum required capitalization (usually invested in the taxicab itself) and carries the minimum insurance required by state law. The drivers themselves are usually judgment proof, so that seriously injured victims of taxicab accidents go largely uncompensated unless they can look to the assets of the shareholders. The theory of "enterprise entity" discussed in section 6.8 of this Nutshell dictates that the separate existence of each minimally capitalized taxicab corporation should be ignored and the entire fleet of taxicabs treated as a single entity; the more difficult question is whether a claim may also be made against the shareholders individually. In Walkovszky v. Carlton the court refused to hold the shareholder liable in the absence of allegations that he or she was conducting business in his or her individual capacity, and "shuttling * * * personal funds in and out of the corporations 'without regard to formality and to suit their immediate convenience.' " However, after the complaint was amended to make this specific allegation, it was upheld on a motion to dismiss; the case was thereafter settled. The reluctance of the defendants to go to a jury in cases of this character is understandable; most of the litigation arises on a motion to dismiss, and the cases are settled if the complaint survives that motion.

§ 6.6 Failure to Follow Corporate Formalities

Anyone reading cases dealing with shareholder liability for corporate obligations will be struck by the emphasis placed by courts on the failure to follow the requisite corporate formalities as a ground for imposing shareholder liability in both contract and tort cases. In many opinions, the court describes the failure to follow normal corporate routine and then concludes that the corporation is the "alter ego" or "instrumentality" of the shareholder or that the "corporate veil should be pierced." While a complete catalogue of dangerous acts is probably impossible to prepare, there appears to be a substantial risk that the separate corporate existence will be ignored when business is commenced without completing the organization of the corporation or without issuing shares and receiving the consideration therefor, when shareholders' meetings or directors' meetings are not held (or consents are not signed), when decisions are made by shareholders as though they were partners, when shareholders do not sharply distinguish between corporate property and personal property, when corporate funds are used to pay personal expenses, when personal funds are used for corporate expenses without proper accounting, or when complete corporate and financial records are not maintained.

It is difficult to see, as a matter of logic, why corporate confusion and informality have been given the importance that they have. In most cases, the confusion and informality are not related to the claim advanced by either tort or contract plaintiffs. As a matter of fact, evidence of informality or commingling of affairs is usually first found during discovery long after the transaction giving rise to the particular litigation took place. To hold shareholders personally liable because of activities which are almost always unrelated to the plaintiff's claim, creates a windfall for the plaintiff. For this reason, some courts have refused to "pierce the corporate veil" despite considerable evidence of confusion. One possible explanation for "piercing the corporate veil" in these cases is that the shareholder should not be permitted first to ignore the rules of corporate behavior and then later to claim the advantage of the corporate shield. In the absence of harm to anyone or to the state, however, it is difficult to see why the premise should lead to the conclusion.

The importance given to corporate formalities as the test for determining whether the corporation's separate existence will be recognized tends to create a trap for unwary shareholders in closely held corporations. Shareholders in a small corporation often find managing the business a full-time occupation; formal corporate affairs such as meetings and the like are put off or ignored because there is full agreement in fact by all interested parties regarding what should be done and who should do it. The play-acting aspects of corporate meetings, elections, and the like in a closely held corporation may also strike businessmen as rather silly. Insistence by an attorney that formal corporate procedures be followed may be dismissed as a subtle attempt at an additional fee. This attitude invites disaster.

When failure to follow appropriate corporate procedures tends to injure third persons, there is little objection to holding the shareholder liable. Procedures within the corporation may be so undifferentiated that a person may believe he or she is dealing with a shareholder individually rather than with the corporation. Similarly, intermingled personal and corporate assets may disappear into the personal coffers of the shareholder to the detriment of corporate creditors. These factors, however, are present in only a small minority of the confusion cases.

§ 6.7 Parent–Subsidiary Cases

Many cases in which shareholder liability has been found concern shareholders that are themselves corporations. In these cases, a parent corporation is being held liable for the debts of a subsidiary. They have a different flavor than cases in which the shareholder defendant is an individual, and some cases even suggest that different tests are being applied depending on whether the shareholder-defendant is an individual or a corporation. When a corporation is the defendant, only a larger corporate entity is being held responsible for the debt; when an individual is the defendant, however, personal liability extending to non-business assets is being imposed. There is therefore a wide-spread belief that "piercing" is easier when the shareholder is a corporation rather than an individual. However, the one empirical study of the actual results reached in litigated cases indicates that this belief is mistaken; that study indicates that corporate shareholders were held liable in 28 percent of the litigated cases while individual shareholders were held liable in about 40 percent of the litigated cases.

Many corporations create subsidiary corporations for the specific purpose of limiting their liability in connection with risky new businesses; if the judicial system is too generous in piercing the corporate veil in parent-subsidiary cases, desirable entrepreneurial conduct may be discouraged, or may not occur at all as corporations decide not to risk their core assets by going into risky, tangential businesses. Whatever the merits of these policy arguments, there does not appear to be any bias in the cases against corporate shareholders. The cases in which corporate shareholders have been held liable for subsidiary obligations include the following situations:

(a) When the subsidiary is being operated in an "unfair manner," e.g., the terms of transactions between parent and subsidiary are set so that profits accumulate in the parent and losses in the subsidiary;

(b) When the subsidiary is consistently represented as being a part of the parent, e.g., as a "division" or "local office" rather than as a subsidiary;

(c) When the separate corporate formalities of the subsidiary are not followed;

(d) When the subsidiary and parent are operating essentially parts of the same integrated business, and the subsidiary is under capitalized; or

(e) When there is no consistent clear delineation of which transactions are the parent's and which are the subsidiary's.

The lack of a consistent clear delineation between the parent's affairs and the subsidiary's affairs is not uncommon. Often the individual acting for the subsidiary is also an agent of the parent; unless the "hat" she is wearing is clear, the argument also may be made that she was actually acting on behalf of the parent rather than the subsidiary or on behalf of both. These cases may phrase the test in terms of agency. Thus the probability of parental liability increases significantly when there are close relationships, informality of operation, and overlapping of personnel employed by the corporations.

Of course, in some cases the failure to delineate between operations of the parent and the subsidiary may actually mislead third persons into believing they are dealing with the parent corporate entity. Most cases, however, impose liability whenever intermingling is present on a wide scale without inquiring specifically whether the plaintiff was actually misled. As a result it is important in every "family" of corporations to maintain the maximum possible degree of separation. In most such families the ties are inherently very close: for example, the parent owns all the shares of the subsidiaries, they have common officers, they have common auditors or attorneys, they file consolidated returns for federal income tax purposes, they share common suites of offices in the same building, and they report their income on a consolidated basis. These close ties are basically consistent with the separate existence of the subsidiary; what creates problems are carelessness and casualness, such as transactions between parent and subsidiary that are not adequately documented, particularly the transfer of funds, common officers and directors who do not specify on whose behalf an action is taken, the failure to maintain independent books and records for each corporation, and the failure of the parent to recognize that the subsidiary is theoretically an independent entity, e.g., by the board of directors of the parent making detailed decisions on behalf of one or more subsidiaries when in theory the decisions should have been made by the board of directors of the subsidiary.

Intermingling of assets is particularly dangerous. Separate accounts may be maintained, but informal transfers or "loans" may be made from time to time to meet the day-to-day needs of the business. Such conduct increases the risk of parental liability. If funds owned by the parent are needed by the subsidiary, the proper procedure is to establish a formal loan, preferably using a promissory note, and then to transfer the funds to the subsidiary's bank account. The corporate books of both parent and subsidiary then reflect the transaction accurately and the risk that the intermingling of assets will result in the two corporations being treated as one is reduced. Many parent corporations have established centralized cash management plans for their subsidiaries: each subsidiary is required to transfer excess cash on a daily basis to a central account managed by the parent where it may be invested, and each subsidiary may draw on this account on a daily basis as needed for its operations. If the cash management plan is properly approved and accurate records of all transfers of cash in both directions are kept, these plans should not be viewed as involving the kind of intermingling that gives rise to potential liability.

Other common features of a parent/subsidiary "family," are participation in a single employee retirement plan, a centralized accounting and legal staff, and centralized control over the raising of capital. Of themselves, these features should not give rise to an inference that the separate existence of corporate subsidiaries should be ignored.

§ 6.8   The Concept of "Enterprise Entity"

"Enterprise entity" refers to the economic unity that is a single business enterprise. Courts are suspicious of attempts to divide what is essentially a single economic enterprise among several different corporations with the intention of minimizing the assets subject to claims of creditors of each enterprise. Perhaps this is because it is not "playing fair" with creditors who may believe that an entire economic enterprise is a single unit; in any event, courts may well "put the enterprise back together" despite the shareholders' attempt to segregate it into separate corporate entities. In this kind of case, a "brother-sister" corporate relationship may be ignored as readily as a parent-subsidiary relationship. Indeed, the empirical study of litigated piercing the corporate veil cases discovered a number of cases in which brother-sister enterprises were combined into a single unit for liability purposes.

Many large corporations are conglomerates consisting of several essentially discrete and independent businesses. The concept of enterprise entity does not apply to these operations. What is dangerous is taking a single business and separately incorporating its component operations. Of course, if one or more independent businesses are conducted as divisions of the parent corporation and are not separately incorporated, the parent is liable for the debts of those divisions.

§ 6.9   Choice of Law Issues in "Piercing the Corporate Veil" Cases

Until about 1980, the law of "piercing the corporate veil" appeared to be independent of the state in which the case arose. Courts resolving piercing cases freely cited cases from other jurisdictions without inquiry into whether different states were more or less liberal in imposing, or had different rules about, shareholder liability for corporate obligations. Indeed, the tests and rhetoric used by courts were so vague and amorphous that differences in formulation, even if they had existed, would have had little or no effect on the results reached. Thus, in the few cases in which courts did discuss whether the law of the state of incorporation, or the law of the state in which the activities giving rise to the claim on which shareholder liability was sought, should apply, a definitive resolution of this conflicts issue was found to be unnecessary.

As litigation in this area has continued to grow, however, different state policies or philosophies with respect to the imposition of shareholder liability have appeared. Some states now seem clearly to be more "liberal" than others in imposing such liability; some states have accepted the distinction between tort and contract cases suggested above, while others apparently have not. Texas has partially codified its law of piercing the corporate veil by enacting a statute that provides that in contract cases "actual fraud" is required for the imposition of liability, and failure to follow corporate formalities or procedures is not ground for imposing such liability. In other states, courts have adopted varying policies with respect to piercing the corporate veil arguments. The development of such identifiably different principles by specific states means that the conflicts of law issue must be addressed.

Many corporations are of course incorporated in Delaware and conduct their business primarily or entirely in other states. The Delaware position with respect to "veil piercing" has been described as very conservative: the separate existence of corporations will be recognized in the absence of fraud. An argument may be made that the law of the state of incorporation should apply to the piercing issue under the generally accepted rule that "internal affairs" of corporations should be governed by the law of the state of incorporation. The scope of shareholder liability for corporate obligations plausibly may be described as involving "internal affairs." Indeed, Texas has a statute that states explicitly that the responsibility of shareholders for corporate obligations is governed by the state of incorporation.

On the other hand, there is a strong policy in favor of applying the law of the state with the most significant contacts with the litigation, particularly in torts cases. Consider, for example, a Delaware corporation that is wholly owned by Illinois residents; the corporation's entire business is conducted in Illinois, and a resident of Illinois is injured because of the negligence of the agents of the corporation. Certainly a strong policy argument may be made that the more liberal Illinois law of "piercing" should be applied rather than Delaware law, since all the important contacts are with Illinois and not with Delaware. If Illinois law would permit "piercing" under the circumstances, it is probably unlikely that an Illinois court would deprive an Illinois resident of a remedy against another Illinois resident merely because the corporation was formed in Delaware. In most cases of this type that have arisen, the court has simply applied local law without considering the possible application of the law of the state of incorporation, but the entire matter cannot be said to be free from doubt.

§ 6.10   The Federal Law of "Piercing the Corporate Veil"

An issue that is related to the choice of law issue discussed in section 6.8 is whether there is a federal law of piercing the corporate veil that is applicable in suits in which the United States is a party.

Clearfield Trust Co. v. United States (S.Ct.1943), held that federal law should govern questions involving the rights of the United States arising from nationwide federal programs. Acting under this general principle, federal courts have held, for example, that in a suit to recover overpayments from a provider of services under the Medicare Program, a federal law of piercing the corporate veil should be fashioned to determine whether shareholders of the provider are personally liable for such overpayments. Other cases agree with this general approach. In fashioning the federal law in this area, courts have generally relied on piercing cases that were in the federal courts because of diversity of citizenship. As a result, the federal law of "piercing" probably does not differ significantly from state law in most respects.

Mention should also be made of the Comprehensive Environmental Response, Compensation and Liability Act (CERCLA). This statute imposes broad responsibility for cleaning up toxic waste sites on both the "owner" and the "operator" of the site. Several cases arising under this statute have held that a corporate controlling shareholder who manages the detailed affairs of a subsidiary may have CERCLA liability as an "operator" of a site owned and operated by a subsidiary. Cases have also applied the *Clearfield Trust* principle to develop a federal law of piercing the corporate veil in CERCLA cases that results in the parent being liable as an "owner" because the corporate veil of the subsidiary owning the property was "pierced." Either theory normally results in substantial environmental clean up responsibilities being imposed on the parent corporation. Not all courts have applied these doctrines liberally; one recent decision states that a parent corporation should not be held liable either as an "owner" or "operator" unless the facts justify piercing the corporate veil of the subsidiary.

§ 6.11 Reverse Piercing

Most cases involve efforts by a creditor to hold the shareholder responsible for corporate obligations. In some cases, the shoe is on the other foot. A shareholder argues in a suit against a third party defendant that the separate existence of the corporation should be ignored on policy grounds. The classic case is Cargill, Inc. v. Hedge (Minn.1985), where a farm family created a corporation to own the land and buildings that comprised their farm. When the Hedge family ran into financial difficulty, a creditor obtained a judgment and sought to execute on the land. Minnesota has a statute that provides an exemption from execution of farm property owned by individual farmers. In order to avoid the sale of their farm, the Hedges argued that the separate existence of their corporation should be ignored, and they should be entitled to the exemption. Based on the strong Minnesota public policy favoring protection of family farms from execution sale, the Minnesota court applied a "reverse pierce" principle to protect the family, but the court cautioned that this principle should be available only in "carefully limited circumstances." Other examples of "reverse piercing" exist; in some cases a person other than the shareholder has made a similar argument.

Some courts have expressed skepticism about the reverse pierce doctrine, arguing in effect that if a person forms a corporation, he should be expected to "take the bitter with the sweet," and not be able to disclaim the corporate existence when it is in his interest to do so. All in all, this doctrine should be viewed to have doubtful validity.

§ 6.12 "Piercing the Corporate Veil" to Further Public Policy

Yet another type of piercing the corporate veil case involves the claim that a separate corporate existence should not be recognized because to do so would violate a clearly defined statutory policy.

To take an illustrative case, the statutes of several states formerly prohibited branch banking. In other words in these states a banking corporation had to stick to a single location and could not open branches around the state. Accepting this statutory policy, may a banking corporation own the voting stock of another bank? Or, may a single holding corporation own a majority of, or all, the voting stock of several banks? Answers to questions such as these must be based on an evaluation of the strength of the state policy against branch banking rather than on policies underlying the separate existence of corporations. If the policy is a strong one, the recognition of a separate corporate existence may provide an unacceptable method of circumvention, and the separate corporate fiction must yield to the state policy. On the other hand, if the policy against branch banking was not a strong one, there was no reason for courts to find a fundamental conflict between the statute and the corporate form and hold invalid relationships that conform with the notion of separate corporate existence.

Public policy is also the critical question in the series of cases involving family corporations organized to obtain social security or unemployment benefits for owners who would not be eligible for such benefits if the business had continued to be conducted in noncorporate form. Several federal decisions have held that social security benefits may not be denied to a person who "incorporates" his or her business assets for the sole purpose of qualifying for the benefits, but decisions at the state level concerning temporary disability insurance, workmen's compensation, and unemployment compensation, are split. A clearer example involves the unemployment compensation statutes which provide for an exemption from the tax for employers having fewer than some designated number of employees, e.g., four. May a single business be divided into several separate corporate units each employing less than the statutory minimum to obtain the exemption for each? Courts have held, not surprisingly, that the state unemployment commissions may disregard the separate corporations, treat the business as a single unit, and impose the tax on it.

Generalization is difficult in such cases. Sometimes, assistance may be gained from statutory language that indicates that the policy should be applied to "direct or indirect" relationships. Nevertheless, delicate judgments are required in these cases, for the policies underlying regulatory statutes must be weighed against the policies supporting the concept of the corporate entity.

§ 6.13 "Piercing the Corporate Veil" in Taxation and Bankruptcy

Given the broad social and governmental policies involved in the federal income tax laws and the federal bankruptcy act, it is understandable that specialized tests have also evolved under these statutes for determining when the separate corporate existence will be disregarded.

Under the Internal Revenue Code of 1954 there is a need to preserve tax revenue and to set aside fictional transactions which have as their sole purpose the minimization of taxes. A corporation's separate existence generally will be recognized for tax purposes if it is in fact carrying on a bona fide business and is not merely a device created for the purpose of avoiding taxes. The taxpayer, however, must accept any tax disadvantages of the corporate form if he or she has elected to choose that form. Further, even if the corporate form is adopted and carefully followed, the Commissioner has broad powers to disallow deductions or exemptions, or reallocate items of income to clearly reflect income.

Entirely different policies are involved in the bankruptcy area. Bankruptcy courts have considerable flexibility in dealing with controlling or dominant shareholders of bankrupt corporations. The bankruptcy court may:

(1) "Disregard the corporate entity" and hold the shareholder personally liable for the corporation's debts if the shareholder's conduct is within the rather vague tests of piercing the corporate veil. The effect of this conclusion is that the controlling shareholder may be responsible for all corporate obligations; all payments made by the corporation to the shareholder before bankruptcy may also be recovered by the trustee since essentially the corporation and shareholder are treated as a single unit.

(2) Refuse to recognize claims by shareholders against the corporation as bona fide debts provable in bankruptcy. If the claim is based on services or intangible benefits provided to the corporation, the claim may be disallowed in its entirety as fictitious or "not proved." If it involves infusions of capital or tangible property, the bankruptcy court may consider payments as contributions to capital rather than as debt. This treatment of shareholder debt is usually limited to loans made at or shortly after the formation of the corporation when the corporation is inadequately or thinly capitalized, and simply reflects that what in fact is equity capital may have to be treated as equity capital in bankruptcy proceedings. A number of decisions follow this approach and there are analogous holdings in the tax field. Yet the application of this principle is elusive: there is no easy way to determine when a corporation is in fact under capitalized, and while most courts have treated the issue on an "all or none" basis and reclassified all the debt as equity, it is arguable that it should reclassify only that portion necessary to make the capitalization adequate. As a general test, where the corporation enters into a new business with sufficient capital so that it can borrow the balance of the needed capital

from a bank or other independent source of funds, the original capitalization for that business is deemed "adequate"; if the shareholder rather than the third party makes the loan under such circumstances, that transaction should be accepted by the bankruptcy court as a bona fide loan.

(3) Under the "Deep Rock" doctrine—so named from the Deep Rock Oil Corp., the subsidiary involved in the leading case of Taylor v. Standard Gas & Electric Co. (S.Ct.1939)—the court may subordinate claims presented by controlling shareholders to the claims of other creditors or preferred shareholders on the ground that the shareholder acted inequitably or unfairly. Examples of inequitable claims include taking unreasonable amounts as salary, manipulation of the affairs of the corporation in disregard of standards of honesty, or selling assets to the corporation at inflated prices. The type of conduct that will result in subordination under the Deep Rock doctrine can only be stated in general terms: the doctrine is based on general principles of equity and fair dealing. It is not necessary to show that the indebtedness was a sham or fiction, since technically what is involved is the order of payment of debts rather than total rejection of the claim. The theory is that a person who has acted unfairly in his or her management of the corporation should step aside so that other creditors may be first satisfied. Of course, usually the assets of the bankrupt estate are inadequate to satisfy all claims and subordination therefore results in the shareholder receiving nothing on his or her claim. Despite this underlying theory, in at least one case the Deep Rock doctrine was applied when the controversy was between innocent creditors of the bankrupt subsidiary and the equally innocent creditors of the bankrupt parent.

The type of conduct that triggers these doctrines differs only in degree rather than kind. In a sense these are alternative weapons in the bankruptcy court's arsenal.

§ 6.14 Other Generalizations About "Piercing the Corporate Veil"

Three final observations should be made about the confusing and result-oriented doctrines discussed in this chapter. First, there is no inherent reason to assume that ignoring the separate corporate existence must be an all-or-nothing affair. Particularly if the dominant question does not involve public statutory policies but merely liability for corporate obligations, a corporation may be viewed as existing for some purposes but not for others. There is some case authority, for example, for piercing the corporate veil to hold shareholders active in the business personally liable, but recognizing the same corporation's separate existence to protect passive investors from the same liabilities. Second, there is a strong judicial feeling that when a person elects to do business in corporate form he or she must take the bitter with the sweet, and cannot later argue that the separate corporate existence should be ignored when it is to his or her benefit. Except in the rare "reverse pierce" cases (see § 6.11) the doctrine of piercing the corporate veil is not available for the benefit of shareholders, but only against shareholders. This view is particularly strongly developed in the tax cases. Finally, where the considerations are not strongly weighted one way or the other, a presumption of separate existence of the corporation should be respected. The fiction of separate corporate existence, in other words, should be the rule not the exception.

[For unfamiliar terms see the Glossary]

CHAPTER SEVEN

FINANCING THE CORPORATION

§ 7.1 Introduction

Perhaps no other area of corporation law is more confusing to law students without prior business backgrounds than corporate securities such as shares of stock, bonds and debentures. The language is new and unfamiliar, the concepts seem mysterious and sometimes illogical, and everything seems to build on historical concepts of dubious relevance today.

While this has been traditionally true, in the 1990s new winds are blowing through the area of corporation finance. The Model Business Corporation Act (1984) and the statutes of about twenty-five states have eliminated the historic concept of par value and have developed new and simplified rules relating to the issuance of stock. These states have also adopted new rules relating to the validity of distributions. The advantages of this new approach are so obvious that it is likely that ultimately all states will abandon the older historical concepts. However, for the foreseeable future, a significant number of states, and attorneys practicing in them, must cope with the historical rules.

The basic purposes of this chapter are, first, to dispel the mystery of the older historical statutes and, second, to introduce the modern approach of the Model Business Corporation Act (1984). The discussion of the older statutes proceeds one simple step at a time. It begins with the issuance of shares of common stock by a newly formed corporation. It then briefly considers other classes of stock that corporations may issue, the use of borrowed capital—that is, debt—as a substitute for contributed capital, and finally, the issuance and reacquisition of shares of stock by an ongoing corporation. Reserved for a later chapter are issues related to the payment of dividends and the making of other distributions to shareholders (Chapter 18 of this Nutshell).

§ 7.2 Basic Definitions: Common Stock; Authorized and Issued Shares

Shares of common stock are the fundamental units into which the proprietary interest of the corporation is divided. If a corporation issues only one class of shares, they may be referred to by a variety of similar names: common shares, capital stock, common stock, or, possibly, simply shares or stock. Whatever the name, they are the basic proprietary units of ownership and are referred to here as simply common stock.

Section 6.01(b) of the MBCA (1984) defines the two fundamental characteristics of common stock: (1) they are entitled to vote for the election of directors and on other matters coming before the shareholders and (2) they are entitled to the net assets of the corporation (after making allowance for debts and senior securities) when distributions are to be made, either during the course of the life of the corporation or upon its dissolution. One important innovation of the MBCA (1984) is that it permits these two fundamental characteristics to be divided or split between different classes of stock (so there may not be a single class that has both of these residual characteristics and, therefore, no class of stock that is unambiguously common stock), but section 6.03(b) requires that at least one share of each class with these basic attributes must be outstanding.

Assuming that a new corporation is going to have only a single class of shares, the articles of incorporation must state the number of shares of common stock the corporation is authorized to issue. This number is known, not surprisingly, as the corporation's "authorized capital" or "authorized stock." (In states with older statutes, the articles of incorporation must also set forth the "par value" of the authorized shares or a statement that the shares are "without par value." The limited significance of "par value" is discussed in the following sections.)

There is no statutory limitation on the number of shares that may be authorized by a corporation and no requirement that all or any specific fraction of the authorized shares be actually issued. Why, then, doesn't every corporation simply authorize millions or billions of shares, and then issue only the number desired? In many states there are practical constraints. Some states impose franchise or stock taxes on the basis of authorized shares; in these states to authorize many more shares than there is an intention to issue simply increases taxes with no offsetting benefit. Also, authorizing a large number of shares may create concern on the part of investors since authorized shares may be later issued merely by the board of directors without shareholder approval. On the other hand, it is generally believed desirable to authorize at least some additional shares over and above what is presently planned to be issued for unexpected contingencies and to avoid the need for amending articles of incorporation if more shares are later needed.

The capitalization of a corporation is based on the number of shares actually issued and the capital received therefor, not on the number of authorized shares. Capital received in exchange for issued shares is usually referred to as the corporation's invested capital (or sometimes its "contributed" capital) and is viewed as being invested in the corporation permanently or indefinitely.

§ 7.3   The Price of Common Shares

Let us assume that a new corporation is authorized to issue 1,000 shares of common stock and it has been agreed that the two investors, A and B, will each contribute $5,000 for 50 percent of the stock. How many shares should be issued and for what price?

Within a broad range, the number of shares and price per share in such a situation can be set at any level. For example A and B might purchase one share each for $5,000, or 10 shares each for $500 per share, or 100 shares each for $50 per share. It is important, of course, that A and B each pay the same amount for each share and receive the same number of shares; however, as between themselves it makes no difference what that amount is per share. It would be undesirable, however, to issue 500 shares each at $10 per share, since that would exhaust the entire authorized capital and would require an amendment to the articles of incorporation if more capital was needed at a later date.

In this simple example it was assumed that the two shareholders had agreed in advance each to contribute $5,000. It would be a breach of this understanding if A were issued 100 shares at $50 per share and B 500 shares at $40 per share. Each would own 50 percent of the outstanding shares of the corporation, but A's interest has been "diluted," since the corporation has only $9,000 of assets, so that A has paid $5,000 for an interest that is worth only $4,500.

Usually all shares in a start up business are issued at the same price per share. A valuation problem clearly arises if one shareholder is to contribute cash while the other shareholder is to contribute property or services, and the possibility of dilution occurring is increased. Dilution may also occur in the case of an ongoing business that decides that it needs additional capital to be obtained by the issuance of more stock. The current value of the shares of the business will usually be uncertain and negotiation will be necessary to determine the appropriate price for the newly issued shares. This negotiation will often be between corporate officers or directors, on one side, and potential investors, on the other. If the price is set too high, the new investor pays more than the proportionate interest he or she is obtaining is worth; if it is set too low, the interest of the current shareholders is being diluted and the new investor is obtaining a bargain. Usually the price that yields total fairness between the old and the new is uncertain or subjective so that any price agreed upon by arms-length negotiation must be accepted.

Usually the board of directors of the corporation determines the price at which new shares are to be issued (subject of course to the willingness of potential investors to pay this price). See MBCA (1984) § 6.21(b). State statutes, however, authorize the shareholders to reserve this power to themselves by appropriate provision in the articles of incorporation. See MBCA (1984) § 6.21(a). As a practical matter, it is unusual for the shareholders to reserve this power to themselves; the board of directors typically sets the price at which shares are to be issued.

If only common sense were involved, the pricing of common shares would end at this point. However, the par value statutes in effect in many states impose an elaborate system of rules relating to the issuance of common shares which have substantive as well as accounting implications for this apparently simple transaction. These rules dealing with par value are the subject of the following six sections.

§ 7.4 Par Value, Stated Capital and Related Concepts

Older state statutes assume that shares will have a "par value" or "stated value" (which is the same thing). The possibility that a corporation may issue "no par" shares or shares "without par value" in states with par value stat-utes should be put to one side for the moment since in most of these states the treatment of such shares is based on the treatment of par value shares. Par value of a share of common stock is simply the dollar amount designated as par value by the draftsman of the articles of incorpo-ration. It may be one mill, one cent, one dollar, ten dollars, whatever the draftsman designates. The par value designation is made in the articles of incorporation as part of the fundamental description of the authorized capital, e.g. "The number of shares the corporation is authorized to issue is 1,000 shares of common stock with the par value of $1.00 per share;" each share certificate then describe the stock represented by the certificate as involv-ing both "common shares" and a "$1.00 par value," both usually in large and conspicuous type.

The use of par value goes back to medieval times. Originally it had considerable importance because it was widely viewed as the amount for which the shares would be issued: shares with a par value of one hundred dollars could be subscribed for at one hundred dollars per share with confidence that all other identical shares would also be issued for $100 per share. This is not the modern practice, however. Today, par value serves only a minor function and is in no way an indication of the price at which the shares are issued, with this one exception: The one basic rule about setting the price for shares of com-mon stock with a par value is that the price must always be equal to or greater than the par value. If this rule is violated and shares are issued for less than par value, the recipient shareholder in most states is automatically liable to the corporation for the difference. This liability is usually called a "watered stock" liability and is discussed in greater detail in § 7.7 of this Nutshell. In par value states today, most attorneys use "nominal par value," in which a low (or "nominal") par value is set but the shares are issued for a significantly higher price. For example, shares with a par value of ten cents per share may be issued for $10.00 or $50.00 per share. In most par value states, "no par" shares may be used but they have not attained the nearly universal acceptance of nominal par value shares. For several reasons the current practice in states with par value statutes runs strongly in the direction of using a "nominal" par value.

Several factors caused the gradual movement away from treating par value as a definitive representation of the purchase price of shares. One factor is the loss of flexibility of pricing shares. When a secondary market for shares develops, a corporation raising capital by selling shares with a par value of $100 for $100 per share in effect competes with that market and would have to stop selling shares if the market price of the previously-issued shares drops below $100 per share. At that point potential investors can get a better price in the secondary market than they can from the corporation which is locked into the $100 price by the par value. A second factor was the federal documentary stamp tax on issuance of corporate securities (since repealed) which, until 1958, was based on the par or stated value rather than actual value. A nominal par value thus reduced federal stamp taxes. Similarly, state franchise and stock transfer taxes also were (and to a limited extent still are) based on par or stated value; in these states a low par value again reduces the corporation's tax liability. Still another factor arises in the situation where property of uncertain value is being contributed; if high par value shares are given in exchange for such property, arguments may later arise that the property was in fact not worth the par value of the shares received and the recipients might be sued for the difference on the theory that they had received watered stock. See § 7.7 of this Nutshell. These various reasons provide adequate practical justification for abandoning high par value shares in every instance. Further, there is very little to be gained from using high par value shares; the principal advantages are possible benefits to the corporation because psychologically investors or creditors may feel more secure dealing with a corporation with a high par value stock. Such an advantage is not very persuasive, however, since there is no reason to believe that investors or creditors pay any attention to par value one way or the other. In any event there has been a virtually universal shift away from the use of high par value shares.

Par value serves an important function in addition to establishing a price floor below which shares may not be issued: it is an essential ingredient in determining the capital accounts of the corporation. In this and the following sections, the terminology of the 1969 Model Business Corporation Act will be followed. While not all states with par value statutes use this terminology, most states do (and those that do not embody similar concepts). In this terminology, par value is an essential ingredient in determining the "stated capital" and "capital surplus" of the corporation.

In order to understand "stated capital" and "capital surplus" and the issues that evolve from them, a brief excursion into fundamental accounting concepts is necessary. The basic syllogism or truism on which financial statements are based is that *net worth* equals *assets* minus *liabilities*. That syllogism is obviously true for an individual such as you or me; it is equally applicable to a corporation that is treated as an entity or fictitious person. By simple arithmetical manipulation of the basic syllogism, assets also equal liabilities plus net worth. This is the formula used in a "balance sheet" where one side of the equation is placed on the left side and the balance on the right side of a ledger.

Assets	Liabilities + Net Worth

A balance sheet balances because it is simply a restatement of the basic equation.

Let us examine a balance sheet for a new corporation immediately after it has sold 100 shares of stock for 1,000 dollars in cash. The balance sheet shows:

Assets		Liabilities	–0–
Cash	$ 1,000	Net Worth	
		Common Stock	$ 1,000
	$ 1,000		$ 1,000

The concepts of stated capital and capital surplus relate to how the common stock item is shown on the right hand side of the balance sheet. "Stated capital" is defined to be the aggregate par value of all issued shares (plus or minus certain adjustments not relevant for present purposes) while "capital surplus" is defined to be the excess (if any) of capital contributed over the par value. Thus, if in our hypothetical the 100 shares of common stock had a par value of $1 per share and were sold at $10.00 per share the balance sheet would be as follows:

Assets		Liabilities		–0–
Cash	$ 1,000	Capital Accounts		
		Stated Capital	$	100
		Capital Surplus	$	900
	$ 1,000		$	1,000

In this balance sheet, the phrase "capital accounts" has been substituted for "net worth" to somewhat more closely reflect accounting terminology used in the old Model Business Corporation Act, but its meaning is the same.

Under par value statutes, there is no requirement that any specific minimum amount be put in in the form of stated capital. Several states establish a minimum capitalization requirement of $1,000 (or some other amount), but these states require only an aggregate capital of the specified amount without differentiating between how much should be stated capital and how much should be capital surplus. Thus, in these states, it is theoretically possible to create a corporation with $0.01 of stated capital and $999.99 of capital surplus.

Now, a logical question that may be asked is what difference does it make if the capital contribution is recorded as stated capital or capital surplus? Rather surprisingly it does make a difference, which can best be appreciated if we first draw up a balance sheet after the corporation (1) has borrowed $1,000 from a bank and (2) has had two years of operations during which it has earned and accumulated an aggregate of $2,000 over-and-above all costs, taxes, etc. Further, for simplicity we will continue to assume that all of the assets are held by the corporation in the form of cash. The balance sheet looks like this:

Assets		Liabilities	$ 1,000
Cash	$ 4,000	Capital Accounts	
		Earned Surplus	$ 2,000
		Stated Capital	100
		Capital Surplus	900
	$ 4,000		$ 4,000

At this point the shareholders decide they want to distribute to themselves some or all of the $4,000. If the balance sheet is to continue to balance, every dollar taken from the left-hand column must obviously be reflected by the reduction of a right-hand column entry. The right-hand entries thus in effect limit or monitor the distribution of assets from the left-hand column. For example, as described in a later chapter, under the 1969 Model Act dividends may be lawfully paid, "out of" earned surplus. This means that amounts may be paid from the cash of the corporation as dividends up to the maximum amount shown in the right-hand column under "earned surplus," or $2,000 in the above example. Of course, a dividend of, say, $500 paid out of earned surplus would in the above example result in the reduction of cash by $500 to $3500, offset by a reduction of earned surplus to $1,500, and the balance sheet will still balance.

Under the old Model Business Corporation Act, corporations have greater freedom to make distributions from capital surplus than from stated capital. The basic concept is that stated capital is "locked in" the corporation and cannot be distributed except upon the liquidation of the corporation; however, assets may be distributed to the extent of capital surplus simply with the approval of the holders of a specified fraction of the common shares. Such a distribution is not a dividend in the normal sense of the word but is called by various names, e.g., "liquidating dividend," "distribution in partial liquidation," or the like. (See § 18.1 of this Nutshell.) Also under the old MBCA, capital surplus but not stated capital may be used to repurchase or redeem outstanding shares previously issued by the corporation. (See § 18.6 of this Nutshell.)

If all the capital is put in the form of stated capital (i.e. the par value of the issued shares equals the consideration received) all the capital is "locked in;" if the bulk of the capital contributed is recorded as capital surplus rather than stated capital there is greater flexibility to distribute unneeded capital to shareholders or reacquire outstanding shares at a later date. In other words, there is greater flexibility in a corporation with this balance sheet:

Cash	$ 1,000	Liabilities		–0–
		Capital Accounts		
		Stated Capital	$	100
		Capital Surplus		900
	1,000			1,000

than there is in a corporation with this balance sheet:

Cash	$ 1,000	Liabilities		–0–
		Capital Accounts		
		Stated Capital	$	1,000
		Capital Surplus		–0–
	1,000			1,000

From the standpoint of the corporation such flexibility is a mildly positive feature and is an additional reason for the wide-spread use of nominal par value which leads to low stated capital and high capital surplus. Of course, a bank that lends money to a corporation might be unhappy if large amounts of capital surplus are available for distribution to shareholders since theoretically the capital of the corporation forms a "cushion" for the creditor and increases the possibility that the corporation will have the liquid assets to repay the loan when it comes due. Lenders, however, do not rely on the corporation statutes for protection against unwise distribution policies; they usually insist on contractual restrictions on the otherwise virtually complete freedom of corporations to distribute their assets. (See § 18.7 of this Nutshell.) Such restrictions are required so routinely by most lenders that they have almost totally replaced the corporation statutes as the operative restriction on the freedom of corporations to distribute their capital to their shareholders.

§ 7.5   No Par Shares

In the early period of corporate history, corporations were only permitted to issue shares with par value. No par shares are a relatively recent wrinkle, first permitted in New York in about 1915, and the rules relating to such shares were developed in the context of the established rules for accounting for par value shares. Obviously, the consideration for which no par shares are issued may be set without any reference to a minimum imposed by a par value. However, the capital received must still be allocated between stated capital and capital surplus. When no par shares are issued under most state statutes based on the old Model Business Corporation Act, the entire consideration fixed by the corporation for the shares constitutes stated capital. However, statutes generally permit the directors to allocate some portion or all of the consideration to capital surplus. Before 1969, the old Model Business Corporation Act limited this power to 25 per cent of the consideration received, but par value states have generally eliminated this restriction. Most states today permit allocation of "any part" of the consideration received for no par shares to either stated capital or capital surplus. Apparently under such a provision it is possible to create a corporation with as little stated capital using no par shares as with nominal par value shares.

For many years no par shares suffered from a tax disadvantage in that federal stamp taxes were computed on no par shares based on the issue price while par value shares were valued at par value for tax purposes. Where this valuation structure is in effect (and it may continue to be in effect in some states) nominal par value shares obviously continue to offer a tax saving over no par shares. Perhaps this historical pragmatic reason explains why no par shares have never become the dominant practice in most par value states.

State statutes provide that the board of directors has the power to fix the consideration for which no par shares are issued but the articles of incorporation may expressly reserve this power to the shareholders. This option was originally based on the long since discredited idea that par value ensures equality of shareholders while no par shares do not. In the modern context, the option for shareholders to set the issuance price of no par shares does not differ in any significant way from the similar election that is available with respect to nominal par value shares. It is doubtful if either is ever elected today.

§ 7.6　Shares Issued for Property or Services

This section deals with the issuance of shares for property (other than cash) or services under both the older par value statutes and the Model Business Corporation Act (1984).

If shares are issued for cash on the barrel head, the cash price of each share is readily established, subject only to the limitation that the price must equal or exceed the share's par value, if any. If the shareholder-to-be is contributing property or services, however, the situation is more complicated.

In the first place, under most state statutes not all types of property or services may serve as acceptable consideration for the issuance of shares. State constitutions in some sixteen states and statutes in at least thirteen additional states provide, in varying language, that shares may be paid for "in whole or in part, in cash, in *other property, tangible or intangible, or in labor or services actually performed for the corporation.*" This quotation is taken from § 19 of the old Model Business Corporation Act, but it is common language. In addition, many state statutes specifically provide that promissory notes or the promise of future services do not constitute permissible consideration. Shares issued for ineligible consideration under these statutes are not validly issued and may be canceled or suit brought by other shareholders; or alternatively, persons receiving such shares may be compelled in a suit by creditors to pay in additional consideration on the theory the shares are "watered." (See § 7.7 of this Nutshell.)

These "eligible consideration" statutes are not part of the par value structure but are independent requirements. A state may eliminate the par value requirements and yet elect to retain these limitations on the types of eligible consideration for shares (as, indeed, California has done).

There is a fair amount of case law under these statutes that provides additional gloss on what is eligible consideration: preincorporation services are "services actually performed;" patents for inventions, "good will" of a going and profitable business, contract rights, or computer "software" constitute "intangible property" if they appear to have real value. On the other hand, a lease or contract right that is subject to a substantial condition may not constitute "property," at least if it is likely that the condition will not be fulfilled. Secret formulas, processes or plans that lack novelty or substantial value have also been held not to constitute "property." A note secured by a mortgage on real estate is usually considered to be eligible "property" rather than an ineligible "promissory note." Further, one case holds that if shares are issued partially for services previously rendered and partially for services to be rendered in the future, the entire issue of shares is invalid since the court will not apportion it if the directors do not. Thus, shares to be issued to employees for services may be validly issued only if the issuance takes place at the end of the employment period. However, one recent decision, Rooney v. Paul D. Osborne Desk Co., Inc. (Mass.App.1995) holds that an employee who actually performs the services is entitled to receive the promised-for stock on a theory of promissory estoppel, the court stating that the corporation statute's purpose is to protect creditors and existing shareholders, and those purposes do not require the invalidation of the agreement to issue stock where the services have been performed.

The Model Business Corporation Act (1984) rejects these limitations on eligible consideration. Under section 6.21(b) eligible consideration may consist of "any tangible or intangible property or benefit to the corporation, including cash, promissory notes, services performed, contracts for services to be performed, or other securities of the corporation." This major change in policy was based on a recognition that the traditional rules often led to anomalous results and that "in the realities of commercial life" there is sometimes a need for the issuance of shares for contract rights or intangible property or benefits. Assume, for example, that Jane Fonda agrees to make a film in exchange for a twenty-five per cent interest in the film. Even though a bank might well be willing to lend $10,000,000 to a new corporation to make the Fonda film, the traditional rule would not permit the corporation to issue Jane Fonda her shares until after she has performed the requisite services. Similarly, John D. Rockefeller would not be able to give his promissory note for shares even though his promissory note is "as good as gold." However, the prohibition against promissory notes presumably would not prevent a third person from using Rockefeller's promissory note as consideration for the issuance of shares to the third person.

One consequence of the provisions of the Model Business Corporation Act is that corporations may issue shares immediately for promises of future service, promissory notes or future benefits that involve possible receipts in the future. What happens if things do not work out as contemplated and the services are never performed, the notes are not paid, or the future benefits are never received? The answer is simple: the shares are still outstanding and the corporation simply has whatever claims it can put forward for the future benefits or under the contract for services or on the promissory notes. If the corporation is not happy with this result, section 6.21(e) permits the corporation to escrow the shares until the services are performed, the benefits received, or the notes paid, and cancel them if there is a default. Alternatively, the corporation may restrict the transfer of the shares until the desired benefits are received.

A second requirement under the old Model Business Corporation Act and the statutes of many states, is that the "value" of the property or services must be determined. Section 18 of the 1969 Model Act required the board of directors to "fix" the "consideration, expressed in dollars" that the corporation is to receive, and many state statutes have identical or analogous language. However, section 20 of the old Model Act provided that "in the absence of fraud in the transaction," the judgment of the board of directors as to the value of the consideration "shall be conclusive." This section took much of the potential sting out of a good faith but erroneously high valuation. These provisions are equally applicable to par and no par value shares. Under these provisions, the resolution of the board of directors accepting property for shares must do two things: it must specify the specific property involved, and it must express or fix the value of the property in dollars. Of course, the value so expressed must exceed the par value of any shares being issued. The purposes of section 18 apparently were to assure compliance with par value requirements and to enable existing shareholders to determine whether their interests were being diluted; the purpose of the "in the absence of fraud" language of section 20 was to give certainty to purchasers of shares; they could invest in shares without concern that the validity of those shares may later be attacked for having been issued for property worth less than what the directors established. The language, however, was broader and might prevent shareholders whose interests were significantly diluted from attacking the valuation placed on property by the board of directors. Presumably, something close to actual fraudulent intent must be shown before the decision of a board of directors as to the value of property received can be overturned under these statutory provisions even at the suit of other shareholders when there are no subsequent purchasers involved.

The Model Business Corporation Act also changes these rules substantially. The board of directors does not have to determine the value of property that is received; it need only determine "that the consideration received or to be received for shares to be issued is adequate." [MBCA (1984) § 6.21(c)]. Further, that determination "is conclusive insofar as the adequacy of consideration for the issuance of shares relates to whether the shares are validly issued, fully paid, and nonassessable." This language is designed to narrow the conclusive nature of the directors' determination to situations in which questions might be raised about the adequacy of the consideration for which shares currently on the market were issued.

§ 7.7 Liability of Shareholders for Watered Stock

This section deals primarily with problems arising under the par value statutes. To a limited extent, however, a similar problem may arise under the Model Business Corporation Act (1984).

The term "watered stock" is a colorful common law phrase describing the situation where shareholders receive shares without paying as much for them as the law requires. The common law defines three classes of such shares—"bonus" shares, "discount" shares, and "watered" shares. "Bonus" shares are par value shares issued free when the shareholder fully paid for shares of another class; "discount" shares are par value shares issued for cash for less than par value; "watered" shares are par value shares issued for property that is worth less than the par value of the shares. All three of these types of shares are often indiscriminately referred to as "watered shares," a convenient generic phrase to describe these transactions.

Much of the early common law relating to watered shares concerned the liability of shareholders receiving watered shares to pay the additional consideration needed to "squeeze out the water." Two alternative theories by which creditors might hold shareholders liable appear in the early cases. The "trust fund" theory in effect treats the stated capital of the corporation as being a trust fund available for the payment of creditors, and failure to pay in the proper amount is therefore actionable by any creditor. As pointed out in Hospes v. Northwestern Mfg. & Car Co. (Minn.1892), this theory is to a large extent a fiction since corporate capital lacks virtually all the elements of a true trust. The "holding out" theory in effect presumes (usually contrary to fact) that creditors rely on stated capital in extending credit. On this theory, creditors with claims arising prior to the wrongful issuance, or subsequent creditors who were aware of the wrongful issuance, cannot compel additional payments by the shareholders on account of the watered stock. Early courts wavered between these two theories, often referring to a trust fund theory, but reaching decisions more consistent with the holding out theory.

Many modern corporation acts now define the liability of shareholders in connection with the issuance of shares in precise though not always unambiguous terms. A widely adopted provision of the 1969 Model Business Corporation Act states that "a holder of * * * shares of a corporation shall be under no obligation to the corporation or to its creditors with respect to such shares other than the obligation to pay to the corporation *the full consideration for which such shares were issued or to be issued.*" [MBCA (1969) § 25.] In effect, this article (1) substitutes a statutory obligation running both to the corporation and its creditors for the obligation based on the trust fund or holding out theories of common law, and (2) measures the extent of the liability on the basis of "the consideration for which such shares were issued or to be issued" rather than par value. This section must be read along with section 18 of the 1969 Model Business Corporation Act which authorizes par value shares to be issued "for such consideration expressed in dollars, not less than the par value thereof, as shall be fixed from time to time" by the directors. The similar provision for no par shares is essentially the same with the omission of the phrase "not less than the par value thereof."

Under these older statutes it seems clear that a shareholder is liable to the corporation if he or she pays less for the shares than the consideration fixed by the directors, and this liability is measured by the difference between the fixed consideration and the amount actually paid. Further, if the consideration is improperly fixed by the directors at less than the par value of the shares to be issued, the shareholder is liable for the difference between whatever he pays and the par value of the shares. If nominal par value shares are used, it is unlikely that a shareholder will end up actually paying less than the par value of the shares; however, even if he or she pays more than par value, liability to the corporation will nevertheless exist if the amount paid is less than the consideration fixed by the directors. Virtually the same risk of liability exists if no par shares are used: there is no possibility that a shareholder will pay less than par, but liability may arise if he or she pays less than the consideration fixed by the directors for the issuance of the shares. Under these statutes there is thus little, if any, difference in potential liability between par and no par shares.

Considerable ambiguity may exist under these modern statutory provisions where property at an excessive valuation is contributed in exchange for either par value or no par value shares. Under the 1969 Model Act, for example, when issuing shares for property, section 18 provides that the directors must set "the consideration expressed in dollars" or the "consideration expressed in dollars, not less than the par value thereof" for no par and par shares respectively. Under section 25, shareholders have no liability to the corporation with respect to shares "other than the obligation to pay to the corporation the full consideration for which shares were issued or to be issued." The key phrase in this section, the "full consideration" for which shares were issued may conceivably refer either to the designated property itself or to the dollar value placed on the property by the directors when it expressed the consideration "in dollars." This is a practical question that arises whenever a previously unincorporated business with lots of different kinds of property of uncertain values is incorporated, and is present where either nominal par or no par shares are used. To take an example, assume that the directors authorize the issuance of 1,000 shares of $1.00 par value stock for specified property which they value at $10,000. Assume further the valuation of $10,000 is fraudulent and the property is actually worth only $5,000. After the shares are issued, the balance sheet of the corporation looks like this:

Assets		Liabilities	–0–
Property	$10,000		
		Capital Accounts	
		Stated Capital	$ 1,000
		Capital Surplus	9,000

At common law the rule in this kind of situation appeared to be that the shares were not watered at all since the value of the property received exceeded the stated capital of the corporation. If the shareholder in such a case did not expressly promise to pay $10,000 but only to contribute the specified property there appeared to be no way to hold the shareholder liable for more than the property itself. Of course, there is something peculiar about this balance sheet because the value of the assets are greatly overstated and the "capital surplus" account contains $5,000 of "water." It may be that a representation that the assets are worth $10,000 to a creditor would be fraudulent in and of itself; however, there is no basis for recovery against the *shareholder* unless he or she actually makes such a representation.

If the statute, like the 1969 Model Act, requires the directors to express the value of the consideration "in dollars," it is likely that the shareholder in the above example is liable for an additional $5,000 since the "full amount of the consideration fixed as provided by law" was $10,000 and he has only contributed property with a value of $5,000.

At common law the issuance of watered, bonus, or discount shares gave rise to liability on the shareholders receiving the shares, not liability on the directors authorizing such shares. It is possible, however, to devise common law theories of liability by which directors might be held liable for authorizing watered shares, particularly in suits brought by other shareholders or creditors who relied on the financial statements thereby created. Yet another possibility is a suit brought by existing shareholders to cancel watered shares as not being lawfully issued. In many states this appears to be the most common way in which watered stock questions arise.

Section 6.22(a) of the Model Business Corporation Act (1984) is superficially similar to section 25 of the old Model Business Corporation Act. It provides that a purchaser of shares from a corporation is not liable to the corporation or its creditors "with respect to its shares except to pay the consideration for which the shares were authorized to be issued." Under this Act the consideration may consist of a promissory note or a contract to perform services in the future (see § 7.6 of this Nutshell); the Official Comment states that the phrase "with respect to its shares" was included to make clear that the shareholder remains liable on the promissory note or contract to perform services without regard to this section.

In a sense, the limited liability of shareholders with respect to shares is closely related to the fundamental concept of limited liability that is central to the modern corporation. The relationship is made explicit in section 6.22(b) of the Model Business Corporation Act (1984) that states that with two exceptions "a shareholder is not personally liable for the acts or debts of the corporation." The two exceptions are first, that the articles of incorporation may expressly provide for such personal liability, and second, that the shareholder "may become personally liable by reason of his or her own acts or conduct." This latter clause is designed to cover both consensual assumption of liability for specific obligations and principles by which shareholders may inadvertently become liable for corporate obligations under the doctrine generally known as "piercing the corporate veil," discussed in chapter six of this Nutshell, or possibly other doctrines as well.

§ 7.8 Treasury Shares as a Device to Avoid Restrictions on the Issuance of Shares

Treasury shares are shares of the corporation that were once lawfully issued but have been reacquired by the corporation (and held in its treasury, hence their name). The status of such shares is an uneasy one under traditional par value statutes. They are given an intermediate status between being issued and being unissued: they are not outstanding for purposes of voting, quorum determinations, or dividends (which would obviously create circularity), but since they were once issued they also are not subject to the restraints on issuance described in the previous sections. In other words they can be resold or reissued presumably without regard to the par value of the shares or the nature of the consideration being received for them. This anomalous result is not accepted in all jurisdictions. However, it is generally the position that treasury shares are not subject to the restrictions applicable to original issuance of shares, and many corporations maintain a supply of treasury shares in part to permit transactions the consideration for which might not qualify under the traditional rules.

Treasury shares are quite unlike shares of other corporations which the corporation may own. Shares of other corporations acquired by a corporation are investments by the acquiring corporation. The acquisition of a corporation of its own shares is a distribution, not an investment. When a corporation acquires some of its own shares, the assets of the corporation are reduced by the amount of the purchase price and all the other owners of shares have a somewhat increased proportional interest in the reduced assets. Treasury shares are economically indistinguishable from authorized but unissued shares. Thus, it is not meaningful to treat the acquisition of treasury shares as anything but a disproportionate distribution of corporate assets to the selling shareholders, or better, a disproportionate dividend. See § 18.4 of this Nutshell.

The Model Business Corporation Act (1984) eliminates the concept of treasury shares and treats all shares reacquired by the corporation as authorized but unissued shares [§ 6.31(a)].

§ 7.9   Current Trends Regarding Par Value

When all is said and done, the concepts of par value and stated capital have relatively little to commend them in the modern era. At best they are historical oddities that provide little real protection to creditors and have been twisted by sophisticated attorneys to squeeze out the maximum flexibility for their corporate creations. At worst, they are confusing if not misleading.

The Model Business Corporation Act (1984) eliminates both the concept of par value (except to the limited extent discussed below) and the distinction between stated capital and capital surplus. The validity of corporate distributions to shareholders is measured by new insolvency and balance sheet tests. (See § 18.6 of this Nutshell.) Further, the MBCA (1984) eliminates the restrictions on eligible consideration discussed in § 7.6 of this Nutshell as well as the concept of treasury shares discussed in § 7.8. The elegance and simplicity thereby created has much to commend it since it returns the issuance of common shares back to a simple, common sense set of rules.

The Model Business Corporation Act (1984) does permit a corporation to elect to create par value for shares if it desires. [MBCA (1984) § 2.02(b)(iv).] The Official Comment indicates that this provision permits parties to elect to be governed by par value provisions as a matter of contract if they so desire. Election of an optional par value may be useful if it is likely that the corporation will at some time in the future transact business in a state in which franchise or other taxes are computed on the basis of par values.

Most practicing attorneys, of course, are familiar with par value statutes, having studied them in law school and practiced under them. In states that have adopted all or significant portions of the MBCA (1984) provisions, there is a tendency by attorneys to follow familiar patterns and continue to use par value provisions. As time goes on, however, it is likely that more attorneys will take advantage of the flexibility and simplicity provided by the MBCA (1984) provisions.

§ 7.10   Other Types of Securities: "Equity" and "Debt" Securities

Securities issued by a corporation may be broadly classified into "equity securities" and "debt securities." "Equity" in this sense is roughly synonymous with "net worth" or "ownership" and is derived from the following, quite common usage: if one subtracts a business's liabilities from its assets, what remains is the owners' "equity" in the business. Equity securities therefore refer to all securities that represent ownership interests in the corporation, while debt securities, such as bonds or debentures, represent interests that must ultimately be repaid. Common shares, of course, are the quintessence of an equity security since they represent the basic residual ownership of the corporation but preferred shares are also equity securities.

Common and preferred shares may also be referred to as the "capital stock" of the corporation, since they both appear in the lower right hand ("equity") part of the balance sheet under the caption "capital."

The distinction between "equity" and "debt" underlies much of the modern law and practice relating to corporation finance. At the simplest level the distinction is easy to grasp. A "debt" is something that must be repaid: it is the result of a "loan," the person making the loan is a "creditor," and if periodic payments are made, they are "interest." On the other hand, "equity" represents an ownership interest in the business itself. One thinks in terms of "shareholders," shares of "capital stock," voting, and "dividends" rather than "interest." It is sometimes not realized, however, that as a matter of economics, there is not a sharp distinction between debt and equity. For example, a 100 year "debenture" with interest payable solely from income if and when earned, and repayment subordinate to other debts of the business is more like an equity security than a debt security. Corporations may create mixed or "hybrid" securities which have some of the characteristics of debt and some of equity. Despite the lack of clear distinction between debt and equity in these situations, legal consequences vary substantially depending on how a particular hybrid security is classified. A hybrid security may be treated as a debt security for some purposes and as an equity security for other purposes, e.g., for income taxation purposes, rights on bankruptcy or insolvency, and the right to participate in management. The classification of hybrid securities for tax purposes, in particular, has given rise to litigation.

§ 7.11   Characteristics of Debt Securities

Debt securities are important sources of capital for publicly held corporations. Typical debt securities are long term debentures, and bonds. (Short term debts are usually represented by promissory notes that are not commonly referred to as "securities.") Technically a "debenture" is an unsecured corporate obligation while a "bond" is secured by a lien or mortgage on corporate property. However, the word "bond" is often used indiscriminately to cover both bonds and debentures and is so used hereafter. Bonds are historically bearer instruments, negotiable by delivery, issued in multiples of $1,000 with interest payments represented by coupons that are periodically clipped and submitted for payment. Bonds may also be registered with the issuer and transferable only by endorsement. Today, bond ownership is usually reflected either by registered instruments, or, increasingly, solely by book entries on the records of brokerage firms rather than by physical instruments.

Interest payments on debt securities are usually fixed obligations, due in any event, and expressed as a percentage of the face amount of the security. A six percent bond means that a $1,000 bond will pay $60 per year. Since the $60 payment is fixed for the life of the bond, the market value of the bond will move inversely with interest rates.

Not all bonds carry a fixed coupon rate. So-called income bonds, in which the obligation to pay interest is conditioned on adequate corporate earnings, are also known. Somewhat rarer are so-called participating bonds, where the amount of interest payable on the bonds increases or decreases with corporate earnings. The 1980s saw the development of novel interest provisions for bonds. "PIK" ("payment in kind") bonds pay interest in the form of promissory notes or additional bonds rather than cash for a stated period of years; cash interest payments begin on a specified date. "Reset" bonds contain provisions that require the issuer to adjust ("reset") the interest rate at a specified date in the future in the event the bonds are selling below face value so as to return the bonds' market value to their face value. These novel provisions have created difficulties for borrowers; in several instances, for example, reset bonds were selling at such a low price as the reset date approached that no adjustment in the interest rate could return the bonds' market price to their face value. In the case of such bonds, default or renegotiation of their terms was inevitable.

Debt securities are usually subject to redemption, which means that the corporation has reserved the power to call in and pay off the obligation before the maturity date, often at a slight premium over the face value. Securities chosen for redemption may be chosen by lot or by some other system. Many debt securities require the corporation to set aside cash, usually called sinking fund provisions, to redeem a part of the issue each year (or purchase securities on the open market and retire them), or to accumulate until the entire issue matures when the proceeds will be used to pay off the principal.

Debt securities may be convertible into equity securities, particularly common stock, on some predetermined ratio. This ratio is usually adjusted for stock splits, dividends, etc. The protection given by such adjustments is often referred to as protecting the conversion privilege from "dilution." When convertible debentures are converted, they, and the debt they represent, disappear and the new equity securities (the "conversion securities") are issued in their place. Convertible debentures themselves are treated as equity securities for many purposes. Convertible debentures are also usually redeemable; when the value of the conversion securities exceeds the redemption price, it is obviously to the holders' advantage to convert when an announcement is made that the debentures will be called for redemption. Such a conversion is usually described as "forced." Conversion in such situations is possible because a redemption privilege is exercisable only after notice is given as specified in the indenture (the underlying contract that defines the rights of the issuer, the holders, and the trustee) while the conversion privilege continues to exist until the instant of redemption. Litigation has arisen over the adequacy of the notice of redemption, the issue typically being whether the issuer need only give the minimum notice called for in the indenture or whether broader public notification must be given.

Some states authorize holders of bonds to participate in the selection of the board of directors either generally or upon specified contingencies, such as default in payment of interest. The inclusion of such powers, of course, blurs the distinction between debt and equity securities. The Model Business Corporation Act (1984) does not permit debenture holders to be given the power to vote (though several state statutes authorize corporations to give the power to vote to bond holders).

§ 7.12 Classes of Equity Securities; Preferred Shares

State corporation statutes give corporations broad power to create novel types of securities or specially tailored classes of common or preferred securities; this flexibility may be utilized to create innovative means of raising capital from third parties and to effectuate intracorporate agreements in closely held corporations. The emphasis in this section, like the preceding one, is essentially descriptive, concentrating on broad classes of equity securities including the principal ones used by corporations to raise capital in the modern era.

(1) *Preferred Shares.* Preferred shares differ from common shares in that they have preference over common shares in the payment of dividends and/or preference in the assets of the corporation upon the voluntary or involuntary liquidation of the corporation. "Preference" simply means that the preferred shares are entitled to receive some specified payment (either a dividend or a liquidating distribution, or both) before the common shares are entitled to anything. Most preferred shares contain preferences both as to dividends and liquidation.

The dividend preference may be described either in terms of dollars per share (the "$3.20 preferred") or as a percentage of par or stated value (the "five per cent preferred"). A dividend preference does not mean that the preferred is entitled to the payment in the same way that a creditor is entitled to payment from his or her debtor. A preferred dividend is still a dividend, and the directors may decide to omit all dividends, common or preferred, and this decision is in no way dependent on whether or not there is current income. Shares preferred as to dividends may be cumulative, noncumulative, or partially cumulative. If cumulative dividends are not paid in some years, they are carried forward and both they and the current year's preferred dividends must be paid in full before any common dividends may be declared. Noncumulative dividends disappear each year if they are not paid. Partially cumulative dividends are usually of the "cumulative to the extent of earnings" type so that the preferred shares continue to have first claim to actual earnings if not paid out as dividends. Unpaid cumulative dividends are not debts of the corporation, but a continued right to priority in future distributions. Since directors (who are elected by the common shareholders) may defer preferred dividends indefinitely if the directors are willing to forego dividends on the common shares as well, it is customary to provide that preferred shares may elect a specified number of directors if preferred dividends have been omitted for a specified period.

Preferred shares may also be participating, though that is not very common. Nonparticipating shares are entitled to a specified dividend before anything is paid on the common but no more, irrespective of the earnings of the corporation. Participating preferred shares are entitled to the original dividend, and after the common receives a specified amount, they may share with the common in any additional distributions. Participating shares are sometimes referred to as "Class A common" or a similar designation reflecting that their right to participate is open-ended.

Like debt securities, preferred shares may be convertible into common shares at a specified price or specified ratio and redeemable by the corporation at a fixed price. Typically, the original conversion ratio is established so that the common must appreciate substantially before it is profitable to convert the preferred. When the price of the common rises above this level, the preferred shares will fluctuate in price in tandem with price fluctuations of the common. The redemption privilege usually does not limit the price of the convertible preferred since the privilege to convert customarily continues for a limited period of time after a call for redemption. A conversion is "forced" when shares are called for redemption at a time when the value of the shares obtainable on conversion exceeds the redemption price. Also like convertible debt securities, convertible preferred usually contain elaborate provisions protecting the conversion privilege from dilution in case of stock dividends, stock splits, or the issuance of additional common shares.

The statutes of some states prohibit the creation of a security which is convertible into shares having superior rights and preferences as to dividends or upon liquidation—in other words, a common may not be made convertible into preferred or into debt. State statutes also may limit the redemption privilege to securities that have a liquidation preference or permit redeemable common shares only if there is another class of common shares that are not subject to redemption. These limitations are virtually the only substantive statutory restrictions on the issuance of classes of shares in most states. The Model Business Corporation Act (1984) does not contain either of these limitations. See § 6.01, and particularly the Official Comment.

The high interest rates of the early 1980s led to the development of novel financing devices, many of which involved preferred stock. For example, many corporations issued preferred stock that was redeemable at the option of the holder, or that became redeemable upon the occurrence of some external event, such as a change in interest rates or the lapse of a specified period of time. Still other corporations issued preferred with floating or adjustable dividend rates that depended on interest rates or some similar measure. Most of these novel preferreds were designed to give corporate holders of the preferred the benefit of the exclusion for intercorporate dividends while at the same time giving the holders most of the benefits of traditional debt. Classes of preferred shares with "PIK" and "reset" provisions also appeared. The validity of some of these novel types of preferred may be questionable under some state statutes; the Model Business Corporation Act (1984) contains provisions designed to assure their validity. See § 6.01(c).

Articles of incorporation may also authorize preferred shares to be issued in *series.* The articles of incorporation in effect create a class of shares without any substantive terms and authorize the board of directors to create "series" from within that class from time to time and to vary any of the substantive terms of one series from another. Where preferred shares in substantial amounts are to be sold by a corporation from time to time to raise capital, the privilege of issuing preferred in series simplifies financing since the price, dividend, liquidation preference, sinking fund provision, voting rights, and other terms of each series may be tailored to then-current market conditions and the need for shareholder approval is eliminated. Shares of different series have identical rights except for the specified business terms which may be varied. Before a series of preferred shares is created, a public filing with the Secretary of State describing the terms of the new series is required. The importance of the power to create series escalated in the 1980s with the development of the so-called "poison pill" defensive tactic against unwanted takeover attempts, which involves the creation of one or more series of preferred shares that have powers dependent on external events, typically the acquisition of some percentage of the corporation's voting shares by outsiders.

There is little or no difference between a "series" or a "class" of shares except their manner of creation—by the articles of incorporation in the case of a class and by action of the board of directors in the case of a series. In recognition of this, section 6.02 of the Model Business Corporation Act (1984) and the statutes of a few states allow the creation of either "classes" or "series" by the board of directors if authority to do so is given in the articles of incorporation.

The various provisions defining the rights of preferred shareholders appear in the corporation's articles of incorporation, bylaws, or directors' resolutions. Collectively they are referred to as the preferred shareholders' "contract" with the corporation and with other classes of shareholders. Rights of preferred shareholders are generally limited to those set forth in this "contract."

(2) *Classes of Common Stock.* State statutes also give corporations broad power to create classes of common stock with different rights or privileges. Such classes are usually designated by alphabetical notations: "Class A common," "Class B common," and so forth. In closely held corporations, classes of common stock are primarily used to effectuate control, voting, or financial arrangements. The following examples illustrate the variety and flexibility that classes of common stock may provide:

(a) A Class A common may be created that is entitled to twice the dividend per share of Class B common, but in all other respects the two classes are identical.

(b) A Class A common may be created that has two votes per share while Class B common has one vote per share (this is permitted under the MBCA (1984) and in most but not all states; some state statutes still have a "one vote per share" principle).

(c) A Class A common may be created that has the power to elect two directors; the holders of Class B common may have the power to elect one, two, or more directors, irrespective of the number of shares of each class outstanding.

(d) It may be required that the president of the corporation be a holder of Class A shares and the vice-president and treasurer be holders of Class B shares.

Classes of common stock may also be used to solve financial, control, or dividend problems in publicly held corporations, though such use is not common. When the Ford Motor Company went public in 1946, it created a special class of common shares to be held by the Ford Foundation. The special shares were convertible into regular common shares when sold by the Foundation. These shares were nonvoting so they permitted control of the corporation to be vested in the public without requiring the Foundation to abruptly liquidate its huge interest in the corporation.

Several publicly held corporations in which specific families have long been associated in a control capacity have sought to combat potential takeover attempts by creating a special class of shares with super voting rights to be issued solely to family members. The terms of this special class provide that shares lose their special voting privileges if they were sold or conveyed to non-family members. Among the corporations adopting this device are the publishers of the New York Times and the Wall Street Journal. The special class assured that voting control resided in the family even though most of the shares were publicly held. In 1988 the SEC adopted rule 19c–4 (usually known as the "one share one vote" rule) designed to prevent such unequal divisions in voting power in the future, though the rule "grandfathered" existing capital structures. This rule was held invalid in The Business Roundtable v. SEC (D.C.Cir.1990), but most securities exchanges have voluntarily adopted similar rules as prerequisites for listing shares for trading.

(3) *Non-voting Shares.* In most states, the articles of incorporation may limit or deny the right to vote to a class of shares. Preferred shares are usually non-voting shares, but the privilege to vote may be extended to such shares, either with the common shares or as a separate class.

Classes of non-voting common shares may also be created. In the closely held corporation, non-voting shares may serve a planning role. For example, the right to vote may be limited or denied to classes of common shares in the election of directors, on other subjects normally submitted to shareholders, or both. In closely held corporations there seems to be no reason why a specific limitation on voting should not be part of the shareholder's overall "contract" with the corporation.

In publicly held corporations, non-voting shares have been treated with greater suspicion. Such shares are somewhat analogous to perpetual voting trusts, and have been criticized on policy grounds for this reason. (See § 9.13 of this Nutshell.) Corporations with non-voting shares held by the public are ineligible for listing on the New York Stock Exchange, and may suffer market and other disadvantages as well. In the early years of this century, many corporations were capitalized by the issuance of non-voting shares to the public while the voting shares were held by the members of the family which founded or controlled the corporation. This practice has declined in importance in recent years. Several corporations that had issued non-voting shares for this reason later converted the non-voting shares into voting shares. This decision itself creates subtle issues as to the relative value of the right to vote and the fairness of the terms on which the privilege to vote is granted to the non-voting shares.

Under most state statutes, even non-voting shares are entitled to vote in connection with certain mergers, share exchanges, and other extraordinary events that may affect the class of nonvoting shares as a class.

(4) *Options.* Options to purchase shares may be used as a capital raising device, to provide employee incentives, and to a lesser extent as part of control devices. Of course, shares under option are not deemed issued and may not be voted until the options are exercised and the purchase price paid, or in some states, a firm commitment to pay the purchase price in the form of a promissory note has been delivered to the corporation.

Many state corporation statutes contain provisions that authorize the issuance of shares in connection with employee stock purchase or stock option plans by the board of directors, and provide that in the absence of fraud the determination by the board of the consideration for such shares shall be conclusive. (MBCA (1984) § 6.24).

"Warrants" are transferable options to acquire shares from the corporation at a specified price. Warrants have many of the qualities of an equity security since their price is a function of the market price of the underlying shares and the specified issuance price. Warrants frequently are issued as "sweeteners" in connection with the distribution of a debt or preferred stock issue; they may be issued in connection with a public exchange offer, or as compensation for handling the public distribution of other shares. Sometimes they are issued in a reorganization to holders of a class of security not otherwise recognized in the reorganization. Warrants may be publicly traded; warrants issued by a number of corporations are listed from time to time on the New York Stock Exchange or other exchanges. "Rights" are in effect short term warrants. They may also be publicly traded and listed on securities exchanges. Rights may be issued in lieu of a dividend, or in an effort to raise capital from existing shareholders.

Closely held corporations that have classes of shares are ineligible for the attractive S corporation tax election except where the classes differ only in connection with voting rights.

§ 7.13   The Advantages of Debt Financing

It is usually advantageous for a corporation to engage to some extent in debt financing. The notion that the best business is a debt-free business, while sounding attractive, is not consistent either with the minimization of income taxes or with the maximization of profits.

(1) *Tax Advantages of Debt.* There are tax advantages for individual shareholders to lend to a C corporation a portion of their investment in the corporation rather than to contribute it outright. Where the shareholders are individuals, such debt reduces the double taxation problem of C corporations discussed earlier. (See § 2.4 of this Nutshell.) Interest payments on such debt are deductible by the corporation whereas dividend payments on equity securities are not. Further, repayment of a debt may be a non-taxable return of capital, while a purchase or redemption of equity securities from a shareholder by the corporation is ordinarily a taxable event. When a shareholder lends a portion of a contemplated investment to the corporation, he or she is hopefully reserving the option of recovering this portion tax free at some later date if the corporation is successful.

There is no tax advantage in debt owed to individuals other than shareholders. However, the deductibility of interest payments to third persons may significantly reduce the cost of borrowed capital as compared to the cost of capital raised through the sale of equity securities. Indeed, the systematic cost advantage that borrowed capital has in the modern American economy has significantly affected the capital structure of all domestic corporations.

Where the contributor of capital is another corporation, somewhat different rules apply. The exclusion of 80 per cent or more of intercorporate dividends may make an equity investment attractive even though the dividend payments are not deductible by the borrowing corporation.

The tax advantages of debt financing have been so substantial for small closely-held corporations in the past that a substantial amount of case law has developed dealing with the question when debt in the corporate structure is excessive so that the Internal Revenue Service may treat the debt as a kind of equity, and disallow interest deductions or treat its repayment as a taxable dividend. (See § 7.14 of this Nutshell.) This problem has diminished in importance with the increased popularity of the S corporation election for such corporations.

(2) *Non-tax Advantages of Debt.* In the non-tax area debt owed both to third persons and to shareholders may be advantageous to a corporation, but for entirely different reasons.

(a) Debt owed to third persons is desirable because of the factor of *leverage.* Leverage arises when the corporation is able to earn more on the borrowed capital than the cost of the borrowing. The entire excess is allocable to the equity accounts of the corporation, thereby increasing the rate of return on the equity invested in the corporation. An example should help to make this clear. Let us assume that a person is considering the purchase of a business which will yield $25,000 per year over and above all taxes and expenses. The purchase price is $200,000. If the person simply buys the business using only his or her own capital, the annual return is 25,000/200,000 or 12.5 per cent.

Let us assume that the same person can borrow 80 per cent of the purchase price at an interest cost of 10 per cent per year. The person will then invest $40,000 of his or her own capital (20 per cent of $200,000), and borrow the remaining $160,000 (80 per cent of $200,000). The interest cost of the loan is $16,000 per year (10 per cent of $160,000). Since the business still makes $25,000 per year, the net profit after interest costs is $9,000 on a net investment of $40,000, and the return on the investment is 9,000/40,000 or 22.5%. In other words, by borrowing 80 per cent of the purchase price, the return per equity dollar invested is increased from 12.5 per cent to 22.5 per cent. If there were five such simultaneous opportunities, a rational investor would take his or her initial $200,000 and invest $40,000 in each of the five rather than buying only one debt-free business. By buying five businesses with 80 per cent loans, he or she will make $9,000 × 5 = $45,000 rather than $25,000. This is leverage, a device well understood by real estate syndicates and promoters who seek to obtain the largest possible mortgage and the smallest possible equity investment of their own. The reason that it is desirable to leverage in the hypothetical is that each dollar invested earns 12.5 per cent but the cost of borrowing is only 10 per cent. The 2.5 per cent difference on every borrowed dollar is allocable to the equity investment—the 20 per cent—thereby increasing the overall return on the equity. The risk involved with the extensive use of leverage, of course, is that the income from the project may not be sufficient to cover the fixed interest charges. The investor would then quickly see his or her return reduced to zero; it is possible that a "negative cash flow" would result and the investor might then have to invest additional amounts to cover the shortfall of income over expenses. Certainly, the investor may be wiped out much more quickly in a leveraged investment than if no part of the purchase price were borrowed.

Since World War II, the United States has suffered an inflationary spiral which may or may not continue in the future. If inflation continues, debt financing is also attractive because the loans will ultimately be repaid with inflated dollars. Of course, the competition for loans in such circumstances may cause high interest charges which will offset, either wholly or partially, this advantage of debt financing.

The Miller–Modigliani theorem states (with certain simplifying assumptions, including elimination of the tax advantage of debt) that the aggregate value of a corporation's securities (the market value of its equity securities plus the market value of its debt securities) is independent of the amount of debt in the corporation's capital structure. In other words, in a perfect world any enhanced value of common stock because of the advantages of leverage is precisely offset by a decline in the market value of the indebtedness.

(b) Leverage can be obtained only by the use of other people's money. Nevertheless, it is often advantageous for non-tax business reasons for shareholders to advance a portion of their investment in the business in the form of loans rather than capital contributions. (The tax advantages of doing this in a C corporation have previously been discussed.) As a creditor, a shareholder may have greater rights upon bankruptcy or insolvency than he or she would have as a mere shareholder. However, if the loans are made as part of the original capitalization of the company, there is a substantial risk that such loans will be subordinated to the claims of general creditors in a bankruptcy proceeding. (See §§ 6.13, 7.16 of this Nutshell.) The basic test in this area is whether the capitalization is such that a third person would have made an arms length loan. If so, the loan by the shareholder should be treated as a loan for bankruptcy purposes. Loans for subsequent business needs also may fare better and stand a good chance of being recognized as bona fide loans.

§ 7.14 Tax Consequences of Excessive Debt Capitalization in C Corporations

The substantial tax advantages of shareholder debt financing in C corporations have led to a large amount of tax litigation as to whether ostensible debt should be reclassified as equity for tax purposes. The judicial decisions in this area do not establish a simple, easily understood test as to when a reclassification from debt to equity is proper. The diversity of possible factual situations is substantial, and there is less than total agreement in the cases as to the applicable legal principles. Perhaps Judge John R. Brown was being somewhat ironic when, in the leading Fifth Circuit case on the question, he stated: "Although the results are diverse, sometimes favoring the taxpayer, sometimes the Government, the cases are in accord in applying with an even hand the controlling legal principles for determining the outcome * * * ." Tomlinson v. 1661 Corp. (5th Cir.1967).

Two interrelated ideas appear to underlie the judicial reasoning in the numerous cases in this area: first, are the legal incidents of the relationship between corporation and shareholder more similar to an equity investment or to a debt relationship? And second, even where the principal incidents of debt exist, is there some paramount policy of federal tax law which requires that particular debt interests be treated as equity investments?

Certainly, many cases may be explained on the ground that despite the label "debt" attached to an interest, the shareholder really created an equity interest. Some of these cases adopt a test of the "intention" of the shareholder in making the investment, but state that this "intention" may be inferred from the provisions of the debenture itself or from surrounding circumstances. The following factors tend to indicate an "intention" to make an equity or capital contribution: (a) use of initial payments, both capital and "loans," to acquire capital assets; (b) proceeds used to start up the corporate life; (c) subordination to other indebtedness; (d) an "inordinately postponed due date;" (e) provision for payment of "interest" only out of earnings; and (f) an express or implied agreement not to enforce collection of the "debt."

At one time it was thought that the talismanic test was the ratio between debt and equity. It was intimated in the Supreme Court decision in John Kelley Co. v. Commissioner (S.Ct.1946) that a ratio of 4:1 (debt equal to four times equity) or more automatically led to the reclassification of the debt as equity. A corporation with a high debt/equity ratio is often called a "thin" corporation. Later cases, however, have rejected the suggestion that the test is a mechanical one based on an arithmetic calculation. In other words, courts have rejected in strong terms the argument by the government that a high ratio of debt to equity automatically indicated an objectionable avoidance of taxes, and therefore grounds for treating the debt as equity. However, high debt/equity ratios are relevant and it is not surprising that most cases in which debt has been reclassified as equity involve debt/equity ratios higher than 4:1, and often higher than 10:1.

§ 7.15　Debt as a Second Class of Stock in S Corporations

An S corporation may not have more than one class of stock outstanding (except classes that differ only in voting rights). A number of early tax cases considered the question whether debt might constitute "a second class of stock," thereby causing the loss of the S corporation election.

After the Internal Revenue Service won several such cases, Congress enacted a definition of "straight debt," the inclusion of which in a corporate capital structure would not cause loss of the S corporation election. The definition of straight debt requires a market interest rate and the inclusion only of terms typical of arms-length debt transactions.

§ 7.16 The Deep Rock Doctrine Revisited

The so-called Deep Rock doctrine has been discussed in a previous chapter (see § 6.13 of this Nutshell). The doctrine, evolved in bankruptcy cases, permits subordination of shareholder-owned debt to the claims of general creditors when the court believes it is fair to do so. It is therefore the bankruptcy analogue to the "thin corporation" problem in tax law described in § 7.14. The shareholder claims which are subordinated may be either secured or unsecured: under this doctrine the court may treat secured shareholder claims either as on a parity with general unsecured claims or as inferior to all other such claims. Obviously, this doctrine, when applied, has the effect of eliminating one major advantage of shareholder indebtedness.

The doctrine has generally been applied in Federal bankruptcy cases, and it has also been recognized in some state insolvency proceedings.

Some cases have held that a mere showing of inadequate capitalization is not enough for disallowance or subordination in the bankruptcy area and that there must be some additional showing of unfairness, fraud, or misrepresentation. The shareholder involved may have the burden of showing "the inherent fairness and good faith of the transactions involved." One court has suggested that "[i]t is only where the conduct of a stockholder or officer toward his or her corporation can be challenged as being detrimental to the creditors that there is any duty on behalf of the [bankruptcy judge] or the courts to recast the voluntary acts of the corporation into something different from what they have in good faith undertaken to engage in." As a practical matter, however, if the initial capitalization is grossly inadequate, some other element of unfairness can usually be found which under this test will permit the court to subordinate the shareholder indebtedness. Also the case law is in disagreement as to whether the adequacy of the initial capital is to be judged in the light of the needs of the particular business, or on an abstract basis of substantiality.

As in the case of tax controversies, subsequent loans needed to keep the business afloat are likely to be accepted by the courts as true loans for bankruptcy purposes, though unfair attempts to obtain security for such loans may still be attacked under the Deep Rock doctrine.

§ 7.17   Equalizing Capital and Services When Forming a Corporation

A recurring problem in financing a close corporation involves the situation where investors have agreed to contribute capital or provide services in varying amounts, and shares are to be issued in some different agreed ratio. Assume, for example, that A and B have agreed to go into business with A providing the necessary capital of $100,-000 with B to work exclusively for the new venture for at least three years. The parties have also agreed that A is to receive 60 per cent and B 40 per cent of the voting shares. The state in question has eliminated par value from its statute but has retained the restrictions on the types of eligible consideration for shares described in § 7.6 of this Nutshell. How can the arrangement be worked out?

(1) B cannot be issued shares immediately upon the execution of a long-term employment contract, since "future services" are not valid consideration for shares.

(2) There is no obstacle, however, to issuing shares for past services. Hence the arrangement may be worked out by issuing A 60 shares for $100,000 immediately, and issuing B 40 shares when the period of employment ends three years from now. Possible disadvantages are (i) until B has completed the services, A is the sole shareholder with total power over the corporation and may exclude B at any time (though such an exclusion may constitute a breach of contract); (ii) B may have to provide services for an extended period without receiving dividends or a salary to live on; and (3) B will have to pay income tax on the value of the shares but will not have received any money from the corporation to do so.

(3) B may propose that he or she sign a promissory note for the $66,667, have the 40 shares issued to him or her immediately, and pay off the note by rendering services under an employment contract. While some states that prohibit contracts for future services to serve as consideration for shares permit promissory notes to serve as consideration, most do not.

(4) Another solution is to issue shares at different prices. A may be issued 60 shares for $100,000 and B 40 shares for $40.00. There is no statutory requirement that all shares of the same class be issued for the same consideration. However, this suggestion is manifestly unfair to A if the business does not do well and the parties desire to liquidate since B in effect has an immediate 40 per cent interest in A's capital.

(5) A more reasonable solution, at least where the S corporation election is not to be made, is to create two classes of common stock with identical rights on dissolution:

(a) Class A common, one vote per share; 6,000 shares issued to A for $100,000 in cash (or $16.67 per share).

(b) Class B common, one hundred votes per share, 40 shares issued to B for $667.00 (or $16.67 per share). If dividends are to be paid on a 60–40 ratio, the dividends on each share of class B stock would have to be set at one hundred times the dividend on each share of class A stock.

This solves the premature liquidation problem. However, multiple votes per share are not permitted in some states. Essentially the same pattern could be created by giving A shares with a fraction of a vote per share, if that is permitted under the specific state statute.

(6) Another solution is to issue A 60 common shares for $60 and B 40 common shares for $40, and have A lend the corporation $99,940. This solves the corporate law and premature dissolution problems but creates others. There is a risk that the debt would not qualify as "straight debt" under the S corporation election, and make the corporation ineligible for that desirable tax election. If the corporation is taxed as a C corporation, it would be viewed as a "thin" corporation for tax purposes, and an attempt by the corporation to deduct interest payments on the $99,-940 "debt" would be disallowed. A also would probably not be able to maintain creditor status in a bankruptcy proceeding under the "Deep Rock" doctrine. B might also object that A should not have a creditor's claim to all his or her capital while B is contributing services for which he or she has no claim at all.

(7) Perhaps the best solution, where the S corporation election is not essential, is this: A receives 60 common shares, for $60.00 ($1 per share) and B receives 40 common shares, for $40.00 ($1 per share). A also receives 500 preferred shares for $50,000 ($100 per share) and "lends" the corporation the remaining $50,000. Since the aggregate capitalization is now $50,100 (combining all the

consideration received for the common and preferred), debt is less than 50 per cent and the debt/equity ratio is about 1:1. The chances of applying the "thin" corporation or "Deep Rock" doctrines are therefore greatly reduced. This pattern was essentially upheld in the Maryland case of Obre v. Alban Tractor Co. (Md.1962), involving a state insolvency proceeding. It may be noted that the dividend preference of the preferred is not specified. Under the circumstances, that is a matter of negotiation between A and B.

If this problem were to arise in a state with a par value requirement, the shares of stock would have to be assigned a par value that is less than the lowest consideration for which the shares are to be issued.

§ 7.18 Issuance of Shares by a Going Concern: Preemptive Rights

The issuance of authorized but previously unissued shares by a going concern must meet the same requirements as to kind and amount of consideration as on the original formation and capitalization of the corporation. The number of shares to be sold and the consideration therefor is set by the board of directors. In addition, however, the issuance of new shares may affect the financial and voting rights of existing shareholders, and as a result additional legal requirements may be applicable. If shares are issued to the current shareholders in strict proportion to their shareholdings, the relative position of each shareholder is obviously unaffected though the aggregate capital invested in the corporation has increased. However, if shares are issued to third persons or to existing shareholders not in strictly proportional amounts, the voting power of some shareholders will necessarily be reduced. Further, if the shares are issued disproportionately and for less than current value (a term that need not here be precisely defined), the financial interest of some shareholders in the corporation will necessarily be diluted.

A "preemptive right" permits existing shareholders, subject to several important exceptions, to subscribe—in preference to strangers and pro rata with other existing shareholders—for their relative proportion of new shares to be issued by the corporation. Ideally, the preemptive right of each existing shareholder protects him or her from injury resulting from the issue of shares. However, in practice it often does not work out that way. For one thing, preemptive rights under modern statutes are permissive rather than mandatory and corporations may limit or deny such rights by provisions in the articles of incorporation. However, even if preemptive rights are excluded, equitable principles may limit the power of corporations to dispose of new shares on an unfair basis.

Shares sold by a going corporation may come from three sources. They may be shares that are newly authorized by the corporation by an amendment to the articles of incorporation. Or, they may be shares that were previously authorized in the articles but never previously issued. Or they may be "treasury shares," that is, shares that have been issued and subsequently reacquired by the corporation. Even though the issuance of any additional shares, no matter what the source, has the same dilutive effect, different legal principles may be applicable depending on the source of the shares and the precise language of the state statute defining the shareholder's preemptive right.

At common law and under the statutes of many states the preemptive right did not extend to the following types of transactions:

(1) Shares that were originally authorized but unissued. The rationale for this exception was that an implied

understanding existed between the original subscribers that sale of the remaining authorized shares to obtain necessary capital may be completed. However, this rationale is not persuasive today in light of the modern practice of authorizing additional shares that are not planned to be sold as part of the original capitalization. As a result some states do not recognize this exception.

(2) Treasury shares. The rationale for this exception is that shareholders are not injured since the shares had previously been issued and their reissuance simply restores a dilution that had existed previously. Again this may not be persuasive, depending on the particular factual situation under consideration.

(3) Shares issued for property or services rather than cash or shares issued in connection with a merger. The theory underlying these exceptions is that preemptive rights in such situations would frustrate or render impractical desirable transactions, or are impossible to work out since existing shareholders may not own, and therefore cannot contribute, property on a proportional basis.

(4) Shares issued to satisfy conversion or option rights.

(5) Shares issued pursuant to a plan of reorganization or recapitalization under court supervision.

Some recent decisions have refused to apply these exceptions mechanically and have looked to the realities of the particular situation. One court, for example, held that preemptive rights should not be denied when property is the consideration for shares except where, because of peculiar circumstances, the corporation has great need for the particular property, and issuance of shares therefor is the only practical and feasible method by which the corporation can acquire it. In many situations, the corporation may pay cash to acquire the needed property; to allow the corporation to acquire it with shares, it was argued, defeats the preemptive right that would exist if shares were issued for cash and the cash used to acquire the property.

Modern state statutes change the common law preemptive right in several respects:

(1) At common law it was generally held that a shareholder's preemptive right was an integral part of the ownership of shares. However, all modern statutes give corporations the privilege of dispensing entirely with preemptive rights if they so choose. The choice must be made by a specific provision in the corporation's articles of incorporation. Statutes may grant preemptive rights unless they are specifically negated in the articles (an "opt-out" clause), or preclude preemptive rights except to the extent specifically granted in the articles (an "opt-in" clause). Section 6.30 of the Model Business Corporation Act (1984) adopts an "opt in" clause, but simplifies the drafting problem faced by an attorney desiring to create preemptive rights by establishing a "standard form" for electing preemptive rights in section 6.30(b). This standard form, which covers such matters as the scope of the preemptive right, waiver, and the duration of the right, may be modified as desired.

(2) They sometimes give preemptive rights more broadly than the common law, e.g., they may extend the right to "authorized but unissued shares," "treasury shares," and securities convertible into common shares, all types of shares to which the common law preemptive right did not extend.

(3) They provide specifically that preemptive rights do not exist between different classes of shares, e.g., holders of preferred do not have a preemptive right to acquire common. The MBCA (1984) standard form of preemptive rights, however, seeks to preserve voting power by providing that common shareholders have a preemptive right to acquire voting or convertible preferred shares.

(4) They provide that shares issued pursuant to employee incentive or compensation plans are not subject to preemptive rights if the plan was originally approved by the shareholders. The MBCA (1984) standard form of preemptive rights does not include this proviso.

What considerations enter into the decision to limit or deny preemptive rights? The argument in favor of preserving preemptive rights is that the shareholder who subscribes for a given percentage of the original issue of the shares of a corporation should be entitled to maintain his or her percentage interest provided he or she is willing to subscribe for the proportion of the additional issue. This sounds like a democratic principle and undoubtedly it is in many cases. There are situations, however, in which preemptive rights are more a nuisance than anything else. Suppose for example that a corporation with a fairly large number of shareholders is in need of immediate funds and can obtain them only by a prompt sale of additional shares to bankers or underwriters. It may well find that compliance with and satisfaction of the preemptive rights of its existing shareholders will be expensive, time-consuming, and only partially successful.

If it is anticipated that the corporation will for some time remain a close corporation, preemptive rights may be retained so as to give each shareholder the maximum protection against dilution, though it is safer to provide such rights by shareholder agreement than by reliance on the state statute. But, if it is anticipated that the corporation will in the near future engage in public financing or will seek to acquire other companies or properties by the issuance of its shares, preemptive rights are often eliminated to avoid legal complications when the time arrives for the sale of additional shares or the acquisition of other companies or properties. In any event, preemptive rights serve little purpose where shares are publicly traded, since additional shares can usually be bought on the open market if desired. Where preemptive rights have been excluded, the directors may always later decide to offer additional shares pro rata to existing shareholders. In fact, in many corporations, existing shareholders are the most logical market, and the one likely to be pursued.

§ 7.19 Oppressive Issuance of Shares

Additional shares of stock may be issued oppressively to dilute the interests of other shareholders in the corporation. Misuse of this power is often referred to as a "squeeze out" or "freeze out."

A number of cases attest that corporate management has a fiduciary duty of taking corporate action according to the best interests of the corporation rather than for personal advantage. This principle amply covers situations where, in the absence of preemptive rights, management dilutes the interests of shareholders simply by issuing additional shares to itself at a bargain price. This principle may also cover situations where management issues shares to itself at a fair price to ensure retention of control without offering the shares more broadly. In the first situation there is dilution of both financial and voting interests; in the second there is only dilution of the voting power.

Much more difficult are cases involving a combination of legitimate and self-serving purposes. Shares may be issued to friendly persons for apparently worthwhile purposes and entirely in accordance with statutory requirements, but the minority shareholders complain that the real purpose and principal effect of the transaction is to freeze them out or dilute their interest. Most cases have permitted such transactions to stand, at least where the ostensible purpose does seem to have substance. Courts are naturally reluctant to second guess decisions by directors and interfere in intracorporate disputes, but will do so if they feel that the ostensible purpose is a sham, and the real purpose of the transaction is simply to benefit management.

Preemptive rights give shareholders considerably less protection against such tactics than is often thought. Indeed, as a practical matter, the protection provided by preemptive rights is often illusory. A minority shareholder may be frozen out if he or she lacks the financial ability to exercise the preemptive right and purchase the additional shares in order to protect his or her proportionate interest. Often, the majority or dominant shareholders may purchase their allotment by offsetting indebtedness owed to them by the corporation (thereby exercising their preemptive rights without further financial investment) while other shareholders have to invest substantial amounts of cash just to stay even. In one case, for example, the court refused to intervene when a shareholder was given the choice of investing an additional $136,000 to preserve his twenty per cent interest or permitting his interest in the corporation to be diluted to less than one per cent. Hyman v. Velsicol Corp. (Ill.App.1951). In another case, where the reduction was from about 32 per cent to less than one per cent, the court applied the test whether the issuance of shares seemed to serve a substantial corporate purpose or whether it was designed simply to benefit management, and over one dissent, concluded that the issuance of shares should be set aside. Browning v. C & C Plywood Corp. (Or.1967). The issue in these cases may come down to an evaluation of the existence of a valid business purpose for the transaction: e.g., the need of the corporation for the additional capital, or where indebtedness is canceled and the corporation receives no additional cash, whether the improvement in the balance sheet caused by the cancellation of indebtedness is a bona fide purpose. There appears, however, to be a trend toward giving minority shareholders protection against the unfair issuance of shares despite the presence of a nominal business purpose on the theory that the majority shareholder owes a fiduciary duty to the minority. See § 12.11 of this Nutshell.

§ 7.20 Circular Ownership of Shares

As indicated earlier, treasury shares—shares of a corporation which have been issued but subsequently reacquired by and belong to the corporation—have an intermediate status in most states. They are treated as issued but not outstanding and may not be voted or be counted in determining the number of shares outstanding.

Shares that are owned by a wholly- or majority-owned subsidiary of the issuing corporation are usually called circularly owned shares. Even though they are not technically treasury shares, they are treated in an analogous fashion. They may not be voted or considered as outstanding for purposes of a quorum. See MBCA (1984) § 7.21(b). In other words, circular control is prohibited under most statutes. On a similar theory, shares held by the issuing corporation in a fiduciary capacity also have sometimes been barred from being voted or counted in determining the number of shares outstanding, though section 7.21(c) and the statutes of a number of states permit such voting.

§ 7.21 A Cautionary Postscript: The Risk of Violating Securities Acts While Raising Capital

The Federal Securities Act of 1933 and state statutes, called "blue sky laws," require corporations to register issues of securities with governmental agencies before they are sold publicly. (The picturesque name, "blue sky laws," is reputedly derived from the practice of certain turn-of-the-century promoters of selling "lots in the blue sky in fee simple absolute.") Initial registration under these statutes, considered at length in advanced courses on securities regulation, is expensive, difficult, and time consuming. Further, selling shares without registration when required gives rise to substantial civil liabilities and may lead to criminal prosecution as well.

When corporations raise capital by selling shares, it is important that the offering not become inadvertently a public one, thereby triggering the registration requirements of these statutes, or that some exemption from registration under these statutes is available. The definition of a "public offering" and the scope of exemptions from registration are often complex legal issues. As a result, the risk of an inadvertent violation of these statutes is often a real one.

When a corporation first registers securities under these statutes it is often said to "go public."

[For unfamiliar terms see the Glossary]

CHAPTER EIGHT

THE DISTRIBUTION OF POWERS WITHIN A CORPORATION: SPECIAL PROBLEMS

§ 8.1 The "Statutory Scheme" In General

Traditional state business corporation acts envision a particular model or norm of management and control within the corporation. The traditional model assumes that shareholders elect directors who "manage" the business and affairs of the corporation and who select the officers to carry out the board's directions. This model is referred to as the "statutory scheme," or "statutory norm." This model assumes that every corporation has certain characteristics, however, manifestly many corporations in the real world do not possess these characteristics.

The traditional statutory model assumes that a corporation has several (or many) shareholders when they provide that the shareholders will hold meetings to select directors pursuant to a notice given a certain number of days in advance of the meeting date. These requirements do not make much sense in a corporation with only a single shareholder. A "meeting" of one person is not very much of a meeting, and the requirement that all shareholders be given ten days' notice of that meeting is slightly ridiculous.

Further, rather surprisingly, a large, publicly-held corporation also does not fit all aspects of the traditional model. In these corporations, shareholders are usually so diverse and poorly organized that their principal participation in business affairs is ratifying the selection of directors made by persons who control the day-to-day operations (and who are collectively referred to as the "management"). Further, the board of directors does not of itself "manage" the business of a large publicly held corporation; that is done by the corporate officers (the "management"). The board of directors participates in corporate affairs through its selection of the chief executive officer and to some extent through the exercise of other functions, such as oversight, the provision of advice to management, establishment of compensation levels, approval of major transactions, and so forth. See chapter 13 of this Nutshell. The large publicly held corporation model fundamentally is quite unlike the traditional corporate model which assumes that the board of directors manages the business.

It is probable that the traditional statutory scheme more or less accurately describes control relationships in many intermediate corporations in the continuum between the very small and the very large.

A question that is critically important is the extent to which the traditional statutory requirements relating to management and control may be varied in corporations that do not closely resemble the traditional model. The modern publicly held corporation management structure developed without express statutory authority; that structure began to be recognized in corporation statutes only in the 1970s and 1980s. See chapter 13 of this Nutshell. In connection with closely held corporations, as late as the 1930s it was accepted dogma that the statutory scheme could not be varied or relaxed by agreement of the shareholders in any significant way even though the number of shareholders was small. Since then, however, a more liberal and relaxed view of what is permitted has become generally accepted.

A small, closely held corporation in practice more close-ly resembles partnerships than publicly held corporations. A person not versed in corporation law might well con-clude that in the absence of harm to some class of persons, businessmen should be permitted to vary the statutory norms to fit the needs of their particular busi-ness relationship. Such freedom is generally available in partnerships, and there seems to be no reason why it should not be equally available in corporations. While the trend mentioned above is clearly in the direction of pro-viding increased freedom within the corporation, it is still not available to the same extent as it is in a partnership.

The reason the development in closely held corpora-tions has been slower is the survival of the theory that the granting of the privilege of limited liability and permission to conduct business in the name of a fictitious entity is a concession by the State: In order to gain the concession one must follow the procedures and rules set forth in the business corporation statutes. (See generally § 1.2 of this Nutshell). Despite criticism of this theory as pure formal-ism, vestiges of it remain embedded in the thinking of judges, and it is therefore unsafe to attempt by agreement substantial variations from the statutory norm that are not expressly authorized by statute. Legislation is the ultimate solution if greater freedom is felt to be necessary, and indeed there is a trend toward relaxing the statutory norms discussed in this Chapter both by general legisla-tion in business corporation statutes and the enactment of special statutes (discussed in Chapter 12 of this Nutshell) to relieve closely held corporations from the strictures of the traditional statutory scheme. However, even under these statutes, it still may be unsafe to attempt to vary the statutory norms in a way not contemplated by these statutes.

The special problems of the closely held corporation are discussed in § 8.10 of this chapter and in Chapter 12 of this Nutshell.

§ 8.2   The Statutory Scheme: Shareholders

The shareholders in the traditional statutory scheme are the ultimate owners of the corporation, but have only limited powers to participate in management and control. The statutes contemplate that they may act through four main channels:

(1) Election and removal of directors;

(2) Approval or disapproval of corporate operations which are void or voidable unless ratified;

(3) Approval or disapproval of amendments to articles of incorporation or bylaws constituting the "contract" between the corporation and its shareholders; and

(4) Approval or disapproval of fundamental changes not in the regular course of business (mergers, compulsory share exchanges, dissolution, or disposition of substantially all the corporate assets).

This list, however, does not fully exhaust the shareholders' powers in fact. For example, statutes also grant shareholders miscellaneous incidental powers, perhaps the most important of which is the right to inspect corporate books and records. See, for example, Chapter 16 of the Model Business Corporation Act (1984), discussed in Chapter 19 of this Nutshell. Section 8.03 of the MBCA (1984) requires shareholder approval of certain major changes in the size of the board of directors. The MBCA (1984) and most state statutes also authorize shareholders to file derivative suits on behalf of the corporation (MBCA (1984) §§ 7.40—7.47) or suits to enjoin ultra vires acts (MBCA (1984) § 3.04). State statutes that embody the traditional par value corporation finance concepts also grant shareholders other powers, e.g., a veto power over repurchases of corporate shares out of capital surplus, a veto power over dividends payable in the shares of the corporation, and the power to approve the consideration for which no par shares are issued. It is also well established that shareholders may adopt resolutions making recommendations to the board of directors, and because of the power to select and remove directors, it is probable that the directors will listen carefully to the views of a majority of the shareholders. (See § 8.7 of this Nutshell.) Further, some matters such as the selection of independent accountants have been vested in the shareholders either by tradition or because of regulations by the Securities and Exchange Commission. Nevertheless, the fact remains that in the traditional corporate model the shareholders have only limited powers to participate in management and control: their principal function is to select other persons—the directors—to manage the business of the corporation for them.

§ 8.3   The Statutory Scheme: Power of Shareholders to Remove Directors

At common law, a director had considerable security of office for the period of his or her election. He or she could be removed only for cause, a procedure technically known as "amotion." Further, a director, threatened with removal for cause, was entitled to some elements of due process including notice of charges, an opportunity to be heard, and a hearing. Of course, in a corporation with shares widely held by the general public, a "trial" of a director by the shareholders at a meeting was unwieldy and impractical. Decision was made in fact by the granting or withholding of a proxy appointment, a fact that was recognized by courts which required that the imperiled director be given access to the proxy machinery to conduct his or her defense. There was also some case law questioning the power of a court to remove a director even for cause if a majority of the shareholders refused to do so. These various common law rules are, of course, basically consistent with the principle that directors' independence of judgment cannot be restricted or interfered with by shareholders.

These common law rules have been virtually totally superseded by statute. Modern corporation statutes permit shareholders to remove directors without cause (see MBCA (1984) § 8.08), though in a few states such a power exists in all circumstances only if specifically reserved to the shareholders in the articles of incorporation. Furthermore, a number of states expressly permit a court to remove directors upon a judicial finding that the director "engaged in fraudulent or dishonest conduct, or gross abuse of authority or discretion," and that removal is in the best interest of the corporation. See MBCA (1984) § 8.09. The power to remove a director by judicial act is appropriate in two circumstances: (1) where the director possesses sufficient voting power as a shareholder to prevent removal, and declines to vote for his or her own removal, and (2) in publicly held corporations where the director refuses to resign despite requests to do so, and the cost of a special shareholders' meeting to remove him or her is substantial.

The statutes permitting the removal of directors without cause subtly change the relation between shareholders and directors. The power to remove for policy or personal reasons (not involving "cause" in the legal sense of misconduct) may be important in several areas, for example:

(1) Where a person has recently acquired a majority of the outstanding shares (or at least working control) and desires to put "his own people" in control of the corporation immediately;

(2) In closely held corporations where a majority (or sole) shareholder may wish to elect friends as directors but ensure their continued loyalty. An unlimited power of

removal without cause goes a long way toward ensuring that loyalty.

Of course, under modern statutes a corporation may voluntarily elect to grant directors the tenure they possessed at common law. Such provisions are not uncommon. For example, a number of publicly held corporations have granted directors this security as part of a defensive plan to make takeovers more difficult, the theory being that a potential purchaser of a working majority of the corporation's voting shares may be deterred if the purchaser is unable to obtain immediate control of the corporation's board of directors. Similar provisions may also appear in closely held corporations as part of a plan to assure continued minority shareholder representation on the board of directors.

A question may exist as to whether an amendment to bylaws granting (or restoring) the power to remove directors without cause may be made effective against incumbent directors who were elected under bylaws that guaranteed them greater security of office. A court may be tempted to argue in this situation that a change in the bylaws during the term of a director is an invalid deprivation of a vested right.

§ 8.4 The Statutory Scheme: Directors

The traditional language of business corporation acts defining the role of the board of directors is that "the business and affairs of a corporation shall be managed by the board of directors." The word "shall" has a mandatory ring, and it is pursuant to this provision that courts have sometimes struck down, as against public policy, agreements between businessmen which purport to dictate how persons shall vote as directors.

In the very large corporation with billions of dollars of assets, it is not realistic to expect the directors actually to manage the day-to-day affairs of the business. That is management's responsibility. In recognition of this, section 141(a) of the Delaware General Corporation Law and section 8.01(b) of the Model Business Corporation Act (1984) (as well as the statutes of many other states) have modified the basic obligation of directors essentially to read: "all corporate powers shall be exercised by *or under the authority of,* and the business and affairs of the corporation *shall be managed under the direction of,* its board of directors, subject to any limitation set forth" in the articles of incorporation. The italicized language authorizes corporations to vest actual management authority in the executive officers of the corporation under the general direction of the board of directors. The final "subject to" clause, it may be noted, authorizes limitations on the scope of the traditional power of directors to be placed in the articles of incorporation.

The scope of the phrase "business and affairs" is not defined in the statutes. Generally, in closely held corporations directors formulate the policy of the corporation, and authorize the making of important contracts. They may delegate details of the actual daily operation of the corporation to officers and agents, but they closely oversee those activities. In the publicly held corporation, most management decisions are delegated to corporate officers subject to the general direction of the board of directors.

Directors have specific statutory authority in numerous areas. For example, the decision to declare dividends is specifically a directoral function, as is the determination of the consideration for which shares are to be issued. Even in the case of important corporate changes, such as mergers or amendments to articles of incorporation, which require shareholder approval, the directors have the responsibility to formulate the proposed change, approve it, and submit it to the shareholders for approval or disapproval. The directors serve a "gatekeeper's role" with respect to such transactions. See § 8.8 of this Nutshell.

The power of directors with respect to the business and affairs of the corporation in the traditional model flows from the statute rather than from the shareholders who elected them. This power is granted to the directors by the statute, it is not delegated to them by the shareholders in the electoral process. As a result, directors may, if they wish, disregard the expressed desires of a majority of the shareholders and act as they think best—subject of course, to the ultimate power of the shareholders to select different directors next time. However, there are only a few recorded illustrations of the exercise of this independent power. As a practical matter, the power of selection and removal of directors is a powerful brake on boards of directors acting independently of the expressed wishes of a majority of the shareholders. In addition, there is perhaps a partially articulated notion that complete independence of action is inconsistent with shareholder democracy in publicly held corporations. This problem occasionally arises immediately after a successful corporate takeover where the shareholders do not possess the power to remove sitting directors.

Perhaps the clearest illustration of the directors' independence from shareholders is their gate keeping function in connection with mergers, amendments to articles of incorporation. If the directors do not approve a proposal and recommend that it be submitted to the shareholders, the shareholders are without power to act on the proposal on their own.

The relationships between directors, shareholders and the corporation are *sui generis*. The shareholders elect directors who are granted broad authority with respect to the corporation and its property. Further, responsibility accompanies power. The directors owe fiduciary and other duties to the corporation and to the shareholders. Such duties include specified statutory liabilities for director misconduct plus broader common law duties—due care, loyalty, corporate opportunity, and the like. A director may conceivably be liable for misconduct even though he or she is following the wishes of a majority of the shareholders of a corporation. Because of this risk of directoral liability, cases involving the role of directors place great importance on their unimpaired independence of decision. Shareholder agreements on matters that are reserved to the discretion of directors are often referred to by courts in antagonistic terms: they are against public policy because they "fetter" the discretion of directors, or in extreme cases, "sterilize" the board.

§ 8.5   Elimination of the Board of Directors

Until relatively recently it was an accepted premise of the corporate model that every corporation had to have a board of directors. The first important exception to this principle occurred in the special close corporation statutes described in Chapter 12 of this Nutshell. The reason underlying the decision to permit such corporations to dispense with a board of directors and have their affairs conducted directly by shareholders runs along the following lines. Why should a corporation with a few shareholders—perhaps only one or two—have to have a board of directors? Why should not such a corporation be permitted to dispense with a board of directors entirely and simply conduct business directly through shareholders? In fact, that is almost always what happens, with the shareholders donning their "director hats" when their lawyer tells them to. There seems to be no good reason why such a corporation should not be able to have its formal structure reflect the reality of the way the business is run, and a number of states enacted close corporation statutes authorizing such a management form.

The close corporation statutes generally require an election by the corporation to adopt those statutes. But why should the option to dispense entirely with the board of directors be limited to corporations that have made that election? If a non-electing corporation has only one or two shareholders, why should it not also be entitled to dispense with its board of directors? It was on the basis of reasoning implicit in these questions that the original draftsmen of the Model Business Corporation Act (1984) added section 8.01(c) that permitted any corporation with 50 or fewer shareholders to elect to dispense with or limit the authority of the board of directors. In 1992, this privilege was broadened even further to permit any corporation to adopt non-traditional governance rules, including dispensing with a board of directors, by a simple written agreement executed by all of the shareholders. It is too early to tell whether this innovative provision will be widely used; certainly it represents a sharp departure from the traditional mores of the corporate form.

§ 8.6   The Statutory Scheme: Officers

Corporation statutes generally do not attempt to define the authority and role of officers. A typical statutory provision merely states that each officer of the corporation "has the authority and shall perform the duties set forth in the bylaws or, to the extent consistent with the bylaws, the duties prescribed by the board of directors or by direction of an officer authorized by the board of directors to prescribe the duties of other officers." (MBCA (1984) § 8.41). In theory, corporate officers administer the day-to-day affairs of the corporation subject to the direction and control of the board of directors. In fact, of course, their authority is often considerably greater, particularly in larger publicly held corporations. Further, the precise scope of the implied authority of officers vis á vis third persons—particularly the president—is somewhat broader, but varies from state to state. (For a discussion see § 11.5 of this Nutshell.) The basic point for present purposes, however, is that corporate officers are visualized in the traditional statutory model as agents carrying out policies established by the board of directors.

In modern statutes, the board of directors is given complete discretion as to the titles for persons filling specific corporate offices. Older statutes often designate that each corporation must have a "president," a "secretary," a "treasurer" and one or more "vice presidents." However, the board of directors was given authority to create additional offices and designate the titles for persons holding those offices.

§ 8.7 Shared Responsibility With Respect to Corporate Operations

As indicated previously, in the traditional corporate governance model, the directors have responsibility for the management of the business and affairs of the corporation. In this model, shareholders also have limited roles on certain business matters. For example, shareholders of publicly held corporations may be called upon to review and approve the selection of accountants, auditors or attorneys who are to evaluate the stewardship of the directors. Also, shareholders are sometimes called upon to approve or refuse to approve specific corporate operations or corporate transactions. Shareholder ratification usually involves transactions in which management is personally interested (see § 14.16 of this Nutshell) or requests by officers or directors for indemnification against liability or litigation costs (see § 15.2 of this Nutshell). It has become almost standard operating procedure, for example, for publicly held corporations to submit incentive compensation plans for officers and high level employees (profit sharing plans, stock option plans, "phantom stock" plans, and the like) to the shareholders for approval. Approval of transactions by shareholders does not totally immunize the transaction from attack since a court may subsequently decide that it involves waste or a gift of corporate assets. Approval by shareholders, however, probably prevents shareholders who voted to approve the plan from later attacking it; approval may also prevent other shareholders from attacking the fairness of the transaction or shift the burden of proof from management to the attacking shareholders. Ratification or approval of transactions, however, does not validate fraudulent, oppressive or manifestly unfair transactions involving officers or directors.

Shareholders are sometimes asked to approve a blanket resolution covering all business and other transactions by management during the period since the last meeting. Such resolutions do not validate improper transactions of which the shareholders have no knowledge.

Independent of statute, shareholders also may make recommendations to the board of directors on corporate matters. While without legal effect, such resolutions express the views of the ultimate owners of the corporation, and are usually followed. For example, in one leading case, Auer v. Dressel (N.Y.1954), it was held proper for shareholders to vote upon a resolution approving the administration of an ousted president and demanding his or her reinstatement. The Court said, "The stockholders, by expressing their approval of Mr. Auer's conduct as president and their demand that he be put back in that office, will not be able, directly, to effect that change in officers, but there is nothing invalid in their so expressing themselves and thus putting on notice the directors who will stand for election at the annual meeting."

§ 8.8   Shared Responsibility: Approval of Fundamental Corporate Changes

Shareholders have the specific statutory power to approve or disapprove fundamental changes in the corporation's structure proposed by the board of directors. In a few states, shareholders have the power both to propose and to adopt such changes, but in most states directors must first approve the action and recommend it to the shareholders before the shareholders may act. While changes subject to shareholder approval vary to some extent from state to state, most states require shareholder approval of the following:

(1) Amendments of articles of incorporation.

(2) Mergers and consolidations.

(3) Dissolution.

(4) Sale of all or substantially all of a corporation's assets not in the ordinary course of business.

(5) Statutory share exchanges where a decision to make an exchange is binding on all holders of shares.

In most states, a majority of all the outstanding voting shares must approve the proposed transaction, though several states retain the older requirement (almost universal thirty years ago) that two-thirds of the outstanding shares (both voting and nonvoting) must approve the proposed transaction.

Under the Model Business Corporation Act (1984) and the statutes of many states, the board of directors has a "gate keeping" function with respect to fundamental transactions: the shareholders may consider such transactions only if the board of directors decides it is appropriate for them to do so. If the board of directors refuses to recommend the transaction to the shareholders, they may not approve the proposal upon their own motion. Thus, decisions on such basic matters in most states are shared between shareholders and directors, and both must concur in the proposal. In a handful of states, including Massachusetts, shareholders have power to effectuate basic corporate changes without the concurrence of the directors, but that is the exception rather than the norm.

In addition to these fundamental changes, state statutes may provide for shareholder approval of less substantial transactions, including distributions in partial liquidation out of capital, reductions of stated capital, or the purchase of corporate shares out of capital surplus.

§ 8.9 Shared Responsibility: Bylaw Amendments

In most states, the initial bylaws of a corporation are adopted by the board of directors or incorporators, whichever group completes the organization of the corporation. Thereafter, the power to amend or repeal bylaws may be vested in either the shareholders or the directors, or very commonly in either group. The 1969 Model Act contained a skeletal and rather ambiguous provision that appears in the statutes of many states; it provides that the power to amend is vested in the board of directors "unless reserved to the shareholders by the articles;" further the shareholders may "repeal or change" bylaws adopted by the directors. (1969 MBCA § 27, second sentence)

The Model Business Corporation Act (1984) devotes three entire sections to bylaw amendments. Section 10.20 is the basic section: it provides that directors may adopt, amend, or repeal bylaws unless (a) the bylaw deals with a subject that the statute or the articles of incorporation reserve exclusively to the shareholders, or (b) the shareholders have previously amended or repealed a bylaw on the same subject and have provided expressly that their action is not subject to change by the directors. Further, section 10.20(b) makes it clear that the shareholders' power in this area is primary since the directors may not declare any bylaw off-bounds to the shareholders in the same way that shareholders can with respect to future action by the directors. Section 10.21 deals with bylaw provisions increasing quorum or voting requirements for shareholders while section 10.22 deals with bylaw provisions relating to quorum or voting requirements for directors.

There are wide variations in the state statutes dealing with the power to amend or repeal bylaws. Generally, the power is shared but the primacy of shareholders in this regard is usually recognized. In a few states directors may not repeal or amend bylaws adopted by shareholders; in others the shareholders may designate bylaws that may not be amended by the board of directors.

§ 8.10 Restrictions on Directors in Close Corporations

Experience has shown that in the real world the participants in a business venture often wish to divide up the powers of management and control in a way that is difficult to fit within the traditional statutory scheme. Doubtless the greatest strain on the statutory scheme occurs in corporations with relatively few shareholders—"close corporations" or "incorporated partnerships." But similar problems also may occur in joint venture corporations and even in publicly held corporations. This section considers the developing law as to the extent to which the statutory scheme can be varied by agreement.

A not uncommon situation arises when two or three persons own a business which is being conducted in corporate form. A minority participant wishes to have a veto power over some specific corporate action. How should this power be created? As with many other corporate issues, there are ways that a veto power may be validly created. However, a veto power in a single shareholder is potentially inconsistent with the statutory scheme since it is a restriction on the broad discretion granted the board of directors by statute, and as a result may be invalid.

A case from the 1960s well illustrates this problem. In Burnett v. Word, Inc. (Tex.App.1967), a minority shareholder in each of two closely held corporations desired to retain a veto over the corporation borrowing money. The shareholders entered into a written agreement that the corporations would not borrow more than $10,000 and $40,000 respectively, except by unanimous approval of the shareholders. The agreement also stated that each party "binds himself to vote as stockholders and directors in such a manner as to carry out bona fide the purposes and intent of this agreement." This agreement obviously fettered to some extent the business discretion of the board of directors, and thereby departed from the statutory scheme. The court invalidated the portion of the agreement relating to the directors: "An agreement by which directors abdicate or bargain away in advance the judgment the law contemplates they shall exercise over the corporation is void. The agreement of the parties to bind themselves as directors is void." In a more recent case, the New York Court of Appeals upheld by a closely divided vote a similar provision. Zion v. Kurtz (N.Y.1980). Cases such as these, whether or not correctly decided, illustrate the pervasive impact of the statutory scheme on judicial thought and the danger of assuming that simply because all parties in interest agree to a variation in the statutory scheme, the variation is valid. It may be noted in passing that the agreement in Burnett v. Word, Inc. was upheld to the extent it constituted an agreement by shareholders to vote as shareholders in a specified manner. Agreements of this type are discussed in § 9.12 of this Nutshell. In other words, the danger lies in agreements that prescribe what the board of directors will do, not agreements between shareholders as to how shareholders will vote as share-holders.

Some courts have upheld variations on the statutory scheme, and the modern trend distinctly appears to be running in the direction of upholding such agreements and away from the strict position of Burnett v. Word, Inc. The leading line of cases with respect to agreements fettering the discretion of directors arose in New York. In McQuade v. Stoneham (N.Y.1934), the Court invalidated an agreement between the majority shareholder and two minority shareholders that one minority shareholder would be retained as treasurer of the corporation at a specified salary. There was a falling out, and the board of directors failed to reappoint the shareholder to the office of treasurer and discontinued his salary. The Court said, "We are constrained by authority to hold that a contract is illegal and void so far as it precludes the board of directors, at the risk of incurring legal liability, from changing officers, salaries or policies or retaining individuals in office, except by consent of the contracting parties. On the whole, such a holding is probably preferable to one which would open the courts to pass on the motives of directors in lawful exercise of their trust." (An independent ground for this decision also existed.)

Two years later the same problem again came before the highest New York court in the case of Clark v. Dodge (N.Y.1936). Clark owned 25 per cent and Dodge owned 75 per cent of the stock of two corporations manufacturing medicinal preparations by secret formulae. Dodge did not actively participate in the management of the business; the secret formulae were known only to Clark, who actively managed the business. In 1921, Dodge and Clark entered into an agreement by which Dodge agreed to retain Clark as general manager of the business and to pay him one-fourth of the income either in the form of salary or dividends. The agreement was to continue so long as

Clark remained "faithful, efficient and competent to so manage and control the said business." Clark, in turn, agreed to disclose the secret formulae to Dodge's son and upon Clark's death without issue to bequeath his 25 per cent interest in the corporation to the wife and children of Dodge. This entirely sensible business arrangement appears to run afoul of the McQuade principle, since Dodge was in effect agreeing that the board of directors would retain Clark as general manager and to pay twenty-five per cent of the earnings to him in the form of salary or dividends. The Court nevertheless upheld the agreement:

> Are we committed by the *McQuade* case to the doctrine that there may be no variation, however slight or innocuous, from [the statutory] norm, where salaries or policies or the retention of individuals in office are concerned? There is ample authority supporting that doctrine * * *. [S]omething may be said for it, since it furnishes a simple, if arbitrary, test. Apart from its practical administrative convenience, the reasons upon which it is said to rest are more or less nebulous. Public policy, the intention of the Legislature, detriment to the corporation, are phrases which in this connection mean little. Possible harm to bona fide purchasers of stock or to creditors or to stockholding minorities have more substance; but such harms are absent in many instances. If the enforcement of a particular contract damages nobody—not even, in any perceptible degree, the public—one sees no reason for holding it illegal, even though it impinges slightly upon the broad provision [vesting directors with the powers of management]. Damage suffered or threatened is a logical and practical test and has come to be the one generally adopted.

> Where the directors are the sole stockholders, there seems to be no objection to enforcing an agreement among them to vote for certain people as officers * * *.

If there was any invasion of the powers of the directorate under that agreement it is so slight as to be negligible; and certainly there is no damage suffered by or threatened to anybody. The broad statements in the *McQuade* opinion, applicable to the facts there, should be confined to those facts.

The Clark opinion arguably rests on two different grounds:

(1) The Court emphasized that in *Clark* all the shareholders were parties to the agreement. In *McQuade,* there were shareholders who were not parties to the agreement. Certainly, non-consenting shareholders may be injured if directors fail to exercise their "honest and unfettered" judgment, and hence it seems reasonable to reconcile the two cases on this ground. On the other hand, the agreement in *McQuade* was not being attacked by a non-consenting shareholder, but by a person who was a party to the agreement, arguably an unenforceable agreement. No emphasis was placed on the presence of non-consenting shareholders in the *McQuade* decision.

(2) The Clark opinion stresses that the arrangement harmed no one, and that "damage suffered or threatened" is a logical and practical test. If this were the sole test adopted in Clark v. Dodge, the courts might accept very substantial variations from the statutory norm—possibly to the extent of permitting the total abolishment of the board of directors. However, subsequent cases in New York indicate that this is too expansive a reading of Clark v. Dodge and that as much stress should be placed on the statement that the impingement in that case was "slight" or "innocuous" as on the language that no damage was "suffered or threatened." In Long Park, Inc. v. Trenton–New Brunswick Theatres Co. (N.Y.1948), all the shareholders agreed that one shareholder should have "full authority and power to supervise and direct the operation and management" of certain theaters, and that sharehold-

er could be removed as manager only by arbitration. The court invalidated this arrangement under *McQuade*: "We are not confronted with a slight impingement or innocuous variance from the statutory norm, but rather with the deprivation of all the powers of the board insofar as the selection and supervision of the manager of the corporation's theaters, including the manner and policy of their operation, are concerned."

In 1982, the New York Court of Appeals put a rather bizarre twist on these cases, which, if accepted generally, may eliminate most of the problems in this area. Zion v. Kurtz (N.Y.1980), involved a complex financing arrangement in which the creditor obtained as part of the security for a loan a minority interest in a closely held corporation and a commitment from the dominant shareholder that the corporation would not enter into transactions or new business without the consent of the creditor. Under the law of Delaware, such an agreement might validly be entered into only by a corporation electing statutory close corporation treatment (see § 12.13 of this Nutshell); however, to be eligible for such treatment the corporation in its articles of incorporation had to expressly elect close corporation status and also to refer to the agreement limiting the discretion of directors. The corporation involved in Zion v. Kurtz had done neither. The court nevertheless viewed these omissions from the articles of incorporation as "technical" defects and within the power of the court to correct by an order of reformation. Three justices dissented vigorously on the ground that the whole theory of close corporation election was that public notice should be provided in the articles of incorporation, and the reasoning of the majority vitiated this important principle. Delaware, itself, has rejected the underlying premise of this decision. In Nixon v. Blackwell (Del.1993) the Delaware Supreme Court held that it was improper to apply special close corporation provisions to a non-electing corporation, "because the provisions of the statute relating to close corporations and other statutory schemes preempt the field in their respective areas."

Section 620 of the New York Business Corporation Law was added in 1961 to overrule the *McQuade* principle in limited circumstances. That section basically provides that a restriction on the discretion of the board of directors is enforceable if it appears in the corporation's certificate of incorporation and is approved by all of the shareholders. While this section would not validate the agreements reached in the cases described above, it does provide a road map for making enforceable agreements restricting the discretion of directors in New York.

The leading case outside of New York that rejects the rather narrow view of McQuade and similar cases is Galler v. Galler (Ill.1964), a decision which enforced a complex shareholders' agreement containing numerous "impingements" of varying degrees of seriousness on the statutory scheme, including a mandatory dividend requirement. After drawing sharply the distinction between closely held and publicly held corporations, the Court called for statutory recognition of the special problems of the closely held corporation, and concluded that "any arrangements concerning the management of the corporation which are agreeable to all" should be enforced if (1) no complaining minority interest appears, (2) no fraud or apparent injury to the public or creditors is present, and (3) no clearly prohibitory statutory language is violated. While this decision has generally been approved and applauded, a subsequent Illinois case refused to extend *Galler* to validate a shareholders' agreement that more or less squarely contradicted a specific statutory provision relating to the amendment of bylaws. Because of this qualification in the *Galler* opinion, there is some lingering doubt as to whether all shareholders' agreements will be upheld.

Earlier it was stated that agreements restricting the discretion of directors may sometimes be made enforceable within the confines of the traditional corporate model. In many states, the corporation statutes permit a corporation to increase voting requirements up to and including unanimity. It may be possible to give a single director a veto power over specific transactions through modification of the voting requirements in the articles of incorporation or the bylaws. Similarly, a provision that the treasurer of the corporation must be a holder of a certain class of stock is enforceable in most states; classes of shares may be created so as to ensure that a specific person will be named as treasurer (though nothing would apparently prevent the corporation from creating a nonstatutory office such as "comptroller" and assign most traditional treasurer duties to that new office). Doubtless other devices may be invented by ingenious counsel to make enforceable specific management proposals even in states that closely follow the traditional management norm.

The most important ameliorating trends, however, are statutory provisions that permit non-traditional management forms for certain corporations. Many state statutes permit the participants in a corporation to adopt nontraditional forms of governance. For example, section 8.01(b) of the Model Business Corporation Act (1984) originally provided that the power of the board of directors to direct (or oversee the direction of) the business and affairs of the corporation was "subject to any limitation set forth in the articles of incorporation." This "subject to" clause authorized all variations to the statutory scheme discussed in this section so long as the appropriate provision appears in the articles of incorporation. In 1992, this clause was eliminated and replaced by a much broader authorization in section 7.32 of MBCA (1984). This section, which is discussed in § 12.9 of this Nutshell, eliminates the requirement that provisions be included in the articles of incorporation but requires that they be approved unanimously by the shareholders.

As a result of the *Galler* decision discussed above, about 20 states have enacted opt-in close corporation statutes. See § 12.13. These statutes also permit electing closely held corporations to adopt non-traditional forms of governance.

§ 8.11 Delegation of Management Powers and the Statutory Scheme

Interference with the discretion of directors has also been used to attack broad management agreements between the corporation and outsiders by which the sole power of management appears to be taken from the board and vested in the managers. There seems to be no inherent reason why a corporation should not be able to appoint a general manager with broad powers over day-to-day affairs subject to the general oversight of the board. The management agreement cases appear to depend on whether the court believes that the board has retained a sufficiently broad power of oversight. Similar arguments have been applied to invalidate agreements that grant a shareholder the sole power to manage a portion of the corporation's assets without review by the board of directors. Potentially over-broad delegation to an executive or other committee of the board of directors may also be attacked on a similar ground, though that question is now usually dealt with by specific statutory provision. (See § 10.10 of this Nutshell.) The test in all these cases is whether the agreement "sterilizes" the board so that it has no managerial role at all or whether reasonable powers of oversight are preserved to the board.

[For unfamiliar terms see the Glossary]

CHAPTER NINE

SHARES AND SHAREHOLDERS

§ 9.1 Annual and Special Meetings of Shareholders

Every state statute contains more or less routine provisions about meetings of shareholders. The Model Business Corporation Act (1984), for example, provides that a meeting shall be held "annually at a time stated in or fixed in accordance with the bylaws," [MBCA (1984) § 7.01(a)], that notice of an annual or special meeting shall be given not less than ten nor more than sixty days before the meeting [MBCA (1984) § 7.05(a)], and so forth. The failure to hold an annual meeting does not "affect the validity of any corporate action" [MBCA (1984) § 7.01(c)], though any shareholder may obtain a summary court order requiring the corporation to hold an annual meeting if one is not held "within the earlier of 6 months after the end of the corporation's last fiscal year or 15 months after its last annual meeting" [MBCA (1984) § 7.03(a)(1)]. So far as notice is concerned, statutes permit written waivers that may be executed before, at, or after the meeting in question [MBCA (1984) § 7.06(a)].

The principal purpose of an annual meeting obviously is the annual election of directors, but the annual meeting may act on any relevant matter that is within the ambit of shareholder control and is not limited to the purposes set forth in the notice. Indeed, under the 1984 Model Act [MBCA (1984) § 7.05(b)] and the statutes of most states, no statement of purposes at all need appear in the notice of annual meeting.

A special meeting is any meeting other than an annual meeting. It may be called by the persons specified in the statute or in the bylaws of the corporation. Typically, such a meeting may be called by the board of directors, the holders of some specified percentage of the outstanding shares of the corporation, or by certain officers. The 1984 Model Business Corporation Act authorizes holders of ten per cent of the votes eligible to be cast at the meeting to compel the holding of a special meeting [MBCA (1984) § 7.02(a)(2)]; this type of provision is controversial since it may result in a shareholders' meeting being held on matters which management might prefer not be considered or even on matters on which it is clear that there is no chance of passage. There is also the possibility that repetitive or unnecessary meetings might be called by small factions of shareholders. The Official Comment to MBCA (1984) § 7.02 suggests that the board of directors has some discretion in calling special meetings at the request of shareholders to meet this last problem.

Unlike the annual meeting, the only subjects that may be considered at a special meeting are matters described in the notice of meeting. MBCA (1984) §§ 7.05, 7.02.(d).

A quorum at any annual or special meeting consists of a majority of the outstanding shares, except that the quorum requirement may be increased or decreased by provisions in the articles or bylaws. Statutes usually prescribe a minimum below which the quorum may not be reduced. The most popular figure is one-third, based on old MBCA § 32; the 1984 Model Business Corporation Act does not contain any statutory minimum. Statutes do not prescribe a maximum number to constitute a quorum, and it is therefore possible to require the presence of all outstanding shares to conduct business at a shareholders' meeting. Unanimous quorum requirements are sometimes adopted in close corporations as a planning device, even though it increases the risk of a deadlock since a single shareholder, no matter how small his or her holding, may prevent the existence of a quorum, and hence the holding of the meeting.

Most state statutes provide that where a quorum is present, the affirmative vote of a majority of that quorum is necessary to bind the corporation. Such statutes may lead to questionable results in situations where votes are present (and counted toward the quorum) but abstain from voting on an issue. Under the traditional statutes abstentions are in effect treated as negative votes since an action can be adopted only if a majority of all the votes that are present vote in favor of the measure. The 1984 Model Business Corporation Act changes the traditional rule: it provides that if a quorum is present a measure is approved "if the votes cast * * * favoring the action exceed the votes cast opposing the action" [§ 7.25(c)]. The example used in the Official Comment to explain why this is preferable posits a meeting of a corporation with one thousand shares outstanding. A quorum is, of course, 501 in the absence of a specific provision in the articles of incorporation. Assume that 600 shares are represented at the meeting and the vote on an action is 280 in favor, 225 opposed, and 95 abstaining. Under the traditional statute, the measure fails since 301 votes are necessary (a majority of the quorum); under the MBCA (1984), the action is approved, 280–225. It may be noted that if the 95 abstaining shares were not present at all, the action would have been approved under both types of statutes.

Somewhat different rules of shareholder voting are often applicable to elections of directors. These rules are discussed in § 9.6 of this Nutshell.

If a quorum is initially present, a disgruntled faction may sometimes lose a vote, and thereafter leave the meeting seeking to "break" the quorum and prevent the victorious faction from conducting further business. The general rule is that a quorum, once present, continues, and the withdrawal of a faction does not disable the remaining shareholders from continuing. The position that a minority faction of shareholders cannot "break" a quorum once it is established is codified in § 7.25(b) of the 1984 Model Business Corporation Act. Because of this rule, a faction that knows it will be in the minority but believes that a quorum will not exist without their presence, should stay entirely away to prevent a quorum from ever being present, rather than appearing and later withdrawing in an attempt to break the quorum.

§ 9.2 Shareholder Action by Consent

Virtually all states today authorize shareholders to conduct business by unanimous written consent without actually holding a meeting. Unanimous consent is particularly helpful in closely held corporations, where most shareholders' decisions are unanimous, and the formality of a meeting may be dispensed with (though to be valid under these statutes the consent must be evidenced by a signed writing).

About a dozen states, including Delaware, have gone a step further and authorized holders of the number of shares needed to act on a matter to act by written consent without a meeting. (Del. Gen. Corp. Law, § 228) As discussed in the chapter on proxy voting in publicly held corporations, elimination of the unanimity requirement is not as radical a proposal as might first be thought since most shareholder votes in such a corporation are cast by proxy in any event, and the same information must be provided for either a vote by proxy or an action by consent. (See section 13.19 of this Nutshell.) In smaller corporations, however, majority consent provisions do not contain the same built-in safeguards. And even in publicly held corporations, the majority consent provision has had some unexpected consequences since it enables a successful aggressor which acquires a majority of the target's voting shares to make immediate changes in management without having to request that the board of directors call a special meeting of shareholders. The majority consent provision in Delaware has led to a fair amount of litigation, including the efforts of corporations to blunt its force by restricting the power to act by majority written consent.

§ 9.3 Record and Beneficial Ownership of Shares

Every corporation retains records of the persons in whose name shares have been issued and every share certificate that is issued refers by name to that person. This person is called the "record owner" and generally the corporation may deal with the record owner as though he were the sole owner of the shares. The theory is that when the record owner sells shares, he normally hands over the certificate to the purchaser with the endorsement on the reverse side of the certificate properly executed; the purchaser may then submit the endorsed certificate to the corporation with a request that a new certificate be issued in a designated name. The old certificate is canceled (and retained with the records of the corporation) and a new certificate is issued in the name of the purchaser (or another name designated by the purchaser) who then becomes the new record owner. While modern practice in the transfer of shares of publicly held corporations is quite different from the theory, record ownership concepts continue to apply to all corporations. The corporate records of the names and addresses of record owners are usually called the "stock transfer books" or "share register" (though they may consist simply of stubs formerly attached to share certificates). The corporation deals only with record owners on matters such as dividends, voting, and notices of meetings. A purchaser who does not obtain the issuance of a new certificate is the "beneficial owner" of those shares; while corporations do not accord beneficial owners the rights of ownership (since they deal only with record owners), the beneficial owner is the "real" owner and can compel the record owner to turn over dividends or to execute appropriate documents to permit the beneficial owner to exercise the power to vote or to become the record owner.

Many state statutes authorize a corporation to issue certificateless shares. Records of share ownership are maintained by the corporation, which provides new owners with a written statement of the information otherwise required on certificates. See MBCA (1984) § 6.26. Apparently certificateless shares are not widely used in states which authorize such shares.

Obviously every publicly held corporation with active trading in its shares must not only have available a large number of new certificates to issue to transferees but also must take steps to ensure that transfers are properly recorded, that new certificates refer to the same number of shares as old certificates, and so forth. These mechanical functions of registering share transfers are handled by "transfer agents" who keep exact records of all shareholders, their names, addresses and number of shares owned. Publicly held corporations also use "registrars," whose function is to make sure the corporation does not inadvertently over issue shares. In an earlier era, the mechanical functions of registration of transfer of shares were quite onerous. However, the modern "book entry" system of recordation and transfer of ownership interests of publicly held corporations simplify the keeping of records and have greatly reduced the practical problems faced by transfer agents and registrars in this area. See § 13.9 of this Nutshell.

§ 9.4 Record Dates

Once the possibility of share transfers is recognized, some rule must be established to determine the point in time that eligibility to vote and the right to receive dividends is determined. This is normally done by corporations establishing a "record date" in advance of the meeting or action. A record date may be established directly by bylaw provision, but it is more customary to authorize the board of directors to set a record date.

With respect to voting, section 7.07 of the 1984 Model Business Corporation Act requires that a date be established in advance and that it be not more than seventy days before the date of the meeting. The record date is usually specified in the resolution of the board of directors calling the meeting. If a record date is established, the corporation continues to register transfers and issue new certificates to transferees, but the persons eligible to vote are those in whose name the shares were registered on the record date.

If the board of directors does not formally set a record date (which often occurs in closely held corporations where shares are infrequently traded), the corporation is deemed to set a record date as of the date the notice of the meeting is mailed, and eligibility to vote is determined as of that date.

Older statutes also usually permit the board of directors, rather than establishing a record date, to order the stock transfer books closed for a stated period, which the old Model Act set as at least ten days but not more than fifty days before the meeting [MBCA (1969) § 30]. If the stock transfer books are closed, the corporation refuses thereafter to register transfers of shares and eligibility to vote is determined by who was the record owner on the date the books were closed. In effect the corporate records are frozen, though, of course, individual shareholders may endorse and deliver certificates to purchasers during the period. This alternative is obsolete since the record date alternative is so much simpler. Certainly in publicly held corporations, it would be completely impractical to allow requested transfers to pile up unrecorded for an extended period before a meeting. The MBCA (1984) does not refer to closing the transfer books as an alternative to setting a record date.

The record date provisions are obviously for the benefit of the corporation. They permit the corporation to give proper notice of the meeting, to prepare a voting list, and to establish precisely who is entitled to vote. They also permit management and other shareholders to solicit votes before the meeting.

Analogous record date provisions are authorized by the Model Business Corporation Act (1984) for a variety of other shareholder actions: who is entitled to receive corporate dividends as between transferor and transferee (see § 18.5 of this Nutshell), who may demand a special meeting, and so forth. In the case of a proposal based on the written consent procedures which involves solicitation of numerous shareholders (see § 9.2 of this Nutshell), the record date for determining validity of consents is the day the first written consent is filed with the corporation. A record date for consent solicitations is necessary because the corporation may receive hundreds or thousands of signed consent forms.

§ 9.5 Preparation of Voting List

A voting list of shareholders eligible to vote must be prepared before each shareholders meeting. Section 7.20 of the Model Business Corporation Act (1984) contains fairly detailed rules about how this list should be compiled and where it must be kept before and during the meeting. Like the statutes of many states, it also requires that this list be available for inspection by shareholders before the meeting; the MBCA (1984) requires that it be available for inspection beginning two business days after the notice of meeting is given. (The theory is that the corporation must compile a list of shareholders entitled to receive notice of the meeting before the notice is actually given and so it is no burden to prepare the voting list at the same time.)

Not all states require that the voting list be available in advance of the meeting; the 1969 Model Act only required that it be available at the meeting itself, though an even earlier version of the Model Act required that it be available for inspection for ten days before the meeting.

Every shareholder has an absolute right to inspect the voting list, and this right is not subject to the qualifications imposed upon a shareholder's right to inspect other books and records of the corporation. (See Chapter 19 of this Nutshell). While the failure to prepare the voting list does not affect the validity of any action taken at the meeting [MBCA (1984) § 7.20(e)], such a failure may lead to a summary court order to create the list and postponement of the meeting.

At the meeting, the share transfer books (rather than the voting list) determines who are the shareholders entitled to vote. In other words, a mistake in the creation of the list does not affect who is entitled to vote at the meeting.

§ 9.6 Election of Directors: Cumulative or Straight Voting

Directors are elected each year at the annual meeting of shareholders. The most common statutory provision is simply that directors are elected by a vote of a majority of the shares (1) present at the meeting and (2) entitled to vote, assuming that a quorum is present. This formulation does not address the situation of three or more factions contending for election (in which case it is quite possible that no faction will obtain a majority of the votes present at a meeting). Section 7.28(a) of the Model Business

Corporation Act (1984) handles this possibility by making the standard for election "a plurality of the votes cast by the shares entitled to vote in the election at a meeting at which a quorum is present." Many states have adopted this sensible modification to a basic voting rule.

Generally, shareholders may only vote in favor of candidates. As in the case of elections of public officials, they may not cast negative votes against candidates.

The articles of incorporation, and in some states, the bylaws, may increase, but may not decrease, the percentage of the shares required for election. In close corporations it is not uncommon to exercise this privilege and require unanimity as a planning device, even though the possibility of a deadlock in the election of directors is thereby obviously increased.

Another important question relating to the election of directors is whether shares may be voted "cumulatively" or must be voted "straight." Cumulative voting (the mechanics of which are described immediately below) has historically had a strong emotional appeal. In several states cumulative voting is mandatory by state constitution or provisions in the state corporation statute. Most states today, however, give a corporation an option to exclude cumulative voting; usually this option requires a specific exclusion in the articles of incorporation (an "opt out" election) though in some states, cumulative voting is not permitted unless specific provision for it is made in the articles of incorporation (an "opt in" election). The Model Business Corporation Act (1984) adopts the latter course [MBCA (1984) § 7.28(c)].

The workings of cumulative voting can be most simply described by an illustration. Let us assume a corporation with two shareholders, A with 26 shares, and B with 74 shares. Further, let us assume that there are three directors and each shareholder nominates three candidates.

A critical point is that candidates run "at large" and do not run for specific places. The three candidates with the most votes in this election are the winners. If only "straight" voting is permitted, A may cast 26 votes for each of any three candidates, and B may cast 74 votes for each of any three candidates. The result, of course, is that if they do not agree on any candidates, all three of B's candidates are elected. If cumulative voting is permitted, the total number of votes that each shareholder may cast is first computed and each shareholder is permitted to distribute these votes as he sees fit over one or more candidates. In the example above, A is entitled to cast a total of 78 votes (26×3) and B is entitled to cast 222 votes (74×3). If A casts all 78 votes for herself, she is assured of election because B cannot divide 222 votes among three candidates in such a way as to give each candidate 79 or more votes and preclude A's election. (If B gives 79 votes to himself and 79 votes to B_1, he will only have 64 votes left for B_2.) Obviously, the effect of cumulative voting is that it increases minority participation on the board of directors. In straight voting, the shareholder with 51 per cent of the vote elects the entire board; in cumulative voting, a relatively small faction (26 per cent in the above example) obtains representation on the board.

The difference between cumulative and straight voting may be vividly illustrated by the deadlock situation where all shares are owned equally by two shareholders—say fifty shares each. If only straight voting is permitted and each shareholder votes only for his or her own candidates a deadlocked election is inevitable. If there are two places to be filled A will vote 50 shares for herself, and 50 shares for A_2; B will vote 50 shares for himself, and 50 shares for B_2. Thus, four candidates will each have 50 votes for two positions, and the result is that no one is elected. If cumulative voting is permitted on the other hand, A may cast 100 votes for herself and she will be guaranteed election (since B obviously cannot give two candidates more than 100 votes each.) If there are an odd number of directors to be elected (say 3) straight voting still leads to deadlock: A_1–50, A_2–50, A_3–50, B_1–50, B_2–50, B_3–50. If cumulative voting is permitted, A and B may each elect one director but the situation is unstable: a deadlock will be created if each tries to elect the tie-breaking director and the other votes rationally. However, the strategy and counter-strategy can become complex. If A gives A_1 76 votes, A_1 will be guaranteed of election since B has only 150 votes and obviously cannot prevent A_1's election; similarly, if B gives B_1 76 votes, A cannot prevent B_1's election. If both shareholders follow this conservative strategy, the result will be A_1–76, A_2–74, B_1–76, B_2–74, with A_1 and B_1 each being elected and a tie existing between A_2 and B_2. However, if B knows that A will follow this strategy in voting, B might be tempted to divide his vote equally between two candidates in order to elect two of the three directors: A_1–76, A_2–74, B_1–75, B_2–75, with A_1, B_1, and B_2 all being elected. A may counter this strategy by also giving her two candidates 75 votes each, thereby creating a four way tie and electing no one. Indeed, it is disastrous if either shareholder deviates from these very precise voting patterns. If B decides to vote only slightly illogically, for example, B_1–77, B_2–73, he delivers control of the corporation over to A even if A follows the conservative strategy of guaranteeing the election of one director: B_1–77, A_1–76, A_2–74, B_2–73, with B_1, A_1 and A_2 elected.

In these and the following illustrations it is assumed that A or B, once they have adopted a strategy and cast their votes, cannot thereafter change them. This is true only to a limited extent in the real world. Balloting for directors is usually by written ballot rather than voice vote so that each shareholder must establish his or her voting strategy without being sure of an opponent's strategy;

however, until the vote is announced, a shareholder may be able to recast his or her votes and thereby correct mistakes in the voting strategy adopted. The traditional rule is that votes may be changed before the results of the election are announced, though this probably depends on whether the person presiding at the meeting permits a change to be made.

As the preceding discussion illustrates, one undesirable aspect of cumulative voting is that it tends to be a little tricky. If a shareholder casts votes in an irrational or inefficient way, he or she may not get the directorships a different voting strategy would have guaranteed; when voting cumulatively it is relatively easy to make a mistake in spreading votes around. The most graphic illustration of this are the cases where a majority shareholder votes in such a way that he or she elects only a minority of the directors. This is most likely to occur when one shareholder votes "straight" and another cumulates. For example, if A has 60 shares and B only 40, with five directors to be elected, B may nevertheless elect a majority of the board if A votes "straight," and B knows that A is doing so. The result might look like this:

A_1–60, A_2–60, A_3–60, A_4–60, A_5–60, B_1–67, B_2–66, B_3–65, B_4–1, B_5–1.

This strategy is daring of B because he is spreading his vote over three persons when he can be sure only of electing two. If A knows that B will try to elect three persons, A, by properly cumulating her votes, can elect four directors, in effect "stealing" one of B's. The results of such an election might be as follows:

A_1–73, A_2–74, A_3–75, A_4–76, A_5–2, B_1–67, B_2–66, B_3–65, B_4–1, B_5–1.

A shareholder generally should not create tie votes among his or her own candidates. If he or she does so, and the tied candidates come in fifth and sixth in an election for five directorships, say, the tie may be broken by a new election for only the fifth seat; the other shareholders may be able to vote their shares in the run-off election for their own candidates, thereby causing the other shareholder to lose a seat.

Section 7.28(d) of the Model Business Corporation Act (1984) and the statutes of many states require shareholders to give advance notice before the meeting if they plan to vote cumulatively. Such a requirement seems plainly desirable because, as the last illustration graphically demonstrates, election results are illogical if some shareholders vote cumulatively while others do not.

The following formula is useful in determining the number of shares needed to elect one director:

$$\frac{S}{D + 1} + 1$$

Where S equals the total number of shares voting, and D equals the number of directors to be elected. The analogous formula to elect n directors is:

$$\frac{\overline{nS}}{D + 1} + 1$$

A minor modification may sometimes be necessary. The first portion of the formula, $\frac{S}{D + 1}$, establishes the maximum number of shares voted for a single person which is insufficient to elect that person as a director. Any share, or fraction thereof, in excess of that amount will be sufficient to elect a director. The formula set forth in the text ignores fractional shares which sometimes may lead to a one share-error. For example, where there are 100 shares voting and five directors to be elected, the first portion of the formula is $\frac{100}{5 + 1}$, or $\frac{100}{6}$. In this example, 16 shares will not elect a director, but 17 shares will, since the first part of the formula yields $16\frac{2}{3}$. The above formula mechanically yields an answer of $17\frac{2}{3}$.

The reason that several states have mandatory constitutional or statutory cumulative voting is that it is believed to be democratic in that persons with large (but minority) holdings should have a voice in the conduct of the corporation. Also, arguably, it may be desirable to have as many viewpoints as possible represented on the board of directors; and the presence of a minority director may discourage conflicts of interest by management since discovery is considerably more likely. Arguments in opposition to this point of view include: (1) the introduction of a partisan on the board is inconsistent with the notion that the board should represent all interests in the corporation; (2) a partisan director may cause disharmony which reduces the efficiency of the board; (3) a partisan director may criticize management unreasonably so as to make it less willing to take risky (but desirable) action; (4) a partisan director may leak confidential information; and (5) cumulative voting is usually used to further narrow partisan goals, e.g., to give an insurgent group a toehold in the corporation in an effort to obtain control.

As a practical matter, cumulative voting in a factionalized, close corporation may be of considerable importance. It is irrelevant, of course, in one-shareholder corporations or corporations in which the parties are in amity and agree upon who should be on the board of directors. In the large, publicly held corporation, it is traditionally considered more of a nuisance than anything else because it complicates voting by proxy, and usually does not affect the actual outcome of an election. It should be observed, however, that where large boards are involved, cumulative voting simplifies the task of institutional investors or "public interest" or other groups whose goal is merely to obtain representation on the board rather than to take over control of the corporation. It also may simplify the task of a person seeking to take over the corporation by giving the aggressor a "toe hold" on the board of directors, though that is debatable. While some groups have advocated that public corporations be required to adopt cumulative voting, management in such corporations tends to oppose cumulative voting, stressing the mechanical and technical complexities of such voting.

In a closely held corporation, representation of minority interests on the board of directors may be ensured by using different classes of common shares that have identical financial rights but are entitled to vote separately as classes for the election of specified numbers of directors. Since cumulative voting tends to be a bit tricky and may be eliminated or minimized by a variety of devices discussed in the following sections, it is generally preferable to use different classes of shares when the business plan contemplates that holders of minority interests in the corporation are to have representation on the board of directors.

§ 9.7 "Classified" Boards of Directors

Most states permit a board of directors consisting of nine or more directors to be "classified" or "staggered" so that approximately one-third of the directors are elected each year, and each individual director is elected for a three year term. In states where cumulative voting is mandatory, and sometimes in corporations formed in other states as well, it is not uncommon to employ this device to minimize the effects of cumulative voting. Classification minimizes the effect of cumulative voting because it takes a larger minority interest to elect one of three directors than it does to elect one of nine directors. For example, if there are nine directors elected each year, ten per cent of the stock can elect a director; if the nine directors are classified and three are elected each year, it takes twenty-five per cent of the stock to elect a director. (If you do not believe these percentages, try them out on the formulas set forth above.)

The theoretical justification for classification is that it ensures "experience of service" on the board, since only one-half or one-third of the board will be elected each year. However, experience of service is usually not a major motivating factor for classifying a board, since as a practical matter, experience of service is usually provided by the simple process of reelecting the same persons as directors year after year.

Another consequence of a classified board is that where an aggressor has acquired a majority of the outstanding shares or where a controlling interest in a corporation has been sold to outsiders, there may be a period during which directors elected by the prior shareholders are continued in office. Where the board consists of three classes, for example, a person becoming a majority shareholder cannot be assured of electing a majority of the board for more than two full years. In some instances classification has been proposed in publicly held corporations primarily for this reason even though the corporation does not have cumulative voting. This consequence does not arise where, as is usually the case today, the shareholders have power to remove directors without cause.

Classifying or staggering the board of directors thus has two basic effects:

(1) It makes it more difficult for a minority faction to elect a director when there is cumulative voting.

(2) It makes take-over attempts more difficult when directors can be removed only for cause.

Under section 8.06 of the Model Business Corporation Act (1984) and most state statutes, the board of directors of a corporation with nine or more members may be divided into two or three classes of as nearly equal numbers as possible, and one class may be elected each year. In a classified board, each director serves for two years (if there are two classes) or three years (if there are three classes). Some states permit a board of three or more persons to be classified into two or three classes if the corporation does not provide for cumulative voting. These statutes make takeovers more difficult but prohibit one or two person classes of directors where cumulative voting is involved.

§ 9.8 Other Devices to Minimize Cumulative Voting

Other devices also limit the impact of cumulative voting. If cumulative voting is not required by statute or constitutional provision, it may be eliminated by an amendment to the articles of incorporation in the same way as any other attribute of shares. (See § 20.1 of this Nutshell.)

Reduction of the size of the board of directors has much the same effect as staggering the election of directors.

Such a reduction may require an amendment to the articles of incorporation, but many states permit corporations to have variable size boards of directors, and the size of the board may be varied by the directors without shareholder approval. See MBCA (1984) § 8.03. Shares may sometimes be tied up in voting trusts or voting agreements; in many states non-voting shares also may be used consistently with a cumulative voting requirement.

It may be possible to remove the minority director without cause and replace him or her with a more congenial person, at least until the next election. Section 8.08(c) of the Model Business Corporation Act and the statutes of many states, however, prohibit the removal of a minority director elected by cumulative voting unless the votes in favor of removal would have been enough to prevent the original election of the director in an election for directors.

The influence of minority directors elected through cumulative voting may be minimized by having informal director discussion in advance of meetings, scheduling board meetings at inconvenient times or places, and delegating functions to committees composed entirely of management directors. While a few instances of the use of such tactics have been reported, they do not appear to be very common. That may be because cumulative voting and the election of minority directors is not required in most states, and corporations generally elect not to have cumulative voting.

§ 9.9   Voting by Proxy

A proxy is a person who is authorized by a record shareholder to vote his or her shares. The relationship is one of principal and agent. Some confusion may arise in terminology since the single word "proxy" may interchangeably be used to designate the document that creates the authority, the grant of authority itself, and the person granted the power to vote the shares. The Model Business Corporation Act (1984) limits the use of the word "proxy" to the person with the power to vote; it refers to the grant of authority as the "appointment" of a proxy, and the document creating the appointment as an "appointment form."

The law of proxy regulation rather neatly divides itself into two areas. On the one hand is the skimpy—almost nonexistent—state law dealing with the legal requirements and duration of a proxy appointment. Under state law, perhaps the most lively issue is whether a proxy appointment that is stated to be irrevocable is in fact irrevocable. That this is not an earth shaking issue is attested to by the fact that the virtual absence of reported litigation on this question. On the other hand is the burgeoning law of federal proxy regulation in publicly held corporations subject to the reporting requirements of section 12 of the Securities Exchange Act of 1934. This is discussed in a later chapter of this Nutshell (see § 13.18).

The standard state statutory provision relating to proxies merely states that a shareholder may vote either "in person or by proxy." MBCA (1984) § 7.22(a). No particular form of proxy appointment is required under this section. Proxy appointments have been ruled valid despite omission of the name of the proxy, the date of the meeting, or the date the proxy appointment was executed. However, the proxy appointment must be in writing, a provision of obvious benefit to the inspector of elections and the corporation. A proxy need not be a shareholder.

The usual state statutory provision relating to duration of a proxy appointment provides in effect that an appointment "is valid for 11 months unless a longer period is expressly provided in the appointment form." [MBCA (1984) § 7.22(c).] Some state statutes limit all proxy appointments to a period of eleven months. The theory of the eleven-month provision is that a new appointment form should be executed before each annual meeting. However, under the MBCA (1984) provision, there is nothing to prevent the parties from agreeing that a much longer period shall be applicable to a specific proxy appointment. Since a proxy is an agent, his or her appointment is normally revocable at the pleasure of the record owner. Thus, even if a long period is designated as the duration of the proxy appointment, it still may be revoked by the record owner.

A proxy appointment may be revoked either expressly or by implication. For example, the execution of a later proxy appointment constitutes a revocation of an earlier, inconsistent appointment. Personal attendance at a meeting may also constitute revocation of an earlier proxy appointment, though this depends on the intention of the shareholder. Since later proxy appointments revoke earlier ones, it is important that appointment forms be dated as of the time of execution. Inspectors of election, where there is a contest, must determine which is the latest appointment form executed by a specific shareholder in order to determine how the shares are to be voted.

§ 9.10 Irrevocable Proxy Appointments

Certain proxy appointments may be irrevocable. Generally a mere recitation that a proxy appointment is irrevocable does not make it so; such an appointment is usually as revocable as any other agency appointment. The general rubric for determining whether a proxy appointment is truly irrevocable is whether it is "coupled with an interest." This phrase, which has its origin in the agency case of Hunt v. Rousmanier's Adm'rs (S.Ct.1823), has no inherent meaning of itself and must be fleshed out with examples and further analysis. It is not enough that the proxy appointment merely be supported by consideration. The clearest example of this is an outright purchase of a proxy appointment for cash by a shareholder seeking to obtain control of the corporation. Such a purchased vote almost certainly would be held to be against public policy and unenforceable; rather than being irrevocable, such a proxy appointment might not be enforceable at all. On the other hand, if a person lends a shareholder money and takes a lien on the shares as security, an irrevocable appointment of the creditor as proxy almost certainly would be enforced against the shareholder. What is the difference between these two situations? A person who purchases a vote presumably intends to recoup his or her investment in the vote by exercising the power to vote in some way. This power may very well be exercised in a manner adverse to the corporation: the proxy's interest is in recouping a personal payment, and in a sense is antagonistic to the corporation. The creditor's interest, on the other hand, is to preserve or increase the value of the shares which constitute the security for the loan. Thus the creditor has a financial interest consistent with that of the corporation which the vote purchaser does not. While this explanation may not justify all irrevocable proxies, it does illustrate the policy considerations that justify recognizing some forms of irrevocable proxy appointments.

To express the same thought in another way, an irrevocable proxy appointment separates the ownership from the voting power. Because of the possibility of injury to the owners by the abuse of a naked voting power unconnected with a financial interest in the well-being of the corporation, the courts have generally refused to recognize the irrevocability of a proxy appointment except where there appears to be little likelihood that the power to vote will be abused. This is the nub of the notion of "coupled with an interest." The following types of proxy appointments have been held to be "coupled with an interest":

(1) A proxy appointment given to a pledgee under a valid pledge of the shares;

(2) A proxy appointment given to a person who has agreed to purchase the shares under an executory contract of sale;

(3) A proxy appointment given to a person who has lent money or contributed valuable property to the corporation;

(4) A proxy appointment given to a person who has contracted to perform services for the corporation as an officer; and

(5) A proxy appointment given in order to effectuate the provisions of a valid pooling agreement (described in the following section).

Some courts have upheld irrevocable proxies in specific situations which do not squarely fall within any of the above categories.

There appears to be a slow trend toward statutory codification of the common law proxy appointment "coupled with an interest" doctrine. New York and California have statutes which define the five situations described above as those in which an irrevocable proxy appointment should be recognized [N.Y. Bus. Corp. Law, § 609(F); Cal. Corp. Code, § 705]. Such a statute resolves possible future disputes very simply, but there is some danger that a reasonable irrevocable proxy appointment might be invalidated because it does not fit squarely into any of the above categories. It was for this reason that section 7.22(d) of the 1984 Model Business Corporation Act, while based generally on the language of the New York statute, makes the list non-exclusive.

§ 9.11 Vote Buying

It was pointed out in the previous section that the purchase of a proxy appointment may be against public policy. Are all purchased proxy appointments against public policy and unenforceable? Most courts that have considered the question agree that purchased votes are invalid *per se*. The one case that arguably reached the opposite result, Schreiber v. Carney (Del.Ch.1982), concluded that a purchased vote should be viewed as a "voidable transaction subject to a test of intrinsic fairness." In that case, a shareholder agreed to withdraw its opposition to a proposed merger in exchange for a favorable loan from a participant in the merger. The loan transaction was disclosed to the other shareholders who voted overwhelmingly in favor of the merger. The court concluded that the loan transaction was entered into primarily to further the interests of the remaining shareholders.

§ 9.12 Shareholder Voting Agreements

A shareholder voting agreement is a contract among the shareholders, or some of them, to vote their shares in a specified manner on certain matters. Such an agreement is usually called a "pooling agreement" because it results in the shares of the participants being voted as a pooled unit. The purpose may be to maintain control, or to maximize the voting power of the shares where cumulative voting is permitted, or to ensure that some specific objective is obtained. The manner in which the shares are to be voted, that is for or against a specified proposal or motion, may be specified in the agreement itself, or be the subject of subsequent negotiation and decision of the shareholders with some method of determining how the shares are to be voted in the event of a failure to agree. The shareholders' pooling agreement extends only to voting on matters that are within the province of shareholders, such as the election of directors, and should be sharply distinguished from agreements that attempt to resolve matters that are vested in the discretion of directors. The latter type of agreement raises serious questions of validity (see § 8.10 of this Nutshell). The pooling agreement does not.

In a pooling agreement, the shareholders retain all the indicia of ownership of shares except the power to vote. In this respect, a pooling agreement differs from a voting trust (discussed in § 9.13 of this Nutshell) which contemplates that legal title to the shares be transferred to the trustees. Generally, the advantages of a pooling agreement over a voting trust are that it is less formal, easier to establish, and there is no disruption of other ownership attributes.

The pooling agreement is generally recognized as a valid contract, subject only to the rules applicable to the validity of contracts in general. A few states have adopted statutes regulating pooling agreements, often limiting the period during which a pooling agreement may continue (e.g. to ten years), requiring that copies of the pooling agreement be deposited at the principal office of the corporation, and so forth. However, in most states, the pooling agreement is essentially an unregulated contractual voting device that may continue for long periods of time. Section 7.31 of the Model Business Corporation Act (1984) basically codifies the common law rules applicable to pooling agreements.

A basic part of a pooling agreement is the manner of resolution of possible disagreements in the future. While the parties to the agreement are presumably in complete accord as to how their shares should be voted today, there is no assurance that they will be in accord tomorrow. Pooling agreements usually specify that participants will consult in advance of the meeting as to how the pooled shares should be voted, and that the shares will be voted as a majority or some other percentage specify. For example, in an important Delaware case, the agreement provided that the six participants in the pool could select eight agents (most selecting one, some two) and the shares would be voted as any seven agents specified. Abercrombie v. Davies (Del.1957). Arbitration was provided for in the event seven agents were unable to agree. While this agreement ultimately was held to constitute an invalid voting trust rather than a pooling agreement, the method of dispute resolution is interesting in that it required a high degree of consensus by the participants. Resolution of disagreements is usually by arbitration or by a decision of some person mutually trusted by all the participants. However, if the pooling agreement covers enough shares to constitute working control of the corporation, arbitration may in fact vest control of the corporation in the hands of the arbiter, a person with no financial interest in the enterprise. A "runaway" arbiter is unlikely because the shareholders may, by agreeing among themselves, retake control over the voting of the pooled shares. Pooling agreements also often provide that the participants in the pool may substitute arbiters by mutual agreement. Instead of arbitration, a pooling agreement may give a participant the option of withdrawing his or her shares if disagreement continues over a period of time. Such a provision, of course, in a sense defeats the original purpose of a pooling agreement.

Enforcement of a pooling agreement creates special problems since the shares are registered in the names of the individual shareholders. Many courts will enforce a pooling agreement by decreeing specific performance. It is not always certain, however, that specific performance will be available. In Ringling Bros.-Barnum & Bailey Combined Shows v. Ringling (Del.1947), the leading Delaware case involving pooling agreements, the agreement itself did not specifically appoint anyone to vote the shares of an objecting shareholder who refused to follow the arbiter's instructions. Nevertheless, the Chancellor found by a process of implication that a proxy appointment existed in favor of the other shareholder. On appeal, the Supreme

Court held that the proper remedy was simply not to count votes cast in contravention of the instructions of the arbiter. Under the circumstances, the result was to defeat utterly the purpose of the pooling agreement, since the minority shareholder who was not a party to the pooling agreement had a majority of the remaining shares after giving effect to the disqualification.

Some state statutes specifically address the enforcement issue either by authorizing irrevocable proxy appointments in connection with pooling agreements or by stating expressly that pooling agreements are specifically enforceable. New York, for example, validates and makes irrevocable a proxy granted in connection with a pooling agreement [N.Y. Bus. Corp. Law §§ 609(e), 620], while section 7.31(b) of the Model Business Corporation Act (1984) simply states that a pooling agreement "is specifically enforceable." The New York statute is less desirable since, to take advantage of that statute, the agreement probably should specifically appoint a proxy. Enforcement of pooling agreements under the New York statute might also create practical problems for inspectors of corporate elections who must decide who is entitled to vote shares based on the pooling agreement rather than on the corporate records. In these circumstances, an inspector probably would insist that a court decree be first obtained determining how the shares should be voted—a result that the Model Business Corporation Act (1984) formulation clearly contemplates.

§ 9.13 Voting Trusts: Purpose, Operation, and Legislative Policy

A voting trust differs from a pooling agreement primarily in that legal title to the shares is vested in trustees, and the shares are registered in the names of the trustees on the books of the corporation. Voting trust agreements usually provide that all dividends or other corporate distributions be passed through to the equitable owners of the shares. The trustees may also issue transferable voting trust certificates representing the beneficial interests in the shares and these certificates may be traded much as shares of stock are traded. While voting trust agreements may limit the power of trustees to vote on certain matters or to transfer the shares held by them to third parties without the consent of the beneficial owners, nevertheless, in a voting trust the legal title to the shares, and usually the entire power to vote, is separated from the equitable ownership of the shares.

At common law there was great suspicion of voting trusts. One commentator described a voting trust as "little more than a vehicle for corporate kidnapping." This attitude has largely disappeared. State statutes now uniformly recognize the validity of voting trusts and they have received a more hospitable judicial reception. Section 7.30 of the Model Business Corporation Act (1984) states that a voting trust may be created subject to minimal requirements:

(1) The agreement may not extend beyond ten years;

(2) The agreement must be in writing and signed by one or more shareholders who transfer their shares to the voting trustee on the books of the corporation; and

(3) The voting trustee must prepare a list of the persons with beneficial interests in the voting trust and deliver that list and a copy of the agreement to the corporation at its principal office. These documents are thereafter available for inspection by shareholders.

Section 7.30(c) deals with the matter of extending a voting trust beyond its ten year maximum life. The statutes of several states permit an extension during the last year of the life of a voting trust; section 7.30(c) adopts the somewhat simpler rule that a voting trust may be extended at any time during its life for a period of ten years running from the date the first shareholder signs the extension of a voting trust. Of course, an extension is binding on shareholders who agree to the extension; a person objecting to the extension is entitled to a return of his or her shares upon the termination of the original term of the voting trust.

Some states have imposed a further substantive requirement on voting trusts that the essential purpose of the trust must be a proper one. For example, a trust created solely for the purpose of securing control of or lucrative employment with a corporation would be invalidated in some states. Obviously, proof of such motives depends on subjective testimony; the cautious, close-mouthed creator of a voting trust in these states may create an enforceable voting trust despite wrongful motives, while a garrulous person with basically good motives may inadvertently make damaging statements about the underlying purpose of the trust. In a majority of the states, the purpose of a voting trust is not inquired into; a voting trust is valid if it complies with all statutory requirements.

A voting trust agreement that fails to comply with all statutory requirements is considered invalid in its entirety in most states. Even though these requirements are basically simple ones that may be easily complied with, a number of cases have arisen in which these requirements have been ignored. The most common failing is not filing a copy of the voting trust agreement in the records of the corporation. In addition, some states take the position that a voting trust that is not by its terms limited to ten years is invalid from the outset because it does not meet the statutory requirements; under the MBCA (1984), a trust that contains no specified term is valid for ten years only.

Courts generally treat voting arrangements that have the essential characteristics of a voting trust to be subject to the formal statutory requirements of a voting trust even though the arrangement is not a formal voting trust. The leading case in this respect is Abercrombie v. Davies (Del.1957). Another case, Hall v. Staha (Ark.1990) holds that a limited partnership formed in order to obtain voting control over the corporation was a voting trust.

§ 9.14 Voting Trusts: Use in Public Corporations

A voting trust, unlike most of the other control arrangements discussed in this Chapter, may be used in publicly held corporations as well as in closely held corporations. For example, a voting trust may be used in connection with the capitalization or reorganization of a corporation to provide for temporary stability of management. A temporary voting trust may be ordered where as a result of the reorganization the voting power is lodged in a large, unorganized group of bondholders who previously had no power to control the corporation. Another possible use is in connection with divestiture orders under the Federal Antitrust laws, where the court desires to order an immediate termination of control, but where the financial details of the divestiture may take a long period to work out. A voting trust may also be used by creditors of a publicly held corporation to remove holders of large blocks of stock whom the creditors mistrust from the control of the corporation. An outstanding example of this use was a 1960 loan of $165,000,000 to Trans World Airlines by a consortium of banks. As a condition to the loan, Hughes Tool Co., then wholly owned by Howard Hughes, was required to place its shares of TWA (amounting to 75 per cent of the outstanding shares) into a voting trust with the banks designating the trustees. In this way, Mr. Hughes was isolated from the actual management of the debtor corporation.

§ 9.15   Voting Trusts: Powers and Duties of Trustee

Voting trusts usually contain precise provisions defining the powers and duties of the trustees. Voting trustees may have working control of the corporation for extended periods of time, but may have little or no financial interest in the corporation. Problem areas that have arisen include:

(1) May the trustees elect themselves as directors and/or officers? The wisdom of permitting dual offices is debatable since it is unlikely that a voting trustee would vote to remove himself or herself as a director.

(2) May the trustees remaining in office fill a vacancy in the trustees? Trustees are often given this power, though it may also be vested in the holders of voting trust certificates.

(3) May the trustees vote on major corporate changes, such as mergers, dissolution, or the sale of substantially all of its assets? Arguably, consent of the holders of voting trust certificates should be obtained on such major matters, but voting trust agreements often provide that the trustees may vote on such matters as they see fit.

(4) May the trustees dispose of the shares subject to the voting trust? Voting trust agreements often provide that no sale of underlying shares may be effected without the prior consent of all, or a designated percentage, of the holders of voting trust certificates.

(5) Should the trustees be relieved of liability for errors in business judgment or nonfeasance? Trustees typically desire broad exculpatory clauses, but these clauses may be inconsistent with the legitimate interest of depositing shareholders. Also, courts may decline to enforce broad exculpatory clauses applicable to fiduciaries or read such clauses very narrowly.

(6) What deductions, if any, may the trustees make from dividends received by them before paying them over to the equitable owners?

(7) Are the trustees entitled to compensation, and if so, in what amount?

(8) What provision, if any should be made for the eventuality that the trustees may disagree among themselves as to how the shares should be voted? Normally, the rule should probably be that majority vote controls, but it is possible that the creators of some voting trusts might prefer a rule of allocating the voting power proportionately among the voting trustees. Provision may also be made for the eventuality that the voting trustees might themselves deadlock on some specific issue.

Generally, courts tend to construe voting trust agreements narrowly or to imply a broad fiduciary duty by which trustees' actions may be tested.

§ 9.16 Creation of Floating Voting Power Through Different Classes of Shares

The common law treated with some suspicion various devices that effectively divorce the privilege of shareholder voting from the ownership of shares: irrevocable proxies (§ 9.10 of this Nutshell), shareholder pooling agreements (§ 9.12 of this Nutshell), and voting trusts (§§ 9.13–9.15 of this Nutshell). While these devices are valid and enforceable within their limited spheres, they are hedged with restrictions or limitations. One device that apparently permits the effective divorce of voting power from ownership of any significant financial interest in the corporation is the creation of classes of shares with disproportionate voting and financial rights. In most states, no limitation is placed on the creation of classes of shares without voting rights, with fractional or multiple votes per share, with power to select one or more directors, and with limited financial interests in the corporation. The leading case involving the use of special classes of stock to create a floating voting power without a significant financial interest in the corporation is Lehrman v. Cohen (Del.1966). Two families, the Lehrmans and the Cohens, owned equal quantities of the voting stock of a major grocery chain. The shares were divided into two classes, denominated AL and AC, and each could elect two directors. Because of internal disputes and disagreements that could not be resolved because of the makeup of the board, both families agreed to the creation of a third class of voting stock, AD stock, consisting of one share with the power to elect one director. The par value of the one share of AD stock was $10; this stock was not entitled to receive dividends, and on liquidation was entitled to receive back only its par value. Further, it could be redeemed or called at any time upon the vote of four directors upon the payment of the par value to the holder.

For several years, this tie-breaking mechanism worked well. The holder of the one share of AD stock was the attorney for the corporation; he elected himself director and participated actively in the meetings of the board. Eventually, the holder of the AD stock allied himself with the Cohen family and together they made the attorney the chief executive officer of the corporation pursuant to a long term employment contract. Despite the fact that the AD stock was little more than a floating vote or tie-breaking mechanism with only a nominal financial interest in the corporation, its validity was upheld against the contentions that it constituted a voting trust or an invalid voting arrangement. One plausible justification for the result upholding the validity of the Class AD stock in this case is that it seems impossible to draw a line between permissible and impermissible classes of shares. The statute gives virtually total freedom to vary voting and financial interests; one cannot say that $10 is too little, but that some other financial interest is enough.

While there has not been very much litigation on this type of arrangement, what there is tends to support the basic conclusion of the Delaware Supreme Court.

§ 9.17 Share Transfer Restrictions: Purposes, Operation, and Effect

In the absence of specific agreement, shares of stock are freely transferable. However, restrictions on free transferability of shares may be of vital importance in both closely held and publicly held corporations.

A. *Closely Held Corporations.* In the closely held corporation share transfer restrictions typically constitute contractual obligations to offer or to sell shares either to the corporation or to other shareholders, or to both successively, on the death of the shareholder or when the shareholder decides he or she wishes to retire or leave the venture. The restriction may take the form of (1) an option in the corporation or shareholders to purchase at a designated price, (2) a mandatory buy-sell agreement obligating the corporation or shareholders to purchase the shares, or (3) merely a right of first refusal, giving the corporation or the shareholders an opportunity to meet the best price the shareholder has been able to obtain from outsiders. The choice between these three forms of share transfer restrictions depends on the business needs of the shareholders. Obviously, an option or a right of first refusal does not guarantee the shareholder a specified price, whereas a buy-sell agreement does. Since investors or participants wish to avoid being "locked in" to an investment, most closely held corporations adopt buy-sell agreements.

In closely held corporations, share transfer restrictions not only enable participants in the venture who wish to leave to liquidate their interests but also enable the continuing participants to decide who shall thereafter participate in the venture. The right of "exit" is particularly important to minority shareholders in a closely held corporation since otherwise their interest is largely at risk of actions taken by the controlling shareholders. In effect share transfer restrictions achieve the corporate equivalent of the partnership notions of dissolution-on-demand and *delectus personae.* They also may ensure a stable management and protection against an unexpected change in the respective proportionate interests of the shareholders which might occur if one shareholder is able to quietly purchase shares of other shareholders. A further advantage of share transfer restrictions in a closely held corporation is that if properly prepared they may materially simplify the estate tax problems of a deceased shareholder. If the corporation or other shareholders are obligated to purchase the shares owned by the deceased shareholder (a buy-sell agreement) the estate may be assured that a large, illiquid asset will be reduced to cash. Further, either an option or a buy-sell agreement, if properly prepared, will be accepted by the Internal Revenue Service as establishing the value of the shares for federal estate tax purposes, thereby avoiding a potentially serious dispute with the tax authorities. Since closely held shares have no market on which value can be based, the Internal Revenue Service is apt to take a very optimistic attitude as to the value of such shares in the absence of an agreement establishing the value.

Share transfer restrictions in closely held corporations may also be imposed to ensure the continued availability of the S corporation election (see § 2.5 of this Nutshell). Restrictions on transfer for this purpose may be necessary to ensure that the thirty-five shareholder maximum is not exceeded and that shares are not transferred to an ineligible shareholder (such as a corporation or trust) that would cause the loss of the election.

B. *Publicly Held Corporations.* In a publicly held corporation, share transfer restrictions are usually used to prevent violations of the Federal Securities Act where the corporation has issued unregistered shares, e.g., in connection with the acquisition of another business. In order to prevent the unregistered shares from immediately being resold in the public market, share transfer restrictions are imposed on the unregistered shares and instructions may be placed with the transfer agent to refuse to accept unregistered shares for transfer unless accompanied by an appropriate attorney's opinion. Share transfer restrictions may also be used to ensure the continued availability of an exemption from registration which may be lost, for example, if the shares are offered for resale to nonresidents. The availability of several exemptions from registration under regulations adopted by the Securities and Exchange Commission are expressly conditioned upon the corporation imposing restrictions on the transfer of shares issued in reliance upon the exemption.

Share transfer restrictions in publicly held corporations differ in nature as well as purpose from share transfer restrictions in closely held corporations. In the latter, restraints usually are of the option or buy-sell variety which require the shareholder to offer or sell his or her shares to the corporation or to other shareholders. In the publicly held corporation on the other hand, restrictions usually take the form of flat prohibitions on transfer unless the transferor can establish that the transfer is consistent with the securities laws or regulations. This may require an opinion of counsel, affidavits by the purchaser or transferee, and the acceptance of further restrictions on transfer by the purchaser or transferee. Such uses of share transfer restrictions are considered fully in courses on securities regulation.

§ 9.18 Share Transfer Restrictions: Scope and Validity

Many early judicial decisions take the position that share transfer restrictions are restraints on alienation and should therefore be strictly construed. As a result it is important to specify clearly and unambiguously the essential attributes of the restrictions and the events that trigger the restraint. In option or buy/sell agreements for example, the death, divorce, or bankruptcy of a shareholder may trigger the restriction. A desire to sell or donate the shares to a third person will also usually trigger the restriction but a transfer by gift to children or grandchildren may be excluded from the restriction. Careful drafting is essential. It has been held, for example, that a restriction against sales "to the public" does not prohibit a sale to another shareholder, or that a prohibition against sale to an "officer stockholder" does not cover a sale to a corporation owned by an officer stockholder. Obviously, such holdings tend to defeat rather than further the basic purpose of share transfer restrictions.

The common law legal test as to the validity of a share transfer restraint is that it "does not unreasonably restrain or prohibit transferability." Under this test, an outright prohibition on transferability would certainly be held invalid. Also dangerous are restrictions which prohibit transfers unless consent of the directors or other shareholders is first obtained; the possibility that consent may be arbitrarily withheld may invalidate the restraint. Language that consent "will not be unreasonably withheld" may validate a restriction of this type. Other questionable types of restrictions include restrictions barring transfers to competitors or to a distinct class, such as aliens; restrictions imposing a penalty, such as a loss of vote or loss of dividend as a consequence of the transfer; or the creation of callable common shares.

The niggardly common law view about the enforceability of share transfer restrictions reflected in the preceding paragraphs has caused several states to adopt legislation broadening the types of restrictions that may be enforced. Section 6.27 of the Model Business Corporation Act (1984) builds on these provisions; it is a carefully drafted statute that attempts to eliminate most of the undesirable restrictive features of the common law. It distinguishes between the purpose of a restriction (subsection (c)) and the type of restriction (subsection (d)). Section 6.27(c)(3) provides that generally the purpose of a restriction must be "reasonable," but restrictions described in subparts (1) and (2)—to maintain the status of the corporation when it is dependent on the number or identity of shareholders and to preserve exemptions under federal or state securities law—are valid without investigation into the reasonableness of the purpose. Phrased differently, the purposes set forth in subparts (1) and (2) are conclusively presumed to be reasonable. Section 6.27(d) lists four types of restrictions—buy-sell requirements, options, consent restrictions, and prohibitory restrictions. The last two are valid if "the requirement is not manifestly unreasonable." This last clause is taken directly from section 202 of the Delaware statute. (Del. Gen. Corp. Law, § 202.) Several other states have adopted similar statutes.

Restrictions are sometimes imposed after the corporation has been created and shares issued. In these situations the question may arise as to whether the shares previously issued are subject to a restraint which is inserted in the articles of incorporation or bylaws. In the absence of statute, the case law has split on whether the restrictions may be imposed retroactively; section 6.27(a) of the Model Business Corporation Act (1984) provides that restrictions are not applicable to previously issued shares unless the holders of the shares are parties to the agreement creating the restrictions or voted in favor of imposing them.

§ 9.19   Share Transfer Restrictions: Duration of Restraints

Unlike voting trusts, which usually have a statutory duration of ten years or less, there is no express restriction on the duration of share transfer restrictions. So long as the type of restriction is limited to the traditional option or buy-and-sell agreement, it is probable that the restriction remains enforceable without regard to the rule against perpetuities or equitable notions of "reasonableness." Less orthodox types of valid restraints normally continue so long as the need or justification for them exists.

Share transfer restrictions may terminate prematurely in one of two ways: by express agreement of the shareholders involved (e.g., when all decide to sell their shares to an outside purchaser despite a restriction against such sales), or by abandonment or disuse. If shares are sold or transferred without compliance with the restrictions and without objection by the various parties, a court may conclude that the restrictions have been abandoned and are no longer enforceable. Isolated sales in violation of the restriction may not be sufficient to support such a conclusion, though a person objecting to the current sale may be estopped if he or she participated in the earlier transaction. A policy of selective enforcement of share transfer restrictions probably will be invalidated.

§ 9.20   Share Transfer Restrictions: Procedural Requirements

In creating share transfer restrictions it is important that the proper formalities be followed and that the requirements of the relevant business corporation act be complied with. Most restrictions appear in the articles of incorporation or bylaws of the corporation, though some may be imposed by simple contract between the corporation and shareholders or between the shareholders themselves. Statutes generally require that a reference to any restriction imposed in corporate documents must also be placed or "noted" on the face or back of each share certificate which is subject to the restriction [MBCA (1984) § 6.27(b)]; generally, however it is not necessary for the full text or a complete description of the restriction to appear on the certificate. Section 6.27(b) also requires the notation to be "conspicuous," a term that is defined in section 1.40 as meaning "so written that a reasonable person against whom it is to operate ought to have noticed it. For example, printing in italics or boldface or contrasting color, or typing in capitals or underlined, is conspicuous. A printed heading in capitals * * * is conspicuous. Language in the body of a form is 'conspicuous' if it is in larger or other contrasting type or color." The requirement of conspicuous notation also appears in article eight of the Uniform Commercial Code, and in many states that is the only place where a "conspicuous" requirement appears.

Unless the procedural requirements described in the previous paragraph are complied with, the restriction is unenforceable against a shareholder who is unaware of the restriction; a person who knows of the restriction at the time the shares are acquired is bound by the restriction whether or not these procedural requirements have been met.

§ 9.21 Option or Buy/Sell Agreements: Who Should Have the Right or Privilege to Buy?

Share transfer restrictions that constitute option or buy/sell agreements to purchase the shares may run either to the corporation or to some or all the other shareholders. The choice is a matter of convenience, though usually it is preferable for the restriction to run to the corporation. The advantages of this are three-fold: the corporation may be able to raise the necessary cash more easily than the shareholders individually, the proportionate interests of the remaining shareholders are unaffected by a corporate purchase, and a corporate purchase is advantageous from a tax standpoint. On the other hand, a repurchase of shares by a corporation is a distribution of assets to shareholders that must meet certain legal requirements; in par value states, the purchase may be lawfully made only if the corporation has the necessary earned or capital surplus at the time the purchase is to be made; under the MBCA (1984), such a transaction is a distribution and must meet the tests of MBCA (1984) § 6.40 (see § 18.6 of this Nutshell). In order to take care of the possibility that the corporation may be legally barred from acquiring the shares, buy/sell agreements may require the shareholders or some of them to agree to buy the shares if the corporation is not legally permitted to do so.

If the corporation purchases all the shares of one shareholder, that transaction is treated as a "sale or exchange" of the stock by the seller, subject to the benefits of the special tax rates on capital gains. Furthermore, the transaction is not treated as an indirect dividend to the remaining shareholders even though their proportionate interest in the corporation has changed. Thus, a repurchase transaction provides a tax free benefit to the remaining shareholders. This tax advantage is so substantial that it is standard operating procedure to retire a shareholder's interest through a corporate repurchase of the shares, if that is practicable.

If the share transfer restrictions run to the other shareholders rather than to the corporation, a problem arises if one or more of the shareholders are unable or unwilling to purchase their allotment of shares. Agreements usually provide that in that situation the shares not purchased should be reoffered proportionately to the remaining shareholders who may or may not be obligated to purchase the shares. The proportionate interests of the shareholders will necessarily be changed if one shareholder is unable or unwilling to purchase his or her allotment. However, the shareholders may not always desire that the shares be offered proportionately to the other shareholders. For example, a majority shareholder with a son and daughter may wish to provide that all shares be first offered to his or her son and then to his or her daughter (or vice versa) rather than be offered proportionately.

If the number of shareholders is large—more than four or five, say—the mechanics of having the restrictions run to the shareholders become complicated, and it usually is preferable for the restrictions to run to the corporation. Many share transfer restrictions provide for sale to the corporation, or then proportionately a sale to the other shareholders if the corporation is unable to purchase them. Finally, if life insurance is to be used to provide funds to purchase shares on the death of a shareholder, it is usually simplest to have the corporation pay the premiums and own the policies on the lives of each shareholder rather than having each shareholder attempt to insure the life of every other shareholder. If there were 25 shareholders, a complete cross-purchase arrangement with life insurance would require 600 policies!

§ 9.22 Option or Buy/Sell Agreements: Establishment of Purchase or Option Price

The price provisions of shareholder option or buy-sell agreements often raise the most difficult and important problems in drafting these arrangements. Since closely held shares by definition have no market or quoted price, one simply cannot refer to a "fair," "reasonable," or "market" price; some definite method of valuation must be provided. Further, since it usually is impossible to know whose shares will be first offered for sale under such an agreement, everyone's goal in establishing a mechanism to determine the price is usually to be as fair as possible. (Of course, this is not universally true; individualized circumstances may well exist which make it reasonably clear that one shareholder's interest will be retired first, and the other shareholders may be tempted to act opportunistically when creating the pricing mechanism.)

The following methods are often used to establish a purchase price usually stated on a per share basis:

(1) A stated price;

(2) Book value;

(3) Capitalization of earnings;

(4) Best offer by an outsider;

(5) Appraisal or arbitration, either by expert, impartial appraisers or arbitrators, or by directors or other shareholders; or

(6) A percentage of net profits to be paid for a specified number of years following the event which triggers the sale.

It is impossible to state definitively which is the most desirable method, since it depends on the nature of the business and assets being valued. The simplest method is for the parties to fix a definite price in the agreement itself. This may be par value, original purchase price, or a price established by negotiation. In the absence of fraud or overreaching, courts have enforced agreements where the price is well below the value of the shares, though there is always a possibility that a court may deem a grossly inadequate price to constitute an unreasonable restraint on alienation or to be "unconscionable." Generally, it is desirable to provide for periodic reevaluation of the fixed price as the fortunes of the corporation rise or fall. One problem that may arise is what happens if the parties fail to agree on a new price, or if they fail to revise the price from time to time as contemplated by the agreement. A willful refusal by a younger shareholder to renegotiate the price under such an agreement might be considered a breach of contract or even fraudulent, as might be a convenient "forgetfulness" on the part of such a shareholder. It is also possible that a court might conclude that there is a sufficient fiduciary relationship between the shareholders to justify a court-ordered price reevaluation whether or not specific provision therefor was made.

By far the most popular method of valuation is "book value," which may be computed by a simple division of a balance sheet figure by the number of outstanding shares. Indeed, it is probable that book value is often used without serious consideration as to its advantages or disadvantages in connection with the specific business. Book value is based on the application of certain accounting conventions to corporate transactions and whether or not book value is a realistic estimate of value depends on the circumstances; it may be appropriate to require that book value be adjusted in certain ways before being used to establish a purchase price. For example, one accounting convention requires assets to be valued at cost and not be reappraised upward to reflect current market values. Thus, a corporation that owns real estate acquired decades earlier at low prices often will have a book value that considerably understates the true value of the assets. Similarly investments in readily marketable securities may be shown on the books at cost even though current market values may be obtained from the financial tables of any newspaper. In these instances, a restatement of such assets in terms of current market or appraised values may be more appropriate than "pure" book value. Accounting conventions also allow corporations to include certain things as assets which may never be realized; for example, costs of initial formation or of "good will" acquired in connection with the purchase of another business. It may be appropriate to eliminate such non-asset "assets" from the balance sheet before computing book value.

A number of accounting techniques have been developed for federal income tax purposes, and it may be undesirable to have a shareholder's interest in a corporation valued on the basis of tax accounting principles. For example, if the corporation utilizes accelerated depreciation schedules for tax purposes, it may be desirable to specify that straight line depreciation should be used to compute book value for valuation purposes. Or, if inventory is valued on a LIFO basis, it may be desirable to require the inventory to be valued at a more realistic figure before computing book value.

Appraisal of the value of closely held stock has its own difficulties. Appraisers tend to prefer to value shares by capitalizing earnings or cash flow, or by making a direct appraisal of the market value of assets, or by a combination of the two, rather than relying on book value. Capitalization of earnings or cash flow is a fairly complex method of estimating the value of a business, though the basic idea is simple enough: if a corporation has average earnings of, say, $50,000 a year, and it is reasonable to capitalize those earnings at ten per cent, the corporation should be valued at $500,000. If the reasonable capitalization ratio were eight per cent, the business would be valued at $625,000 (625,000 × .08 = 50,000); if it were fifteen per cent, it would be valued at $333,333 (333,333 × .15 = 50,000). One may quite legitimately ask where both the $50,000 and the ten per cent figures came from, particularly since different earnings estimates or capitalization ratios have a significant effect on the overall valuation. An appropriate capitalization ratio may be justified on the basis of earnings ratios of comparable publicly held businesses, the appraiser's general experience with valuing businesses in the particular industry, or simply the appraiser's intuitive "feel" as to how risky a specific business is. Valuation based on capitalization of earnings may also be affected by different assumptions about the level of average earnings in the future, and whether different assets should be capitalized at different rates.

Normally, an appraiser or arbitrator will consider all the various possible methods of valuation, and in fact the price he or she sets may reflect an average of various possible values, for example, the average of book value, the capitalized value, and the estimated liquidation value if the assets were sold. The logic of averaging the results of discretely different techniques is doubtful, since if a corporation, for example, is worth more as a going concern than it is liquidated, it should be valued as a going concern without regard to the liquidation value.

After the value of the overall business is obtained, the per share value is usually obtained by a simple division by the number of outstanding shares. However, complications may involve the basis on which senior securities are valued and whether a further discount from the per share value should be taken if the shares are an isolated minority block with no chance of sharing in control. There is an extensive body of decisions (and law review commentary) on the priority of specific discounts and premiums in the valuation process.

§ 9.23 Option or Buy/Sell Agreements: Life Insurance

The unexpected death of a shareholder may cause serious disruption in a close corporation. Two things are essential if the corporation is to pass smoothly through such difficult periods: planning and money. A properly drafted buy-and-sell agreement or option may provide the former; life insurance is often the simplest way of providing the latter. It is possible, of course, to provide that the estate of a deceased shareholder is to be paid out over a period of time from anticipated future earnings. This may not be satisfactory from the standpoint of an estate, faced with large tax liabilities and a desire to wind matters up promptly. Life insurance, usually owned by the corporation, may provide the necessary funds to allow the estate's interest to be retired promptly. Of course, this assumes that the shareholder is insurable, that his or her age is not such that the cost of premiums is prohibitive, and the corporation's cash flow will support the necessary premiums without adversely affecting business operations.

§ 9.24 Selection of the Purchaser in Deadlock Buyouts

A mandatory buy-sell arrangement is often recommended as the best solution in possible deadlock situations, where (usually) two equal shareholders own and manage the business but fear that there may be disagreements in the future. As described in some detail in a later chapter, (Chapter 12 of this Nutshell), the remedies for deadlock in the absence of agreement are not entirely satisfactory. In the event of significant, unresolvable disagreement, it seems much neater and cleaner that one shareholder should buy out the other. In addition to important questions about price and timing, additional problems in working out deadlock-breaking arrangements include who is to buy out whom if both desire to continue the corporate business? Often the senior should buy out the junior, though if the age discrepancy is large, it may be more sensible to reverse the order and have the junior buy out the senior. One variation, which somewhat resembles roulette, or the classic children's device for cutting up a pie evenly, is to have one shareholder set a price at which he or she is willing to buy out the other shareholder or to sell his or her own shares, at the election of the other shareholder. While there is nothing inherently improper with this device, it should be utilized with caution since it may be necessary to persuade a court of its reasonableness in order to obtain judicial enforcement by a decree of specific performance. Another issue is precisely what events trigger the power to buy? Some kind of objective standard is usually desirable, such as the failure to agree on a slate of directors for some specified period. Yet another issue is which of the various pricing formulas should be used and which should be avoided? In light of the possible deadlock it seems important to choose a formula that does not rely on a cooperative effort to set the price; it also seems desirable to use a formula that will yield as "fair" a price as possible rather than one that appears to create a bargain for one faction or the other.

§ 9.25 Deferred Payment of the Purchase Price

Many share transfer restrictions provide that the purchase price of shares shall be paid in annual or more frequent installments extending over several years upon the retirement of a shareholder or on his or her separation from the business. The theory behind these provisions is that they enable the business to pay for the shares out of future profits or future cash flow without incurring indebtedness for this purpose. The withdrawing shareholder may or may not be entitled to interest on the deferred payments. Under modern statutes such debts are on a parity with general trade creditors. See § 18.11 of this Nutshell.

Where payments of the purchase price are deferred, the parties may also agree that the aggregate amount of the price may be adjusted upward or downward depending on the profitability of the business in the years following the exercise of the share transfer restriction. In effect, this is a form of "work out," widely used in connection with the purchase of businesses generally to adjust the purchase price to reflect the future success of the business. A "work out" may avoid an impasse over valuation of the business, as the seller believes a high valuation is appropriate while the buyer is much more pessimistic. A "work out" permits the actual operation of the business to determine which estimate was more reasonable.

[For unfamiliar terms see the Glossary]

CHAPTER TEN

DIRECTORS

§ 10.1 Number and Qualifications of Directors

Historically, virtually all statutes required that there be at least three directors, and many statutes required that each director have certain qualifications, such as being a shareholder or a resident of the state. Mandatory qualification requirements have been almost universally eliminated and most states now permit boards of directors to consist of one or two directors.

The privilege of having a board of one or two directors in many states is limited to corporations with one or two shareholders, but under section 8.03(a) of the Model Business Corporation Act (1984) and the statutes of an increasing number of states, any corporation may elect to have a board consisting of one or two directors without regard to the number of shareholders. The notion that only corporations with one or two shareholders may have boards of directors consisting of one or two members seems superficially plausible. Presumably the shareholders will be the directors. In some situations, however, these statutes create unnecessary problems. Consider, for example, a corporation that is owned entirely by one person, and the sole shareholder is the single director. Assume further that the shareholder desires to make gifts of shares of stock to his two minor children. Under these statutes, the board of directors would have to be increased to three members when the first gift of shares is made since there are then three shareholders!

Even though mandatory qualifications for directors have universally been abolished, corporations are free to provide for special qualifications, such as requiring each director to be a shareholder or to be a holder of shares of a specific class. Qualifications for directors may appear either in the articles of incorporation or the bylaws. However, only "individuals" may serve as directors. MBCA (1984) § 8.03(a). In some countries, corporations or other entities may serve as directors; this practice has apparently never taken root in the United States.

The number of directors of a corporation may be "specified in or fixed in accordance with the articles of incorporation or bylaws." MBCA (1984) § 8.03(a). It is quite common to permit the board of directors to fix its own size. The bylaws may expressly give this power to the board, or the number of directors may be fixed in the bylaws but the board of directors may be given the general power to amend bylaws. (See § 8.9 of this Nutshell.) Section 8.03(b) restricts the power of the board of directors to fix its own size by requiring shareholder approval of changes in the board of directors that increase or decrease its size by 30 per cent or more. Alternatively, the articles of incorporation or bylaws may create a variable range size for the board of directors and the board of directors may set the size of the board within that range; shareholder approval is required for changes in the outer limits of that range or for a change from a fixed to a variable size board, or vice versa. MBCA (1984) § 8.03(c). The purpose of these provisions is to give the board of directors power to add desirable members to the board without shareholder approval, or to decide not to fill a vacancy, but to prevent the board from manipulating its own size in a substantial way without shareholder approval. These provisions were added because of policy considerations; relatively few states restrict the power of the board of directors to alter its size.

Some cases have recognized that bylaws setting the number of directors may be amended informally, as for example by the shareholders electing four directors when the bylaws specify that the board shall consist of only three directors. However, that is not a desirable practice, injecting future uncertainty as to the number of directors to be elected and reducing the value of the written bylaws.

§ 10.2 Directors' Meetings: Notice, Quorum, and Similar Matters

Detailed provisions relating to directors' meetings appear in corporate bylaws and only skeletal provisions are set forth in business corporation statutes. Regular meetings of the board of directors may be held weekly, monthly, quarterly, or at any regular interval. The bylaws usually specify when such meetings are to be held, or may authorize the directors themselves to specify, by resolution, when regular meetings are to be held. It is customary to hold a regular meeting of directors either immediately before or immediately after the annual meeting of shareholders. Special meetings are meetings other than regular meetings. The principal difference between regular and special meetings is that a regular meeting may be held without notice, while a special meeting "must be preceded by at least two days' notice of the date, time, and place of the meeting." MBCA (1984) § 8.22(b). However, even these modest notice requirements may be dispensed with by a corporation if an appropriate provision is placed in the articles of incorporation or bylaws. Directors may also waive notice (if such notice is required at all) in writing before, at, or after the meeting. MBCA (1984) § 8.23(a).

Unlike a shareholders' meeting, any relevant business may be transacted at a special meeting of directors even though not referred to in the notice. The theory behind this distinction is that directors' meetings routinely consider a variety of business matters under varying degrees of urgency whereas shareholders meet only to consider a limited number of matters. As a result the only practical difference between regular and special meetings of directors is the notice requirement.

In a board of directors with a fixed size, a quorum consists of a majority of the number so fixed; if the board does not have a fixed size (i.e. it is a board with a variable range), a quorum consists of a majority of the directors in office immediately before the meeting. MBCA (1984) § 8.24(a). The articles of incorporation or the bylaws, however, may authorize a quorum to consist of as few as one-third rather than a majority of the number described in the preceding sentence. MBCA (1984) § 8.24(b). This provision is patterned after § 707 of the New York Business Corporation Law; in most states, a quorum of directors may not be set at less than a majority. MBCA (1984) § 8.24(a) and the statutes of all states permit the articles of incorporation or bylaws to specify that a number greater than a majority, including all directors, may constitute a quorum. Where a quorum is present, the act of the majority of the directors present at the meeting is the act of the board, again unless the articles of incorporation or bylaws require a greater number. MBCA (1984) § 8.24(c). Under this section, the quorum must be actually present when the action is taken; many state statutes are silent on the question whether a quorum must be present throughout the meeting in order to take action. It may be recalled that a different rule is applicable to meetings of shareholders: once a quorum is present at a shareholders' meeting it is deemed to exist throughout the meeting even if some shareholders withdraw. (See § 9.1 of this Nutshell.) The opposite rule was made applicable to boards of directors in view of their management and fiduciary responsibilities; it also encourages management to present important issues early in the meeting when a quorum is more likely to be present than toward the end of the meeting when some directors may have left.

Provisions that a quorum consists of all directors often appear in articles of incorporation of closely held corporations. Unanimity requirements for voting also may appear in these documents. These provisions are obviously intended as control provisions to grant a veto power to a single director; as practical matter, they create potential deadlocks at the directoral level, since the refusal of a single director to attend or vote affirmatively on a matter prevents the corporation from acting.

With a single exception, if a quorum is not present the board of directors may not act. The only exception is where the directors are filling a vacancy; section 8.10(a)(3) of the Model Business Corporation Act (1984) provides that "if the directors remaining in office constitute fewer than a quorum, they may fill the vacancy by the affirmative vote of a majority of all the directors remaining in office." Many state statutes contain a similar provision based on the language of the 1969 Model Act that a vacancy "may be filled by the affirmative vote of the remaining directors *though less than a quorum.*" Unlike the MBCA (1984), an ambiguity hides in the italicized language of the older statute. Even though there are vacancies, the number of directors in office may still be greater than a quorum. However, if two factions are vying for control, the smaller faction may stay away from a meeting called by the larger faction to prevent a quorum from being present. At such a meeting the directors present are less than a quorum even though the directors in office are greater than a quorum. The cases are split as to whether the faction present at such a meeting, "though less than a quorum," may fill the vacancies. In Tomlinson v. Loew's (Del.1957), bylaw language similar to the phrase "though less than a quorum" was held to refer to the directors in office rather than to the directors present at the meeting. Several other cases, however, adopt the opposite construction.

§ 10.3   Compensation of Directors

The traditional view is that a director is not entitled to compensation for his or her ordinary services as director unless specific provision is made by the board of directors. The theory is that either directors are acting as trustees or that they are motivated by the prospect of increasing the return on their own shares. However, a director may be entitled to compensation pursuant to contract entered into in advance or for extraordinary services beyond normal directoral functions, or for service as a corporate officer or agent. These principles are based on tradition not legal power. In the early years of this century the practice developed in many corporations of paying small honoraria to "outside" or "nonmanagement" directors for attending meetings. With the increasing use of nonmanagement directors, particularly in publicly held corporations, the practice has grown of providing substantial remuneration ($50,000 per year or more) to all directors who are not officers of the corporation. In addition, many corporations provide incentive plans (such as stock options) or "golden parachutes" to outside directors in order to induce them to serve. Some corporations offer retirement plans to outside directors. Many corporations believe these compensation plans improve the quality and interest of outside directors, though some shareholder-oriented groups have complained that these plans are too generous.

Many state statutes give express recognition to the modern practice of compensating directors. The Model Business Corporation Act, for example, provides that "unless the articles of incorporation or bylaws provide otherwise, the board of directors may fix the compensation of directors." MBCA (1984) § 8.11.

§ 10.4　Filling of Vacancies on the Board

Modern statutes authorize vacancies in the board of directors to be filled either by the shareholders or by the board of directors. MBCA (1984) § 8.10(a). Directors elected to fill vacancies must stand for election at the next annual meeting of shareholders even if the term otherwise would continue beyond that meeting. MBCA (1984) § 8.05(b). Some states follow earlier versions of the Model Act and provide that directors elected to fill a vacancy remain in office for the term of their predecessor. This has application only if the terms of the board are staggered. (See § 9.7 of this Nutshell.)

Older statutes distinguish between an "old" and a "new" vacancy. An "old" vacancy is created by the death or resignation of a director and may be filled by the remaining directors. A successor director in an "old" vacancy serves the unexpired term of his or her predecessor. A "new" vacancy, on the other hand, is created by an increase in the number of directors by amendment of the bylaws or articles of incorporation. A "new" vacancy may be filled only by the shareholders, not the directors. The distinction between "old" and "new" vacancies arose in decisions from the State of Delaware, and was reflected in the 1950 version of the Model Act but was eliminated by an amendment in 1962. This history explains why section 8.10(a) of the MBCA (1984) expressly treats a "vacancy resulting from an increase in the number of directors" the same way as other vacancies. Many but not all statutes reflect this simpler and more sensible approach.

A common device to ensure minority representation on boards of directors of closely held corporations is to provide that separate classes of shares are entitled to elect specific numbers of directors. MBCA (1984) § 8.10(b) preserves this concept when vacancies are to be filled by limiting the shareholders authorized to fill vacancies to those that would be entitled to vote for the original election of the directors. Otherwise all shareholders might be able to vote on filling the vacancies. If such vacancies are filled by the board of directors, all directors, including those elected by other classes of shares, may vote on filling the vacancies. However, the damage this might do to the interests of the class of shares entitled to elect the original directors is limited because directors elected to those positions may be thereafter removed without cause solely by the class of shares entitled to vote in the original election under section 8.08(b). Section 8.10(c) makes it clear that a vacancy that will occur in the future, as by a dated resignation, may be filled immediately, with the resigning director participating in the decision. This provision may be of importance in corporations with closely divided or deadlocked boards of directors.

§ 10.5   Hold–Over Directors

Statutes provide that despite the expiration of a director's term, he or she continues to hold office until a successor is "elected and qualified." MBCA (1984) § 8.05(e). As a result, the failure to hold an annual meeting does not affect the power of a corporation to continue to transact its business since the directors presently in office continue in office with power to act.

The hold-over director provision is particularly important in situations where the shareholders are deadlocked in voting power and unable to elect successors to directors whose terms have expired. In this situation, those who are "in" remain as directors apparently forever; however, the ultimate solution is the involuntary dissolution of the corporation (or a mandatory buyout of one faction's shares at a judicially determined price) if the deadlock cannot be broken. See section 12.9 of this Nutshell.

§ 10.6   Necessity for Meeting and Personal Attendance

Numerous early cases refer to the rule that the "power invested in directors to control and manage the affairs of a corporation is not joint and several, but joint only," and that therefore action by directors must be "as a body at a properly constituted meeting." The underlying theory was that the shareholders were entitled to a decision reached only after group discussion and deliberation. Views may be changed as a result of discussion, and the sharpening of minds as a result of joint deliberation improves the decisional process. Several corollaries arise from this theory: first, the independent, consecutive approval of an act by each of the individual directors is not effective directoral action; second, directors may not vote by proxy; and third, formalities as to notice, quorum, and similar matters must be fully adhered to.

These corollaries make very little sense when applied to a close corporation where all the shareholders are active in the business, and even the requirement of a formal meeting of the directors in that situation is likely to be considered a meaningless formality. Further, rigid application of the doctrine often permits a corporation to use its own internal procedural defects as a sword to undo undesired transactions. This basic injustice is heightened because persons dealing with the corporation usually have no way of verifying that the formalities were in fact followed.

As a result, the broad historical principle of group decision-making was vitiated by judicially created exceptions even as it was being articulated. The basic exceptions are "estoppel," "ratification," and "acquiescence." Even though informal directoral action may be ineffective to formally authorize a transaction, it may be considered acquiescence in and ratification of the transaction. "Ratification" or "acquiesence" is usually implied where the corporation accepts the benefit of the contract without objection or where all the shareholders are aware of the contract and voice no objection. "Estoppel" is usually applied where the secretary of a corporation certifies that a meeting took place when it in fact had not; the corporation is "estopped" from questioning whether the requisite formalities were followed. It may also apply where responsible corporate officers accept the benefits of a transaction that they later regret. While it is dangerous to assume that the historical principle that directors may act only at meetings is totally obsolete, it is probable that one or more of the exceptions will be found applicable in specific situations.

§ 10.7   Telephonic Meetings

The Model Business Corporation Act (1984) authorizes members of the board of directors or a committee of the board to participate in a regular or special meeting through the use of a means of communication "by which all directors participating may simultaneously hear each other during the meeting." Most states have similar statutes that at least extend to the most ubiquitous "means of communication": the conference telephone call. The MBCA (1984), however, goes somewhat further than most of these statutes since it is broadly phrased in anticipation of possible advances in communications technology and expressly authorizes "a meeting" through the use of such technology at which no two directors are in the same room. Participation through one of these "means of communication," the statute adds, constitutes presence in person at a meeting.

This provision may be of considerable practical usefulness where directors are widely scattered, or where one or more of them are distant from the location where regular meetings are held. However, the fact that specific statutory authorization was felt to be necessary for a common sense idea such as telephonic meetings illustrates the persistence of the common law notion that directors can act only in meetings and through communal participation.

§ 10.8   Action Without a Meeting

Section 8.21 of the Model Business Corporation Act (1984) permits directors to act by unanimous written consent without a formal meeting "unless the articles of incorporation or bylaws provide otherwise." Most states have similar statutes.

Action by written consent under the MBCA (1984) has the same effect as a unanimous vote and may be described as such in any document. MBCA (1984) § 8.21(c). This modest and sensible provision solves most problems created by the rule requiring actions to be taken at directors' meetings. Problems still may arise, however. For one thing, obtaining a written consent signed by all the directors is itself a formality which may be overlooked by a careless attorney. There is also the problem of timing; action by consent is effective when the last director signs the consent under MBCA (1984) § 8.21(b), so that it is difficult to argue that such a consent is retroactive. Of course, arguments may then be made based on the doctrine of ratification, but it is always possible that by the time the last director signs one or more other directors may have changed their minds. And, of course, the procedure is inapplicable if one of the directors objects to the transaction in question and refuses to execute the consent; a formal meeting is then essential. All in all, it may be simpler to set a relatively low quorum level and act only through called meetings.

§ 10.9   Directors' Objections to Actions

Directors are sometimes faced with the difficult problem of what to do when a majority insists on authorizing the corporation to enter into transactions which the director feels to be precipitate, risky, a breach of fiduciary duty, or outright illegal. The concern of such a director is not theoretical, since in some circumstances all acquiescing directors may be held personally liable even though some of them may have had serious mental reservations about the action. To avoid this result a director must make sure that his or her dissent appears in writing in one of the ways set forth in section 8.24(b) of the Model Business Corporation Act: a dissent or abstention from the action must be entered in the minutes of the meeting or the director must deliver written notice of dissent or abstention "to the presiding officer of the meeting before its adjournment or to the corporation immediately after adjournment of the meeting."

Filing of a dissent not only eliminates liability, but also obviates later questions of proof and may have a psychological effect upon the other directors who realize that at least one director considers the conduct sufficiently questionable as to require legal protection. Also, it affords notice to shareholders or others examining the records that at least one director questioned the propriety of a specific transaction.

Rather than filing a notice of dissent, directors may take other steps to delay an action believed to be unwise. For example, they may request that the corporation obtain an opinion of counsel as to the propriety of the proposed transaction. While directors may rely in good faith on the opinion of counsel [MBCA (1984) § 8.30(b)(2)], an unqualified reliable opinion may be difficult to obtain as a practical matter if the transaction is questionable. Another option is resignation from the board before the action is taken; if the resignation occurs after the transaction is approved, liability may be avoided only if the director files the appropriate dissent. Presumably, a written resignation because of disagreement over an action taken by the board of directors would be viewed as a dissent from that action.

Even though a meeting is called without proper notice, a director waives any objection to the notice by attending the meeting and participating in it. Indeed, any participation by such a director is likely to be considered a waiver even though the director objects at the outset to the lack of notice. Section 8.24(d)(1) also addresses this issue in part by providing that such a director must object "at the beginning of the meeting (or promptly upon his arrival) to holding it or transacting business at the meeting."

§ 10.10 Committees of the Board of Directors

Many corporations utilize committees of the board of directors to consider in detail technical matters, to consider corporate transactions that in some way affect the personal interests of one or more directors, and to make directoral decisions during periods when the board does not meet. In addition to the committees discussed here, some corporations have utilized committees that may be composed of directors (and sometimes outsiders) to provide advice and perspective to the board of directors or to corporate management. Corporations also may form committees of management personnel to consider business-related problems; these committees form part of executive management rather than part of the management structure of the board of directors. The committees discussed here are not purely advisory or part of management; they are committees of directors that have the power to act to some extent in lieu of the board or directors.

Where a board of directors is large and meets relatively few times per year, it may be convenient to appoint an executive committee to perform the functions of the board of directors between meetings of the full board of directors. Executive committees are usually composed of inside directors who are officers or employees of the corporation (or at least are likely to be available upon call or upon short notice). The executive committee is probably the best known type of committee of directors; the earliest corporation statutes that recognized the need for committees of the board of directors apparently had this type of committee in mind. The scope of the authority of an executive committee is discussed below.

In the last thirty years, a strong trend has developed toward creating additional committees within the boards of directors of publicly held corporations. The three most popular standing committees are the audit committee, the compensation committee, and the nominating committee; in many corporations they are primarily or exclusively composed of outside directors, that may predominantly be composed of outside directors, i.e., directors not affiliated with management. Other committees that may predominantly be composed of outside directors include strategic planning, public policy, environmental compliance, management development, technology, and employee benefits. In addition, special ad hoc committees may be created to consider the merits of specific issues, such as derivative litigation filed on behalf of the corporation, requests for indemnification for expenses incurred by directors or officers in connection with litigation, or on the ratification of conflict of interest transactions between a director and the corporation.

Many state statutes permit committees of directors to be formed only if there is express authorization to do so in the articles of incorporation. The Model Business Corporation Act and modern statutes generally permit the creation of committees unless expressly prohibited by the articles of incorporation or bylaws. Many statutes require that the creation of a committee be approved by an absolute majority of the directors (as contrasted with a majority of the directors present at a meeting at which a quorum is present, the test applicable to normal directoral decisions). See MBCA (1984) § 8.25(b). The MBCA (1984) and the statutes of many states require that a committee consist of at least two directors, though some statutes permit a committee to consist of one or more members.

A question that has received a fair amount of legislative attention is what limits should be imposed on the delegation of power to directoral committees. The early statutes dealing primarily with executive committees limited the authority of committees to routine matters relating to the business of the corporation. Many statutes also expressly negated the power of committees to act on behalf of the board on such important or extraordinary matters as approving mergers, declaring a dividend, and authorizing the sale of shares. The concerns apparently were to obviate the possibility of a "runaway" committee and ensure that the full board of directors considered important matters. Section 8.25(e) of the Business Corporation Act (1984) contains a list of prohibited functions that was developed on a somewhat different theory: delegation of authority to committees should be prohibited only where the actions substantially affect the rights of shareholders among themselves as shareholders and are irrevocable when completed, are likely to become irreversible within a brief period of time, or are likely to involve significant changes of position by others that cannot be rectified. The test basically is to prohibit delegation of important actions that cannot be overruled or overturned by the board of directors. Among the nondelegable matters listed in section 8.25(e) are authorizing distributions, filling of vacancies on the board of directors, amending bylaws, authorizing the repurchase of shares, authorizing the issuance of shares, or recommending approval of transactions that the statute requires be approved by the shareholders.

[For unfamiliar terms see the Glossary]

CHAPTER ELEVEN

OFFICERS

§ 11.1 Statutory Designations of Officers

Traditional corporation statutes require every corporation to have certain designated officers. Typically, these statutes require that each corporation have a president, one or more vice presidents, a secretary, and a treasurer. The apparent need for four different officers in even small corporations is significantly tempered by the further provision that any two offices (other than secretary and president) may be held by the same individual. The requirement that the president and secretary be different individuals is apparently based on the perceived need for two officers to execute contracts and other formal documents; some statutes that require designated officers allow all the offices to be held by a single individual. Even though these statutes designate the titles of the offices, most of them do not purport to define what the roles of these officers are or what the inherent powers of the various offices are.

The Model Business Corporation Act (1984), following the Delaware statute, eliminates all mandatory titled officers. Section 8.40(a) provides simply that each corporation shall have the officers described in its bylaws or appointed by its board of directors. The reasons underlying this change were that some corporations desire to have officers with different titles, and there seems to be no good reason to require such corporations to fit into the statutory mold in this regard. Also, there was some concern that implications of authority might be drawn from the statutory titles that might be inconsistent with the corporation's desires.

The Model Business Corporation Act (1984) did find it necessary to define the duties of one corporate officer in section 8.40(c). The responsibility for preparing minutes of meetings and authenticating records referred to in that section are traditionally viewed as part of the responsibility of the secretary of a corporation, and the MBCA uses the designation "secretary" in the statute when referring to the officer with those responsibilities. MBCA (1984) § 1.40(20). However, it is not necessary that a corporation use this designation for the officer with this responsibility. The definition of "secretary" in the MBCA is intended to be used only for internal cross references within the statute itself.

Closely held corporations tend to use traditional descriptions for specific offices. Thus, even in a corporation formed under the Model Act, the senior executive officer is likely to be designated as the "president," and the principal financial officer as the "treasurer."

Publicly held corporations usually use a different nomenclature for senior officers. Officers are usually given titles such as chief executive officer (CEO), chief operating officer (COO), chief legal officer (CLO), and chief financial officer (CFO). The chief executive officer is generally viewed to be the title of the individual ultimately in charge of the management of the business; that person is often, but not always, also designated as the "chairman of the board of directors." Publicly held corporations in traditional states that designate the titles of officers usually use this designation and may assign the statutory office of president to an intermediate management position rather than the CEO.

§ 11.2 Express Authority and Power to Act In General

The source of express authority of corporate officers should first be sought in the state's business corporation act, second in the corporation's articles of incorporation, third in the corporate bylaws and, fourth, in corporate resolutions adopted by the board of directors. The first two sources rarely shed light on the authority of officers. As described above, even the older statutes that designate required offices do not typically describe the authority of those officers. A typical statutory provision (section 50 of the 1969 Model Act) simply provides that each designated officer "shall have such authority and perform such duties in the management of the corporation as may be provided in the bylaws, or as may be determined by resolution of the board of directors not inconsistent with the bylaws." Compare the similar language of section 8.41 of the Model Business Corporation Act (1984). Modern articles of incorporation generally do not refer at all to corporate officers, so that one is remitted to the bylaws and to express resolutions of the board. Bylaw provisions are usually fairly general and give little specific or reliable practical guidance (see § 11.3 of this Nutshell), so that as a practical matter express authority is apt to be found solely in authorizing resolutions of the board of directors.

In addition to express authority, corporate officers possess implied actual or apparent authority, either from the nature of the office held or the manner in which business was conducted in the past. Finally, amorphous doctrines of "ratification," "estoppel," or "unjust enrichment" may sometimes allow third persons to hold corporations responsible for actions by officers despite the absence of express, implied, actual, or apparent authority when the action occurred. These various sources of authority are discussed in the sections that follow.

§ 11.3 Roles of Corporate Officers

The following descriptions of roles of corporate officers are drawn from model bylaws intended for use under a statute that requires designated officers, and therefore represent normal "boilerplate" descriptions.

(1) The president is "the principal executive officer of the corporation" and, subject to the control of the board, "in general supervises and controls the business and affairs of the corporation." He or she is the proper officer to execute corporate contracts, certificates for securities, and other corporate instruments.

(2) The vice president performs the duties of the president in the absence of that officer or in the event of his or her death, incompetence, or inability or refusal to act. Vice presidents act in the order designated at the time of their election, or in the absence of designation, in the order of their election. Vice presidents may also execute share certificates or other corporate instruments.

(3) The secretary has several different functions: he or she keeps the minutes of the proceedings of shareholders and the board of directors, sees that all notices are duly given as required by statute and the bylaws, acts as custodian of the corporate records and of the corporate seal and sees that the seal of the corporation is properly affixed on authorized documents, keeps a register of the names and post office addresses of each shareholder, signs, along with the president or vice president, certificates for shares of the corporation, and is in general charge of the stock transfer books of the corporation.

(4) The treasurer has "charge and custody of and is responsible for" all funds and securities of the corporation, and receives, gives receipts for, and deposits, all moneys due and payable to the corporation. The treasurer may be required to give a bond to ensure the faithful performance of his or her duties.

Traditional statutes also usually provide that the board of directors may assign additional duties to any statutory corporate officer, and the president may also assign additional duties to any vice president, the secretary, or the treasurer. In states that designate titles of officers in the statute, corporations may create assistant secretaries, assistant treasurers, and other officers not specifically referred to in the statute.

In publicly held corporations, the roles of CEOs, COOs, and the like may be described in organization manuals or the like that describe the management structure for the specific corporation. These manuals typically are prepared by the management rather than the board of directors.

§ 11.4 Express Authority Delegated by Board of Directors

When a person negotiates with a corporation, he or she deals with a flesh-and-blood human being. That person may represent, either expressly or by implication, either that she is authorized to bind the corporation, or that approval of a more senior officer is required. How does one make certain that the corporation—a fictional entity—is in fact bound by a specific transaction? It is possible, of course, to trust to appearances, implied authority, general descriptions of authority set forth in the previous section, blind luck, and the like, but that is very dangerous since litigation may be necessary to prove that the person in fact had authority to bind the corporation, and, because the doctrines are vague and amorphous, it is always possible that one may lose.

The most foolproof way to ensure that the corporation is bound by a specific transaction is to require the person purporting to act for the corporation to deliver, prior to the closing of the transaction, a certified copy of a resolution of the board of directors authorizing the transaction in question and directing the named officer to enter into the transaction on behalf of the corporation. The certificate should be executed by the secretary or an assistant secretary of the corporation, the corporate seal should be affixed, and the certificate should recite the date of the meeting (or a statement that the resolution was approved by unanimous written consent) and quote the resolution itself. The corporation is estopped to deny the truthfulness of facts stated in a secretary's certificate relating to the records in his or her custody. Or to put the issue in a somewhat different way, keeping and certifying corporate records is within the actual authority of the secretary and the act of certification therefore binds the corporation. Further, since the binding nature of the certificate rests on an estoppel, an inquiry into the background behind the certificate may possibly destroy the basis of the estoppel. And a third person who has reason to know that the facts recited in the certificate are not true is not able to rely on a theory of estoppel. However, in the absence of such knowledge, one can deal with a corporate officer with confidence upon the production of a duly executed secretarial certificate. This procedure is fine, so far as it goes, but it does not cover many small transactions that are never taken before the board for review and approval. Of course, if the corporation receives the benefit of a contract it will be bound on a theory of ratification, and will not be able to lack of authority.

Attorneys required to give an opinion that a major transaction has been duly approved by a corporation will normally review articles of incorporation and bylaws, and will inspect the minutes of the meeting of the board of directors at which the action was approved. However, they normally rely on the certificate of the secretary of the corporation that the minutes accurately reflect who was present and what action was taken; such reliance seems entirely consistent with the attorneys' obligation to investigate with due diligence.

§ 11.5 Inherent Power of the Corporate President

Most non-lawyers are apt to think that the person holding the office of president of a corporation is the most important single person within the corporation and that he or she therefore must have authority to enter into normal business transactions, and probably has authority to enter into extraordinary transactions as well. In fact, these widely held views are often erroneous: the present state of the law in many jurisdictions is that the president has only limited authority which may not extend beyond minor, ordinary, routine transactions. Essentially, the focus of power to approve more significant transactions is in the board of directors, not the president.

This narrow construction of the president's authority is based primarily on older cases and may readily lead to injustice. Persons relying on reasonable appearances may discover that their reliance was ill-advised, and that the corporation is not obligated on a relatively routine transaction authorized by the corporate president. Persons aware of the rule are forced virtually to insult the president by demanding an exhibit of his or her authority.

Some courts have broadened the implied authority of the president or chief executive officer, and there appears to be a general trend in this direction particularly in large, publicly held corporations. Broader authority of the president is likely to be found in cases where the corporation later regrets the transaction and seeks to hide behind the lack of authority of its nominal chief officer. Some courts have suggested that a president presumptively has any powers which the board could give him or her. Others have given that officer authority to enter into transactions "arising in the usual and regular course of business," and construe that phrase broadly. This may include, for example, the power to hire or discharge all employees. However, the inherent authority test is at best uncertain in its application to specific facts so that all unusual or extraordinary contracts should be authorized by the directors—including such matters as lifetime or long-time employment contracts and settlement of material litigation.

§ 11.6 Implied Authority, Apparent Authority, Ratification, Estoppel, and Unjust Enrichment

Even where the authority of an officer purporting to act for a corporation is not within the inherent authority of officer, and has not been authorized by a previous action of the board of directors, the doctrines of ratification, estoppel, implied actual authority, or apparent authority may be available to a third person seeking to hold the corporation. These various doctrines, described below, are closely interrelated.

(a) *Ratification and Related Doctrines.* The board of directors of a corporation may learn that an officer has entered into a transaction in the past without being specifically authorized to do so. If the board does not promptly attempt to rescind or revoke the actions previously taken by the officer, it is probable that the corporation will be bound on the transaction on a theory of "ratification." Ratification may arise merely from knowledge of the transaction and failure to disaffirm or rescind it; usually, however, there are also elements of retention of benefits by the corporation and/or known reliance by the third party on the existence of the contract. "Estoppel" or "unjust enrichment" might equally well be found in such cases. Estoppel differs from ratification mainly in that attention is placed on the reliance of the third person, and the inequitableness of permitting the corporation to pull the rug out from under a person who reasonably relied on the corporation's silence.

(b) *Implied Authority.* Most problems involving implied authority of corporate officers arise when the third person seeks to hold the corporation on a current transaction by showing that the directors accepted or ratified prior similar transactions in the past. The argument is that the acquiescence of the board of directors indicates that an actual grant of authority was informally made. The same facts which support a finding of ratification of transaction A_1 may be used to conclude that a later similar transaction, A_2, was impliedly authorized. This is, of course, implied actual authority.

(c) *Apparent Authority.* Apparent authority bears somewhat the same relationship to the concept of estoppel as implied authority bears to ratification. To show apparent authority, one must prove such conduct on the part of the principal as would lead a reasonably prudent person, using diligence and discretion, to suppose that the agent has the authority he or she purports to exercise. A third person, knowing that an officer has exercised authority in the past with the consent of the board of directors, may continue to rely on the appearance of authority, and the doctrine of apparent authority may protect that reliance. For apparent authority to exist, there must be some conduct on the part of the principal, i.e., the corporation, which creates the appearance of authority; a mere representation by an agent that he or she possesses the requisite authority is not sufficient. However, conduct may consist of silence when the principal is aware that the agent represents the existence of authority, or it may consist of acquiescence in, and ratification of, acts performed in the past.

The principal practical difference between apparent authority and implied actual authority is that for apparent authority, the third person must show that he or she was aware of the prior acts or holding out and relied on appearances, while implied actual authority may be found even in the absence of knowledge or reliance on the part of third persons. However, the same conduct may often be cited to prove either implied actual authority or apparent authority.

* * *

In view of the close interrelationship between the various doctrines referred to in this section, it is not surprising to find that courts sometimes slip from one doctrine to another, sometimes perhaps not being fully aware of the differences.

The various doctrines discussed in this section may be applicable to situations other than silence and acquiescence. For example, a corporation may expressly ratify a transaction, or a corporation may be estopped to deny that a transaction was authorized if it expressly creates the appearance of authority but withholds actual authority. Similarly, implied authority or apparent authority may arise from a variety of affirmative circumstances as well as silence on the part of the directors.

Courts may be reluctant to find ratification of an unauthorized act by an officer where the act is fraudulent, unfair to minority shareholders, or against public policy. Often, in such situations, the court may conclude that the corporation lacked the requisite full knowledge to ratify the act. Of course, to avoid such an act the directors must offer to return any benefits obtained by the corporation.

§ 11.7   Fiduciary Duties of Officers and Agents

Corporate officers and agents owe a fiduciary duty to the corporation. The common law standard imposed involves a high degree of honesty, good faith, and diligence because corporate officers and agents render services for pay, and are often full-time employees. The officer or agent should act for the sole benefit of the corporation and give to it his or her best uncorrupt business judgment. Full disclosure of possibly conflicting transactions may be required, and the officer or agent may be found to hold in trust for the corporation profits made personally in competition with, or at the expense of, the corporation. When all is said and done, however, general statements about the scope of fiduciary duties rarely decide specific cases.

Section 8.42 of the Revised Model Business Corporation Act imposes a standard of conduct for officers that is essentially identical to that imposed on directors. See Chapter 14 of this Nutshell. However, the scope of an officer's obligation to the corporation is determined in part by the nature of the performance required of him or her. The duty of subordinate officers or agents may be somewhat narrower than the analogous duty of a director. However, most of the litigation relating to fiduciary duties involve directors, and such cases are often relied on to establish the duties of high-level or managing corporate officers and agents.

A corporate officer or agent may also be liable to the corporation if he or she exceeds his or her actual authority and binds the corporation in a transaction with a third person. Such a transaction, of course, must be within the officer's or agent's apparent authority if the corporation is to be bound.

§ 11.8 Liability of Officers and Agents to Third Parties

A corporate officer or employee who acts within the scope of his or her authority as the corporation's representative in a consensual transaction is not personally liable on the transaction if he or she acted solely as an agent. This statement of a basic agency principle is little more than a truism; what is significant are ways in which a corporate officer or employee may, despite this general agency principle, make himself or herself liable on a corporate obligation. There are several possibilities:

First, the agent may expressly guarantee the performance by the corporation, intending to be personally bound on the obligation. Such a guarantee may be written or oral, and may or may not be supported by consideration, depending on the sequence of events and what is requested. Of course, to be enforceable, a promise must be supported by consideration. Whether or not it must also be in writing usually depends on the proper scope of the provision of the statute of frauds dealing with promises to answer for the indebtedness of another. For example, an oral promise by the president of a corporation to a supplier of merchandise that he or she would assume the obligation of payment if goods were delivered might be enforced despite the statute of frauds on the theory that the president was the primary obligor. Similarly, the so-called "main purpose" or "leading object" exceptions to the suretyship provision of the statute of frauds may in some circumstances make an oral guarantee by a corporate officer enforceable.

Second, the agent may not intend to be personally bound, but may in fact bind himself or herself by creating the impression that he or she is negotiating on an individual rather than corporate basis, or by executing the agreement in such a way as to indicate personal liability. Even if the existence of the corporation is disclosed, joint liability of the corporation and the officer may be created because of informality in the manner of execution. The proper manner for an officer to execute a document in the name of, and on behalf of, a corporation is as follows:

ABC Corporation

By:_____
President

Any variation from this form is dangerous, since the mere designation of the corporate office may be deemed a description of the signing party rather than evidence that he or she signed as agent. For example, the following form of execution:

ABC Corporation

_____
President

is ambiguous since the corporation and the president may be either joint obligors or the president may have intended to sign only in a representational capacity. The word "president" does not resolve the ambiguity since it may be either an identification of the individual obligor or an indication that he or she signed only as a representative. In cases involving ambiguous forms of execution courts appear to be more willing to allow corporate officers to testify about the "real intention of the parties" in executing general contracts than in executing promissory notes.

Third, if an officer negotiates a transaction without disclosing he or she is acting as an agent on behalf of a corporation, the actor is personally liable to the third person on general agency principles relating to undisclosed principals.

Fourth, if the agent is acting beyond the scope of authority, he or she may be personally liable on the transaction unless the corporation takes the agent off the hook by ratifying the transaction. A person acting as an agent generally warrants he has authority to bind his principal to the transaction; this principle, of course, does not apply where the third person is aware the officer or agent lacks authority and the transaction must be submitted to the board of directors for approval.

Finally, liability may arise because imposed by statute. Failure to pay franchise taxes or to publish a notice upon incorporation may, in some circumstances, lead to individual as well as corporate liability on corporate obligations. The federal income tax statutes provide for a penalty of one hundred per cent of the tax for failing to pay over income taxes withheld from employees. This penalty tax may be imposed on "any person required to collect, truthfully account for, and pay over" the tax. (IRC § 6672.) There are perhaps other statutes as well that impose personal liability for failing to comply with the statute.

§ 11.9 Imputation of Knowledge to Corporation

In the foregoing discussion, there have been several references to "corporate knowledge" or understanding that appear to ignore the fictional nature of a corporation. Of course, a corporation can "know" or "have notice of" something only if one or more persons who represent the corporation know or have notice of the thing. Usually, knowledge acquired by a corporate officer or employee while acting in furtherance of the corporate business or in the course of his or her employment is imputed to the corporation. Thus, if the president knows of a transaction, the corporation ratifies it if the corporation accepts the benefits of the transaction, even though one or more directors or other officers may not know all the details. Service of process on an authorized agent of the corporation will support a default judgment against the corporation even though the agent fails to forward the papers to the corporation's attorney.

Difficult problems arise when it is sought to impute knowledge of an agent to the corporation if the agent is acting adversely to the corporation. Generally information or knowledge may be imputed from an agent who has ultimate responsibility for the transaction to the corporation even if the agent is acting adversely to and in fraud of the corporation. Similarly, if a corporate officer learns that a low level employee is defrauding the corporation, the officer's knowledge may be imputed to the corporation even though the officer does not disclose the information to other officers or directors.

Generally, an agent's wrongful intention may be imputed to a corporation so that a corporation is subject to civil or criminal prosecution, including prosecution for traditional crimes such as murder or rape. Of course, for the corporation to be prosecuted such acts must be connected with, or be in furtherance of, the corporation's business and the agent's position with the corporation must be such as to justify imputation of the wrongful intent to the corporation.

§ 11.10   Tenure of Officers and Agents

Corporate officers and agents generally serve at the will of the person or board having authority to elect or appoint the officers or agents. Corporate officers are elected or appointed by the board of directors, and corporation statutes generally provide that they may be removed by the board of directors with or without cause. MBCA (1984) § 8.43(b). So far as agents appointed by the president or chief executive officer are concerned, the power to discharge is implicit in the power to employ. Corporate bylaws usually explicitly grant the power to remove or discharge as part of the power to appoint.

Many state statutes refer to the "election" or "appointment" of officers. The Model Business Corporation Act (1984) uses only the word "appointment," reserving the word "election" for the selection of directors.

Of course, an officer or agent may be given an employment contract, and removal of that officer or agent may give rise to a cause of action for breach of contract. Typically, the remedy for breach of an employment contract is damages and not reinstatement. Further, the mere election or appointment of an officer or agent, even for a definite term, is not usually held of itself to give rise to a contract right. MBCA (1984) § 8.44. The validity of employment contracts in light of corporate bylaw provisions is discussed in the following section.

§ 11.11   Long–Term Employment Contracts

Long-term or lifetime employment contracts have given rise to litigation primarily in the context of closely held corporations.

(1) *Validity.* Corporate bylaws usually provide that officers are to be elected or appointed by the board of directors for a term of one year. Does that bylaw restrict or limit the power of a corporation to grant an officer an employment contract extending beyond the term of that office? Generally, the answer is "no" since an officer or employee may be relieved of his duties at any time even if he has an employment contract. Of course, the corporation may be liable for breach of contract for the premature termination of the employment period. MBCA (1984) § 8.44(b). On a parity of reasoning, long-term contracts, e.g., leases, have been upheld despite the fact that they "bind" subsequent boards of directors. A second argument may also be made if the board has power, as most boards of directors do, to amend the bylaws. An employment contract for more than one year may be deemed to be an implied amendment of the bylaws by the board, since the board could first amend the bylaw and then enter into a long term employment contract. While some courts have accepted this argument, there is a practical

problem with implied amendments of bylaws since one cannot then rely on the written bylaws as being the current and complete rules governing the corporation's internal affairs.

(2) *Lifetime Employment Contracts.* The claim that a person has been given a life time employment contract by a closely held corporation has been treated with hostility by the courts. Claims that a lifetime employment contract was created are usually based on oral statements within the context of a family-run business. While such a contract is not within the statute of frauds, courts may feel that the factual basis for such an open-ended and long-term commitment is inherently implausible. Also, lifetime contracts may subject a corporation to a substantial liability which may run for a long and indefinite period during which circumstances may substantially change. Even where the promise of lifetime employment is unambiguous, courts may refuse to enforce the contract on the ground the person authorizing the arrangement had neither actual nor apparent authority to do so. However, there is nothing inherently illegal about a lifetime contract if it is duly authorized by the board of directors

(3) *Discharge for Cause.* It is clear that an officer or employee with a valid employment contract may nevertheless be discharged for cause. "Cause" may consist of acts of dishonesty, negligence, refusal to obey reasonable orders, refusal to follow reasonable rules, or a variety of other acts such as engaging in an unprovoked fight. In effect, this conduct constitutes a breach of an implied—if not express—covenant in the employment contract. Of course, officers that do not have employment contracts may usually be discharged with or without cause.

(4) *Basis of Compensation.* Employees sometimes request that they be compensated on the basis of a percentage of sales or corporate earnings or profits rather than at a flat rate. No particular legal problem is raised by these

arrangements, though questions sometimes arise as to how earnings and profits are to be measured. The simple phrase "net profits" may be ambiguous and its meaning elusive.

(5) *Miscellaneous.* Employment contracts for highly paid personnel in publicly held corporations often provide for deferred compensation, options to purchase shares at bargain prices, reimbursement of business expenses, and other tax-related benefits. The high levels of compensation for CEOs of public corporations have been a matter of political controversy during the 1990s. Congress has acted to limit income tax deductions for salaries in excess of $1.0 million dollars per year in certain situations.

In the closely held corporation, an employment agreement may be an integral part of the basic planning arrangement between shareholders. Terms relating to employment may be placed in shareholder's agreements so that they will be binding on the other shareholders as well as on the corporation. There is a greater possibility of specific performance of a shareholders' agreement than of a simple employment contract; and it is therefore possible that a court may order reinstatement of the shareholder/employee rather than damages. Specific enforcement may be significant in a close corporation where the right to participate in management is an important aspect of the control arrangement agreed to by the shareholders.

[For unfamiliar terms see the Glossary]

CHAPTER TWELVE

THE CLOSELY HELD CORPORATION

§ 12.1 The Meaning of "Closely Held" and "Publicly Held"

The term "closely held corporation" normally signifies that the corporation has only a few shareholders. This simple definition of "closely held" seems intuitively satisfactory, but creates a serious problem at the margin. There are nearly four million active corporations in the United States; when these corporations are classified solely by the number of shareholders, they form a continuum from one-owner corporations, at one end of the spectrum, to corporations with hundreds of thousands shareholders at the other. It is not possible to define precisely what is meant by a "few" except on a purely arbitrary basis. Whatever number is chosen to define "few", there will always be indistinguishable corporations that have precisely one more shareholder than whatever number has been chosen.

A more useful definition may be obtained by first defining the essential characteristic of a "publicly held" corporation and then defining a "closely held" corporation negatively as a corporation that is not "publicly held." It turns out that this approach leads to a more useful classification system. A "publicly held" corporation may be defined as one that has a sufficiently large number of shareholders that there has developed an active established market in which shares are traded. The existence of an active trading market for shares means that outside investors always have a power to "enter" or "exit" simply by buying or selling shares in these public trading markets. In contrast, where an active trading market for shares does not exist, the power to "enter" or "exit" is usually circumscribed and may not exist at all. This is the essential difference between publicly held and closely held corporations.

Under the definition suggested here, most closely held corporations will be small and will be owned by one or a few persons. However, some may be large in terms of assets and may have a substantial number of passive shareholders. But so long as there is no active trading market for the ownership interests, the business does not have the most fundamental characteristic of a publicly held business.

This chapter discusses the special problems of closely held corporations. Chapter 13 discusses publicly held corporations.

§ 12.2 Management and Control of the Closely Held Corporation

It is useful to consider first problems of management and control in a closely held corporation in which there has been no advance planning. It is assumed that there are two or more shareholders, and that one shareholder (or an allied group of shareholders) owns a majority of the shares of the corporation. There are thus "majority shareholders" and "minority shareholders" and in a closely held corporation the difference between these two groups of shareholders may be great.

In the absence of advancing planning, management and control of a closely held corporation is governed by the "default" provisions of the corporation statutes or, as it is sometimes phrased, the "standard model" of the corporation. In this standard model, the majority shareholders have the power to determine who will serve on the board of directors and therefore they have complete control over management decisions and decisions with respect to distributions. Any right that a minority shareholder has to participate in decision-making is at the sufferance of the majority. Furthermore, in the standard model a minority shareholder does not have the power to compel either the purchase of his shares by the corporation or by other shareholders or the dissolution of the enterprise. Dissolution requires the affirmative vote of a majority of the outstanding voting shares. Essentially, therefore, the standard model places broad powers in the majority shareholders and gives minority shareholders no assurance of the right to participate in the financial returns of the business, to participate in decision-making, or to withdraw from the enterprise at will. Any rights to "voice" or "exit" on the part of minority shareholders exist in the unplanned closely held corporation only at the sufferance of the majority shareholders.

It is of course possible (and quite common) for majority and minority shareholders to operate the corporation cooperatively and for their mutual benefit with little or no dissension or disagreement. The most serious problems in closely held corporations occur when this is not the case, when there is dissension between the majority shareholders and the minority, or when for some reason the majority shareholders have exercised their power to exclude some or all minority shareholders from participation in the enterprise.

When dissension exists the practical importance of the control of a corporation cannot be overstated. Control means the power to determine what business the corporation should engage in, how it shall be pursued, who will run the day-to-day affairs of the business, who will be employed by the corporation and who will not, how much each employee will be paid, and what his or her responsibilities will be. The board of directors may determine that all shareholders will be employees of the corporation, or that some will not be so employed. If a shareholder-employee does something that irritates the majority shareholder, she may be fired as an employee, thereby losing her salary. Since the payment of dividends is essentially discretionary with the board of directors, control also means power to make distributions to shareholders, to determine their amount, or to withhold all such distributions. Majority shareholders may omit dividends but continue to pay themselves a salary as officers and employees, thereby depriving minority shareholders of all return from their investment but continuing to receive benefits from the corporation themselves.

There are of course limits and exceptions to this general picture of total control by the majority. Cumulative voting rights may in some states give substantial minority shareholders a place on the board of directors. (See § 9.6 of this Nutshell.) Suits to compel the payment of a dividend or to involuntarily dissolve a corporation may succeed in sufficiently egregious cases. Come the millenium and the corporation is voluntarily dissolved, minority shareholders are entitled to participate in liquidating distributions. In addition, some courts have imposed fiduciary duties on controlling shareholders when dealing with minority shareholders, though Delaware courts have refused to do so. See § 12.11 of this Nutshell. However, as a generalization minority rights are virtually non-existent in the standard form closely held corporation.

§ 12.3 "Oppression" and "Freeze–Outs"

Oppression and freeze-outs may be major problems in closely held corporations. These terms refer to the actual use by controlling shareholders of the power they possess to exclude minority shareholders from participation in the management of the business and to deprive them of significant economic return on their shares. The term "oppression" is a comparative term that assumes a minority shareholder originally had certain minimum rights of participation that she is now being deprived of by the majority shareholders. This minimum right of participation is usually judged, where applicable, by the terms on which the minority shareholder originally became involved with the corporation or the promises which induced her to invest. "Freeze-outs" (or "squeeze-outs" as they are often referred to) entail the use of control to deprive the minority of all benefits of share ownership in an effort to persuade the minority to sell their shares at an unfavorable price.

Oppression and freeze-outs are possible because of the combination, first, of the power of controlling shareholders to exclude minority shareholders from participation in the financial benefits of the corporation and, second, the absence of any meaningful right of "exit" from the corporation. In theory, the shares of stock of any corporation are freely transferable. Shares of publicly held corporations are of course traded in large and active securities markets and therefore are salable simply by a telephone call to one's broker. The reality is far different when one is dealing with shares of a closely held corporation. The power to sell shares is meaningless if there is practically no one interested in buying them, or if the only persons who are interested is willing to offer only a ridiculously low price. And that is usually the case with respect to closely held shares in oppression and freeze-out situations.

A minority shareholder who is receiving little or no financial return from the corporation can dispose of his shares only through voluntary transactions with the corporation, with one or more other shareholders, or with some outside third party. However, because closely held shares cannot be purchased or sold in an active market, the value of minority shares is a matter of negotiation and judgment. Neither majority nor minority shareholders have an obligation to pay a generous price for the shares if they decide to purchase them at all. On the contrary, they have strong economic incentives to offer a shareholder who desires to sell a low price because they receive little immediate benefit from the purchase of minority shares:

(1) Controlling shareholders usually do not need the additional minority shares to cement or preserve that control. By purchasing minority shares they do not materially improve their economic position with the corporation but they do reduce the amount of their personal liquid assets. Controlling shareholders who do decide to purchase minority shares will normally do so by arranging for the corporation to make the purchase.

(2) Similarly, minority shareholders have little incentive to purchase minority shares since the purchase does not generally improve their position significantly vis á vis each other or the majority shareholder. They become larger minority shareholders. As is the case with the controlling shareholders, their investment in the corporation increases but their influence does not.

(3) Finally, if the corporate shareholders have no incentive to pay a fair price for minority shares, there is little reason for them to cause the corporation to purchase the shares either, since the corporation is in effect a surrogate of the shareholders in this connection. Where a purchase has been agreed upon by some or all of the shareholders it is usually desirable for the corporation to make the purchase for tax reasons and to preserve the remaining shareholders' proportionate interest in the corporation.

Shareholders do have an incentive to eliminate minority shareholders if they can do so at an acceptably low price. Disaffected minority shareholders have rights that may prove troublesome in practice. They have the power to inspect corporate books and records and to file direct or derivative lawsuits charging the controlling shareholders with self-dealing or the breach of fiduciary duties. They may claim the directors are acting in bad faith when they refuse to pay dividends. Disaffected minority shareholders may become, in short, real nuisances, and their elimination at a favorable price is therefore attractive. Further, if the corporation is dissolved and its assets distributed, all shareholders are entitled to a pro rata portion of liquidating distributions; elimination of minority interests increase the amounts received by the remaining shareholders upon dissolution. As a result, controlling shareholders desire to eliminate minority interests, if the price is "right." However, from the selfish interest of the other shareholders, there is little incentive to offer much more than the nuisance value of the minority shares.

Controlling shareholders may "soften up" minority shareholders by depriving them of all return on their shares for an extended period before opening negotiations with them. The controlling shareholders are in no hurry. Time is usually on their side. While there is a market of sorts for minority shares, it is a distress market not at all like a market involving the traditional willing buyer and willing seller contemplated by economic theory.

(4) Sales of minority interests to third parties also are unlikely to occur unless the purchaser is acceptable to the controlling shareholders and is able to negotiate an arrangement with them. For one thing, most closely held corporations include share transfer restrictions designed to ensure that controlling shareholders have a veto over who may purchase the shares. See § 9.17. Even where the closely held minority shares are not subject to legal restriction, third parties are unlikely to be interested in purchasing them, since the purchaser may find himself in exactly

the same position as the shareholder desiring to sell. It is unlikely that an outsider would even consider the purchase of minority shares without some assurances from the controlling shareholders, and the outsider may insist on reaching a firm agreement with the controlling shareholders. If an advance agreement with the controlling shareholders cannot be reached, the outsider will most likely look elsewhere for an acceptable investment, though conceivably the outsider may agree to purchase the shares at distress prices as a speculative gamble.

§ 12.4   Advance Planning in Closely Held Corporations

Law and economics scholars tend to view problems of oppression and freeze-outs in closely held corporations as of little practical importance since rational investors may readily obtain protection against such tactics by negotiation in advance. It may be helpful to consider briefly the typical negotiation model favored by these scholars. An investor is considering whether to invest in a closely held corporation as a minority shareholder. The potential investor has alternative investment opportunities and is therefore free to "walk" away from the negotiations if a satisfactory deal with the majority shareholders cannot be agreed upon. Similarly, the corporation is able to attract other similarly situated investors if this specific investor cannot be satisfied. There is arms length negotiation by parties who are under no compulsion to enter into the transaction and who are rational, adequately informed and under no compulsion to enter into the transaction. In this model the parties may be trusted to hammer out a mutually acceptable arrangement with adequate protections for the investor/minority shareholder. If an acceptable arrangement cannot be worked out, there will simply be no transaction. In this model, judicial or legislative intervention is not justified since whatever arrangements are agreed to by the consenting parties should be respected.

There can be little criticism of this conclusion where the assumptions that underlie this model are valid. However, these assumptions are by no means always true. Regrettably every corporation lawyer regularly encounters situations in which for one reason or another minority shareholders do not have adequate contractual protection against abusive conduct by controlling shareholders. An unsophisticated investor may be overly trusting of the controlling shareholder. An investor who is in amity with the controlling shareholders at the outset may see no reason to negotiate for protections. However, over a period of time changes in personnel are likely through deaths or withdrawals, and the possibility that adverse and hostile interests will develop within a closely held corporation should therefore be quite foreseeable.

Further, in some situations, particularly those involving family corporations, no advance planning may take place at all. The paradigm situation is the unexpected death of the controlling or sole shareholder in a successful business leaving two or three heirs who promptly form controlling and minority factions. A surprisingly large number of oppression and freeze-out cases involve family corporations. While perhaps controlling shareholders may be criticized for not making rational plans for succession, these cases nevertheless are not uncommon.

§ 12.5 Traditional Protection Devices in Closely Held Corporations

Oppression and freeze-outs may be avoided through the use of a variety of traditional and accepted control devices. A variety of devices are discussed in chapter 9 of this Nutshell. A right of "exit" may be granted to minority shareholders through the device of option or buy/sell agreements. See §§ 9.17 through 9.25 of this Nutshell. A right to a "voice" in corporate affairs may be assured through shareholder voting agreements, voting trusts, and the use of different classes of shares that grant different voting rights.

Care must be taken that a control device will in fact be respected and will protect the non-controlling shareholders. Section 8.10 of this Nutshell has discussed the limited validity of shareholders' agreements *inter se* that restrict the discretion of directors; that rule of law of uncertain scope obviously limits the usefulness of a simple contract as a control device. On the other hand, many state corporation statutes validate shareholder agreements that eliminate or restrict boards of directors. In some states, these agreements are validated only for corporations that have made the special close corporation election; in others these agreements are valid if they are in writing and agreed to by all the shareholders. Perhaps the most general and useful provision in this regard is section 7.41 of the Model Business Corporation Act (1984), approved in 1991. This section is discussed below. See § 12.14.

§ 12.6 Classes of Shares as Control Devices

A most flexible and fool-proof device to establish representation on the board of directors of a corporation or a veto power over certain types of decisions is the use of different classes of shares, usually different classes of common shares (see generally §§ 7.12, 9.16 of this Nutshell). Classes of common shares may be used effectively to create a variety of different control devices independent of the financial interests in the corporation. The following examples illustrate the flexibility of this device:

(1) A corporation is to have two shareholders, one putting in $100,000, the other $50,000. They desire to share equally in control but in the ratio of their contributions (2:1) for financial purposes. The attorney suggests that an equal number of shares of two classes of common

stock, Class A common and Class B common, be authorized. Each class is entitled to elect two directors, but the dividend and liquidation rights of the Class A are twice those of Class B. The corporation then issues all the Class A common to one shareholder for 100,000 dollars and all the Class B common to the other shareholder for 50,000 dollars. In this structure, the S corporation election would be unavailable because of the two classes of stock but the desired financial relationship is ensured.

(2) Alternatively in the same situation, if shares with multiple votes per share are authorized in the particular state, the shares may be identical in all financial respects, with the class received by the smaller contributor having two votes per share and half the number of shares being issued. In this structure, the S corporation election is available, since different classes of stock do not disqualify a corporation from that election if the classes differ only in voting rights.

(3) A minority shareholder wishes to be assured of being treasurer of the corporation and to have a veto over all amendments to the articles of incorporation. The attorney suggests that a special class of common shares be issued to the minority shareholder, and the articles of incorporation provide that (1) the treasurer must be a holder of that class of shares, and (2) the articles may be amended only by an affirmative vote of two-thirds of each class of shares, voting by classes. In other respects the classes have equal rights.

(4) There are three shareholders, each contributing the same amount of capital, but C is also contributing the basic idea and wants the same voting power as A and B combined. One simple solution is to issue voting and non-voting common shares (with equal dividend and liquidation rights) in the following amounts:

	Voting	**Non-voting**
A	50	50
B	50	50
C	100	–0–

Somewhat the same result may be obtained by the use of nonvoting preferred shares or indebtedness rather than non-voting common shares. If the classes of shares differ other than in voting rights the S corporation election is unavailable.

(4) A, B, and C have each contributed the same amount of capital, but A wants to be sure that B and C will not combine to oust her and cut off her income. The attorney suggests that A execute a five-year employment contract with the corporation guaranteeing her the specified income, renewable for a second five years at the option of A. To assure that A will be assured of a right to participate in the board deliberations, the attorney suggests that three classes of stock be created with identical financial rights but each with the power to elect one director. The S corporation election remains available to a corporation with this capital structure.

There seems to be little doubt about the validity of control arrangements based on different classes of shares. While there has been litigation on the outer bounds of the power to create specialized classes of shares, recent decisions are uniformly favorable. In perhaps the most startling case, Lehrman v. Cohen (Del.1966), the Delaware Supreme Court upheld a class of common shares which consisted of one share having a par value of $10; the share (1) could elect one of the five directors (the other four were elected by two equal factions), (2) was not entitled to receive dividends, (3) could share in the proceeds of dissolution only to the extent of the par value of the one share, and (4) could be redeemed by the corporation at any time by paying the shareholder the par value of the share, upon approval of four of the five directors. This share comes close to a naked vote completely divorced from ownership, yet was upheld. This one-share class was designed to avoid a potential deadlock between the two principal shareholders and was issued to the attorney representing the corporation; after several years, the attorney and one of the other two shareholders combined forces to take over working control of the corporation, a situation which was cemented by a long term employment contract for the attorney. This arrangement was upheld in its entirety. (See § 9.16 of this Nutshell for a discussion of the same case in a somewhat different context.)

§ 12.7   Increased Quorum and Voting Requirements

A second useful device in effectuating shareholder control arrangements is increased voting requirements in order to give minority interests a veto power. This veto power may be applicable at the shareholder level, at the board of directors level, or both. In all states today, it is possible to increase the percentage needed to approve a measure to any desired number; usually unanimity is imposed, but in some circumstances a lesser percentage may be sufficient or have the same effect. While a requirement of unanimity was held invalid by a few courts, most notably Benintendi v. Kenton Hotel (N.Y.1945), the language of modern statutes is broadly permissive, and there is no doubt today about the validity of increased voting requirements.

It is usually important to increase both the quorum requirement and the minimum vote requirement in order to make sure that it is impossible for the corporation to act without the assent of all shareholders or all directors. Where the voting requirement has not been increased it is sometimes possible for the minority shareholder or director to prevent action by staying away from the meeting if that makes it impossible to obtain a quorum. In one case, such conduct was held to constitute a breach of fiduciary duty. Gearing v. Kelly (N.Y.1962). This decision seems questionable given the dynamics of the closely held corporation.

If the increased voting requirement is set forth in the articles of incorporation or bylaws, the provision creating the increased voting requirement should itself expressly be made non-amendable except by the increased voting requirement. Some state statutes provide this protection automatically, but many do not. See MBCA (1984) § 7.27(b).

The use of classified common shares and unanimity requirements through enhanced voting and quorum requirements increase the possibility of a deadlock within the corporation.

§ 12.8 Deadlocks

A "deadlock" involves situations in which a closely held corporation finds itself on dead center and unable to act. Deadlocks may readily be avoided by advance planning. The fact that cases involving deadlocks continue to arise with some regularity simply demonstrates that planning sometimes does not occur when it should.

A corporation is potentially subject to deadlock in a variety of circumstances. (1) Two factions may each own exactly fifty per cent of the outstanding shares. Equal ownership may be preplanned, e.g., by two equal partners deciding to incorporate their ongoing business, or by two entrepreneurs deciding they wish to share equally in all aspects of the business. It may also arise from planning decisions by a prior shareholder, as when she gives or bequeaths one half of her holdings to each of two descendants. (2) There are an even number of directors, and two factions each have the power to select the same number of directors. (3) A minority shareholder has retained a veto power through the device of increased quorum or voting requirements and there is a substantial disagreement among the shareholders. In each of these situations, the corporation may in effect be unable to make any decision at all, and thus be unable to function as a corporation.

A deadlock may occur either at the shareholders' level or at the directors' level. A deadlock does not necessarily mean that the corporation is unable to continue to conduct its business. If the shareholders are deadlocked, the corporation may continue to operate, since the board of directors in office when the deadlock arose remain in office indefinitely and may continue to manage the business. While a deadlock at the directoral level may prevent the corporation from functioning, it is more likely that some corporate officers, usually the president, general manager, and treasurer, may continue to operate the business either alone or in cooperation with each other, often to the complete exclusion of the deadlocked board of directors and the shareholders. At a subsequent election of directors the deadlock may be broken, though that is probably unlikely.

The most practical solution for the truly deadlocked corporation is usually for one faction to buy out the other in a negotiated transaction. If they cannot agree on a sale, they may be able to agree to dissolve the corporation. However, it is almost always preferable to preserve a going corporation rather than to dissolve it. The business assets of a corporation, including intangible good will, are ordinarily worth more as a unit than fragmented and sold.

While it sometimes may be possible for deadlocked parties to work out a sale after the deadlock has arisen, the more logical solution is to address the problem when the parties agree to the potential deadlock arrangement and are in amity, and to work out an agreement in advance by which one faction should buy out the other at a fair price in the event of a deadlock. Buy-sell agreements in this context were discussed earlier (see § 9.24 of this Nutshell).

§ 12.9 Involuntary Dissolution

The earliest general corporation statutes provided no special remedy for intracorporate conflict within a closely held corporation. As a result, minority shareholders were largely defenseless against abusive conduct and deadlocks could be resolved, if they could be resolved at all, only by negotiation. Today, statutes in every state provide the ultimate remedy of involuntary dissolution at the request of a shareholder. The language of § 14.30(2) of MBCA (1984) is typical of these state statutes. Under this section a shareholder seeking involuntary dissolution must establish that

(1) The directors are deadlocked in the management of the corporate affairs, the shareholders are unable to break the deadlock, and "irreparable injury to the corporation is threatened or being suffered, or the business and affairs of the corporation can no longer be conducted to the advantage of the shareholders generally, because of the deadlock;" or

(2) The directors or those in control of the corporation "have acted, are acting, or will act in a manner that is illegal, oppressive, or fraudulent;" or

(3) The shareholders are "deadlocked in voting power," and have failed, for a period that includes at least two consecutive annual meeting dates, to elect successors to directors whose terms have expired; or

(4) The corporate assets are being "misapplied or wasted."

Early cases state that there is no general common law right of dissolution. Hence the initial attitude of courts toward these statutes was to construe them strictly and require strong showings of potential or actual abuse or harm before granting dissolution. Further, these statutes are addressed to the discretion of the court, so that a court might decline to grant dissolution even if the shareholder proved that conduct falling within these provisions had occurred.

The early attitude toward strict construction of these statutes is disappearing and a much more flexible attitude developing. Courts have been willing to construe broadly language such as "oppressive" or "irreparable injury" in order to protect minority shareholders against oppression or freeze-outs. "Oppressive conduct," for example has been virtually equated by some courts with "fair dealing" or "fair play." Conduct may be found to be "oppressive" upon a showing that action has been taken that is inconsistent with the expectations of the shareholders as to their roles in the corporation. Another definition that is widely quoted is "burdensome, harsh and wrongful conduct," or "a visible departure from the standards of fair dealing, and a violation of fair play on which every shareholder who entrusts his money to a company is entitled to rely." Baker v. Commercial Body Builders (Or.1973).

There are problems with statutes that make involuntary dissolution the standard or sole remedy available in cases involving oppression of minority shareholders or deadlocks. Involuntary dissolution is not an attractive remedy when it leads to the destruction of a valuable and profitable business. Less extreme remedies should be available. Further, involuntary dissolution often causes significant hardship to one party or another on an erratic basis. For example, if a single shareholder's personal abilities largely explain the corporation's current success, she may well desire liquidation of the corporation. By performing services for the corporation, the dominant shareholder is in effect sharing the fruits of his or her ability with other shareholders who presumably made a contribution at an earlier time. If the corporation were dissolved, presumably the dominant shareholder could start up a new business that is virtually identical with the old one, capture the fruits of the good will that has been generated in the existing corporation, and not share those fruits with anyone. In most situations, the dominant shareholder cannot simply abandon the existing corporation and start a new business in competition with the corporation since such action might be deemed to constitute unfair competition or an usurpation of a corporate opportunity by the dominant shareholder. A classic example of the attempted use of dissolution by a dominant shareholder in this manner is In re Radom & Neidorff, Inc. (N.Y.1954). Whether or not dissolution unfairly benefits a shareholder in such a situation is debatable.

Several states have adopted statutes that supplement the traditional involuntarily dissolution remedy by authorizing a judicially imposed buy-out at an appraised or judicially determined price as an alternative to involuntary dissolution. These newer statutes are based on recognition that the remedy of involuntary dissolution often unreasonably benefits one faction of shareholders at the expense of another. Even in states with statutes that refer exclusively to involuntary dissolution, courts are increasingly willing to provide remedies short of dissolution: usually a mandatory buyout of the interest of a minority shareholder at a judicially determined price. In this respect, courts appear to be influenced by the flexible remedies provided in special close corporation statutes discussed in § 12.13 of this Nutshell, and in effect are extending these remedies to non-electing corporations by expansive construction of involuntary dissolution statutes. These developments led to the development of section 14.34 of the Model Business Corporation Act (1984), discussed in the following section.

§ 12.10   Section 14.34 of MBCA (1984)

In 1991, the Committee on Corporate Laws, recognizing the trend away from exclusive reliance on involuntary dissolution, adopted a new section of the Model Business Corporation Act (1984) that codifies the buyout remedy discussed in § 12.9 of this Nutshell. However, section 14.34 is less flexible than the remedies devised by the courts. A major limitation of section 14.34 is that it is triggered only if a shareholder brings suit for involuntary dissolution under the traditional statute, and when such a suit is filed, the only available option is that corporation or the remaining shareholders may elect to purchase the shares owned by the plaintiff. There is no reciprocity or discretion here; the shareholder who files the suit must be the seller if the corporation or the remaining share-holders make the election to purchase. As a result, a lawsuit to force involuntary dissolution becomes a high risk enterprise. In the case of a deadlocked corporation with two fifty percent shareholders it is easy to visualize a situation where neither party is willing to file the suit and thus assent to be the seller. In this situation, paradoxically, the effect of MBCA § 14.34 may be to chill attempts to obtain judicial assistance in resolving permanent dead-locks.

Section 14.34 gives little guidance as to how fair value should be determined. It is clearly an issue of fact on which expert testimony may be appropriate. The section does authorizes the court to order the purchase price to be paid in installments and to allocate or apportion shares among the various shareholders of various classes "to preserve the existing distribution of voting rights among holders of different classes insofar as practicable." If the price and other terms determined by the court are unac-ceptable to the corporation or its controlling sharehold-ers, the corporation may elect to dissolve rather than complete the purchase.

§ 12.11   Fiduciary Duties of Shareholders of Closely Held Corporations

Until relatively recently it was generally accepted that shareholders in general did not owe duties to other shareholders, and that the fiduciary duties of directors of a closely held corporation in particular were no different than fiduciary duties in corporations generally. The first indication of change in these fundamental principles occurred in early judicial opinions and law review articles that discussed problems of oppression and deadlock; they referred to closely held corporations as "incorporated partnerships" and urged greater use of partnership-type duties in resolving disputes between shareholders of such corporations. The decision in Galler v. Galler (Ill.1964) was particularly influential in this regard.

The decision in Donahue v. Rodd Electrotype Co. (Mass. 1975), held that the shareholders in a closely held corporation owed a fiduciary duty to other shareholders that is substantially the same as the duty partners in a partnership owe to each other. A number of state courts have cited *Donahue* approvingly. In states that recognize this principle, non-controlling shareholders facing oppressive or unfair conduct may have a cause of action against the corporation and the controlling shareholders on the basis of this fiduciary duty to ensure fair and equal treatment of minority interests.

The paradigm situation in which courts have found a fiduciary duty of controlling shareholders is where the controlling shareholders decide to cause the corporation to purchase some of their shares—but not enough shares to effect control—at a favorable price while refusing to offer the same opportunity to the minority shareholders (or offering to purchase minority shares only at a much lower price). This was the precise situation involved in *Donahue*, and most courts that have addressed this specific situation have held that the principle of equal opportunity must be applied to give an equal opportunity to the minority shareholders to have shares purchased on the same terms. Courts have also applied a fiduciary duty to controlling shareholders who negotiate to purchase shares of minority shareholders without disclosing relevant information to them about the value of their shares or that the controlling shareholder has already obtained a right to resell the shares at a higher price.

Many cases applying this fiduciary duty concept do so in broad terms that literally may apply to all sorts of business transactions. While it may be that injustice in fact occurred in some specific cases, a broad fiduciary duty in the close corporation context has a significant capacity for mischief since it often leads to judicial review of the validity of many business decisions. For example, several Massachusetts decisions after *Donahue* have involved minority shareholders who were fired as employees of the corporation. It is of course possible that a firing of a minority shareholder may be part of a planned freeze-out or squeeze-out. However, it also may have been because he regularly drank too much alcohol at lunch and was ineffective for the rest of the day. It may have been because the nature of the corporation's business has changed and the skills of the minority shareholder are no longer needed by the corporation. It may have been because the corporation has hired a younger person who turns out to have superior skills so that the minority shareholder has become superfluous or redundant. Yet these clear business decisions may become litigable issues by a broad application of the fiduciary duty concept. Law and economics scholars have criticized the Donahue principle on this ground.

Law and economics scholars have also criticized the *Donahue* principle on the ground that it imposes an *ex post* duty that the parties to the transaction almost certainly would not have selected if they had considered what term to include in their corporate "contract."

In Nixon v. Blackwell (Del.1993), the Delaware Supreme Court refused to accept the holding of the cases described in the previous paragraphs. It took the position that it was inappropriate to create special judicially-created duties for closely held corporations in the absence of legislative direction. It may be, of course, that the traditional duties of directors, particularly the restrictions against self dealing (see §§ 14.10–14.14 of this Nutshell) may cover many of the more egregious transactions invalidated by cases involving the *Donahue* principle.

§ 12.12   Resolution of Intracorporate Disputes by Arbitration

Mandatory arbitration is sometimes used as a device to resolve intracorporate disputes. In most states today, arbitration is generally available to resolve future disputes without regard to their justiciability. Arbitration, of course, requires either a current willingness to arbitrate a dispute or a pre-existing agreement by the shareholders to submit the issues to arbitration. In considering the desirability of arbitration for intracorporate disputes, two questions should be considered: first, what kinds of controversies is the arbitrator likely to face, and second, what kinds of solutions will he or she be permitted to adopt?

The advantages of arbitration are speed, cheapness, informality (as contrasted with a court proceeding), and the prospect of a decision by a person with knowledge and experience in business affairs. Where the reason for deadlock is a question not involving a basic personal or policy matter, arbitration may satisfactorily resolve a dispute and permit the corporation to continue. For example, in Vogel v. Lewis (N.Y.1967), the issue was whether a corporation should exercise an option to purchase contained in a lease of real property. The court held that this issue should be submitted to arbitration, a result which seems reasonable under the circumstances.

However, many intracorporate disputes involve personality conflicts or broad differences in policy. An arbitrator may have no criteria for resolving such disputes, and even if he or she does resolve a specific dispute, it is unlikely that the decision will have cured the basic disagreement which led to the specific dispute. In Application of Burkin (N.Y.1956), a well-known New York case, a minority shareholder in a corporation sought arbitration of a claim that the majority shareholder should be removed as director. The corporation's governing documents required unanimity but the majority shareholder not unnaturally refused to vote in favor of his own removal. The court refused to order arbitration on the theory that the dispute was not justiciable, a result which was later overruled by statute. It is certainly doubtful that arbitration is a suitable remedy for a dispute such as this.

§ 12.13   Special Close Corporation Statutes

Some 18 states, including California, Delaware, and Texas, have adopted special statutes designed specifically for closely held corporations. The genesis of these special statutes is the famous decision in Galler v. Galler (Ill. 1964), in which the court upheld an highly unorthodox shareholder's agreement in a two person corporation. The opinion contains a strong plea to state legislatures to consider the unique problems and needs of closely held corporations.

While the special close corporation statutes vary widely from state to state, they have the common characteristic that they are optional and must be specifically elected by an eligible corporation by inclusion of a statement in the articles of incorporation that "this corporation is a statutory close corporation" or some other similar statement. Eligibility is usually defined by the number of shareholders: a maximum number of 25, 30 or 35 is typical. These statutes also usually deal with what happens when the number of shareholders exceed the maximum number set forth in the special statute. Indeed, many statutes have rather elaborate provisions dealing with how the election is to be made, which corporations are eligible for the election, and how the election may be revoked.

Special close corporation statutes permit an electing close corporation to dispense entirely with a board of directors and have the business conducted by the shareholders either following the partnership format or by adopting some other system of governance. Bylaws, meetings, and elections of managers may also be dispensed with. Shareholders' agreements are validated even though they interfere with the discretion of boards of directors. A provision expressly prohibiting the application of the piercing the corporate veil doctrine for informal conduct by electing corporations appears in many of these statutes. A variety of judicial remedies for oppression, dissension or deadlock are specifically authorized. In the event of a deadlock at the directoral level, courts are specifically empowered to break the deadlock by the appointment of impartial "provisional directors." This provision is designed to provide a simpler, more flexible and less drastic solution to deadlocked corporations than either the appointment of a receiver or involuntary dissolution. This provision may be applicable to all electing close corporations and may not be opted out of by a specific corporation. In the event of deadlock at the shareholders' level or oppressive conduct, courts are invited to fashion a remedy that is suitable under the circumstances. Some statutes list as many as eleven different types of remedies that a court may invoke, such as removal from office of any director or officer or the appointment of any individual as a director or officer. Special dissolution provisions also may be included.

These special close corporation statutes have been widely praised by commentators but rather surprisingly they do not appear to be widely used "on the ground" by corporate practitioners. Studies in various states indicate that exercise of the close corporation election is relatively uncommon. This may indicate only that old habits of corporate lawyers die hard. It may also indicate, however, that the need for special treatment of close corporations has been overstated. In part because of this lack of widespread use of these special elections, the drafters of the Model Business Corporation Act withdrew a special "close corporation supplement" in 1991 and substituted a new section 7.32, a much simpler provision broadly validating all shareholder agreements relating to management within closely held corporations. This provision is discussed in the following section of this Nutshell.

The attractiveness of these special close corporation statutes has been reduced in part because most states have modified the standard corporation form to some extent to resolve the peculiar problems of the closely held corporation. Provisions allowing action by written consent, increasing quorum and voting requirements, reducing the size of the board of directors to one person, and permitting most traditional directoral functions to be reserved to the shareholders, are now very common. Section 7.32 of the MBCA (1984), discussed in the following section of this Nutshell, carries this trend to its logical conclusion.

§ 12.14   Section 7.32 of MBCA (1984)

In 1991, the Committee on Corporate Laws of the American Bar Association withdrew its "Close Corporation Supplement" to the MBCA (1984) and substituted a new section of general applicability. Section 7.32 is a broad provision authorizing shareholders' agreements that depart completely from the traditional statutory scheme. An agreement entered into by all the shareholders at the time of the agreement may, among other things, eliminate the board of directors entirely, authorize distributions not in proportion to share ownership, establish who shall be directors or officers and specify their manner of selection, delegate the authority of the board of directors to one or more shareholders or other persons, require dissolution on demand of one or more shareholders or upon the occurrence of a specific contingency, and so forth. The Official Comment states that these provisions are illustrative and not exclusive. A further example given in that Comment approves a system of weighted voting for directors based on shareholdings. However, there are outer limits. The Official Comment suggests that a shareholder agreement that provides that the directors of the corporation have no duties of care or loyalty to the corporation or the shareholders would be beyond the purview of section 7.32. If the powers of directors are vested in persons other than directors, the directoral duties are imposed on those other persons.

Shareholder agreements valid under section 7.32 are not legally binding on the state, on creditors, or on third parties. For example, a shareholders' agreement that provides that only the president has authority to enter into contracts would not preclude third persons from relying on other corporate officers under general principles of agency. Special rules are also provided for persons who subsequently acquire shares in the closely held corporation. A purchaser of shares who is unaware of the existence of the agreement is bound by the agreement, but she is granted an unqualified power to rescind the purchase upon discovering the agreement. However, if the shares are represented by certificates that contain a proper legend, the purchaser is presumed to have knowledge of the existence of the agreement and has no power to rescind. Persons acquiring shares through gift or bequest also are bound by the agreement and have no power to rescind unless the contrary is provided in the agreement itself.

Agreements under this section are valid for ten years unless the agreement provides otherwise. Section 7.32 also provides that the agreement terminates automatically if the corporation makes a public offering of its shares.

It remains to be seen whether this innovative provision becomes widely accepted as the most desirable solution to the problems created by close corporations.

[For unfamiliar terms see the Glossary]

CHAPTER THIRTEEN

THE PUBLICLY HELD CORPORATION

§ 13.1 The Publicly Held Corporation in Perspective

As described in § 12.1 of this Nutshell, the most important difference between a publicly held corporation and a closely held corporation is that there is a public market for the shares of a publicly held corporation. That market may be the New York Stock Exchange, the American Stock Exchange, the vast over-the-counter market known as NASDAQ, or one or more regional exchanges. Nevertheless a shareholder of a publicly held corporation who desires to sell his or her shares may do so simply by calling a securities broker. An investor who decides to become a shareholder of a specific publicly held corporation also may do so simply by calling a broker and placing an order to buy.

Many publicly held corporations are huge economic entities with billions of dollars of assets, tens or hundreds of thousands of employees, and millions of shares outstanding. These corporations differ from closely held corporations in several fundamental respects:

(1) *Economic Power.* These large publicly held corporations wield immense economic power in the United States and world-wide. They may decide what products to develop, what safety devices to incorporate in them, what environmental pollutants to create and how to handle them (subject of course, to overriding governmental regulation), who to employ, where to locate plants, whether to move production facilities to Mexico or the Pacific Rim, and so forth. The manner in which such decisions are

made and the relationship between such private, presumably profit-oriented decisions, and the broader goals of social and governmental policy have been the subject of intense speculation and analysis for nearly a century.

(2) *Diffusion of Ownership.* The ownership of very large corporations is divided up among thousands of different investors and there is no clear group of persons that can be described as the "owners." These investors typically are passive in the sense that they do not have a voice in management except indirectly by voting for directors. Even though shares are widely owned by thousands of different investors, a significant fraction of the outstanding shares may be held by a relatively few institutional investors (described in § 13.8 of this Nutshell).

(3) *Professional Management.* The managers of the business are professionals who receive the bulk of their compensation from their managerial services and not from their share ownership. While managers own shares, they are typically a fraction of one percent of all the voting shares. Even in corporations whose names are associated with specific individuals or families, it is relatively uncommon today to find that management control is based squarely on share ownership. The exceptions usually involve corporations that are relative newcomers on the public scene; they are often the modern success stories in which the founders of the business have decided to "go public" but have retained, singly or collectively, a controlling interest in the shares of the corporation.

(4) *Bureaucratic Structure.* The management structure within the business is highly bureaucratic in nature, with very substantial amounts of discretion with respect to ordinary business transactions lodged in individuals below "the top."

(5) *Public Availability of Information.* Because the corporation is publicly held, it is required by federal law to

make publicly available a considerable amount of information about its affairs, including periodic audited financial statements and interim disclosure of important developments that materially affect the business. It has been stated that the management of a publicly held corporation operates in a goldfish bowl; that is an overstatement, but certainly these corporations have an obligation to make public disclosure of significant developments, both good news and news that the management would probably just as soon not be widely disseminated.

(6) *Sources of Capital.* Very large corporations may readily obtain substantial amounts of capital either through the public sale of securities to individuals and sophisticated institutional investors or through the placement of loans with banks and other financial institutions.

"Publicly held" of course refers to whether a market exists for the shares of its stock. Size itself is not a reliable criterion. A few publicly held corporations are relatively small and a few closely held corporations rival the larger publicly held corporations in size. However, these corporations are exceptional and unusual cases. The number of publicly held corporations has been estimated to be in the range of only 10,000, or so. In contrast there are nearly four million closely held corporations. Nevertheless, in terms of wealth, power, and economic importance, publicly held corporations own the great preponderance of business assets.

§ 13.2   The Internal Structure of Large Corporations

Large corporations are so large that they almost defy imagination; they rival many governments in terms of wealth, size, and economic power. One large corporation may have hundreds of plants and offices, a dozen or more discretely separate lines of businesses, and tens of thousands of products. Hundreds of thousands of employees and their dependents may depend directly or indirectly on the continued success of the corporation for their livelihoods. If one counts suppliers and their employees, customers, communities and even entire states, the success or failure of a large corporation affects millions of persons.

A large corporation may have operations in foreign countries that rival in size their American operations. Manufacturing plants may be located in Mexico, Malaysia, Taiwan, England, and a number of other countries. Sales offices numbering in the thousands may be located in all major countries and in many minor ones as well. The most intense competition may come from foreign enterprises rather than domestic ones.

Since the total number of employees of a very large business is in the tens or hundreds of thousands, the mere keeping of personnel records is a daunting task. Among the employees may be a legal staff of hundreds of lawyers—larger than many major law firms. General Electric's legal staff consisted of 440 lawyers at the end of 1993. Consider also the obligation of a large corporation to file a tax return each year with the federal government. A tax return for such a large entity is certainly going to be complex. The 1992 tax return for one major corporation alone ran to 21,000 pages and 30 volumes. Such a corporation is under almost continuous audit by Internal Revenue Service agents assigned exclusively to review its transactions, and a cadre of tax attorneys, accountants, and tax specialists are employed by the company to make sure that its activities are reported in a way most favorable to the company. Control over such a large and complex entity involves a hierarchy of employees, a private bureaucracy so to speak.

As with any bureaucracy, the very large corporation may be slow to react to changes in technology and innovation, to changes in consumer tastes, and to the development of competitive products. This may be a product of simple inertia: The bureaucratic structure may resist change and simplification, accumulating rust, as it were. However, it may also reflect imperfect markets that fail to react promptly to economic changes. The 1980s and 1990s have seen many well-known large American corporations falter and lose their preeminence in familiar markets. Some have recovered, some have not. A large firm succeeds only if its managers are able to effectively coordinate and match people and inputs with current technologies and changing markets. It will fail, or at least decline slowly, if the business remains static and continues to follow standard operating procedures that were successful a decade ago but are obsolete today. The 1990s has seen massive down-sizing within management structures by numerous corporations. Whole layers of management have been eliminated in an effort to reduce costs and improve overall efficiency. Management and innovation are the keys to success in the modern era, but controlling costs and keeping the enterprise "mean and lean" appear to be the watchwords of the 1990s.

§ 13.3 Profit Centers

A large corporation is built around organizational charts, targeted goals, and delegated responsibilities. Generally, successively higher levels of management are given increasingly broad discretion and responsibility. The bureaucratic structure is complicated, however, because large corporations are involved in numerous activities and product lines, and decision-making is diversified and diffused. Several large internal hierarchical structures exist simultaneously within the lower levels of the bureaucracy. Starting at the lowest level of business management, such as shop foreman or a similar position, successive layers of broader responsibility can be traced up through successive levels of management. If this process is followed, it may culminate in a single person or, in rare instances, a small committee, that has responsibility for one or more areas of operations. A single person may be "President of the Plastics Division" or "Manager of the Chemicals Sector" of a large corporation. That person may have virtually complete responsibility for the profitability of a multi-plant business with sales of billions of dollars per year and yet be several hierarchical levels below the highest management level within the corporation itself. This intermediate manager may have broad discretion with respect to the management of the division or sector on a day-to-day basis; however, commitments and decisions above a stated level may be made only with the approval of more senior managers.

These divisions into business areas may be called "profit centers." They may be structured as a separate wholly owned business entity, typically a corporation, or they may not have any independent legal existence of their own, but legally be a part of the corporation itself. The words "department" or "division" usually connote that the profit center is not an independent legal entity while the word "subsidiary" connotes that the profit center has independent legal existence. However, usage is not uniform, and one sometimes sees references to a "division" when the word "subsidiary" would have been more accurate, and vice versa.

As a practical matter, these differences in legal form do not make a great deal of difference in the day-to-day operation of profit centers. Subsidiaries must have boards of directors consisting usually of management personnel drawn from the operating components and the higher levels of the corporate bureaucracy. In some wholly owned subsidiaries the role of the board of directors is purely a formal one; in others, the board provides significant input and advice to the manager of the division. Precisely the same function may be served in a "department" or "division" by a committee without independent legal standing. The parent corporation may appoint a "shareholder's representative" to deal with major issues in a subsidiary but have direct reporting in the case of a division. One minor difference is that the amount of paperwork to record decisions is somewhat greater for a separate legal entity than it is for a department or division. It is important that the paperwork be done properly to avoid later arguments in litigation that the separate legal existence of the subsidiary has been abandoned by the parent corporation.

The typical profit center functions as a largely autonomous business having wide discretion over research, product development, advertising, sales policies, and other matters. The head of the profit center has the ultimate responsibility for the operations of that profit center; if the profit center does poorly or has internal difficulties or problems, that person may lose his or her job. One characteristic of a profit center is that it is sufficiently discrete and self-standing that it can usually be bought or sold as a unit to a third party without causing a major reshuffling of assets, employees, and records.

The various profit centers—the "Plastic Division" or "Chemicals Sector," for example—have their own "central" offices. Commonly this office is at one of the major plants or sales offices operated by that center, though it may be free-standing, at a location where the division or sector has no other facilities. In some instances, these offices may also be located at the same physical location as the "home office" described below.

Even though there is considerable decentralization of management and day-to-day control within large corporations, the results of operations are reported on a company-wide basis. The financial statements of all profit centers are "consolidated" into a single financial statement for the entire enterprise. For internal purposes, however, accounting statements for individual profit centers may be created on an annual, monthly, weekly, or even daily basis.

§ 13.4 The Corporate Headquarters

Above profit centers there is an "umbrella organization," that may be defined as the "home office" or "corporate headquarters" of the corporation itself. In this home office there is a centralized bureaucracy that has general oversight of all the various profit centers. In addition, the home office handles various core operations such as accounting and fund raising that affect all the profit centers.

The headquarters organization is also hierarchical in form. At the highest levels are managers, usually with responsibility for specific functional areas; these managers have ultimate authority over broad areas of business activities. They have titles that describe their areas of responsibility: "chief legal officer," "chief operations officer," "chief financial officer," "chief accounting officer," and so forth. These offices appear so commonly in very large corporations that everyone understands their acronyms: "CFO," "COO," "CAO," "CLO," and so forth. The senior management official, the top of the management pyramid to which all the functional managers report, is the chief executive officer, or the "CEO."

Many state corporation statutes require that every corporation have certain specified officers: usually a president, a secretary, a treasurer, and one or more vice presidents. In order to comply with these statutory requirements the statutory title may be appended to a specific office: the CFO may have the title "chief financial officer and treasurer," for example, and the CEO may have the title "President and Chief Executive Officer." However, the statutory titles may also be given to persons lower in the hierarchy. The COO, or an employee in the COO's office, may be given the title "president," for example. By and large, the functional titles rather than the statutory titles are used. The titles of "vice president," "assistant secretary," and "assistant treasurer" may be given to numerous employees in the various offices and plants operated by the corporation in order to permit contracts to be entered into and other corporate actions performed in each office or plant without involving the home office personnel.

One important function of the home office is the selection of top operating managers for individual profit centers and the monitoring and review of their performance. The home office also provides a variety of centralized services that experience demonstrates is more efficiently provided on a centralized basis than by allowing each profit center to develop its own system. Areas of central direction and control typically include the provision of auditing and legal services; the raising of capital; the maintenance of pension plans, health benefit plans, and the like for all employees; the provision of incentive compensation plans for top managers; and ultimate decision-making with respect to the long-term direction of the enterprise.

Since the corporation must prepare and publish periodic financial statements, it is obviously desirable to require all profit centers to use a common accounting system prescribed by the home office. Similarly, the home office may have the responsibility of assuring the overnight investment of available funds and minimizing borrowing costs. This may lead to a "cash concentration" system in which all funds available throughout the entire enterprise are deposited on a daily basis in accounts handled by the home office. Profit centers, in other words, may not have their own bank accounts or banking connections, though they may withdraw funds for operations as needed from central accounts. The advantage of this system from the standpoint of the enterprise is that excess funds may be available to be "lent" to a specific profit center, thus avoiding the possibility that one profit center may be seeking a bank loan when another profit center has excess funds that are invested in low yielding bank deposits.

Another function generally handled by corporate headquarters is raising capital from various sources and allocating it among the various profit centers. While many profit centers may have the capability of borrowing funds on their own from commercial sources, the main office itself should be able to borrow on more favorable terms than any single profit center. Concentrating capital raising at the home office also permits centralized review and approval of proposed capital investments by profit centers. This, in turn, permits the corporation to divide its huge— but ultimately limited—resources among competing proposals put forth by the profit centers in a rational manner in order to maximize overall return.

Compensation levels for senior managers of the various profit centers are typically determined by the home office. In this way, good performance may be rewarded and yet consistent compensation levels for mid-level managers may be maintained across the entire business of the corporation.

The home office is "the corporation" for purposes of shareholder relations, interaction of the board of directors with management, dividend payment decisions, and the like.

The home office may be located in any state without regard to where the corporation is incorporated. While Delaware is the most popular state of incorporation, very few Delaware corporations have their home offices in that small state.

§ 13.5　The Chief Executive Officer

At the apex of managerial control within a large corporation is an individual referred to almost universally as the "chief executive officer" or "CEO." The CEO has responsibility for the management team that directs the enterprise, and is himself ultimately responsible to the board of directors for the success of the enterprise. If, for example, the CEO loses confidence in the CFO, the CEO must replace him and find a more satisfactory one. In theory, the CEO has power to call the shots in the corporate bureaucracy on narrow issues as well as broad ones, where and when he wishes. In practice, the CEO, as the head of a large bureaucratic organization, cannot hope to run details of the business operations; if he is to be effective, authority over day-to-day operations, including personnel, financing, advertising, and production must be entirely delegated to subordinates, and the CEO must concentrate on the broadest issues relating to the business.

The typical CEO is a professional manager. Rarely does he own an appreciable fraction of the corporate stock. His power arises from his position at the top of the bureaucracy rather than from his ownership interest or voting power at the shareholder level. His tenure is ultimately determined by the board of directors of the corporation.

Because the CEO has ultimate responsibility for the success or failure of the corporation, he—and quite possibly he alone—may make the final decision on whether to embark upon a radical change in business strategy. If the change turns out to be disastrous, the CEO may lose his job through a process described below. The CEO may decide, for example, to close fifteen plants in order to redirect the primary emphasis of the corporation, or to develop a new product such as a state-of-the-art airplane or modern computer that will strain the economic resources of any very large corporation. If unsuccessful, such a strategy may call into question the long term viability of the enterprise: in effect "betting the company." These decisions are usually the ultimate responsibility of the CEO even though it may be necessary to obtain the approval of the board of directors that has the power to reject the CEO's proposal. In rare instances, the board of directors may actually exercise this power despite the recommendation of the CEO; this is clear evidence that the CEO has lost the confidence of the board of directors and his resignation is the normal consequence. This is well understood both by the CEO and the members of the board of directors. Where the CEO has the confidence of the board of directors, the board will normally approve a proposal even though individual directors may have reservations about the wisdom of the proposal.

During much of the Twentieth Century, the CEO's power was viewed by most observers as virtually absolute. Whether or not the power of the CEO was truly absolute in the past, it was certainly greater in the past than it is today; there are many indications that the power of the typical CEO has declined in the 1980s and 1990s for a variety of reasons.

§ 13.6 Compensation of Senior Executives

One visible and controversial aspect of modern corporation law is the level of the compensation of senior executives, particularly the CEO. In the 1990s the average salary of CEOs and other senior executives of Fortune 500 corporations was in the high six or low seven figures; but this was usually supplemented by stock options, bonuses, and incentive compensation arrangements. The aggregate compensation paid to some CEOs was in the tens or even the hundreds of millions of dollars in a single year. A survey of 350 corporations in early 1995 revealed that levels of CEO compensation had increased by 8.1 per cent from 1992 to 1993 and an additional 11.4 per cent from 1993 to 1994. During the same two years, white collar salaries generally had increased by only a total of 4.2 per cent, and in many instances work forces had been "downsized" or salary levels reduced by changing the work force from employees to "contract workers." Senior executive salary levels in the United States are much higher than the salaries of their European or Asian counterparts. Compensation thus has become a major political issue. Visible consequences of this controversy include the following:

1) Congress enacted the Revenue Reconciliation Act of 1993, one provision of which limited the income tax deductibility of salaries in excess of one million dollars per year. However, since the provision excluded performance-based compensation, it appears to have had only minimal effect on actual levels of compensation. Some corporations have continued paying compensation in excess of $1,000,000 per year despite the loss of the tax deduction; others have apparently *increased* the levels of compensation from the high six figures to the million dollar level. This tax legislation involves corporate governance more than tax law. In order for payments to be treated as performance based, the corporation's outside directors must approve performance criteria at the beginning of the performance period; the underlying compensation arrangement must be adequately disclosed to, and approved by, the shareholders; and the outside directors must certify in writing that the performance criteria have been met before the compensation is paid. The proposed regulations contain standards for determining whether a specific director qualifies as an "outside director" under this section. The SEC requires the compensation committee to discuss the corporation's policies with respect to the one million dollar cap in the proxy statement. See § 13.19 of this Nutshell.

Corporations have exhibited some reluctance in seeking approval of performance compensation plans by shareholders. They are perhaps concerned about the possible use of this information in later class action or derivative suits brought by shareholders.

2) In 1992, the Securities and Exchange Commission mandated more elaborate and complete descriptions of compensation levels, requiring a "specific discussion" of compensation levels compared with profitability and shareholder return.

3) The SEC required corporations to place shareholder proposals with respect to compensation levels in proxy statements. See § 13.20 of this Nutshell.

4) The SEC required footnote disclosure of the value of stock options granted to senior executives.

§ 13.7 Shareholders as "Investors" or "Owners"

Assume you buy one hundred shares of stock of General Motors Corporation. In January, 1996, such a purchase would have cost about $5,000, including brokerage commissions. In one sense you are now a partial owner of a major automobile business; or at least that is how the New York Stock Exchange has historically wanted small investors to view their own roles. However, that is not a very realistic way of looking at your role. General Motors has some 600 million odd shares outstanding; your one hundred shares is not a very large percentage interest in General Motors. Also, there certainly is not very much you can do to influence what GM does. Why does someone such as yourself invest $5,000 in this way? Almost all investors view the purchase of shares of stock as purely a financial one: Will I make money if I invest my $5,000 in General Motors? The sources of a potential gain are two-fold: (1) the investor will receive dividends (in 1995, GM was paying a dividend of $1.20 cents per share per year, or $120.00 per year on a $5,000 investment), and (2) if GM does well, the price of the stock may go up and the investor will profit by selling it for more than he paid for it. A quick calculation shows that the dividend yield on GM stock in 1995 was a little over 2 per cent per year. The possibility of price escalation is obviously a very important consideration since an investor at the same time could obtain a yield of 5 percent or more in a totally riskless savings account. Also, GM is traded on the New York Stock Exchange and GM stock can be sold simply by a telephone call to your broker. This is a liquid investment.

If GM turns downward or management does something you do not like, the sensible thing to do is simply to sell your GM stock and invest the funds somewhere else. This is generally known as "exercising the Wall Street Option."

Of course, a shareholder does have the right to vote for the election of directors and from time to time she may have limited additional rights to participate in management. For example, shareholders are entitled to vote for or against the appointment of a specific accounting firm to audit GM's books and report the result of the audit. Shareholders may vote on some proposals that appear in proxy statements. Shareholders also have some additional rights, for example, to bring derivative suits, to vote on mergers and other fundamental transactions, and so forth. However, it does not take a genius to see that the actual participation in corporate decision-making by small shareholders in large corporations is nominal at best. The interest of the average small shareholder in a publicly held corporation is purely economic.

Of course, exercising the Wall Street Option is not a neutral act, particularly if a large number of shareholders decide to do so at about the same time or if several large investors conclude at about the same time that they no longer want GM in their portfolios. The price of GM stock will go down, a result which management is not going to be happy about. Low stock prices harm management to the extent that their compensation is incentive-based (since incentives are usually measured by increases in stock prices). More seriously, the loss of investor confidence may reflect itself in loss of confidence in top management within the board of directors, and the CEO and top management may be in danger of losing their jobs.

In light of the truly nominal role that most shareholders play in managing the corporate enterprise, it is questionable whether small investors should be viewed as the "owners" of the business at all. Indeed, as described in § 1.3 of this Nutshell, modern economic theory visualizes the very large business as a "nexus of contracts" and rejects the assumption that investors—shareholders in publicly held corporations, typically—should be viewed as "owners" at all. Rather they are viewed as contributors of capital having the right to receive the residual cash flow and capital of the business, and being the first to suffer the consequences of losses. Implicit in this analysis is the assumption that the managers of the business—the CEO and his subordinates—are the central organizers and the central component of a business with investors being contributors of capital much like commercial lenders. Capital is of course only one of numerous inputs in a business (albeit a very important one) and there is no inherent reason to denominate the contributors of this input as "owners."

§ 13.8 Institutional Investors

In the early 1930s, Berle and Means published a seminal book entitled *The Modern Corporation and Private Property*. Its principal thesis was that a fragmented ownership carries with it none of the control that ownership normally provides. Berle and Means drew from this thesis the conclusion that the managers of many publicly held corporations had dictatorial power over the corporation and the owners had no power. This picture was probably never completely accurate, but certainly modern trends in securities ownership and the role of boards of directors are moving strongly away from the corporate world envisioned by Berle and Means.

Since Berle and Means wrote, there has been an important—almost revolutionary—change in the patterns of ownership of publicly held corporations. Today, "institutional investors," a concept that was virtually unknown sixty years ago, dominate stock ownership of many corporations and transactions on many securities markets, including the New York Stock Exchange. The major categories of institutional investors are private pension funds, public employee pension funds, mutual funds, banks, university endowments, life and casualty insurance companies, and private investment funds. As of 1996, institutional investors owned about 55 percent of all the stock of the one hundred largest corporations traded on the New York Stock Exchange. It is not uncommon for the hundred largest shareholders in a very large corporation—all institutional investors—to own more than 50 percent of the voting shares of that corporation. In some very large corporations that are highly popular investment vehicles, institutional investors as a group may own 80 percent or more of all the voting shares of that corporation.

In one respect institutional investors differ from the typical small individual investor. Most institutional investors are in effect investing other people's money in a fiduciary capacity—for example, pension funds manage money set aside for the retirement of specific individuals, insurance companies manage the proceeds of insurance premiums that ultimately will have to be paid out to beneficiaries of insurance policies, and mutual funds make investment decisions on behalf of individuals who have opted to have other people invest their money for them. Since these institutional investors owe fiduciary duties to third persons, they may make investment decisions with respect to portfolio securities in response to those duties rather than on the basis of long term investment goals of maximizing the gain from ownership of specific stocks. This was particularly true during the late 1980s, a period of extremely high levels of takeover activity in which large premiums of 50 per cent or more over current market prices were regularly offered by aggressors. Institutional investors faced with fiduciary duties to their members or participants usually desired takeovers to succeed so that they could take advantage of the extremely attractive prices that were being offered. Some institutional investors—most notably the California Public Employees Retirement System (CalPERS)—decided to oppose management's defensive tactics. In doing so, it quickly became apparent that management ignored recommendations or suggestions from individual institutional investors with respect to takeover defensive tactics, when management's tenure was at stake.

Clearly the holdings of institutional investors today could lead to control over much of American industry if they can work together as a group. Even where control is not in fact exercised, their collective influence on management could be great. Collective effort, however, has not been easy to obtain. There are legal impediments to any one institutional investor (or any one investor of any kind, for that matter) owning more than five percent of the voting stock of any issuer. As a result, most institutional investors own considerably less than five percent, usually less than two percent of the stock of a single issuer. Therefore, there is a large number of institutional investors owning shares in any one issuer.

Institutional investors are also generally subject to a major "free rider" problem that limits the ability of institutional investors to actually wield the power their ownership interest potentially creates. A free rider problem arises whenever a number of persons have small interests in a venture whose return may be improved only by the investment of costly collective time and effort. Each person would prefer that others invest the necessary time and effort, thereby obtaining a "free ride" from the efforts of others. The result may be that no one actually takes the necessary steps.

In addition, most institutional investors diversify their portfolios, that is they spread their funds around among many different investments and many different companies, so that any one issuer is always a relatively small part of their aggregate portfolio even though the number of dollars invested in single issuers may be very large. An investor with a diversified portfolio tends to have little incentive to participate actively in management (since changes in the price of any one stock will have a small effect on its aggregate wealth). Rather they tend to vote their shares in support of management and the status quo.

Finally, until recently there were substantial legal impediments to any group of more than ten shareholders agreeing to work cooperatively together in an effort to elect directors or otherwise influence management. The SEC proxy regulations required anyone who was involved in influencing voting of shares by more than ten shareholders to go through an expensive registration process. In 1992, the SEC loosened these restraints. The principal change permitted institutional investors to communicate directly with each other and with corporate directors with respect to voting of shares (so long as they did not solicit the votes of others) without concern about possible violation of the SEC proxy rules. Anecdotal evidence indicates that many institutional investors have taken advantage of this additional freedom. Stories appear from time to time, for example, that one or more institutional investors plan to communicate their dissatisfaction with the performance of specific portfolio companies with management or with specific directors. A corporation with more than fifty percent of its stock owned by institutional investors can hardly ignore the implications of such a communication.

This growth in activism by institutional investors has increased in part because many of them recognize that they are in fact long term investors. It is difficult for individual institutional investors to exercise the Wall Street option if they are dissatisfied with the performance of a portfolio company: Large blocks of shares as a practical matter may be salable at an acceptable price only if other institutional investors are willing to buy them. On the other hand, this may be a strength when dealing with an issuer: Institutional investors now make up such a large portion of the trading market for a specific stock that a sale by several of them may have a dramatic (and traumatic) negative effect on the price of that stock. Issuers may well take seriously warnings that several institutional investors are dissatisfied with their economic performance.

§ 13.9 Registration of Securities in Street Name or in the Name of Nominees; Book Entry

Institutional investors routinely record their ownership interests in publicly held corporations in the names of "nominees" rather than in their own names. They usually use a partnership of employees using names such as "Abel and Company." This practice developed to avoid onerous transfer requirements placed on corporations or fiduciaries selling shares.

Most smaller shareholders who invest in securities on a speculative basis also do not register the transfer of shares into their own names. Increasingly, shares owned by

individual investors are being registered in the name of
Cede and Company, the nominee for the New York Depository Trust Company and ownership is reflected by
book entry. Cede is today the registered owner of approximately 70 percent of all shares traded on the major
exchanges. The book entry system, described below, greatly simplifies the trading of publicly held securities, but it
has the effect of rendering largely irrelevant the record of
shareholders maintained by transfer agents of publicly
held corporations. Indeed, the corporation itself may not
know the identity of most of the beneficial owners of its
securities. These widespread practices, that mask to a
considerable extent the true ownership of a large part of
publicly held securities, have developed for entirely innocent and desirable reasons.

Beneficial owners of securities today is reflected by
simple book entry in the records of the brokerage firm
with whom the investor deals. Purchases and sales of
securities are reflected solely by transaction confirmations
and monthly statements from the brokerage firm to its
customers. The brokerage firm, in turn, also does not hold
record title to its customers' securities. Assuming that it is
a participant in the central clearing service maintained by
the Depository Trust Company, shares owned by the
brokerage firm are reflected by book entry in DTC's
records. Transactions with other brokerage firms within
the central clearing service are reflected simply by book
entries on DTC's records. The process does not record
individual transactions in DTC's books; rather all transactions in a specific stock by customers of firm A—both
purchases and sales—are netted together each day and
only a single entry, plus or minus, is made on DTC's
books. The same is true for firm B and for all other
member brokerage firms of DTC. If a customer of firm A
buys 100 shares of stock while another customer of firm A
sells 100 shares of the same stock on the same day, no

entry at all is made on DTC's records, though the books of the brokerage firm will, of course, reflect that a different customer now owns the 100 shares. If the purchaser of shares owned by a customer of firm A is a customer of firm B, there will be an adjustment on the records of DTC. It depends on how many offsetting transactions there are in that security that day. This system of trading is undeniably efficient and it permits the recording of trades of hundreds of millions of shares each day with a minimum of paper flow. It also interposes two intermediaries—Cede and Co. and the brokerage firm—between the issuer of securities and the beneficial owner, and makes largely irrelevant the traditional learning on the rights of persons with respect to share certificates.

More and more shares each year are being registered in the name of Cede and Co., and entering the book entry form of ownership. Relatively few shares each year are withdrawn from the central clearing system and reissued in the name of a beneficial owner. Thus, fewer and fewer certificates are held by individuals, and the record owner who is also the beneficial owner is becoming more and more rare.

The book entry system is efficient not only for trading but also for the distribution of dividends, which are transferred by wire from the issuer to DTC to brokerage firms on the day the dividend is payable, and deposited into the accounts of customers on the same day. There are problems, however, in communicating through two sets of intermediaries for various types of shareholder actions, particularly actions that must be taken within narrow and clearly defined time limits.

Article 8 of the Uniform Commercial has been revised to provide a reasonable set of rules for book entry transfers. Considerable protection against insolvency of brokerage firms is provided by the Securities Investors Protection Corporation, a federal corporation that insures against securities losses of up to $500,000 for each brokerage firm customer of a brokerage firm that becomes insolvent owning less securities than reflected in its customer records.

§ 13.10   The Board of Directors: Theory and Reality

"Management" of very large corporations of course generally refers to the CEO and the bureaucratic structure under him by which control of the enterprise is effected. See sections 13.2–3.5. Management power, however, is subject to the control of, and significantly influenced by, the power of general oversight possessed by boards of directors. The board of directors serves an essential function in corporation law and theory, since it is the representative of passive investors when dealing with the managers. It is elected by the shareholders and it selects and monitors management, and fixes the compensation of the CEO and other high level managers.

As with many other areas of business law, one has to separate the theory from the reality when discussing the roles of directors in publicly held corporations. The board of directors in theory has plenary power over management. Traditional corporation statutes provide that the corporation "shall be managed by" the board of directors. Under this unambiguous directive, the board certainly has the power to manage the business and affairs of the corporation itself and reduce the CEO to little more than an errand boy. In theory, the board of directors has power to "trump" management on any specific issue that it chooses to involve itself with. It is very unusual, however, for a board of directors in a large publicly held corporation to actually become involved in direct business management. Public corporations are huge entities; boards of directors are usually part-time overseers.

The most fundamental power of the board of directors is to monitor the performance of the CEO, to set his compensation, and to fire him and replace him with someone else in the expectation that the management and profitability of the business will be thereby improved. However, removal of a CEO is not an every-day event. In fact, the relationship between a CEO and the corporation's board of directors is complex because CEOs have historically had a major voice in deciding who should actually serve on the board of directors. The manager is usually directly involved in the selection of his overseers while the shareholders can only vote for or against the overseer so selected. Clearly, the relationship between management, the board of directors, and the shareholders is more complicated than theory would suggest.

Modern business corporation statutes recognize the reality that the board of directors of publicly held corporations do not directly manage the business. They provide that management of the corporation shall be "by or *under the direction of*" of the board of directors. MBCA (1984) § 8.30. The italicized phrase was added specifically with the role of the typical board of directors of the very large corporation in mind. In other words, boards of directors of publicly held corporations do not "manage;" the management "manages." It is almost always misleading to assume or suggest that there is actual management "by" the board of directors in large publicly held corporations.

Modern boards of directors are composed primarily of outside directors, who are busy persons often with their own businesses to run. One cannot realistically expect exhaustive continuous involvement in corporate affairs from those directors. Furthermore, in publicly held corporations, a modern board of directors is a part-time board. It may meet ten or twelve times a year, for perhaps for an average of four hours each. Much of that time is devoted to routine matters dealing with the board's activities, discussion of financial results, and reports of committees. Clearly, the board of directors of a large publicly held corporation is not going to be able to review a number of specific matters in depth at a meeting.

§ 13.11   The Election of Directors in Publicly Held Corporations

Again it is useful to separate theory from the reality. In theory, individual members of the board of directors are elected by the shareholders at meetings. Each director must be nominated and must receive, depending on the specific statute involved, either a majority or a plurality of all votes cast in the election. The theory is that shareholders select directors. The reality is quite different.

First of all, virtually all shareholders in publicly held corporations vote by proxy; only a handful of them actually attend meetings in person. (Indeed, there is no building in the world large enough to hold all the shareholders of GM). The decision as to who is to be elected is not made by the vote taken at the shareholders meeting; it is really resolved some time earlier by the filling out of proxy forms by the owners of shares that are voted by proxy. Further, shareholders voting by proxy can only vote with respect to persons who have been nominated, and the usual sole nominator is the corporation.

Second, shareholders voting by written proxy must rely primarily on information supplied by the corporation in a proxy statement. This statement and the form of proxy document must meet stringent SEC standards but information is provided only about the candidates for board of directors nominated by the corporation. Furthermore, proxy documents only contemplate a vote in favor of the management-sponsored directors or a withholding of the vote. A shareholder voting by proxy cannot direct that his vote be cast for himself or some other person not identified as a candidate in the proxy form. Proxies signed and returned will be voted for the management candidates unless the proxy is specifically directed to withhold the vote.

Third, it is difficult for other persons or groups to nominate alternative candidates. A shareholder at the meeting theoretically can nominate candidates on her own but that is a forlorn enterprise, since she cannot expect to get the votes of any shareholders (except perhaps the handful that are personally present at the meeting). It is possible for some outside group of shareholders also to solicit proxies in competition with management—a "proxy fight." However, because of the substantial cost of soliciting thousands of shareholders it is quite unusual for any competing group to make a serious solicitation in an effort to elect a majority of the directors in opposition to management. Further, a solicitation of proxies from more than ten shareholders requires compliance with the complex SEC proxy regulations, itself a costly process. As a result, genuine proxy fights for control occur in only a small handful of publicly held corporations every year. Much more likely is a negotiated take-over or an unfriendly cash tender offer made directly to the shareholders, though it is not uncommon for a proxy fight to be threatened as part of the negotiation process.

In the routine election for directors, in short, the management of the corporation designates (or extensively participates in the designation of) the candidates for directors. The information available to shareholders is provided by management, solicitation is undertaken at the expense of the corporation, and the return of the proxy form prepared by management is simplified by enclosing a return envelope with prepaid postage. Most shareholders, acting like sheep (or like responsible corporate citizens, if one prefers that image), sign the management's proxy form and return it in the convenient envelope provided by the corporation. The result of such an election is absolutely a foregone conclusion.

As one reflects on the reality of the selection process for members of the board of directors, it is clear that the selection of candidates is the critical step in the election process, not the election itself—that is ordinarily a foregone conclusion. Until relatively recently the CEO largely dominated the process of selecting management's candidates. Hence it is not surprising that Berle and Means, writing before World War II, viewed the typical board of directors as being totally under the control of management and therefore impotent or irrelevant in monitoring the management of the enterprise—the aspic on the fish, to use one graphic phrase of that era. As described in the following sections, however, the role of the board of directors has materially changed in many corporations since the Watergate scandals of the early 1970s.

§ 13.12 "Inside" and "Independent" Directors

A useful classification of directors is between "inside" directors and "outside" or "independent" directors. "Inside" directors consist of directors who are high level employees of the corporation or who who have some significant economic relationship to the corporation so that they are subject to influence by management. Examples include a banker affiliated with the major bank used as a depository by the corporation, a lawyer who was a partner in the law firm used by the corporation as its principal source of outside legal assistance, or executives of corporations that are suppliers to the corporation. "Outside" or "independent" directors are directors who do not have an employment or other significant economic relationship with the corporation. Today, all boards of publicly held corporations consist of both inside and outside directors, and their degree of independence from management dominance is clearly increasing.

In some classifications of directors, a three-fold distinction is made between "inside" directors—employees of the corporation, "affiliated outside directors"—outside directors with significant economic relationships with the corporation—and "unaffiliated outside directors." Affiliated outside directors are classed as inside directors in the discussion that follows.

§ 13.13. Relationships Between the CEO and the Board

Prior to 1970, the boards of directors of some publicly held corporations consisted entirely of inside directors. In corporations that as a matter of policy included independent directors on the board, the CEO would interview candidates he did not personally know and develop a social and personal relationship with them. The CEO also had power to drop independent directors from the board if they failed to agree with the views of the CEO. A CEO might limit outside directors to friends, college roommates, fraternity brothers, and the like. Such a board was stacked with "yes men" and good friends. Some literature from this period commented acidly that management believed the best kind of director to be one who could be expected to reliably say "yes" or "no" on cue. In corporations with management dominated boards, the board of directors would awaken from somnolence only when faced with dire emergency: the unexpected death or disability of the CEO when there was no clear heir apparent, a financial disaster of such a magnitude that it threatened the continued viability of the corporation, or something like that. While this picture is undoubtedly overdrawn in some respects, it was quite plausible since the CEO had such a dominant role in the selection of individual directors that the board was largely viewed as "his" board of directors.

Another important aspect of CEO dominance of corporate boards was the fact that the chief executive officer was usually also the chairman of the board of directors. He therefore was physically present at meetings of the board of directors and controlled both the agenda and whatever information was circulated to the members of the board of directors before or at the meeting. In this environment significant external input and oversight was difficult to obtain, and frank discussion and review of the CEO's performance was virtually impossible. A decision to request the CEO to resign involuntarily required a "palace coup," a virtual conspiracy by persons whose positions on the board, and sometimes their jobs, were at stake if the plot was revealed prematurely.

The principal catalyst for adding truly independent directors (though many corporations had added such directors many years earlier) was the Watergate-related scandals of the early 1970s. As a result of those scandals, the SEC required all publicly held corporations to create audit committees composed of independent directors to review financial reporting, the relationship with outside auditors, and the controls over unlawful conduct within each corporation. Corporations found it necessary to add independent directors to meet this requirement. The New York Stock Exchange, the National Association of Securities Dealers and the American Stock Exchange amended listing requirements to require that a majority of directors be independent directors. Influential organizations interested in corporate governance added their voice.

By 1980, influential organizations such as the Business Roundtable and the Business Law Section of the American Bar Association were recommending not only that boards of directors of all publicly held corporations should be predominantly composed of outside directors, but also that the critical function of selecting candidates for the board of directors should be vested in a nominating committee also composed predominantly of independent directors. The CEO is usually involved in the work of these committees on the theory that he must be able to work effectively with all outside directors. However, his influence in the actual selection process has declined. Nominees for outside directors are therefore not personally and exclusively selected by the CEO (though he continues to have a voice in their selection).

Not all publicly held corporations have created nominating committees. In these corporations, and possibly some which have created such committees as well, the CEO may continue to be the dominant voice in who should be nominated to serve as directors.

§ 13.14   The Modern Board of Directors

The average board of directors today may consist of 9 or 11 individuals; large boards of 15 or 17 persons are becoming less common. Perhaps one-third of the directors will be inside directors. The other two-thirds consist of independent directors: CEOs of other publicly held corporations, retired CEOs or high level executives of other publicly held corporations, perhaps a University president, a former public official, a successful small businessman, an independent investor, and so forth. Most corporations have one or more female directors; many have at least one minority director as well.

CEOs and former CEOs of other corporations are the most popular independent directors. The usual justifications for the predominance of CEOs of other corporations in the ranks of directors are that they understand the complexities of managing a large enterprise, they appreciate the complex relationship between the CEO and the board of directors and the need of the CEO for both support and disinterested recommendations and advice, and they understand the broad discretion that the CEO must have to run the enterprise. Also, CEOs and former CEOs have the practical experience and background necessary for them to provide useful and sophisticated advice when necessary. This may be a weakness as well as a strength. CEOs of other companies may sympathize with the incumbent's problem and give him the benefit of the doubt on a "there but for the grace of God go I" theory.

In any event, the modern CEO has to deal with a board of directors that is in part composed of persons with considerable business sophistication who are not employed by the corporation and who have a fair amount of independence from the CEO.

The roles of boards of directors since 1970 have moved significantly in the direction of increase oversight, participation, and monitoring the performance of the CEO. Illustrative of this change is the fact that in the 1990s a large number of CEOs of under-performing or marginal corporations have been dismissed abruptly by the board of directors. Companies involved include General Motors, Compaq Computer Corporation, General Electric, American Express, Apple Computing Company, and many others. There has been no similar period of CEO dismissals during the Twentieth Century, even during the depths of the Great Depression; clearly, what has changed today is the increased monitoring of the CEO's performance by independent directors.

Economic factors undoubtedly contributed to these decisions to replace sitting CEOs. The 1990s have been a period in which many corporations faced difficult economic and competitive conditions. Many businesses, large and small, found it necessary to close down unprofitable lines of business, to eliminate management level employees, and to increase the use of modern technology in order to remain competitive. Price increases were impractical in many industries; improvement in profit depended on a reduction in costs without loss of efficiency. Some CEOs found it difficult or impossible to adjust to these changed circumstances.

Also contributing to this development has been the increased activism of certain institutional investors commented upon earlier. which often leads to direct communications between independent directors and unhappy investors. See § 13.8 of this Nutshell. Large shareholders today may prefer to talk with independent directors rather than with the CEO or with management about problems they see with the management and success of the business. A good illustration of the tremendous changes in relationship between the CEO and the board of directors is the fact that independent directors in many publicly held corporations now meet separately from the CEO and inside directors at least once a year to discuss the performance of management. Proposals have also been floated to mandate a separation of the offices of CEO and chairman of the board of directors. While it is unlikely that this will be imposed as a mandatory requirement in the foreseeable future, the mere suggestion of it indicates the extent to which the CEO's power of control has shifted. Such a proposal would have been unthinkable a couple of decades ago. General Motors, perhaps the most traditional corporation in the automobile industry, has publicly released a "GM Board Guidelines for Corporate Governance Issues" which embodies and approves many of these developments.

What is the desired relationship between the CEO and a modern board of directors composed predominantly of independent directors? The CEO has direct responsibility for the conduct and financial success of the business and he must be supported by the board in this respect. The relationship between CEO and board of directors ideally should be a cooperative and mutually supportive one with the board providing advice and assistance on business matters as requested by the CEO. If monitoring is to be successful the relationship should be cooperative but not too close.

One basic function of the board of directors is to assure itself that there always is in place a command structure for the business of the corporation and that some one is in command. Some provision must be made for the catastrophic event in which the bulk of the senior management of the firm is wiped out in an accident. A second basic function is to assure itself that there is an accounting and reporting system in place that assures that transactions are being appropriately recorded and monitored by responsible managers. Indications that there are breakdowns in the accounting and reporting system must be taken as seriously as breakdowns in the command structure.

Modern boards periodically review the performance of the CEO, typically in connection with the issue of compensation. A modern board of directors will have a compensation committee composed of independent directors to deal with compensation matters for high level employees in general, and the CEO in particular. There may also be a separate committee to consider periodically the CEO's overall performance. However, the difficult and painful process of replacing the CEO if his stewardship of the business is unsatisfactory is largely independent of the committee review process. Basically, the CEO's continued tenure today is dependent on his ability to retain the confidence of the board of directors as a whole, particularly the independent directors on the board. Today the CEO is viewed as the highest level employee as much as he is viewed as the leader of the enterprise.

While CEOs are sometimes fired or forced to resign by the board of directors, boards exercise this ultimate power reluctantly and usually only after an extended period of less than satisfactory performance. If the business incurs losses of a magnitude that threaten its continued existence or becomes involved in massive unlawful conduct, individual independent members of the board of directors will act quickly and the CEO may depart very shortly. However, where performance is less than ideal, but the corporation continues to be at least marginally profitable, the process may be painful and drawn out. The first indications of dissatisfaction by one or more directors or institutional investors may be expressed privately only with other independent members of the board. As the concerns are shared with other directors the process slowly moves forward. It is a major step for an independent director to request that a special board meeting be called expressly without the presence of the CEO, or to request that the CEO who is present at a meeting to leave the room so that the directors may discuss openly his performance in his absence. In corporations where independent directors meet regularly by themselves out of the presence of the CEO the process may be quicker.

Inside directors do serve useful functions on a board with a majority of independent directors. Inside directors are familiar with what is going on inside the corporation and can give informed advice and assistance in decision-making on issues relating to the business of the corporation that come before the board of directors. They also may become aware that the CEO is aging or becoming less effective before independent members of the board of directors become aware of this. The issue of succession or replacement may be quietly raised with independent directors before the issue becomes acute, though there may be some personal risk in doing so. The members of management who serve as directors are also likely to be the leading candidates to succeed the incumbent CEO on his death or retirement. Independent directors thus become familiar with the likely successors.

§ 13.15 The "Chicago School" of Law and Economics

In the last three decades there has developed a law and economics analysis of the publicly held corporation that challenges many of the traditional beliefs about the role of management, the importance of takeover attempts by outsiders, and the efficacy of many legal rules. This analysis has come to be associated with scholars at the University of Chicago and will be referred to here as the "Chicago school" of analysis; it is appropriate to point out, however, that scholars with this analytic approach today teach at many different law schools. Central to the Chicago school analysis is the treatment of the corporation described in § 1.3 of this Nutshell as a "nexus of contracts" in which the shareholders are viewed as contributors of capital rather than ultimate owners of the business.

From a common sense viewpoint, it should be obvious that the interests of the CEO and top management might diverge from the interests of shareholders generally. The professional managers of the corporation—the CEO and his subordinates—are interested in keeping their positions, the power they have to direct a huge enterprise, their "perks," and their compensation. Shareholders on the other hand are interested in high dividends and high stock prices. During the last half of this century an analysis has developed that analyzes and rigorously identifies this divergence. As presented by Jensen and Meckling, Theory of the Firm: Managerial Behavior, Agency Costs, and Ownership Structure, 3 J. Fin. Econ. 305 (1976), this demonstration is both simple and elegant. One begins with an arrangement under which one or more persons (the principals) engage another person (the agent) to perform some function that requires delegation of decision-making authority to the agent. One further assumes that each party in the relationship is a rational utility maximizer, that is, that each attempts to obtain the most beneficial mix of (1) his own personal wealth to the extent he lawfully may do so and (2) the various non-pecuniary benefits that he prefers. Non-pecuniary benefits might include "the physical appointments of the office," "the level of employee discipline," "the kind and amount of charitable contributions," "personal relations ('love,' 'respect,' etc.) with employees," "a larger-than-optimal computer to play with," and "purchase of production inputs from friends." These non-pecuniary benefits of course have a cost to the enterprise, they are not free. If one first assumes that the owner of the business is also the manager, the owner will operate the business at a level and in a manner so the marginal utility to the owner of the pecuniary benefits he obtains from his ownership interest in the business equals the marginal utility to him of the non-pecuniary benefits. If the manager owns 50 percent of the residual equity interests in the business, on the other hand, a divergence from this optimal point will occur. The manager will again rationally maximize his utility, but since he bears only one half of the cost of the non-ownership benefits he will increase the consumption of those benefits to the point where the marginal utility of those benefits equals the marginal utility of fifty cents of increased purchasing power. As one posits that the residual interest of the manager declines (to less than one percent as is often the case in real life), the emphasis by the manager on non-ownership benefits increases. In other words, professional managers seek to maximize their own utility by increasing the emphasis on benefits that are charged to the entire enterprise and rely less on their proportional interest in the ownership of the business. The tendency of management to overconsume is often described in the literature as "shirking" by top management.

The divergence between the interest of professional managers and the interest of shareholders is described by economists as being part of a larger problem referred to in economic literature as "agency costs." Agency costs arise because of the separation of ownership and control, because of management's tendency to consume available perquisites, take excessive compensation, and shirk their responsibilities in search of maximizing their own personal utility. Jensen and Meckling define "agency costs" as the sum of (1) the "monitoring expenditures" by the principal, (2) the "bonding expenditures" by the agent, and (3) the residual loss (equal to the dollar loss caused by the manager's decisions that do not optimize the wealth of the owners). "Monitoring expenditures" include budget restrictions, compensation policies, operating rules, and so forth, imposed by the owners to limit the power of the manager to obtain non-pecuniary compensation. "Bonding expenditures" include contractual guarantees that the accounts will be audited by a public auditor, explicit bonding against malfeasance on the part of the manager, and contractual limitations on the decision-making power of the manager. In response, owners must spend resources to increase the fidelity of the managers to the enterprise and to the owners. These expenditures reduce the value of the enterprise and are the third part of the agency costs associated with the separation of management from ownership.

Agency costs may be reduced by aligning the interests of management with the owners. Thus, agency costs may be reduced by increasing the manager's financial interest in maximizing share prices through grants of options to purchase stock or plans that base compensation in part on the return to shareholders. Long term incentive compensation based on earnings and remuneration that is tied to long term increases in the stock price have the same effect. Thus compensation obtained through long term incentive compensation plans in the tens or hundreds of millions of dollars for a very successful CEO may be in the interests of shareholders since they may reduce agency costs by a greater amount. Recent proposals that have received some degree of acceptance are (1) to pay directors in shares rather than cash and (2) eliminate pension or retirement plans for directors.

Certainly a major contribution of economic analysis to the law of corporations has been rigorous analysis of this divergence in goals which in turn has led to extensive discussion as to how the interests of management may be more closely aligned with the interests of the shareholders.

Other aspects of economic analysis of legal rules should be briefly mentioned. When approaching legal rules, members of the Chicago school do not usually start with an already-existing problem and seek to devise a rule that does substantial justice to the persons involved in that problem. This approach is usually referred to as an "ex post" establishment of rules; the Chicago school prefers to adopt an "ex ante" approach that assumes the rule is already in place and asks how the presence of the rule will affect prospective transactions or behavior.

In a few articles or books written by law and economics scholars, there are references to the "shareholders" in publicly held corporations deciding to do X (or do not X), where X is a management decision that affects the value of the corporation's shares. These are almost always references either (1) to decisions rational shareholders would make if they actually voted in their own self-interest, or (2) to decisions made by managers of the corporation who are rationally acting in the best interest of shareholders generally. In some instances, they may be references to market consequences when shareholders exercise their "Wall Street Options." These decisions may be referred to as "implicit decisions." "Implicit" decisions are decisions that a rational investor would make if given a free choice as to alternatives, not real ones.

A final important contribution of the Chicago school is recognition of the importance of the securities markets as a disciplining device for management. The decisions by shareholders to sell their shares (the "Wall Street option") is in a sense a vote. A poor operating performance by management will result in shareholders selling shares, thus depressing share prices and leading indirectly to the ouster of management. Ouster may occur by forced dispossession by proxy fight, public tender offer, or exchange offer. Or it may be the merger or voluntary acquisition by outside interests under the veiled threat of a tender offer if the proposed transaction is rejected. Or it may be the result of the power of large institutional shareholders to threaten to exercise the voting power inherent in their holdings to oppose rather than to support management. Or it may be the threat by other members of the financial community—commercial or investment bankers—to limit the sources of the corporation's long and short term financing unless operating improvements are made. In addition, a palace coup may be a possibility in extreme situations.

Non-economic sources of pressure against under-performing corporations also exist. The threat of shareholders' derivative suits produces pressure. The disclosure requirements of federal law also may exercise a cautionary effect on management. Widespread publicity in the financial press produces pressure on the outside directors to take steps to correct current problems. While the threat that management will be turned out by an irate band of voters—as often occurs in political elections—is largely illusory in the large publicly held corporation, there is a very real possibility that incumbent management may lose the confidence of a majority of the directors and be forced to resign. The possibility of being ousted from a position of power for less than optimal performance is not, in the modern scene, purely theoretical.

§ 13.16 Share Prices and The Changing Body of Shareholders

One feature of publicly held corporations is that the composition of the body of shareholders is changing every day. Modern computerized securities trading programs permit major investors to sell their entire holdings instantaneously in order to capture an additional 25 or 50 cents per share. Many shareholders, particularly institutional investors that owe fiduciary duties to third parties to maximize gain, have a short term profit horizon; this gives management an incentive to keep the shareholders happy by making the short term share price as high as possible and preserving the flow of dividends at all costs even though the actions may not be in the long term best interest of the enterprise. Indeed, management sometimes take actions solely in order to bolster the market price of the stock. The announcement of a planned share buy-back by the corporation is a well known method of bolstering market price. The announcement of a plan to reduce the number of publicly traded shares outstanding through a buy-back usually has a positive effect on share prices even if the plan is never fully effectuated in the form it is announced.

Modern economic analysis suggests that management should act to maximize the intrinsic value of shares, acting as though it is "blissfully ignorant" of the effect of various decisions on the stock's market price. The phrase "blissfully ignorant" is taken from Hu, Risk, Time, and Fiduciary Principles in Corporate Investment, 38 U.C.L.A. L.Rev. 277. However, it is likely that many managers do not do so, and it is probably not reasonable to expect them to do so given the importance that share prices have in the eyes of sophisticated investors.

§ 13.17　The Takeover Movement of the 1980s

The 1980s saw a wave of third party offers to purchase control of large corporations at premium prices significantly above the then current market prices. (This wave ended abruptly in about 1990 but a new and somewhat more rational wave of takeovers is taking place in the latter half of the 1990s.)

Law and Economics scholars suggest that these takeover transactions constitute a market device that disciplines managements that are not maximizing shareholder value. The theory is that anyone willing to borrow billions of dollars to purchase control of a large corporation must believe that he or she can produce greater shareholder value than is currently being produced by the incumbent management. Most economics scholars appear to accept this analysis as the most plausible explanation for most transactions of this period. However, other less optimistic explanations have also been put forth. The takeover movement has been described as an example of speculative excess with little social value similar to the tulip boom in Holland or the American stock market in the late 1920s. Still other explanations suggest that the takeover movement of the late 1980s was largely driven by the benefits of substituting tax-deductible interest payments for taxable distributions. But economists believe that some takeovers in fact did improve efficiency and therefore provided significant benefits to corporate governance by automatically eliminating less efficient managers and that the takeover movement to that extent at least was beneficial from an efficiency standpoint.

In struggles for control where an unfriendly offer to purchase a majority of the voting shares has been made, the blocks controlled by institutional investors may be absolutely critical. The votes of institutional investors (or decisions whether or not to sell) may effectively determine who should ultimately control the corporation.

Many economists view the end of the takeover era in 1990 as a most unfortunate development. These scholars suggest that in the absence of market forces to purge inefficient managers, renewed emphasis must be placed on the roles of (1) independent directors, and (2) large institutional investors to monitor the CEO and assure the effectiveness of management. However, these monitoring devices are viewed as more problematic in monitoring managers than the powerful market device of outside takeovers.

§ 13.18 Proxy Regulation in Publicly Held Corporations

Most modern law of proxy regulation is of federal rather than state origin. Section 14(a) of the Securities Exchange Act of 1934 makes it unlawful for any person to use the mails or any means or instrumentality of interstate commerce or the facilities of a national securities exchange "in contravention of such rules and regulations as the [Securities and Exchange] Commission may prescribe as necessary or appropriate in the public interest or for the protection of investors" to solicit any proxy appointment in respect of any security registered under section 12 of the Act. Pursuant to this broad grant of authority to regulate proxies, the SEC has issued comprehensive and detailed regulations that define not only the form of proxy solicitation documents but also require the distribution of substantial information about issuer, the the backgrounds of candidates for directorships and other issues to be voted upon by shareholders.

Section 12 of the Securities Exchange Act requires the following corporations to register securities: all corporations a) with shares registered on a national securities exchange or b) having assets in excess of $5,000,000 and a class of equity securities is held of record by 500 persons or more. It is not the total number of security holders that is significant, but the number of holders of the specific class of security for which registration is being considered. For example, a corporation with 400 shareholders of record holding common stock, and another 400 shareholders of record holding preferred stock is not required to register either class under section 12, and therefore is not subject to proxy regulation (unless, of course, a class of shares is registered on a national securities exchange). However, once a corporation is required to register under section 12, its registration may be terminated only if (a) the number of shareholders of the class drops below 300, or (b) the assets drop below $5,000,000 and the shareholders of the class below 500.

The constitutional basis for federal proxy regulation is the use of the mails or an instrumentality of interstate commerce. As a practical matter, it is probably impossible to solicit proxies in connection with a security registered under section 12 without using the mails or facilities of interstate commerce. Congress gave the SEC this very broad grant of rulemaking authority because in 1934 it was concerned about abuses in the proxy process but was uncertain about what the remedies should be.

The SEC proxy rules may be broken down into four broad categories—

(1) Requirements of disclosure of full information to shareholders relating to (a) proposals for action by shareholders presented by management through the proxy solicitation machinery, and (b) to a lesser extent, general information about the operations of the corporation.

(2) Prohibitions against the use of fraud or deceptive nondisclosure in the solicitation of proxies.

(3) Requirements that appropriate proposals submitted by shareholders be included in the proxy solicitation materials prepared by management, so that shareholders have an opportunity to consider them.

(4) Special requirements applicable only to proxy fights.

§ 13.19 Disclosure Requirements in Connection With Proxy Solicitations

The SEC proxy regulations (rule 14a–3) provide that with certain exceptions no solicitation of a proxy appointment may be made unless each person is furnished at the same time a proxy statement setting forth detailed information about the corporation's affairs (if management is making the solicitation), about the background of all directors and nominees, about remuneration and other transactions with management and with others, and about any matter on which the vote of shareholders is sought. Proxy statements are not required for solicitations that involve less than ten persons and solicitations by brokers to beneficial owners to determine how to vote shares held in the name of the broker. The term "proxy statement" has been broadly construed to include newspaper ads and informal communications among shareholders with respect to voting plans. In 1992, the SEC narrowed its regulations to permit communications that may specify how the writer plans to vote but does not itself solicit proxies. (This is the provision that has permitted institutional investors to take an increased role in corporate governance.) Proxy statements under rule 14a–3 are one of the major sources of shareholder information about corporate affairs.

Before 1992, the SEC conducted a presolicitation clearance and review process for proxy documents. This process was discontinued in 1992 and currently the SEC only requires that preliminary proxy statement forms be filed before a solicitation begins, and that no proxy be actually solicited until after the filing of a definitive proxy statement. SEC staff reviews preliminary proxy statements to ensure proper disclosure; in this respect it is a "neutral umpire" in the proxy process.

The SEC disclosure requirements also indirectly require the distribution of annual reports. Rule 14a–3(b) provides that if a solicitation is made on behalf of management relating to an annual meeting of shareholders at which directors are to be elected, the proxy statement must be accompanied or preceded by an annual report of the corporation. This is the only basis in most states to require the distribution of an annual report, perhaps the most helpful informational document to shareholders generally.

Corporate management usually must solicit proxy appointments in order to assure that there is a quorum at the meeting. (As a practical matter, the number of shares voted by shareholders who appear personally plus the number of shares owned by management is likely to be numerically insignificant and much less than the minimum required for a quorum). In some corporations subject to registration under section 12, however, major shareholders who will be present in person at the meeting may own enough shares to constitute a quorum without any solicitation of public shareholders. A special section of the Securities Exchange Act of 1934 requires that section 12 corporations that plan to conduct a shareholders' meeting without making a qualified proxy solicitation must supply shareholders with the same information that would have been required if a solicitation had been made. This section graphically illustrates that a major purpose of SEC proxy regulation is to ensure that significant information is made available to shareholders, whether or not they are requested to approve or disapprove some matter. It may be noted in passing that state corporation statues require notice of

a shareholders meeting be given to all shareholders entitled to vote but usually do not require the disclosure of
specific information.

Section 13.9 of this Nutshell discussed the practice of
holding shares in book entry form or in the names of
nominees. This practice creates a problem for the SEC
proxy disclosure process since the beneficial owners of
such shares do not directly receive proxy statements or
annual reports and are not entitled to vote directly (since
they are not the record owners). SEC regulations require
that brokers and dealers transmit proxy material to the
beneficial owners of shares that are held in book entry or
street name form, and either (i) execute proxy appointment forms in blank, and deliver them to the beneficial
owners so that the shares may be voted by them, or (ii)
directly vote the shares as the beneficial owners direct.
The distribution of proxy statements and appointment
forms is now usually handled by private companies spe-
cializing in that activity. The counting of votes (particularly
if a controversial issue is under consideration) also may be
undertaken by specialized firms. Studies by the SEC have
concluded that these indirect methods of distribution of
proxy information and the counting of votes work reasonably effectively. Nevertheless, section 7.23 of the Model
Business Corporation Act (1984) sets forth an alternative
(and experimental) device that permits corporations to
establish procedures to treat beneficial owners of shares
as traditional registered owners. Such procedures have
been discussed but no effort made to implement them
widely.

SEC regulations also require record holders and intermediaries to disclose the names of beneficial holders
directly to the issuer (unless the beneficial holder objects)
so that the issuer may communicate directly with the
beneficial owners. Some brokerage firms recommend that
their customers object to the disclosure of their identities.

Beneficial owners who permit their identities to be disclosed are called "NOBOs," non-objecting beneficial owners.

SEC regulations also prescribe the proxy appointment form itself and prohibit certain devices such as undated or post-dated proxy appointment forms or broad grants of discretionary power to proxies in such forms. Shareholders must be given the option to vote for or against candidates for directors, and proxies must actually vote the shares as shareholders direct for the election of directors and on other issues presented for decision to the shareholders.

Non-compliance with the SEC's proxy regulations entails significant risks. The SEC has authority to assess monetary penalties for non-compliance with its regulations under the Securities Enforcement Remedies and Penny Stock Reform Act of 1990. It may also issue cease and desist orders.

§ 13.20 Shareholder Proposals

Rule 14a–8 establishes a procedure by which shareholders may submit proposals for inclusion in the registrant's proxy solicitation material. If the proposal is an appropriate one for shareholder action, and is timely, registrant must include the proposal even if opposed to it. This is one of the few ways that small minority shareholders may communicate with fellow shareholders. Users of this device include church, public interest, and advocacy groups in an effort to obtain support for their views on public issues, for example levels of executive compensation, discrimination, affirmative action, the treatment of minority groups, the use of nuclear power and environmental concerns. Such proposals are openly political in nature. These proposals are almost never approved by a majority of the shareholders, but the process does require the corporation to address the concerns of these groups. It is therefore widely believed that even defeated proposals relating to corporate matters have an indirect educational effect and may call top management's attention to some problem area that exists in the corporation's activities. Certainly some shareholder proposals decisively rejected at the polls have been subsequently quietly accepted and implemented by management. Nevertheless, concern has sometimes been expressed that the costs imposed by the shareholder proposal rule outweigh the benefits of that rule.

Institutional investors have sometimes utilized this process in their effort to influence management decision-making. Proposals presented by institutional investors usually deal with issues of direct concern to the electorate: secret ballot procedures, the adoption of cumulative voting, rotating the location of annual meetings, and actions with respect to "poison pill" defenses implemented by the board of directors without shareholder vote. These proposals not uncommonly receive substantial support, and have been approved in some instances. At the present time, however, most institutional investors prefer to discuss problems with independent directors directly on an informal basis rather than utilize the shareholder proposal device, though a few institutional investors continue to use the rule 14a–8 process.

When a corporation does receive a serious shareholder's communication, it will usually respond and seek to reach a mutually acceptable accommodation. (In the past, many corporations as a matter of policy refused to discuss matters with shareholders on the theory that business decisions were for management and the board of directors; this attitude is changing.) Many proposals are settled at a preliminary stage before the filing of a formal shareholder's proposal. For example, in 1994, the New York City pension funds were able to persuade corporations to adopt 13 of their proposals without submitting them to shareholders. If that is not possible, management may seek to obtain a "no action letter" from the SEC stating that the staff will not recommend that action be taken by the SEC because the proposal falls within one or more of the permissible exclusions described below. An important recent decision by the Second Circuit holds that a no action letter is not formal agency action that may be subject to immediate judicial review.

If management does oppose a proposal, the proposing shareholder may include a statement of not more than 500 words in support of his or her proposal. A shareholder may submit only one proposal in a proxy statement. Even though the proponent is limited to 500 words, management may explain the basis of its opposition without limitation.

Because shareholders may seek action on proposals of dubious relevance or propriety, or simply for personal publicity, the SEC has imposed specific requirements and limitations on shareholder's proposals. The application of these requirements and limitations has resulted in some litigation, and a substantial body of administrative rulings by the SEC. The SEC has also issued policy statements from time to time with respect to issues raised by shareholder proposals.

Under present SEC regulations, a shareholder's proposal may be omitted in a variety of circumstances. The most important reasons for omission are:

(1) It is not a proper subject for action by security holders under the law of the issuer's domicile;

(2) It relates to the enforcement of a personal claim or the redress of a personal grievance, against the issuer, its management, or any person;

(3) It deals with a matter that is not significantly related to the issuer's business;

(4) It deals with a matter relating to the ordinary business operations of the issuer;

(5) It relates to an election to office;

(6) It is substantially the same as a proposal by another shareholder which will be included in the proxy materials;

(7) Substantially the same proposal has previously been submitted to the shareholders within the previous five years and failed to receive specified percentages of the vote, depending on the number of times it was submitted previously;

(8) It relates to specific amounts of dividends.

Over the years the SEC has issued numerous rulings applying many of these exclusions; as a result, phrases such as "proper subject" or "ordinary business operations" have been given considerable practical content, and the tests are not as open-ended as the language might indicate. For example, the SEC has ruled that important business related proposals are "proper subjects" for shareholder action under state law if they are phrased as recommendations to the board rather than specific directions. See the discussion of state law on this subject in § 8.2 of this Nutshell.

§ 13.21 Private Actions for Violations of Federal Proxy Rules

Rule 14a–9 makes it unlawful to distribute proxy solicitation information that contains "any statement which, at the time and in the light of the circumstances under which it is made, is false or misleading with respect to any material fact, or which omits to state any material fact necessary in order to make the statements therein not false or misleading." This broad prohibition was held to create a private cause of action by shareholders. J. I. Case Co. v. Borak (S.Ct.1964). The Court argued that rule 14a–

9 created a private cause of action since, "private enforcement of the proxy rules provides a necessary supplement to Commission action. As in antitrust treble damage litigation, the possibility of civil damages or injunctive relief serves as a most effective weapon in the enforcement of the proxy requirements." Subsequent decisions by the United States Supreme Court have refused to follow this reasoning when determining whether private causes of action arise under other statutory provisions; however, despite occasional criticism, the Court appears to be unwilling to reconsider *Borak* itself.

Since *Borak* there has been a substantial volume of private litigation under rule 14a–9. Such litigation is within the exclusive jurisdiction of the Federal courts so that state "security for expenses" statutes are inapplicable (see § 16.8 of this Nutshell). Rule 14a–9 litigation has largely been shaped by three subsequent decisions by the United States Supreme Court. In TSC Industries, Inc. v. Northway, Inc. (S.Ct.1976), in an opinion widely read as heralding a narrowing of the scope of the private cause of action under rule 14a–9, the Court defined a "material fact" in language that has been widely cited in other contexts:

An omitted fact is material if there is a substantial likelihood that a reasonable shareholder would consider it important in deciding how to vote.

The competing test that was rejected would have defined material facts to include all facts "which a reasonable shareholder *might* consider appropriate." While the difference between the rejected and adopted tests may seem primarily semantic, the Court's distinction constituted a warning to lower courts to limit rule 14a–9 to substantial misstatements. Prior to this decision some courts had tended to find relatively minor misstatements or omissions to be "material" and therefore violations of rule 14a–9.

The other two important cases are Mills v. Electric Auto–Lite Co. (S.Ct.1970) and Virginia Bankshares, Inc. v. Sandberg (S.Ct.1991). *Mills* involved the question of the required nexus between a material misstatement or omission and the approval of the proposal. It held that it was unnecessary to show a direct causal relationship between the violation and the vote; it was only necessary to show that the proxy solicitation was itself an essential step in the transaction under attack. It therefore concluded that examination of the reliance by individual shareholders on a specific misstatement should not be inquired into, and that reliance should be presumed if the vote was necessary for the completion of the merger under consideration. *Mills* also discusses at some length the remedies available for a violation of rule 14a–9 after the transaction in question has been consummated, and the right of the plaintiffs attorney to recover attorneys' fees in rule 14a–9 cases. *Virginia Bankshares* concludes that the following statement was a statement of fact and not a statement of opinion that could be made the basis of a 14a–9 claim: "The plan of merger has been approved by the Board of Directors because it provides an opportunity for the Bank's public shareholders to achieve a high value for their shares." In fact the directors did not believe that the price offered was a "high" price. *Virginia Bankshares* also holds that a 14a–9 claim cannot be maintained if the vote of the shareholders could not block the transaction in question.

§ 13.22 Proxy Contests

A traditional proxy contest is a struggle for control of a public corporation in which most of the high cards are typically held by management. A non-management group (usually referred to as "insurgents") compete with management in an effort to obtain sufficient proxy appointments to elect a majority of the board of directors and

thereby obtain control. Management has several advantages in a proxy fight: (1) it has the current list of
shareholders, while the insurgents may have to go to
court to get it (while this was a major advantage at an
earlier time, the growth of book entry and street name
registration makes this of little importance today); (2)
within a broad range, management may finance its solicitation from the assets of the corporation, while the insurgents must finance their campaign from outside sources;
and (3) for the reasons discussed earlier, shareholders
may have a pro-management bias. (See § 13.7 of this
Nutshell.) For many years, these advantages appeared to
be overwhelming and relatively few proxy fights were
instituted. Insurgents wishing to take over another company preferred to use cash tender offers rather than proxy
fights. With the growth of the shareholdings of institutional investors and their increased activism (see § 13.8 of this
Nutshell), however, there has been a resurgence in interest in the proxy fight as a device to get management's
attention, if not to oust it outright. In these modern proxy
fights, the roles of institutional investors are usually critical. The willingness of institutional investors to support
insurgents in specific instances undoubtedly contributed
to an increase in the number of such contests during the
late 1980s.

In the traditional proxy fight, an insurgent group, desiring to contest management control, usually first purchases
a substantial block of shares in the open market before
openly announcing its intentions. Under the Williams Act,
a person or group acquiring more than five per cent of the
voting stock of a registered company must file a disclosure
statement within ten days after the acquisition that puts it
over the five per cent figure. The insurgents must then
obtain a list of important shareholders in order to conduct
what is essentially a political campaign to persuade major
shareholders to make proxy appointments in their favor. A

shareholders' list may be sought, though a good deal of information is publicly available about the holdings of institutional investors many of them publish their portfolios on a regular basis, and if a limited solicitation of large shareholders is contemplated, the corporate shareholders' list may not be necessary. Specialized proxy contest firms are available to assist both management and insurgents in the campaign. Advertisements in the financial press are regularly used in an effort to reach smaller shareholders. Large shareholders are contacted individually. The process can be expensive, running into the hundreds of thousands or millions of dollars.

Traditional proxy fights may occur in relatively small publicly held corporations. Today, they are more likely to be used (or threatened) in conjunction with tender or exchange offers. The aggressor may acquire a substantial minority position in the target by public tender offer and then use a proxy contest to obtain sufficient additional votes to replace incumbent management. This tactic has been used when the aggressor lacks sufficient resources to acquire a majority of the target's shares outright. It may also be used when management's defenses against a purchase-type takeover appeared to be impregnable, and the aggressor feels compelled to seek proxy appointments to force the dismantling of those defenses.

Proxy fights for public corporations subject to section 12 of the Securities Exchange Act of 1934 are subject to regulation by the Securities and Exchange Commission. State law on the subject tends to be rudimentary and there are very few reported state cases dealing with proxy fights. However, issues such as the validity of proxy appointments and the propriety of allocating expenses to the corporation may be governed by state law, presumably the law of the state of incorporation under the "internal affairs" rule.

The costs of a proxy fight is usually largely born by the corporation. There appears to be no doubt that the corporation should pay for printing and mailing the notice of meeting, the proxy statement required by Federal law, and the proxy appointments themselves. These are legitimate expenses because without the solicitation of proxy appointments it is unlikely that a quorum of shareholders may be obtained. Most courts have gone further and allowed the corporation to be charged for the reasonable expenses of management of educating shareholders if the controversy involves a "policy" question rather than a mere "personal" struggle for control. Since virtually every proxy fight may be dressed up as a "policy" rather than "personal" dispute, the net effect is substantially all of the management expenses may be paid by the corporation. While some judges have suggested that a narrower test should be applicable to management expenses, these suggestions have not prevailed.

A different question is presented if the insurgents are successful and seek to have the corporation reimburse them for their expenses. Reimbursement of successful insurgents has been permitted if (a) approved by the shareholders and (b) the dispute involved "policy" rather than "personalities." Where these tests are met, the corporation ends up paying for the expenses of both sides since losing management will normally reimburse itself before leaving office. Again, there is a strong undercurrent of judicial opinion which would sharply limit or totally preclude insurgents' reimbursement, but this view has not prevailed.

Law review writers have sometimes suggested that reimbursement should be permitted for unsuccessful insurgents since they may perform a socially useful function but there is apparently no authority for doing so. Most economists view proxy fights as basically desirable phenomena that help rid corporations of inefficient or ineffective management.

§ 13.23 Federal Regulations Relating to Proxy Contests

The Securities and Exchange Commission has promulgated special regulations applicable to proxy contests. These regulations require "participants" other than management in a proxy contest to file specified information with the SEC and the securities exchanges at least five days before a solicitation begins. "Participant" is defined to include anyone who contributes more than $500 for the purpose of financing the contest. The information that must be disclosed relates to the identity and background of the participants, their interests in securities of the corporation, when they were acquired, financing arrangements, participation in other proxy contests, and understandings with respect to future employment with the corporation.

The general philosophy of the proxy contest regulations is well expressed by Judge Clark, of the Second Circuit: "Appellants' fundamental complaint appears to be that stockholder disputes should be viewed in the eyes of the law just as are political contests, with each side free to hurl charges with comparative unrestraint, the assumption being that the opposing side is then at liberty to refute and thus effectively deflate the 'campaign oratory' of its adversary. Such, however, was not the policy of Congress as enacted in the Securities Exchange Act." SEC v. May (2d Cir.1956).

§ 13.24 The Modern Takeover Movement

The growth of cash-oriented takeover techniques has been perhaps the most spectacular development in corporate and securities law since World War II. Cash purchases of publicly held corporations became feasible as a result of a major economic development in the 1960s: the growth of very large pools of capital. This takeover movement not only shook the complacency of management to its core but also enriched the vocabulary of corporate law, led to statutory enactments at both the federal and state levels, and raised important issues of state and federal power.

An appropriate starting point for describing the modern takeover movement is the classic cash tender as it evolved in the 1960s. A cash tender offer is a public invitation to the shareholders of the "target" corporation to tender their shares to the "aggressor" corporation for purchase at a specified price, originally about 20 percent in excess of the then current market price, but later 50 percent or more above that price. In the late 1960s, there were numerous cash tender offers, the success of which were largely based on the element of surprise, virtually blitzkrieg tactics since management had not developed defenses.

The element of surprise was largely eliminated by the Williams Act (technically not a separate statute but a series of amendments to the Securities Exchange Act of 1934 that were adopted in 1968 and 1970). Under the Williams Act, any person who makes a cash tender offer for a corporation registered under section 12 must disclose information as to the source of funds used in the offer, the purpose for which the offer is made, plans the aggressor have if successful, and contracts or understandings with respect to the target corporation. The Act also requires the issuer to respond to the offer. The Act also imposes miscellaneous substantive restrictions on the mechanics of these offers, as well as including a broad prohibition against the use of false, misleading, or incomplete statements in connection with such an offer. In Piper v. Chris–Craft Industries, Inc. (S.Ct.1977), the Court held that a defeated tender offeror did not have standing to sue for damages under this provision of the Williams Act. This Act also requires filing and public disclosure by anyone who acquires more than 5 per cent of the outstanding shares of any class of securities of a section 12 corporation. These requirements eliminated the element of surprise. Similar requirements are also imposed upon (1) issuers making an offer for their own shares, or (2) issuers in which a change of control is proposed to be made by seriatim resignations of directors.

The Williams Act did not halt the takeover movement, but led to increasingly sophisticated tactics by aggressors. The success of takeover bids was largely due to the large premiums over market price offered by aggressors rather than the element of surprise. These premiums virtually assured that profit-conscious institutional investors would tender into the takeover bid. When a cash offer to purchase was made, the open market price for the shares immediately increased dramatically so that it was close to the tender offer price. (Whether it equaled or exceeded the tender offer price depended on a complex variety of factors, including the probability that a competing offer at a higher price might be made, whether the offer was likely to be over-subscribed, and so forth.) Persons owning shares had the choice of selling their shares in the open market or tendering them into the offer. Most shares sold on the open market were ultimately tendered as a group of speculators, known as arbitrageurs, purchased shares in the open market at prices below the tender offer price in order to tender them and profit by the difference between the two prices. In several spectacular incidents, competing bids from different aggressors were forthcoming. If another bidder entered the battle, the arbitrageurs would accumulate shares to await the ultimate winner and then tender the shares, profiting even more. The volume of transactions effected by arbitrageurs during this period was very substantial.

A company that was made the target of a takeover attempt was said to be "in play;" once in play, Wall Street wisdom went, the company was sure to be taken over by somebody, though this was not invariably true.

A great deal of attention has been given to the economic effects of these cash-type acquisitions of huge publicly held corporations in the 1970s and 1980s. There seems to be general agreement that the shareholders of the target corporation benefited; there was less agreement about the effect on the aggressor, whose shares often declined in price if the offer was successful. By combining these two effects, the gain usually outweighed the losses. Economists argued that such transactions increased value but the source of this increase was the subject of considerable speculation. The most common suggestions were the elimination of less efficient management, synergy, or the development of monopoly power. After a company was taken over, portions of the business might be sold off in order to pay down the debt incurred to acquire the business (a "bust up" acquisition). In many instances, the sum of the value of the parts of the target substantially exceeded the cost of the whole. This clearly seemed to be unlocking the value in an under-priced company. However, skeptics suggested that takeovers fundamentally had nothing to do with efficiency but were profitable only because the securities markets systematically under-valued non-controlling blocks of corporate stock. Another suggestion was that these transactions were profitable because they involved transfer payments from other constituencies in the corporation, particularly bondholders. Yet another suggestion was that many of these transactions were either tax-driven or were motivated by a desire for power on aggressors, or both, and therefore had no positive long term effect. In some cases, empire building or ego-gratification were pointed to.

Public takeover activity reached its peak in the 1980s. Aggressors were able to obtain access to billions of dollars of capital to purchase publicly held companies. This period saw the development of a new kind of transaction, the "leveraged buyout" (LBO). An LBO involved the purchase of all the outstanding shares of a publicly held corporation for cash raised by the issuance of "junk bonds" to institutional investors and others, and through temporary or "bridge" loans from commercial banks. Multi-billion dollar cash transactions became common-place. The expected source of repayment of these loans was the earnings and cash flow of the target corporation. LBOs are "bootstrap" acquisitions: the acquired business provides the funds to finance its own purchase. In many instances, incumbent management participated in the buyout, and managed the business after the public shareholders were eliminated. The fear of becoming the target of such a takeover led many publicly held corporations to reduce their attractiveness as an LBO candidate by distributing excess cash and by voluntarily restructuring their capitalization by substituting debt for equity. This might be done by borrowing funds in order to make an extraordinary dividend payment or by distributing debt instruments directly to shareholders. Whether or not all this was desirable from a social or economic perspective is extremely controversial.

In LBO situations the aggressor almost always planned to restructure the target company in a way that required the aggressor to own 100 percent of the outstanding shares of the target. Following a purchase offer, there will always remain a handful of shareholders who did not sell into even the most attractive and successful offer. These remaining minority interests are readily eliminated by a "cash out merger" of the type described in chapter 20 of this Nutshell.

The era of leveraged buyouts and unsolicited takeover attempts came to a crashing halt at the end of the 1980s with the collapse of the Drexel Lambert securities firm and the subsequent drying up of sources of capital to finance such transactions. A number of LBOs failed, the cash flow not being sufficient to carry the load of debt added by the LBO. "Junk bond" offerings had to be withdrawn because of lack of interest; some banks that had made "bridge" loans to finance an LBO discovered that they in fact were permanent lenders rather than interim ones.

Following this collapse, the takeover movement remained quiescent for about four years. In late 1993, takeover transactions began to occur, and the volume increased significantly by 1996. But these transactions differ both qualitatively and quantitatively from the transactions of the 1980s. They are not financially driven, hostile takeovers and leveraged buyouts. Rather, they involve major United States corporations that are acquiring smaller companies or merging in an effort to acquire the size and resources to compete in the United States and abroad with major foreign competitors. Size hopefully assures the ability to invest in new technology, to develop new products, and to guarantee access to world-wide markets. Computer hardware and software companies, banks and entertainment companies have been the most visible participants in this new movement: for example, Chase Bank and Chemical Bank, Disney and American Broadcasting Company, Time Warner and Turner Broadcasting Company. However, these mergers are also appearing in diverse industries, including drugs, paper products and consumer products. This trend is in full swing as of the time this is written.

§ 13.25 Defensive Tactics

With the increasing success of cash tender offers during the 1980s, a great deal of attention was paid to defensive tactics designed to make takeover bids more difficult. These tactics, varying from the blunt to the sophisticated, clearly increased in sophistication over time. Popular tactics included: finding a more congenial suitor (a "white knight"); buying a business that increased the chances that the threatened takeover will give rise to anti-trust problems; adopting voting procedures that made it difficult for an offeror who acquires a majority of the voting shares to replace the board of directors; instituting suit to enjoin the offer for violations of the Williams Act, the antitrust laws, or on other grounds; issuing or proposing to issue additional shares to friendly persons to make a takeover more difficult (a "lockup"); increasing the dividend or otherwise driving up the price of shares to make the takeover price unattractive; amending the basic corporate documents to make a takeover by even a majority shareholder more difficult; buying off the aggressor; buying up the corporation's own shares in the market to drive up the price; creating new classes of stock that increase in rights if any person acquires more than a specified percentage of shares ("poison pills"); and imposing restrictions in connection with the creation of debt that thwart attempted takeovers. Of these varying devices, the poison pill was developed into the most effective defensive tactic. A poison pill threatened to make an unwanted takeover unduly expensive to the aggressor and therefore encouraged the aggressor to negotiate with the incumbent management.

Many cases have considered the validity of defensive tactics in different contexts. Of particular importance are a series of Delaware cases that have largely shaped the permissible area of takeover defenses. Moran v. Household International, Inc. (Del.1985), upheld under Delaware law the adoption of a "poison pill" as a defensive tactic in advance of a specific takeover attempt. In Unocal Corp. v. Mesa Petroleum Co. (Del.1985), the Court set forth the basic test for evaluating defensive tactics: to be protected by the business judgment rule, a defensive tactic must be reasonable in relation to the threat posed to the corporation. This evaluation requires "enhanced judicial scrutiny" over and above the traditional business judgment rule standard. See § 14.7. In Revlon, Inc. v. MacAndrews & Forbes Holdings, Inc. (Del.1985), the court held that when the board of directors concludes that the sale of the business is inevitable, its role shifts from a participant in the contest to a more neutral stance ensuring that the shareholders get the best possible price for their shares. In Paramount Communications, Inc. v. Time, Inc. (Del.1989) the court modified the Revlon/Unocal test and adopted a "range of reasonableness" test. In Paramount Communications, Inc. v. QVC Network, Inc. (Del.1994) the court held that the lower court should apply its "enhanced scrutiny" to determine whether defensive measures were "draconian," defined as either "coercive or preclusive." And, in Unitrin, Inc. v. American General Corp. (Del.1995) the Court required the lower court to consider, first, whether the defensive measures were draconian, and if not, whether they were reasonable responses to the threat presented.

These decisions by the Delaware Supreme Court elaborating upon the basic rules about defensive tactics have been difficult to predict in advance, holding in some cases that the defensive tactic was proper and in others enjoining the use of specific tactics.

§ 13.26   State Legislative Responses to the Takeover Movement

From the outset of the takeover movement, individual states believed that they were directly and adversely affected by takeover attempts by outside interests to take over large local corporations. In part this was probably due to the political power of large local corporations. The first wave of antitakeover statutes, called Business Take–Over Acts, required a pre-offer notification period, a filing of a registration statement, review and a public hearing by the Secretary of State, and approval or disapproval by that office if it concluded the transaction was fair to domestic shareholders. In Edgar v. MITE Corp. (S.Ct.1982), the United States Supreme Court held the Illinois statute of this type unconstitutional under the Commerce Clause.

The states promptly turned to other statutory devices to protect local corporations against unwanted takeover attempts. In CTS Corporation v. Dynamics Corp. of America (S.Ct.1987), the Supreme Court upheld the Indiana Control Share Acquisitions Act, a statute that was clearly enacted to make unwanted acquisitions of Indiana corporations more difficult. Under this statute, a person who purchased shares that increased his percentage of ownership above specified limits was prohibited from voting the additional shares without the prior approval of the remaining shareholders. The opinion of Justice Powell In *CTS* is particularly note-worthy because it carved out a broad area of state regulation in the takeover area, rejecting the argument that there was a "market for control" that was protected from state interference by the Commerce Clause. The Court also rejected the argument that state-created defenses for domestic corporations were preempted by the Williams Act. Since *CTS*, more than forty states have adopted statutes designed to make more difficult the acquisition of publicly held corporations incorporated in that state.

Another type of antitakeover statute are called "business combination" statutes. These statutes restrict the right of persons who acquire more than a specified percentage of stock from engaging in a variety of transactions with the target corporation for a specified period after the acquisition without the prior consent of the pre-acquisition board of directors. In 1988, Delaware adopted such a statute [§ 203 of the Delaware General Corporation Law]. That statute provides that if a person acquires 15 percent or more of a corporation's stock it may not engage in a wide variety of transactions with the corporation for a period of three years, with several exceptions. Because of the importance of Delaware as the state of incorporation of publicly held corporations, this statute has had wide impact. This statute has been upheld by lower courts relying on the broad language of *CTS*.

[For unfamiliar terms see the Glossary]

CHAPTER FOURTEEN

DUTIES OF DIRECTORS, SHAREHOLDERS AND OFFICERS

§ 14.1   The Director as a "Fiduciary"

The duties of directors may be divided into two broad categories: a duty of care and a duty of loyalty or, as it is sometimes phrased, a duty of "fair dealing." The latter duty is often referred to as a "fiduciary" duty.

Because of their broad powers of management, directors occupy a unique position within the corporate structure. They undoubtedly owe a high degree of fidelity and loyalty to the corporation in connection with their actions. These duties are often referred to as "fiduciary duties," and directors are sometimes referred to as "fiduciaries" and their duties are analogized to those of a trustee of a trust. References to the "fiduciary duties" of directors commonly appear in cases involving conflict of interest or self dealing, where the director has entered into transactions of some kind with his or her corporation. However, it is important not to carry this analogy very far: directors of corporations are not strictly trustees, and their duties and liabilities are not identical with those of other fiduciaries. Directors are expected and indeed encouraged to commit the enterprise to risky ventures in order to maximize the return to shareholders; trustees are usually charged with preservation and maintenance of the assets under their control and may be surcharged if they commit the trust assets to speculative ventures. Acts which might be considered breaches of trust by other fiduciaries are therefore often not so regarded in cases of corporate directors. The relationship between director and corporation, in short, is a unique one that cannot be analyzed by reference to other types of fiduciary relationships.

In most instances, directors owe duties to the corporation as a whole rather than to individual shareholders or to individual classes of shareholders. However, if a director deals with a shareholder directly, or acts in a way which injures the economic interest of a shareholder, he or she may become directly liable to that shareholder.

§ 14.2 Duties of Shareholders and Officers

Since shareholders as such have no power to manage the business and affairs of the corporation, it is not surprising that the relationship of a shareholder to the corporation differs from the relationship of a director or officer to the corporation. It is often said that a shareholder owes no fiduciary duty to the corporation or the other shareholders. These statements, however, are too broad. While shareholders may usually vote as their own self-interest dictates, they may owe a duty to the corporation or their fellow shareholders in some circumstances. Controlling shareholders, for example, owe duties to creditors, holders of senior securities and minority shareholders when they transfer control of the corporation to a third party. See § 14.19 of this Nutshell. Some cases have found fiduciary duties akin to those existing in a partnership in closely held corporations. And, even minority shareholders do not have an open license to abuse or sell their voting power, or exercise it fraudulently.

The relationship between corporate officers and agents who are not directors and the corporation depends to some extent on the position occupied by the officer or agent and the type of liabilities that are being imposed. A managing officer may owe substantially the same duties to the corporation as a director. Officers or agents in subordinate or limited positions may owe a correspondingly lesser degree of duty, though even the lowest agent owes the principal certain minimum duties of care, skill, propriety in conduct, and loyalty in all matters connected with his or her agency. The fiduciary duties owed by officers and agents are largely those imposed by the law of agency. See § 11.7 of this Nutshell.

§ 14.3 Sources of Law Relating to Duties—Common Law, State and Federal Statutes, "Federal Common Law"

The basic relationship between a corporation and its directors traditionally has been established by common law decision rather than statute. Many of the duties hereafter discussed are common law in origin: (1) a duty of exercising care in administering the corporation's business; (2) a duty of loyalty to the corporation; and (3) as a subdivision of the general duty of loyalty, a prohibition against usurping business opportunities belonging to the corporation. These common law duties have given rise to a great deal of litigation; they define fundamental obligations in a complex relationship. State corporation acts address certain aspects of these common law duties, and also supplement them by imposing liability on directors for certain specific acts, such as paying dividends when the corporation may not lawfully do so or making loans to directors in certain circumstances. Indeed, directoral liability to the corporation is the principal or exclusive method by which many statutory prohibitions are enforced.

Federal law is also an important source of legal principles relating to duties and obligations within a corporation. The federal securities acts are the genesis of this development with much of it based on rule 10b–5 promulgated by the Securities and Exchange Commission under the Securities Exchange Act of 1934. Rule 10b–5 is the principal source of law with respect to insider trading and the "fraud on the market" theory by which misleading corporate publicity affecting securities prices is regulated. See Chapter 17 of this Nutshell. It is clear that both federal and state law will continue to have their place in the area of duties of directors.

§ 14.4 Duty of Care

A director owes a duty to the corporation to exercise proper care in managing the corporation's affairs. The formal test that is usually quoted is set forth in section 8.30 of the Model Business Corporation Act (1984): duties must be discharged "(1) in good faith; (2) with the care an ordinarily prudent person in a like position would exercise under similar circumstances; and (3) in a manner he reasonably believes to be in the best interests of the corporation." Some states have eliminated the "reasonably believes" standard and substituted a standard of decisions "in accordance with his good faith business judgment of the bests interests of the corporation." Va. Code Ann. § 13.1–690. Another test that is often quoted is that degree of diligence, care, and skill "which ordinarily prudent men would exercise under similar circumstances in their personal business affairs." This language is taken from a leading Pennsylvania case, Selheimer v. Manganese Corp. of America (1966). There probably is little practical difference in these formulations; general language of this sort rarely helps to resolve concrete cases.

The formal standard of section 8.30 of the MBCA (1984), however, is not the operative test for determining whether directors are liable in damages for failing to exercise reasonable care. Evaluation of the reasonableness of a decision must take into account what was known at the time of the decision. One must carefully guard against assessing blame with the benefit of hindsight. Directors must usually make complex decisions on the basis of partial, incomplete, or inaccurate information, and there is always a possibility that unexpected events may occur in the future that change a plausible decision into a disastrous one. Furthermore, judges are not typically business experts and may lack competence in evaluating the reasonableness of a specific business decision made at some earlier time. Courts are reluctant to second-guess corporate managers by holding them personally liable for losses incurred by the corporation. This reluctance finds expression in an important doctrine known as the "business judgment rule." See § 14.5 of this Nutshell. Furthermore, most states have enacted statutes limiting the liability of directors for monetary damages under broad circumstances. See § 14.6 of this Nutshell.

In a word, one may violate the standard of care set forth in section 8.30 of MBCA (1984) and yet not be personally liable for the consequences.

Most cases in which liability for damages has been imposed involve some element of self-dealing as well as negligence or misjudgment. There are relatively few cases in which liability has been imposed on directors in the absence of self dealing, and these cases involve egregious misconduct. The strongest kind of case for imposing personal liability on a director is where the director knowingly participates in a wrongful act. Thus, personal liability has been imposed on directors where they authorize the improper use of corporate funds, knowing that the use is not in furtherance of corporate affairs, or where they assent to the corporation's use of a financial statement to obtain credit when they know that it is false or fraudulent. On the other hand, attempts to hold directors or officers personally liable for antitrust fines imposed on the corporation or for bribes or improper payments made by the corporation have generally been unsuccessful, despite evidence in some cases of the directors' or officers' personal involvement in the conduct or payments in question.

A few cases involve situations where the directors failed to do anything at all even in the face of some evidence of wrongdoing. These cases typically involve directors who view themselves as "figureheads" or "honorary" directors without any responsibility. They may involve a spouse who agrees to be a director in order to meet a statutory requirement that the board consist of three directors as a favor to the other spouse. Some directors may erroneously believe that since they are a minority of the board they have no responsibility for what is happening. A failure to direct at all is a clear violation of the duty of care. One case imposing liability because of the failure of a director to direct is Francis v. United Jersey Bank (N.J.1981). The sons of the deceased founder of the corporation, an "insurance reinsurance" firm, siphoned large sums of money from the corporation in the form of unsecured loans and other improper payments to family members. Ultimately the corporation became insolvent, and suit was brought by the bankruptcy trustee against the estate of Mrs. Pritchard, the widow of the corporate founder, who was a director during the period the improper payments and family loans were made. Mrs. Pritchard was not active in the affairs of the corporation; she was elderly and alcoholic, and stricken at the loss of her husband. She was also unfamiliar with the insurance reinsurance business generally and the affairs of the corporation in particular. Even though the improper transactions were clearly reflected in the financial statements prepared by the corporation, Mrs. Pritchard was unaware of them since she did not examine the financial statements. The court upheld a judgment against her estate for more than $10,000,000 since "she never made the slightest effort to discharge any of her responsibilities as a director." The court further concluded that her failure to fill the minimal responsibilities of her office was a proximate cause of the loss, since consultation with an attorney and threat of suit would have deterred the misconduct. A failure to respond to obvious problems, in short, is one way for a director to be held personally liable for losses suffered by the corporation.

What should a director who is aged, ill, resident of a distant state, or merely lazy or unduly trusting, do in order to avoid liability? As an abstract matter the answer is plain: When a person agrees to be a director he or she accepts certain responsibilities and obligations, and if these are too burdensome, the proper course is to resign rather than fail to meet them.

The issue of causation in the failure of the director to direct cases (discussed in Mrs. Pritchard's case) is sometimes a difficult one. Barnes v. Andrews (N.Y.1924), is the leading case holding that a direct causal relationship must be shown between the director's failure and the specific loss. If this is correct, the burden of proof will often be difficult if not insuperable, since in most cases it may be plausibly argued that the loss would have occurred even if the director had met his or her responsibility.

Also, often helpful to defendants in duty of care cases are the principles (1) that directors, in the absence of other information, may assume that managers and officers are honest, and (2) that directors are not liable if they rely in good faith on information, opinions, reports or statements prepared by responsible corporate officials, counsel, or committees of the board. MBCA (1984) § 8.30(b). However, a director is not considered to be acting in good faith "if he has knowledge concerning the matter in question that would cause such reliance to be unwarranted." In other words, the standard of good faith reliance does not permit a knowledgeable director "to bury his head in the sand" and rely on information or advice he or she should know is erroneous. An attorney who is a director cannot ignore his or her legal background; the same is true of an accountant or banker. On the other hand, a person without specialized knowledge may rely on specialists if acting in good faith, and be immune from liability upon doing so.

All in all, these various principles, when coupled with the broad immunity from liability discussed in the following sections, reduce significantly, but do not eliminate entirely, the risk of liability of directors for breach of the duty of care.

Courts have sometimes buttressed their conclusion that directoral liability does not exist in specific due care cases by arguing that too stringent a test would discourage able and competent persons from agreeing to serve as directors of publicly held corporations.

§ 14.5   The "Business Judgment Rule"

The phrase, "the business judgment rule" is a helpful shorthand description of basic principle applicable to business decisions by boards of directors: that decisions made by the board of directors upon reasonable information and with some rationality do not give rise to directoral liability even if they turn out badly or disastrously from the standpoint of the corporation. A variation of this doctrine, sometimes called the "business judgment doctrine" states that such decisions are valid and binding upon the corporation and cannot be enjoined, set aside, or attacked by shareholders In the balance of this section both of these principles are collectively referred to simply as the "business judgment rule."

Most statements of the business judgment rule add the further qualification that a decision is not protected if the directors making it have "a disabling conflict of interest" or are involved in self-dealing transactions. The rule thus has its principal application to claims based on alleged mismanagement or misjudgment unaffected by any claim that personal gain was sought.

In a broad sense, the business judgment rule codifies the basic principles referred to in the previous section that directors are granted discretion with respect to the management of the corporation, that the rational exercise of that discretion is generally not subject to judicial review, and that most judges are not businessmen capable of second-guessing effectively the exercise of that discretion.

The precise relationship between the duty of care and the business judgment rule is not addressed in the Model Business Corporation Act (1984). It sets forth the duty of care in section 8.30 in traditional negligence terms but does not attempt to codify the business judgment rule. The Official Comment, however, recognizes the existence of that rule outside of the statutory language and suggests that at some future time the business judgment rule will also be codified in the Model Act.

Section 4.01(a) of the Corporate Governance Project of the American Law Institute also sets forth the duty of care in traditional language similar to section 8.30 of the MBCA (1984). Section 4.01(c) defines the business judgment rule as follows: a "director or officer who makes a business judgment in good faith fulfills his or her duty" under section 4.01(a) if (1) he or she "is not interested in subject of the business judgment," (2) he "is informed with respect to the subject of the business judgment to the extent the director or officer reasonably believes to be appropriate under the circumstances," and (3) he "rationally believes that the business judgment is in the best interests of the corporation." This language is the classic description of the business judgment rule. There have been other attempts at formulation of the business judgment rule in the case law that use somewhat different language, but these three basic principles appear essentially in all of them.

It should be noted that the business judgment rule involves a decision or a judgment. Doing nothing without more can never be protected by the business judgment rule. However, a positive decision to do nothing about some issue is protected by the business judgment rule if in fact the directors are informed about the issue and rationally believe that a decision to do nothing is in the best interest of the corporation.

Also, the business judgment rule does not primarily involve a court in the substantive evaluation of the business judgment. Rather, it examines the process or procedure by which the judgment was made rather than the judgment itself, though the "rational belief" portion of the test may be viewed as in part substantive.

The business judgment rule protects many types of actions from suit even though they turn out badly from the standpoint of the corporation. Examples include:

(1) A reorganization of a subsidiary company, including a distribution of surplus, reduction of capital, and distribution of a share dividend;

(2) Election of a manager and president;

(3) A sale of part of the assets of a telephone company;

(4) Acceptance of a note for a judgment rather than enforcing it by execution; and

(5) The closing down of an unproductive mine.

The most controversial case that tested the scope of the business judgment rule is Smith v. Van Gorkom (Del. 1985). The court's opinion in Van Gorkom sets forth the facts in great detail, and the correctness or incorrectness of its holding depends in large part upon how one categorizes those facts. The majority opinion adopts this categorization: Van Gorkom was the chief executive officer of Trans Union Corporation, a publicly held corporation. Van Gorkom owned 75,000 shares out of 20,000,000 outstanding. During review of the future of the corporation, the possibility of taking the company private through a leveraged buyout or of selling it outright was discussed. Van Gorkom, who was close to retirement age, stated that he would accept $55 per share for his stock; during this period the stock was trading in the $24–$39 range. The $55 figure was apparently an intuitive judgment by Van Gorkom of what he thought an attractive price was, given his knowledge of the corporation's business. Studies were run by management to determine whether the cash flow of the corporation at the present level of operations could support the debt needed to support a $55 price in a leveraged buyout. (see § 13.24 for a description of a "leveraged buyout.") On the basis of projections run by the corporation's chief financial officer, it appeared that the cash flow might not be adequate for this purpose. Without further investigation into the value of the company, and without seeking other possible buyers, Van Gorkom contacted Pritzker, "a well-known corporate takeover specialist and a social acquaintance" and pointed out that a leveraged buyout of Trans Union might be feasible at $55 per share. Pritzker promptly offered to buy the corporation in a straight purchase at $55 per share with a decision required within three days. Some members of Trans Union management opposed the proposed sale on the grounds that the price was too low and not supported by adequate appraisals. The board of directors was then presented with the $55 proposal as an emergency matter with a strict three day deadline for approval; Van Gorkom urged approval of the transaction, stating that the company would consider other offers for a period of months as a "market test" of the adequacy of the price. The chief financial officer stated that the price was "fair but at the beginning of the range." The board approved the transaction without asking questions or without extended discussion. Van Gorkom thereafter actively worked to obtain shareholder approval of the transaction without considering other possible alternatives, and the transaction was eventually completed at $55 per share. At one stage, a preliminary feeler was received from a third party offering $60 per share, but was not investigated. Based essentially on these facts, the Delaware Supreme Court by a 3–2 vote concluded that the directors had not adequately informed themselves about the value of the company and the proposed transaction and therefore were not entitled to the protection of the business judgment rule. The basic test of the duty of care, the court stated, was "gross negligence." The dissenters, and much of the subsequent critical commentary about the case, argued that the directors should be able to evaluate a proposed sale of the company on the basis of their own financial experience and background, and in reliance on Van Gorkom's experience and background. Other factors relied upon by the critics of the decision as indicating that the directors had acted properly was the substantial difference between the $55 offering price and the market range in which Trans Union stock had traded in the recent past, and the general financial sophistication of the outside directors of the corporation. The mathematics of the court's holding also received attention: if the measure of damages is $5 per share (not an unreasonable conclusion considering that Trans Union received an apparently serious "feeler" of $60 per share), then the joint and several liability of the directors is 5 dollars times approximately 12,700,000 shares, or a cool $63,500,000. Following the Delaware Supreme Court decision, the case was actually settled for a payment of approximately $22,000,000 from insurance proceeds and funds supplied (apparently voluntarily) by the purchaser in the transaction under attack. The fees payable to the attorneys for the plaintiffs were about $18,000,000.

A decision to sell the business of a publicly held company is the most important decision that ever comes before a board of directors. It may be suggested that *Van Gorkom* is basically correctly decided because such an important decision should not be made without investigation and in blind reliance on the judgment of a single person who will benefit significantly from the transaction, no matter how confident the directors in that person's abilities and objectivity. On the other hand, a person considering this scenario might well raise the question why the outside directors should be liable when Van Gorkom and the other members of his management team appear to have been the persons primarily responsible for the decision. A plausible argument might be made that the outside directors reasonably relied upon Van Gorkom and other members of management, and that that reliance met the requirements of the business judgment rule. The Supreme Court of Delaware was also aware of possible distinctions among the defendants and at least twice asked the defendants' attorney during oral argument whether a difference in treatment for the outside directors might be justified. Apparently for strategic reasons, however, the defendants adopted a "one for all and all for one" strategy and refused to address the question whether some defendants might have defenses not available to other defendants.

The immediate consequences of the Van Gorkom decision on the business community were disturbing. Lawyers and law firms sent out memoranda to their clients warning them of the risk of liability in the absence of a careful investigation and recommending that experts be hired and a "paper trail" be created to demonstrate that a sufficient investigation was made to comply with the requirements of the business judgment rule. Some outside directors began to reassess their decision to be directors, and isolated instances of resignations were reported. The number of lawyers serving on the boards of directors of their clients declined. And some people reported that it was becoming increasingly difficult to persuade desirable persons to serve on boards because of the potential risks involved, despite the level of compensation and the availability of indemnification and insurance.

§ 14.6   Section 102(b)(7) of the Delaware GCL

The response in Delaware to the decision in *Van Gorkom* was prompt. In 1986, section 102(b)(7) of the Delaware General Corporation Law was amended to authorize corporations to amend their certificates of incorporation to eliminate or limit the personal liability of directors for monetary damages, with certain important exceptions. These exceptions are (i) for breach of the director's duty of loyalty to the corporation, (ii) for acts or omissions "not in good faith or which involve intentional misconduct or a knowing violation of law," and (iii) for any transaction from which the director derived an improper personal benefit. Thousands of Delaware corporations promptly amended their articles of incorporation to take advantage of this new provision, which was quickly copied in many other states. In Delaware the section 102(b)(7) amendment requires a vote of shareholders since it is an "opt in" election. Some states "improved" upon the Delaware statute either by making a similar amendment automatically applicable to all corporations or by narrowing or eliminating some of the exceptions, thereby broadening the protection accorded to directors by the statute.

One major effect of this statute doubtless was to permit individuals to become directors with additional peace of mind, and hence effectively it reversed the trend created by a broad reading of *Van Gorkom*. In terms of the effect on suits for due care violations, the statute probably has encouraged suits to enjoin transactions before they are consummated rather than seeking damages after the transaction has taken place. This is probably desirable because the imposition of monetary damages on individual directors seems out of proportion to the nature of the claim.

Suits to enjoin transactions are not affected by section 102(b)(7), since they do not involve the imposition of personal liability. Further, claims based on self-dealing or breach of the duty of fair dealing are also not covered by section 102(b)(7) since they involve the "duty of loyalty."

§ 14.7 The Business Judgment Rule in Takeover Contests

The business judgment rule has been involved in numerous cases brought against directors of corporations which face unwanted takeover attempts and adopt defensive tactics designed to defeat the takeover. See the discussion of defensive tactics in section 13.25 of this Nutshell. In Panter v. Marshall Field & Co. (7th Cir.1981), Marshall Field successfully fended off an unwanted takeover bid by another retail chain primarily by acquiring or opening additional stores that created serious antitrust problems for the aggressor. Following the withdrawal of the offer because of the legal complications created by the expansion policy, the price of Marshall Field shares dropped precipitously, and minority shareholders brought suit against the directors for damages. The court applied the business judgment rule in this case in a broad and expansive manner; there was a vigorous and forceful dissent that argued that the majority's opinion permitted incumbent management to entrench themselves in office without limitation to the detriment of the public shareholders.

The leading cases arise in Delaware, which has taken a narrower and more variable approach. The leading Delaware case permits directors to adopt a "poison pill" preferred stock in advance of any takeover attempt [Moran v. Household International, Inc. (Del.1985)] as a matter of business judgment. In addition, a selective stock repurchase plan that was designed solely to defeat an aggressor who was making an "inadequate and coercive two-tier tender offer" was upheld as a valid exercise of business judgment in the circumstances [Unocal v. Mesa Petroleum Co. (Del.1985)]. In this case, the Delaware Supreme Court recognized that selective stock repurchases (excluding the aggressor but including all other shareholders) had the capacity to defeat every tender offer, and adopted a modified business judgment rule: "A further aspect is the element of balance. If a defensive measure is to come within the ambit of the business judgment rule, it must be reasonable in relation to the threat posed. This entails an analysis by the directors of the nature of the takeover bid and its effect on the corporate enterprise." Shortly following the *Unocal* decision, the Securities and Exchange Commission adopted rule 14d–10 under the Williams Act, generally known as the "all holders rule" that prohibits selective stock repurchases. Nevertheless, the standard of "balance" set forth in *Unocal* has been applied by the Delaware courts to a wide variety of defensive tactics.

The Delaware Supreme Court adopted yet another twist to the business judgment rule in Revlon, Inc. v. MacAndrews & Forbes Holdings, Inc. (Del.1985). In this case, the directors of Revlon vigorously fought an attempted takeover, but eventually it became clear that the sale of the company to one aggressor or another was inevitable. In this situation, the Supreme Court stated, the directors no longer may exercise business judgment to prefer one bidder over another, but instead they have the duty of obtaining the best possible price for the company. A decision to use a "lock up" to defeat a higher bidder and favor a lower bidder violates this duty and thus cannot be protected by the business judgment rule. This last holding, in particular, is broadly consistent with the rationale underlying *Van Gorkom* that when the company is being sold, the directors must try to get the best price rather than simply selecting one bidder and dealing exclusively with it.

The general principle of *Revlon* has been considered and applied by the Delaware Supreme Court and Chancery Court in an important series of cases that address a number of subsidiary issues, such as whether this duty requires an auction, and if so, how long it must continue. The application of the business judgment rule in connection with defensive tactics in takeover situations raises a broad question as to whether the directors, or at least some of them, should be viewed as having a "disabling conflict of interest" and thus not protected by the business judgment rule. Incumbent management, of course, has lucrative positions with the target corporation that are likely to disappear if the aggressor is successful and takes over the target. When they propose strategies to defeat the aggressor, is that a conflict of interest? The answer to this is "probably yes." Similarly, outside directors have positions that carry with them considerable prestige as well as financial benefits, all of which would almost certainly disappear if the aggressor is successful. But to disqualify all of the incumbent board in this manner may well be counterproductive, since the shareholders may then receive no informed advice as to the desirability of the takeover.

In cases where the court has concluded that the board has gone too far in protecting the position of its members, the court is likely to talk about decisions that tend to "entrench management." Such decisions therefore involve a conflict of interest and are not entitled to the protection of the business judgment rule. Recent Delaware opinions have indicated that approval by independent directors of defensive tactics will be given greater deference by courts then decisions in which inside directors participate.

§ 14.8   The Business Judgment Rule in Derivative Litigation

Another area in which the application of the business judgment rule has been controversial in recent years is in connection with the dismissal of derivative litigation. Basically the question is whether the business judgment rule should be applied to decisions by an "independent" committee of the board of directors to discontinue derivative litigation (see § 16.10 of this Nutshell) brought by shareholders seeking recovery in favor of the corporation against one or more officers or directors for alleged misconduct. Typically, the decision whether or not to seek to discontinue such litigation is delegated to a "Litigation Committee" composed of outside directors who are not themselves principal defendants or involved in the acts complained of. The recommendation to discontinue the litigation is made following an investigation by the committee into the merits of the litigation and the advantages and disadvantages to the corporation of pursuing it.

If decisions by litigation committees are protected by the business judgment rule, the decision to discontinue litigation is binding on the plaintiff shareholder who is foreclosed from litigating the merits of his or her case because of the impartial directors' business judgment; the plaintiff may only litigate issues such as the independence and lack of involvement of the members of the committee recommending discontinuance of the litigation, or of the adequacy of the underlying investigation. At first blush it is somewhat startling to put forward the proposition that a court should dismiss litigation without considering its merits because of the actions of a group of independent directors. However, decisions to discontinue or pursue litigation involve business considerations quite as much as decisions such as to go into a new business or to hire a new executive officer.

Major policy arguments against applying the business judgment rule to decisions to discontinue derivative litigation against other directors are the fear of "structural bias," i.e. the concern that directors "will look out for their own," or the possibility that they will take the attitude that "there but for the grace of God go I." It may perhaps be no coincidence that in virtually every instance in which there has been a referral to an independent litigation committee, the committee has concluded that it was in the best interest of the corporation not to pursue the matter.

While early decisions, including decisions by the United States Supreme Court and the Court of Appeals of New York, uncritically applied the business judgment rule to litigation committee decisions, recent decisions have been more cautious. The decision by the Delaware Supreme Court in Zapata Corp. v. Maldonado (Del.1981) may have marked a turning point in this regard. The court there held that before applying the business judgment rule in a case in which a demand on directors was excused (see § 16.10 of this Nutshell), a court should not only consider the independence and good faith of the "Independent Litigation Committee" but also exercise its own "independent business judgment" as to whether the litigation should be terminated. However, the Delaware Supreme Court subsequently held in Aronson v. Lewis (Del.1984) that this standard only applied in "demand excused" cases and the straight business judgment rule should be applied in "demand required" cases. As a result, in Delaware today, the application of the business judgment rule is determined by whether the case is viewed as a "demand required" or "demand excused" case. This approach has been criticized on the ground that it places excessive importance on what should be a preliminary issue, and requires a decision at the pleading stage when there has been absolutely no discovery. Further, because of the critical nature of the demand required/demand excused decision, an interlocutory appeal is almost certain to follow. The test applied by the Delaware courts to determine whether demand is excused is whether the plaintiff has pleaded "particularized facts" that tend to show that the decision complained of is not protected by the business judgment rule. As a global observation, the decisions since *Zapata* in Delaware appear to have made it more difficult and expensive to dispose of unwanted derivative litigation in Delaware by the independent litigation committee route, but that in appropriate cases the business judgment rule may be applied to decisions by such a committee.

This derivative litigation issue continues to arise in the Delaware courts and a number of important additions and embellishments have been added. For example, if a plaintiff makes a demand, that is a concession that it is a demand required case, and the plaintiff cannot thereafter contend that it is really a demand excused case. If a demand is made and is refused, the plaintiff may not obtain discovery on the basis that the refusal was erroneous unless he is able to allege particularized facts that tend to show that the decision was not protected by the business judgment rule.

The Delaware solution has been subjected to substantial criticism, particularly the use of the preliminary demand required/demand refused issue to define the scope of subsequent review of litigation committee decisions. The most widely favored proposal is to make demand required in essentially all cases, and then provide a judicial standard for the scope of review of litigation committee decisions. This is the approach adopted by the Model Business Corporation Act in 1989. Demand is required in all cases, but binding effect of the litigation committee decision should be given only where the directors making the decision are truly independent. The American Law Institute's Corporate Governance Project also adopted a universal demand requirement, but provides a broader scope of judicial review and oversight over decisions to dismiss derivative litigation against officers or directors.

Most decisions involving litigation committees have arisen under Delaware law. However, there are a smattering of decisions in other states. These decisions have generally not followed the Delaware approach and have refused to give binding effect to litigation committee decisions based on the demand required/demand excused distinction. While the stated tests varies, most courts appear to judge the validity of litigation committee decision not solely on the basis of the business judgment rule but also in terms of whether the decision appears proper on the record before the committee.

§ 14.9   The Duty of Loyalty

The duty of loyalty has produced a steady stream of litigation in which transactions have been set aside or directors and officers have been held liable for breach of duty. These cases may be divided into four broad types: (1) cases involving transactions between a director and the corporation (self-dealing); (2) cases involving transactions between corporations with one or more common directors; (3) cases involving a director taking advantage of an opportunity which arguably may belong to the corporation; and (4) cases in which the director competes with the corporation in its business.

The duty of loyalty is referred to as the duty of fair dealing in the Corporate Governance Project. Virtually all states have statutes that deal with some aspects of the duty of loyalty.

§ 14.10   Self Dealing

The danger of self-dealing transactions between a corporation and one or more of its directors is the risk that the corporation may be treated unfairly in such a transaction. Since these transactions are usually voluntary, it is not surprising that, when a self-dealing transaction is questioned, the burden is typically placed on the director as a fiduciary to prove the propriety of the transaction rather than on persons questioning the transaction. The form the transaction takes is not significant. The courts apply essentially the same test to transactions involving the sale of corporate property to a director, the sale of property to a director's spouse, the sale of property by a director to a corporation controlled by the director, a contract between the corporation and a director for the director to perform services (such as selling stock or managing the business), or a transaction between the corporation and a child or close relative of the director. Self dealing is also involved if a director is also an officer and participates in the determination of his salary or other emoluments. See §§ 13.6, 14.12 of this Nutshell.

The early common law took the position that all self-dealing transactions were automatically voidable at the election of the corporation. It was eventually recognized, however, that a black-and-white rule of this type did not fit business needs. Even though self-dealing transactions may be suspect, many of them in fact are entirely fair and reasonable; indeed, in many situations directors may give their corporations benefits that are more favorable than the corporation might obtain elsewhere. For example, loans by directors to the corporation may be made when the corporation could not borrow elsewhere; such transactions should obviously be encouraged and not invalidated. The case law on self dealing transactions basically recognized that transactions that were approved by disinterested directors or shareholders were presumptively enforceable and that other transactions were not voidable if the interested director could establish that they were fair.

Since 1975, a number of states have adopted statutes dealing with conflict of interest transactions. The Model Business Corporation Act, as adopted in 1984, contained a section based on these state statutes [old § 8.31], but in 1988 that section was repealed and a new subchapter F [§§ 8.60 through 8.63] was added to deal more precisely with conflict of interest transactions. It is important to consider old § 8.31 first because most state corporation statutes have provisions similar to this section.

Section 8.31 provides that a conflict of interest transaction is not voidable "solely" because of the conflict of interest if any one of three requirements are met: (1) the transaction was ratified or approved by the board of directors or a committee of the board after full disclosure and without the participation of interested directors, (2) the transaction was ratified or approved by the shareholders as provided in section 8.31(d) (which required the exclusion of shares owned by or voted under the control of the interested directors), or (3) the transaction was fair to the corporation. There is an unfortunate linguistic trap in this language (which also appears in most similar statutes): the purpose of directoral or shareholder ratification is not intended to be limited only to transactions that cannot meet the test of "fairness," i.e. only to unfair transactions. Rather, they are intended to be alternative ways to establish the enforceability of a conflict of interest transaction without going into the question of fairness at all. This pattern makes sense only if it is realized that a judicial inquiry into fairness may involve a complex and expensive hearing and inquiry into difficult business issues; hence, director or shareholder ratification may be utilized to avoid the need for such a hearing. Ratification by disinterested corporate participants is a "safe harbor" that "sanitized" self dealing transactions without the necessity of a complex trial on fairness.

Furthermore, § 8.31 and similar statutes do not state that "sanitization" automatically and conclusively validates all transactions. Rather, it simply removes any possible impediment arising from the fact that a director was involved in the transaction. Thus, ratification under section 8.31(a)(1) or (a)(2) does not validate transactions that involve waste, fraud, or actions in excess of authority, though the burden of proving fraud or waste was on the plaintiff attacking the transaction. This important principle is clearly set forth in the Official Comment and was implicit in the language of the statute itself.

The new subchapter F is a much more ambitious undertaking than old § 8.31. Its basic structure is similar: a conflict of interest transaction is not voidable by the corporation if (1) it has been appropriately approved by disinterested directors or shareholders, or (2) the interested director establishes the fairness of the transaction. Unlike § 8.31, however, subchapter F creates a series of "bright line" principles that increase predictability and enhance practical administrability of the "safe harbor." Thus it defines with some precision (1) the transactions to which subchapter F is applicable, (2) the types of "interests" that constitute "conflicting interests," and (3) the directors that may vote on other directors' conflict of interest transactions. "Qualified directors" may vote on other directors' conflict of interest transactions; a "qualified director" is one that does not have a direct financial interest or "a familial, financial, professional, or employment relationship with a second director who does have" a direct financial interest, "which relationship would, in the circumstances, reasonably be expected to exert an influence on the first director's judgment when voting on the transaction." [MBCA (1984) § 8.62(d)] In addition subchapter F gives preclusive effect—i.e. there is to be no judicial review—to decisions by directors qualified to act under Subchapter F if those decisions satisfy the requirements of the business judgment rule (established in cases such as *Van Gorkom*). However, the Official Comment adds a caution: "If the directors who voted for the conflicting interest transaction were qualified directors under subchapter F, but approved the transaction merely as an accommodation to the director with the conflicting interest, going through the motions of board action without complying with the requirements of section 8.30(a), the action of the board would not be given effect ... Board action on a director's conflicting interest transaction provides a context in which the function of the 'best interests of the corporation' language in section 8.30(a) is brought into clear focus." Official Comment to § 8.61(b).

Let us assume for a moment that a self-dealing transaction is ratified by the board of directors (or a committee of the board) pursuant to subchapter F. The transaction does not involve fraud or waste, but nevertheless is attacked as being unfair to the corporation and unnecessarily favorable to the interested director. Since it was ratified by the directors, a full fairness inquiry is not necessary. Further, if all directors who are acting are "qualified directors" and the process followed by the board (or the committee) meets the standards of the business judgment rule, the transaction is binding on the corporation and there is to be no further judicial review of the decision itself or the process by which it was reached.

Is this degree of finality and immunity from judicial review desirable, or should the court make some kind of residual fairness inquiry before accepting the decision? Or to put the issue in another way, does the act of ratification by "qualified" directors "sanitize" the transaction entirely from judicial scrutiny? The answer provided by subchapter F is "yes." The American Law Institute's Corporate Governance Project addresses the same issue but permits judicial inquiry into the directors' decision to the extent of determining that "it could reasonably be believed to be fair to the corporation at the time of such authorization." The question of the scope of judicial inquiry into director-approved conflict of interest transactions was immensely controversial within the American Law Institute, and to a lesser extent within the Committee on Corporate Laws of the American Bar Association. The difference in formulations, however, may not be as great as might first appear, because under the Official Comment to subchapter F quoted above the court can always inquire into whether the standards of the business judgment rule were met, and among those standards is the requirement that the directors could rationally believe that the action is in the best interests of the corporation.

The Delaware courts permit additional judicial scrutiny of transactions that have been "sanitized" under section 144 of the Delaware GCL, a statute somewhat similar to old § 8.31. The leading case is Fliegler v. Lawrence (Del. 1976), which involved ratification by interested shareholders. The court stated that section 144 of the Delaware General Corporation Law does not provide a "broad immunity," but "merely removes an 'interested director' cloud when its terms are met and provides against invalidation of an agreement 'solely' because such a director or officer is involved. *Nothing in the statute sanctions unfairness* to Agau [the complaining shareholder] *or removes the transaction from judicial scrutiny.*" A footnote dictum in Marciano v. Nakash (Del.1987) states that "approval by fully-informed disinterested directors * * * permits invocation of the business judgment rule and limits judicial review to issues of gift or waste with the burden of proof upon the party attacking the transaction." However, in Kahn v. Lynch Communications Systems (Del.1994), the Court held that compliance with the terms of section 144—ratification by disinterested shareholders or directors—only has the effect of shifting the burden of proof of unfairness to the plaintiffs; the self dealing transaction is not to be validated merely because the ratification decision itself was made consistently with the business judgment rule. Where a majority of the directors making the judgment are interested, only the entire fairness standard is available: Ratification requires the decision of a "neutral decision-making body."

Two critical issues in this area are (1) who may be considered disinterested for purposes of determining who may act on a self-dealing transaction, and (2) what degree of specific knowledge or notice of the underlying facts (and, indeed, of the existence of the conflict of interest itself) is required to constitute an effective authorization or ratification? These issues are discussed with precision in MBCA (1984), section 8.60. Under the earlier statutes there is a considerable degree of flexibility on these issues.

§ 14.11 Interlocking Directors

Transactions between corporations with common directors may lend themselves to the same evil as self-dealing transactions between a director and the corporation, since the interest of a common director may be small in one corporation and large in the other. The common law standard for setting aside transactions between corporations with common directors is simply one of manifest unfairness to one corporation. The role of the common director in approving the transaction also is inquired into. If the corporation on the losing side of the transaction relied on the views of the common director without a full evaluation of the risks, or without disclosure that the director was interested in the other corporation, the chances that the transaction will be set aside are greatly improved. The stated test, however, is an objective one of fairness, not a procedural test based on the degree of the common director's participation.

Section 8.60(1)(ii) treats a transaction between corporations with a common director as a conflict of interest transaction if "the transaction is brought (or is of such character and significance to the corporation that it would in the normal course be brought) before the board of directors of the corporation for action." This provision recognizes that routine business transactions between large corporations should not be made subject to attack simply because the two corporations happen to have a common director. Even transactions that involve millions of dollars are often routine transactions not considered by the board of directors of large corporations. The quoted language is designed to limit conflict of interest transaction to those that are of sufficient importance to the corporation that they are or should be considered by the board of directors.

§ 14.12　Executive Compensation

The compensation of directors who also serve as corporate officers or agents is a specific application of the principles relating to self dealing. Many publicly held corporations have sought to avoid these problems through the use of compensation committees composed of independent directors to monitor compensation levels. Amendments to the Internal Revenue Code have encouraged the use of such committees. See § 13.6.

In publicly held corporations, independent directors usually receive compensation in the form of directors' fees, and also may be eligible to participate in various deferred compensation plans or retirement plans. Some corporations pay independent directors in stock rather in cash. Section 8.11 of the Model Business Corporation Act (1984) allows the board of directors to establish compensation programs for directors. Presumably, the fairness of these amounts may be inquired into under Subchapter F.

Much modern law relating to executive compensation is directly or indirectly related to the federal income tax. The Internal Revenue Code allows deductions for ordinary and necessary business expenses, including a "reasonable allowance" for services actually rendered. Thus, the standard for self-dealing transactions and for deductibility of compensation for tax purposes is not precisely the same. The issues differ in publicly owned corporations and in closely held corporations. Within closely held corporations, the S corporation election creates further strategic considerations.

(1) In a closely held corporation, all the shareholders may be employees of the corporation; if so, and the corporation does not elect S corporation tax status, the salaries paid to the shareholders are likely to be set so as to minimize the aggregate tax liabilities imposed on the corporation and the shareholders. A salary payment may be deductible by the corporation while payment of the same sum in the form of a dividend is not, so there is strong incentive in a C corporation to set shareholders' salaries as high as possible. In a closely held C corporation, the Internal Revenue Service routinely reviews the reasonableness of corporate salaries and may disallow deductions for unreasonably large salaries or for salaries that are clearly being paid in proportion to share holdings. The total amount paid by the corporation to the shareholders is still taxable to the shareholder-recipients either as a dividend or as compensation; the issue is the deductibility of the payments at the corporate level. The same tax-minimization motive is not present in S corporations where earnings are allocated automatically to shareholders for tax purposes.

If some shareholders of a closely held corporation are not employed by the corporation, they are adversely affected by the payment of generous salaries to other shareholders and obviously would much prefer that the same sum be distributed pro rata in the form of a dividend, even though the tax obligations of the corporation may thereby be higher. The adverse effect of generous salaries to some but not all shareholders is independent of the S corporation election. If a salary payment is treated as a dividend for tax purposes, it does not necessarily follow that it should also be treated as a dividend under corporation law and distributed pro rata to all shareholders, though the disallowance of a salary deduction may suggest to a minority shareholder that the payment may also have been improper under general corporate fiduciary principles as well.

In an S corporation, all shareholders must pay tax on corporate earnings allocated to them, whether or not actually distributed. Corporations generally distribute at least an amount equal to the increased taxes owed by shareholders; the failure to do so for all shareholders places a considerable burden on individual shareholders not receiving a salary from the corporation and may give rise to claims of breach of fiduciary duty.

(2) In publicly held corporations, executive compensation is not usually considered to be a manner of distributing earnings. The executive is receiving "other people's money," and the effect of his or her compensation on earnings per share is likely to be minimal. However, compensation in public corporations may be very substantial and the question has arisen as to the circumstances under which a court may set aside compensation on the ground that it is excessive and therefore improper. The tests applied by the courts to determine whether compensation is excessive in a publicly held corporation is whether the payments constitute "spoilation or waste." Rogers v. Hill (S.Ct.1933). Courts, however, have been reluctant to conclude that executive compensation is excessive, particularly if procedures are adopted which minimize the appearance of self-dealing. As a result, there apparently

has been no recent case applying the test of Rogers v. Hill. The rationale underlying this reluctance is set forth in an often-quoted statement from the leading New York case of Heller v. Boylan (N.Y.1941):

"Yes, the Court possesses the power to prune these payments, but openness forces the confession that the pruning would be synthetic and artificial rather than analytic or scientific.

"If comparisons are to be made, with whose compensation are they to be made—executives? Those connected with the motion picture industry? Radio artists? Justices of the Supreme Court of the United States? The President of the United States? Manifestly, the material at hand is not of adequate plasticity for fashioning into a pattern or standard.

"Courts are ill-equipped to solve or even to grapple with these entangled economic problems. Indeed, their solution is not within the juridical province. Courts are concerned that corporations be honestly and fairly operated by its directors, with the observance of the formal requirements of the law, but what is reasonable compensation for its officers is primarily for the stockholders. This does not mean that fiduciaries are to commit waste or misuse or abuse trust property, with impunity. A just cause will find the Courts at guard and implemented to grant redress."

Total compensation must bear at least some minimal relation to the services rendered. If it does not, the payment constitutes waste of corporate assets. Rogers v. Hill involved a compensation plan for executives of the American Tobacco Company which used a formula based on profits in excess of a fixed number. This formula yielded the president of the corporation more than $680,-000 of extra compensation in 1929 and more than $1,300,000 in 1930. The United States Supreme Court held that these payments were so excessive as to be subject to examination and revision by the courts, even though the formula was reasonable and valid in 1912 when it was approved by the shareholders; subsequent developments, however, resulted in payments so large as to raise the question that they constituted waste. In another case, a complaint attacking a very generous pension granted to a CEO shortly before his or her retirement, and funded by a single cash payment of several million dollars by the corporation, was held to state a cause of action for waste. However, examples of the exercise of this power are rare. Furthermore, incentive compensation in a publicly held corporation is usually tied to share prices. A CEO who increases the aggregate value of shares of a corporation by billions of dollars is not likely to be begrudged incentive compensation measured in the tens of millions of dollars.

§ 14.13   Corporate Opportunities

The corporate opportunity doctrine requires a corporate director to render to Caesar at the best possible price that which is Caesar's. As a fiduciary, a director owes a duty to further the interest of the corporation and to give it the benefit of his or her uncorrupted business judgment. He or she may not take a secret profit in connection with corporate transactions, compete unfairly with the corporation, or take personally profitable business opportunities that belong to the corporation.

Very often the application of the doctrine of corporate opportunity to a specific situation comes down to a judicial evaluation of business ethics. Serious problems of definition and evaluation lie close to the surface—when is an opportunity a corporate opportunity? When may a director take advantage of a corporate opportunity on the ground that the corporation is unwilling or unable to take advantage of it? Under what circumstances may a director enter into a business which competes with the corporation? These questions are considered below.

The basic test established by modern cases as to when an opportunity is a corporate opportunity combines a "line of business" test with the pervasive issue whether it is unfair for the director under the circumstances to take advantage personally of the opportunity. Some courts have in effect collapsed the "line of business" requirement into the fairness test and stated that the single test is simply whether it is fair under the circumstances for the director to take advantage of the opportunity. It is probably helpful, however, to recognize that there are two tests: one for determining whether the corporation has a legitimate interest in the opportunity at all (the "line of business" test) and, second, if it does, under what circumstances may the director nevertheless take advantage of it (the "fairness" test).

The "line of business" test typically compares the closeness of the opportunity to the types of business in which the corporation is engaged. The closer it is, the more likely it is to be a corporate opportunity. Some courts have articulated narrower tests as to the necessary relation between the opportunity and the corporate business, for example, the opportunity must involve "property wherein the corporation has an interest already existing or in which it has an expectancy growing out of an existing right," or that the opportunity must in some sense arise out of the corporation's business as it is then conducted. Both of these tests are somewhat narrower than the "line of business" test, but in the last analysis, the verbal formulation of the test is less important than the court's sensitivity to reasonable business ethics as to what belongs to the corporation and what does not.

Other factors may also be important in determining whether an opportunity is a corporate opportunity. For example, weight should be given to (1) whether there were prior negotiations with the corporation about the opportunity, (2) whether the opportunity was originally offered to the corporation or to the director as an agent of the corporation, (3) whether the director learned of the opportunity by reason of his or her position with the corporation, (4) whether the director used corporate facilities or property to take advantage of the opportunity, and (5) how substantial was the need of the corporation for the opportunity. Even if an opportunity is not within a corporation's "line of business," it may be viewed as a corporate opportunity if it was originally offered to the corporation.

Section 5.05(b) of the American Law Institute's Corporate Governance Project defines a "corporate opportunity" to be one that (1) the director should reasonable believe was offered to the corporation, (2) the director believes would be of interest to the corporation, or (3) is "closely related" to a business in which the corporation is engaged or expects to be engaged.

Even if an opportunity is classified as a corporate opportunity, directors are not necessarily precluded from taking advantage of it. The corporation may voluntarily relinquish it and permit the directors to take advantage of it, though such a relinquishment should be viewed as a self-dealing transaction subject to the tests described earlier. See § 14.10. A persuasive policy reason for the relinquishment, e.g., a decision that under the circumstances it would be unwise to expand the corporation's business, helps to establish that the corporation voluntarily decided not to pursue the opportunity. Directors may also take advantage of a corporate opportunity if the corporation is incapable of taking advantage of the opportunity, e.g., on the ground the opportunity is in violation of law, or because the third person refuses to deal with the corporation.

Directors have often sought to justify their utilization of a corporate opportunity on the ground that the corporation was financially unable to capitalize on the opportunity. This defense is a troublesome one, since directors may be tempted to refrain from exercising their strongest efforts on behalf of the corporation if they can thereafter take advantage personally of a profitable opportunity. There is some support for a "rigid rule" prohibiting directors from taking advantage of a corporate opportunity on this ground; in this view, if the directors do not wish to lend the necessary funds to the corporation to permit it to take advantage of the opportunity, they must entirely forego the opportunity. Such a rule seems unnecessarily strict, however, and most courts have permitted directors to utilize corporate opportunities upon a convincing showing that the corporation indeed lacked the independent assets to take advantage of its opportunity. An important case involving this issue, Klinicki v. Lundgren (Or.1985), concludes that a director may not rely on financial inability of the corporation to justify taking a corporate opportunity unless the opportunity is first presented to the corporation for its consideration. A director who secretly takes advantage of an opportunity obviously has greater difficulty justifying his or her conduct than one who advises the corporation of the existence of the opportunity, and the corporation takes no steps to capture the opportunity.

Directors generally may engage in a similar line of business in competition with the corporation's business where it is done in good faith and without injury to the corporation. A number of cases, however, have found a competing director guilty of a breach of fiduciary duty on several possible theories: conflict of interest, corporate opportunity, misappropriation of trade secrets or customer lists, or wrongful interference with contractual relationships. In this area, tort concepts of unfair competition are close to fiduciary duties. Unfair competition with the corporation may involve business activities generally, or may involve specific corporate transactions, such as the director who competes with the corporation in selling shares of stock or who acquires at a discount claims against the corporation when the corporation could have done so. Again, judicial notions of fairness or fair play seem dominant, and a close appraisal of the fiduciary's conduct in light of ethical business practice is necessary.

§ 14.14 Fairness to Minority Shareholders

The preceding sections dealing with various aspects of the director's fiduciary duties to the corporation demonstrate that a test of fairness is an important criterion for evaluating the propriety of specific transactions. This test is explicitly a criterion in evaluating transactions between corporations with common directors and in determining whether a director may take advantage of corporate opportunities; it is also the test in evaluating the propriety of self-dealing transactions generally, at least in the absence of approval of the transaction by independent directors under the business judgment rule. The test of fairness generally serves the interests of the corporation, since well meaning officers and directors should not be discouraged from dealing with the corporation and reasonable transactions should not be set aside merely because of some formal or technical defect in corporate procedure. Further, the fairness test protects shareholders and creditors alike from overreaching or unwise transactions. The major problem with a fairness test is that it tends to be subjective and elastic; a judicial proceeding testing the fairness of a transaction may be broad-ranging and complex.

The test of fairness is applicable to a variety of transactions which defy precise categorization, but which may be lumped loosely under the title "fairness to minority share-holders." For example, in closely held corporations, an important line of cases have held that shareholders owe one another a fiduciary duty in the operation of the enterprise. The leading case is Donahue v. Rodd Electro-type Co. (Mass.1975). This duty could equally be phrased as a duty of fairness owed by directors in such an enter-prise to the minority shareholders. For example, it is unfair for a controlling shareholder to redeem a portion of his holdings at a higher price than offered to minority shareholders. In the absence of preemptive rights, it is unfair for a controlling shareholder to cause the corpora-tion to issue to the shareholder new or treasury shares at a fair price in order to affect or preserve voting control.

A principle of fairness is applicable to transactions af-fecting different classes of stock. In Zahn v. Transamerica Corp. (3d Cir.1947), for example, the directors of the Axton–Fisher Tobacco Company knew that the inventory of the corporation had appreciated greatly in value over the value reflected on the books of the corporation. To obtain the greatest portion of this appreciation for itself, the majority shareholder, Transamerica Corporation, caused the corporation to call a senior security (a convert-ible participating preferred). The corporation did not dis-close the inventory appreciation and, as a result, most of the holders of the senior securities permitted their hold-ings to be redeemed at $80.80 per share rather than converting them into common shares worth considerably more. The court held that the transaction violated a duty owed to the minority shareholders: in effect, the directors are required to treat fairly each class of stock and may not take actions which are designed to enhance the value of one class at the expense of another.

It is important, however, that the fairness principle be put into context. Directors elected by the common share-holders may declare extra dividends on common shares so long as the required provision is made for the senior securities; the directors may call a senior security for redemption in order ultimately to improve the position of the common shareholders. These powers are specifically granted to the directors by the articles of incorporation and are part of each shareholder's "contract" with the corporation. Thus, in *Zahn*, the holders of senior securities have no complaint if these powers are exercised ultimately to benefit the common shareholders who have the power to elect the directors. The holders of senior securities, however, may legitimately expect to be given accurate information so that they will not be misled and may make an intelligent selection of the various options available to them. The original opinion in the *Zahn* case contained language which intimated that the mere call for redemption constituted the breach of fiduciary duty, but on a subsequent appeal on the issue of damages, the Third Circuit adopted the theory that the failure to disclose relevant information constituted the breach. Speed v. Transamerica Corp. (2d Cir.1956).

§ 14.15 "Fairness" and the "Business Judgment Rule"

There is potential overlap between the cases in which the "fairness" test described in the previous sections is applied and the cases described in §§ 14.4 through 14.8 of this Nutshell dealing with the business judgment rule. This is illustrated by two cases involving transactions between parent corporations and their subsidiaries.

In Sinclair Oil Co. v. Levien (Del.1971), a case involving transactions between a parent corporation and its 97 per cent owned subsidiary, the minority shareholders of the subsidiary attacked several transactions, including decisions (1) to pay large dividends by the subsidiary solely in order to ease the cash needs of the parent, (2) to channel oil development in other countries into other subsidiaries of the parent, and (3) to cause the subsidiary not to pursue claims for breach of contract against the parent. The alternative rules potentially applicable, the court noted, are the standards of "intrinsic fairness," on the one hand, or of "business judgment" on the other. Under the latter, actions will be upheld unless there is a showing of "gross or palpable overreaching." The court held that the questions of the excessive dividends and channeling of business opportunities should be evaluated by the "business judgment rule" while the refusal to enforce the contract claim should be judged on the basis of "intrinsic fairness." The basic distinction, the court stated, is whether the transaction involves self-dealing, that is, whether the parent received something from the subsidiary "to the exclusion and detriment of the minority shareholders." Since the dividends were paid proportionally to all shareholders, there was no self-dealing and the business judgment rule should be applied. So far as the business opportunities were concerned, there was no showing that they were ever corporate opportunities of the subsidiary and thus were not taken improperly by the parent. Giving up a contract claim by the subsidiary against the parent, however, constituted self-dealing since the minority shareholders did not participate proportionally, and should be judged by "intrinsic fairness."

The requirement that transactions between parent and subsidiary must be evaluated on the basis of "intrinsic fairness" may sharply limit the power of the parent to utilize the subsidiary's assets most efficiently. For this reason, parent corporations may wish to eliminate the minority shareholders from the subsidiary in a "freeze-out" or "cash-out" merger. Modern statutes permit the involuntary elimination of minority shareholders (see § 18.3 of this Nutshell). On the other hand, such a merger is itself a conflict of interest transaction that requires establishment of the intrinsic fairness of the transaction.

In Weinberger v. UOP, Inc. (Del.1983), the court held that a cash-out merger transaction between a parent corporation and its partially owned subsidiary failed to meet the standard of intrinsic fairness. Intrinsic fairness, the court stated, had two basic aspects: fair dealing and fair price. Fair dealing involved fairness in the initiation, structuring, negotiation, and disclosure of the transaction to the minority shareholders of the subsidiary corporation. Fair price, on the other hand, required an examination of the economic and financial considerations underlying the proposed merger: assets, market value, earnings, future prospects and all other elements that affect the intrinsic or inherent value of a company's stock. Fair dealing and fair price should not be considered separately; the test is "not a bifurcated one" and "and all aspects of the issue must be examined as a whole since the question is one of entire fairness." The burden to establish intrinsic fairness, the court held, was on the parent corporation. In a footnote, however, the court stated that "the result here could have been entirely different" if the subsidiary had appointed an independent negotiating committee of its outside directors to deal with its parent. The court added that "fairness in this context can be equated to conduct by a theoretical, wholly independent, board of directors acting upon the matter before them," and that "particularly in a parent-subsidiary context, a showing that the action taken was as though each of the contending parties had in fact exerted its bargaining power against the other at arm's length is strong evidence that the transaction meets the test of fairness."

Following *Weinberger*, independent directors have been added to the boards of many partially owned subsidiaries to permit arms-length bargaining in the event the parent wishes to enter into a transaction with its subsidiary that implicates the intrinsic fairness standard. Of course, if independent directors are available, their decision must be consistent with the business judgment rule if their action is to have any effect. In Cinerama, Inc. v. Technicolor, Inc. (Del.1995), the Court explained that the business judgment rule has both procedural and substantive aspects: It is procedural because it places the initial burden of proof on the defendants to establish that the business judgment rule is applicable to the decision of the independent. If the business judgment rule is not satisfied then the defendants have the burden to establish the entire fairness of the transaction. A decision that the business judgment rule is applicable does not necessarily validate the transaction, it merely shifts the burden of proving the lack of intrinsic fairness to the plaintiff.

In these cases involving cash out mergers of partially owned subsidiaries, Delaware case law strongly suggests not only that independent directors be placed on the board of the subsidiary to negotiate independently with the parent corporation but also that approval of the transaction be conditioned upon its approval by a majority of the minority shareholders. There should be a full and fair disclosure of all material facts within the control of the parent corporation that would have a significant effect upon the shareholder vote.

§ 14.16 Shareholder Ratification

Ratification by shareholders of a transaction between a director and his or her corporation will sometimes validate a transaction that otherwise might be invalid. Clearly, many self-dealing transactions cannot be ratified by majority vote. Transactions that involve fraud, undue overreaching, or waste of corporate assets (e.g., a director using corporate assets for personal purposes without paying for them) can only be ratified by a unanimous vote, and even then may be attacked by representatives of creditors if the corporation becomes insolvent. The theory is that all the shareholders may dissipate the corporate assets as they wish, so long as creditors are not injured, but that any individual shareholder may object to a clearly improper use of corporate assets even though a majority of the shareholders are in favor of that use.

The test of transactions that may be ratified by shareholder action is traditionally phrased in terms of whether the transaction is "voidable" or "void." Only the former may be ratified. However, as discussed in *In re Wheelabrator Technologies, Inc.* (Del.Ch.1995), the rules are more complicated than a simple "go"/"no go" test. The term "ratification" may apply to transactions which the board of directors could theoretically have approved without shareholder action. It may also apply to situations where approval by shareholders is legally required, e.g., a merger. In the latter case a distinction may be drawn between cases where shareholder approval is required by statute and cases where approval is required by contract, e.g., the "majority of the minority" approval required in parent-subsidiary mergers where the parent owns a majority of the outstanding shares. *Wheelabrator* holds that the effect of independent shareholder approval is to validate actions in duty of care cases but to shift the burden of proof of fairness, or lack thereof, in duty of loyalty cases involving parent/subsidiary mergers or interested transactions between the corporation and a director to the plaintiff.

§ 14.17 Exoneratory Provisions

Provisions are sometimes placed in the articles of incorporation of a corporation that purport to permit transactions between directors and the corporation which otherwise might be voidable under the principles described elsewhere in this chapter. These clauses are not construed literally to validate fraudulent or manifestly unfair acts. Such clauses may (1) permit an interested director to be counted in determining whether a quorum is present, or (2) exonerate transactions between corporation and director "from adverse inferences which might be drawn against them." Some go even further and provide that self dealing transactions may not be subject to rescission and no liability may be imposed on directors arising from such transactions. Despite such clauses, courts examine with care transactions that may involve conflicting loyalties, and thus the usefulness and effectiveness of such clauses are limited.

§ 14.18 Statutory Duties and Statutory Defenses

State business corporation acts impose liabilities on directors for certain transactions that violate specific statutory provisions. This liability is in addition to other liabilities, and usually is not dependent on bad faith. While provisions vary from state to state, liability for the following actions are typical:

(1) Paying dividends or making distributions in violation of the act or of restrictions in the articles of incorporation. See MBCA (1984) § 8.33. Liability is usually limited to the excess of the amount actually distributed over the amount that could have been distributed without violating the act or restriction.

(2) Purchasing its own shares in violation of statute. The liability again is usually limited to the consideration paid for such shares which is in excess of the maximum amount which could have been paid without violating the statute. The Model Business Corporation Act (1984) in effect treats this prohibition as part of (1) since a "distribution" under MBCA (1984) is defined to include both dividends and repurchases of shares.

(3) Distributing assets to shareholders during the liquidation of the corporation without paying and discharging, or making adequate provision for the payment and discharge of, all known debts, obligations, and liabilities of the corporation. The Model Business Corporation Act does not directly address this kind of misconduct. See MBCA (1984) § 14.05(a)(3).

(4) Permitting the corporation to commence business before it has received the minimum required consideration for its shares. With the elimination of minimum capital requirements in MBCA (1984) and the statutes of most states, this provision is of little practical importance. In states that continue to require minimum capital, the liability is limited to the unpaid part of the minimum capital, and the liability terminates when the required minimum capital has actually been received. Earlier statutes in some states extended liability to all debts or liabilities incurred before the required capital has been paid in. Such a provision obviously created a serious trap for the unwary director.

(5) Permitting the corporation to make a prohibited loan to an officer, director, or shareholder of the corporation. MBCA (1984) has eliminated all restrictions on loans to officers, directors or shareholders; in states where these restrictions continue to exist, liability of directors who approve the loan is usually imposed up to the unpaid amount of the loan.

The Model Business Corporation Act (1984) greatly reduces the importance of these various statutory liability provisions, in part because it eliminates some of the underlying restrictions on which the liabilities are based and in part because it provides a simpler test for the lawfulness of corporate distributions, the provision most likely to be violated.

Business corporation acts also usually provide for joint and several liability imposed on all directors present at the meeting at which the transaction giving rise to the liability is taken, and a director held liable may be entitled to contribution from other directors who assented to the transaction. In addition shareholders who received the unlawful distribution may be compelled to return the distribution. See MBCA (1984) § 8.33(b). Under the MBCA (1984), however, only shareholders who accept "knowing the distribution was made in violation of the Act or the articles of incorporation" are liable for contribution. The theory is that shareholders who receive a distribution in ignorance of its illegality are entitled to keep it. In this situation, of course, the possibility of detrimental reliance by shareholders receiving the distribution is quite high.

The directoral liabilities imposed by these statutes may be subject to defenses available to directors generally. For example, in some states it is a defense that the directors met their standard of due care or they relied in good faith upon financial statements or advice given by appropriate corporate officials, attorneys, or others. Not all states recognize such defenses, however, and directors may possibly be liable for violation of statutory duties even though they acted in good faith and with due care. The Model Business Corporation Act (1984) further reduces the significance of these statutory liabilities by making all general statutory defenses applicable to them. It is probable that states will follow the MBCA (1984) in this regard in the future.

There has been virtually no litigation over the scope of these defenses. Indeed, there has also been very little litigation over the statutory liabilities for unlawful distributions or other actions that might lead to imposition of these statutory liabilities.

§ 14.19 Purchase or Sale of Shares or Claims Under State Law

This and the following sections deal with the potential liability of directors and officers when buying or selling shares of the corporation. These transactions involve both state and federal securities law provisions. The state law relating to transactions in corporate shares by directors and officers, or by the corporation itself, discussed in this section until recently has been largely overshadowed by the development of federal law, particularly rule 10b–5, discussed in the following section of this Nutshell. However, there are indications that these state law rules will become more important in the future than they are today.

(1) *Purchase or Sale of Shares by an Officer or Director on the Basis of Undisclosed Information.* An officer or director of the corporation may have knowledge about corporate affairs that is unknown to the general public or to the shareholders. He or she may be tempted either to purchase or to sell shares, depending on the nature of the information, without disclosing the information in order to make a personal profit. These transactions may be effected either by a personal negotiation or by an anonymous transaction using the facilities of a securities exchange. An officer or director who capitalizes on inside corporate information for personal gain violates rule 10b–5 and most cases of this type are currently brought in federal court under that rule.

The common law did not develop a simple test for handling these situations. If an affirmative misrepresentation was made in direct negotiations, of course, normal fraud principles dictate that the defrauded person might rescind the transaction. Furthermore, in personal dealings, some courts found an affirmative duty on the part of the insider to disclose specific facts which were of critical importance and peculiarly within the knowledge of the insider. In the leading case of Strong v. Repide (S.Ct. 1909), the Supreme Court found a duty to disclose "special facts" without attempting to define which facts are "special." In this case the insider concealed his or her identity from the purchaser and failed to disclose material facts about the value of the shares being purchased. In a related line of cases, Kansas adopted a general fiduciary duty to disclose relevant facts on the part of officers or directors when entering into transactions with shareholders. This position, sometimes described as the "minority" rule, appears to have become the majority rule, at least in cases involving closely held shares and personal dealings between the parties. A good recent example is Van Schaack Holdings, Ltd. v. Van Schaack (Colo.1994).

Diamond v. Oreamuno (N.Y.1969) holds that the corporation may recover "profits" made by insiders in securities selling on the basis of internal corporate information that costs would increase materially in the future and the value of the corporation's securities would decline in price. Relying on analogies with the federal securities laws, the court in effect concluded that inside information was corporate property and the insider should not be permitted to profit from the use of that corporate property even though the corporation was not injured thereby. This view has been accepted by some courts and rejected by others. This case involves a publicly held corporation and transactions effected anonymously on a securities exchange. Some courts have indicated skepticism about the correctness of this case.

(2) *Purchase at a Discount of Claims Against the Corporation.* A corporate officer or director may purchase claims against a *solvent* corporation at a discount, and enforce them at face value, though in some circumstances the opportunity to acquire a claim at a discount may itself be a corporate opportunity. It follows that claims validly bought at a discount when a corporation is solvent may

share at face value in a subsequent distribution in insolvency or bankruptcy. A different rule, however, is applicable to claims purchased at a discount when the corporation is insolvent, and on the verge of, or in, bankruptcy or liquidation. The theory is that when insolvency, liquidation, or reorganization has occurred or is imminent, corporate directors should attempt to settle or discharge claims against the corporation on the best possible terms from the corporation's standpoint in order to benefit other creditors and the shareholders, rather than seeking to profit personally from the distribution.

(3) *Purchase or Sale of Shares in Competition With the Corporation.* In some circumstances an officer or director may attempt to sell his or her personal stock in competition with the corporation's attempt to raise capital by selling additional stock. Such conduct is actionable if the opportunity to sell shares to a third person is itself a corporate opportunity. The same principle should be applicable to corporate opportunities to repurchase its own shares as well.

(4) *Purchase or Sale of Shares by a Corporation in a Struggle for Control.* If outsiders are seeking to wrest control of a public corporation away from incumbent management, the incumbents may attempt to use the corporation in order to preserve their position. They may cause the corporation to make open market purchases of its own shares in order to drive up the price and reduce the available supply of shares. Or they may cause the corporation to buy out the insurgents at a premium price in order to eliminate them. (This strategy is usually described as "green mail.") Or they may issue additional shares to themselves or to friendly persons in order to cement their position. Similarly, in a closely held corporation, the majority may decide to have the corporation purchase at a generous price the shares owned by a

particularly obstreperous minority shareholder in order to be rid of him or her. The general test of propriety adopted by the courts to evaluate all such transactions is one of underlying purpose:

"[I]f the actions of the board were motivated by a sincere belief that the buying out of the dissident stockholder was necessary to maintain what the board believed to be proper business practices, the board will not be held liable for such decision, even though hindsight indicates the decision was not the wisest course * * *. On the other hand, if the board has acted solely or primarily because of the desire to perpetuate themselves in office, the use of corporate funds for such purposes is improper."

Cheff v. Mathes (Del.1964). This test may be criticized on the ground that it is possible to dress up virtually every transaction as a "proper business practice." However, a number of cases have invalidated transactions of the type described, so that the test obviously has some teeth. In addition, a special penalty tax has been enacted by Congress to discourage green mail transactions; several states have also enacted statutes attempting to prohibit such transactions.

In the early 1980s, "green mail"—the purchase of a block of shares by a potential aggressor pursuant to a plan to compel the issuer to repurchase shares at a premium price—was viewed as a serious evil. Such a strategy in Delaware would be evaluated under the *Cheff* standard or the *Unocal* standard of "proportionality." See § 13.25 of this Nutshell. Heckman v. Ahmanson (Cal.1985) holds that the greenmail recipient was an aider and abettor of directors' breach of duty of loyalty.

§ 14.20   Duties of Directors of Financially Distressed Corporations

In general terms, directors owe duties of care and fiduciary duties of loyalty to the corporation itself. They are to act in good faith and with the honest belief that the action taken is in the best interests of the corporation. In effect this means that their primary goal is to maximize the wealth of the shareholders. Courts also generally hold that directors of solvent corporations owe no duty to the creditors of the corporation. Indeed, if directors take discretionary steps to favor creditors at the expense of shareholders, they may become liable to shareholders for breach of duty to them.

If a corporation files for reorganization under Chapter 11 of the Bankruptcy Code, these duties immediately shift. Under the Bankruptcy Code the "debtor in possession"— the corporation—owes a fiduciary obligation to protect the interests of creditors. Since court approval of many actions by the debtor in possession is required, directors may take close or difficult questions of fiduciary duty to the court for approval before action is taken. Hence it is unusual for directors of a corporation in Chapter 11 to be surcharged for actions taken that benefit the shareholders rather than creditors. Where the corporation is insolvent, the sole recourse of a corporate creditor is against the corporation or the representative, and not by a direct suit against a director or officer. Such a suit in effect would permit the creditor to obtain a priority or other advantage over other creditors.

Geyer v. Ingersoll Publications Co. (Del.Ch.1992) holds that directors owe fiduciary duties to the creditors when the corporation is "in fact" insolvent. Insolvency in fact was defined as "a corporation in which the value of its assets has sunk below the amount of its debts." In Credit Lyonnais Bank Nederland, N.V. v. Pathe Communications

Corp. (Del.Ch.1991), the Court held that directors of a corporation "in the vicinity of insolvency" owe fiduciary duties to both shareholders and the corporation's creditors, and its responsibility is to "maximize the corporation's long-term wealth-creating capacity." In footnote 55 the Court appended a famous footnote describing how conflicts between shareholders and creditors arise in connection with such a corporation. The "vicinity of insolvency" is obviously a difficult concept to apply in real life.

§ 14.21   Rule 10b–5

Rule 10b–5, promulgated by the Securities and Exchange Commission under section 10(b) of the Securities Exchange Act of 1934, is the source of most current principles relating to transactions in securities by officers, directors, and others. Rule 10b–5 has some of the attributes of a roller coaster: a dizzying growth followed by a sudden decline as the United States Supreme Court sharply limited the growth of the jungle of case law. The deceptively simple language of rule 10b–5 should be quoted—

"It shall be unlawful for any person, directly or indirectly, by the use of any means or instrumentality of interstate commerce, or of the mails or of any facility of any national securities exchange,

"(1) to employ any device, scheme, or artifice to defraud;

"(2) to make any untrue statement of a material fact or to omit to state a material fact necessary in order to make the statements made, in light of the circumstances under which they were made, not misleading, or

"(3) to engage in any act, practice, or course of business which operates or would operate as a fraud or deceit upon any person, "in connection with the purchase or sale of any security."

Rule 10b–5 is a federal regulation and claims arising under it are federal claims. There is no need for diversity of citizenship, suit may be brought only in federal court, and state security-for-expenses statutes (see § 16.8 of this Nutshell) are not applicable. While many rule 10b–5 cases probably could have been brought in state court on state fiduciary or fraud principles, the federal forum has been traditionally preferred by plaintiffs for several reasons. The procedures may be simpler and discovery procedures broader. There is nationwide service of process and broad venue provisions. The doctrine of pendent jurisdiction permits the joinder of both state and federal claims in a rule 10b–5 suit, but a rule 10b–5 claim cannot be joined with state causes of action in a state court. Further, in the past at least, the principles applicable under rule 10b–5 have been more favorable to plaintiffs than the correlative principles of state law. There are also more rule 10b–5 precedents than state court precedents and hence "more law" on which to build one's case. Finally, there is also the feeling, perhaps no longer justified, that federal judges may be more sympathetic to minority shareholder complaints than state court judges. For all these practical reasons, rule 10b–5 was traditionally preferred over state-based claims, and as a result rule 10b–5 prospered while state law languished. In the 1990s, however, the Supreme Court decided two securities cases which indicated that the Court was moving toward a narrower and more literal construction of securities law and regulations. These two opinions held (1) that no "aiding and abetting" liability existed under rule 10b–5 (despite the fact that all lower courts had found that such liability did exist under the securities acts) and (2) the word "prospectus" had a narrow meaning in section 12(2) of the Securities Act of 1933 despite the fact that the Act itself defined "prospectus" very broadly. These two opinions may signify a much narrower construction in Rule 10b–5 in the future.

The present contours of rule 10b–5 should be stated. A private cause of action exists for violations of the rule. This was established in 1946, only three years after rule 10b–5 was promulgated. Only persons who are purchasers or sellers of securities may take advantage of rule 10b–5; however, defendants may be liable under rule 10b–5 even though they themselves were neither purchaser nor seller. The plaintiff must establish that defendants acted with "scienter," that is, "intentional wrongdoing" or a "mental state embracing intent to deceive, manipulate or defraud." However, in some circumstances recklessness may satisfy the scienter requirement. Further, rule 10b–5 only prohibits deception, not unfairness. In other words, a transaction (e.g., a merger) that is adequately disclosed cannot be attacked under rule 10b–5 no matter how unfair its terms.

The jurisdictional basis of rule 10b–5 has been construed very broadly. It is triggered by the use of facilities of interstate commerce—e.g. the telephone—or by use of the mails. To use a classroom example, a violation of rule 10b–5 occurs if the president of a small Denver corporation offers over the telephone to purchase the shares owned by a shareholder living in Denver on the basis of a misrepresentation. The president has violated rule 10b–5 without ever leaving his Denver office. Rule 10b–5 proscribes not only affirmative misrepresentations but also half-truths; in addition, in limited circumstances a failure to disclose "material facts"; mere silence may constitute a violation, e.g., by failing to correct a statement that was accurate when made but is now false. The test of what is "material" is whether a reasonable person would attach importance to the information in determining his or her course of action—in other words, if the information would, in reasonable and objective contemplation, affect the value of the securities, it should be considered "mate-

rial." Examples of material information are a significant
ore strike, a resale contract for the shares or corporate
assets, or a merger opportunity.

Rule 10b–5 has been applied in a variety of different
contexts described in the following sections.

§ 14.22   Rule 10b–5 as an Anti-Fraud Provision.

It is now firmly established that rule 10b–5 is applicable
in private transactions that involve closely held shares if
the jurisdictional requirements have been met and a misrepresentation or half-truth has occurred in connection
with the transaction. Rule 10b–5 thus provides a federal
cause of action for private transactions involving securities
which is an alternative to fraud claims under state law.

Rule 10b–5 is also involved in numerous class actions
involving claimed fraud or misrepresentation relating to
information about publicly traded shares. These lawsuits
became so numerous and controversial that Congress in
1995 enacted the "Private Securities Litigation Reform
Act" to deal with this type of litigation. President Clinton
vetoed this legislation but his veto was overridden by
Congress. These developments are described in detail in
Chapter 16 of this Nutshell.

§ 14.23   Rule 10b–5 as a Prohibition Against Insider Trading.

Rule 10b–5 has been applied to transactions in which
persons with non-public information have sought to capitalize on that information by entering into securities transactions before the information becomes public.

The first statement that trading on the basis of inside
information in the anonymous securities markets might
violate rule 10b–5 appeared in In the Matter of Cady

Roberts & Co. (1961), an SEC broker discipline case. Its first widely-publicized application occurred in Securities and Exchange Commission v. Texas Gulf Sulphur Corp. (2d Cir.1968), where the court held unlawful, under rule 10b–5, the purchase of common shares of Texas Gulf, and call options on those shares, by a number of employees, officers, and directors of Texas Gulf based on a preliminary core that revealed a major ore discovery drilled in an area near Timmins, Ontario. Rule 10b–5 was also held to have been violated by transactions entered into very shortly after the news of the ore strike had been released at a press conference called by the corporation but before the market had had a chance to react to the disclosed information. After this decision, the New York Stock Exchange published guidelines as to when it was appropriate for an insider to purchase shares of the corporation. These guidelines suggest periodic investment purchases (e.g. buying a few shares every month) or limiting transactions to brief periods after public information is released. However, where a development of major importance has occurred, uncertainty may exist as to when an insider may trade even after the information has been released. Since it is usually impractical for the insider himself to disclose material facts (since that is a corporate function), the result is that insiders with material information about corporate matters simply must forego the transaction until after the facts are made public and have been reasonably disseminated by wire services and the like.

The modern law of insider trading has been largely shaped by three decisions of the Supreme Court of the United States: Chiarella v. United States (S.Ct.1980), Dirks v. SEC (S.Ct.1983), and Carpenter v. United States (S.Ct. 1987); and by the enactment of two statutes addressing the insider trading problem: the Insider Trading Sanctions Act of 1984 (ITSA) and the Insider Trading and Securities Fraud Enforcement Act of 1988 (ITSFEA). Both of these statutes are amendments to the Securities Exchange Act of 1934; they clearly assume that there is an effective legal prohibition against permitting insider trading. These developments are described in the following paragraphs.

(i) In *Chiarella*, the Court set aside a criminal conviction under rule 10b–5 of an employee of a printing plant printing documents for securities transactions who traded on information obtained through his work. The information related to proposed tender offers by aggressor corporations; while the names of both aggressors and targets were left blank (or false names were substituted), Chiarella was able to ascertain the identities of the corporations involved and then use the information to profit on the shares of the target corporations. A majority of the Supreme Court held that Chiarella owed no duty to the general public to disclose the information he obtained since he was not an insider and received no information from the target corporation. There was, furthermore, no general rule that prohibited all persons with inside information from trading.

Shortly after *Chiarella* was decided, the SEC adopted rule 14e–3 which prohibits trading by anyone with undisclosed information about pending tender offers. Thus, even an eavesdropper who overhears discussion of a proposed offer at a restaurant or while walking in the street violates this rule if she trades on the basis of the information. On the facts, Chiarella would have violated rule 14e–3 even though he had not violated rule 10b–5. The Second Circuit has upheld the validity of this rule. United States v. Chestman (2d Cir.1991).

(ii) In *Chiarella*, the possibility that a criminal conviction under rule 10b–5 might be based on Chiarella's duties to his employer was suggested by a dissent but not squarely addressed by the majority. Following this decision, the Second Circuit on several occasions has held that a violation of a duty to employers or persons other than the issuer may be used to ground a rule 10b–5 violation. The leading case involving this theory, usually called the "misappropriation theory," is *Carpenter;* in this case, Winans, a reporter for the Wall Street Journal and writer of the daily column "Heard on the Street," was tipping associates about the content of the column before it was published. Favorable mention of a stock in this column usually led to a run-up in price of the stock; Winans and his associates purchased the stock in advance of the column and profited from the increase in price. Winans was convicted of a criminal violation of section 10(b) and rule 10b–5, and the Second Circuit affirmed primarily on the misappropriation theory. The Supreme Court divided 4–4 on this branch of the case, leaving the status of the misappropriation theory in doubt. However, the Supreme Court in Carpenter went on to hold, 8–0, that the misuse of other persons' confidential information may serve as the basis of a criminal prosecution under the mail fraud statute, a criminal statute carrying substantial penalties. Violation of the mail fraud statute usually leads to a sentence of imprisonment.

In United States v. Bryan (4th Cir.1995), the Court held that the misappropriation theory was not valid under Rule 10b–5, though conviction under the mail fraud theory was affirmed. Thus, the continued existence of the misappropriation theory remains in doubt.

(iii) *Dirks* involved a broker who was given information by an insider about a major fraud that was occurring within Equity Funding Corporation, a life insurance and mutual fund corporation. Dirks "blew the whistle" on the fraud only after advising his clients to dispose of their Equity Funding stock. Dirks was a "tippee," that is a person who receives information from a person within the corporation (the "tipper"). Such a person differs from the printer in *Chiarella* in that the tippee is acting on information obtained directly from the corporation. In *Dirks,* the Court held that a tippee was subject to the constraints of rule 10b–5 only if the tipper breached a fiduciary duty in giving the information to the tippee. This question, in turn, is to be resolved on the basis of whether the tipper received a direct or indirect personal benefit from the disclosure, such as a pecuniary gain or a "reputational benefit." In a footnote, the Court also suggested that some nominal "tippees" who receive corporate information in a legitimate manner—such as underwriters, accountants, attorneys, or consultants working for the corporation—should be viewed as temporary insiders so that if they disclose confidential information it is as a tipper and not a tippee.

The requirement of *Dirks* that a tippee is liable under rule 10b–5 only if the tipper obtained an improper benefit from the disclosure, has lead to some unusual allegations. In one case, for example, the former CEO of a major corporation was charged with providing inside information to several friends as well as his mistress; the SEC charged that the former CEO received a direct personal benefit from his "close personal relationship" with his mistress!

(iv) The Insider Trading Sanctions Act (ITSA) constituted the first Congressional recognition of the existence of restrictions on insider trading. That Act authorized the SEC to recover up to three times the amount of trading profit from persons who engage in unlawful insider trading. Under this authority, the SEC has settled a number of insider trading cases, charging the violator with a penalty equal to twice or three times the amount of the trading profit, depending apparently on the degree of culpability. Of course, in addition to this civil penalty, criminal sanctions may be, and often are, imposed.

(v) The Insider Trading and Securities Fraud Enforcement Act (ITSFEA) increased the criminal penalties for securities violations, created a statutory remedy by which contemporaneous traders may bring private actions against persons engaged in unlawful insider trading, added a bounty provision by which informants could receive up to ten per cent of any penalty recovered under ITSA and ITSFEA, and imposed limited civil penalties on persons who directly or indirectly control an inside trader. Probably the most important of these provisions is the one relating to controlling persons: the test for liability is whether such person "knew or recklessly disregarded the fact that such controlled person was likely to engage" in unlawful insider trading or "knowingly or recklessly failed to establish, maintain or enforce" policies or procedures designed to prevent such trading. Under this section, law firms, accounting firms, issuers, financial printers, newspapers and magazines, and others, are required to implement policies designed to prevent insider trading.

Neither ITSA nor ITSFEA contains a definition of insider trading. The test for what triggers the civil penalty and other sanctions under those statutes is based on the Supreme Court cases described above.

A major area of controversy in this appear is the liability of tippees, a person receiving inside information either directly or from another tippee. There is a possibility that both tipper and tippee may be liable for profits made by the tippee in a transaction that violates rule 10b–5. Indeed, one facet of the *Texas Gulf Sulphur* case involved a holding that a tipper was liable for the profits made by his tippees. While the tippees were not parties to that proceeding, the court noted that their action was at least as reprehensible as that of their tipper; today multiple liability is certainly likely under the tests of the *Dirks* case. If the tipper is liable for the tippee's profits, it is doubtful whether the tipper has an "action over" because of the *in pari delicto* principle. In its administration of ITSA and ITSFEA, the SEC has accepted settlements based on the tipper paying a civil penalty equal to or in excess of the profits made by his or her tippee.

The SEC has made the enforcement of the prohibition against insider trading one of its major priorities. Where trading in advance of a major transaction indicates that persons may have been trading on information before it was released publicly, the SEC has consistently investigated even relatively small transactions. Many of these investigations are terminated by settlements in which the person trading, as well as persons who provided the information, have agreed to return all profits and pay an additional civil money penalty. In some cases, criminal prosecutions have been instituted and other types of penalties imposed.

The case law has also considered the liability of a tipper who gives his tippee knowingly false information, and the tippee lost money trading. In Eichler v. Berner (S.Ct. 1985), the Court held that *in pari delicto* should be applied only where "the plaintiff bears at least substantially equal responsibility for the violations he seeks to redress."

In transactions involving publicly traded shares, it is usually impractical for the insider to disclose material facts since that is a corporate function. The result is that insiders with material information about corporate matters simply must forego the transaction until after the facts are made public and have been reasonably disseminated by wire services and the like. Nevertheless the temptation to make a profit on what may well be a "once in a lifetime chance" is often strong, and there is a steady stream of federal insider trading cases.

§ 14.24 Rule 10b–5 as a Protector of the Issuer

Rule 10b–5 is potentially applicable when a corporation issues or acquires its own shares. In other words, the phrase "purchase or sale" is literally construed to cover transactions by the corporation in its own shares as well as transactions by third persons. If shares are issued or acquired by a corporation as a result of deception or a failure of some persons to disclose material facts to the corporation, the corporation may have a claim under rule 10b–5, and this claim may be asserted derivatively by a minority shareholder. For example, stock options granted to officers of Texas Gulf Sulphur Corporation who knew of the major ore strike were canceled since the recipients did not advise the members of the option committee of the material information (the ore strike). Similarly, a rule 10b–5 violation occurs if the corporation is fraudulently induced to issue shares for inadequate consideration even though such conduct also may constitute a violation of state-created fiduciary duties. Of course, in all cases of this type, there must be both deception and scienter in order to meet the fundamental requirements of rule 10b–5.

§ 14.25   Rule 10b–5 as a General Prohibition Against Wrongful Conduct

At an earlier time courts permitted rule 10b–5 to be cast adrift from its mooring as an anti-fraud provision, and applied the rule to situations in which bad conduct occurred and there was some relationship either to the securities market or to trading in securities. The leading case involving this free wheeling approach is Superintendent of Ins. of New York v. Bankers Life & Cas. Co. (S.Ct.1971), where the United States Supreme Court found a rule 10b–5 violation when a corporation sold treasury bonds and the proceeds were fraudulently diverted to third parties. Thus, for a relatively brief period rule 10b–5 appeared to have an apparently limitless growth potential. However, in the 1970s, the United States Supreme Court firmly embraced the doctrine that the last clause of rule 10b–5 ("in connection with the purchase or sale of any security") required the plaintiff to be a purchaser or seller of securities in order to state a rule 10b–5 violation. This doctrine is sometimes called the "Birnbaum doctrine" based on the name of an earlier Court of Appeals decision.

§ 14.26 Section 16(b) of the Securities Exchange Act of 1934

Section 16(b) of the Securities Exchange Act of 1934 is an *in terrorem* provision designed to prevent specified persons from trading in a corporation's securities on an in-and-out basis on the strength of inside information. The following comments outline the scope of this statutory liability:

(1) Unlike rule 10b–5, section 16(b) is only applicable to corporations with a class of securities registered under section 12 of the Securities Exchange Act—that is to corporations (i) with securities traded on a national securities exchange or (ii) with assets of more than $5,000,000 and more than 500 shareholders of record of any class of equity security.

(2) Section 16(b) is only applicable to specified persons, namely officers, directors, and ten per cent shareholders of the issuer. Rule 10b–5 may be applicable to any person.

(3) Section 16(b) is applicable only if there is an offsetting purchase-and-sale or sale-and-purchase of an equity security of the issuer within any six-month period. For example, if there is a sale on January 1, section 16(b) is applicable if there is an offsetting purchase made at any time from six months before to six months after the sale. The sequence of the transactions or the fact that different certificates are involved, is irrelevant. However, a transaction on July 2, six months and one day after the original transaction on January 1, cannot be matched.

(4) The words "purchase" and "sale" are construed broadly. A gift may be a sale, as may be a redemption, conversion or a simple exchange of shares pursuant to a merger or consolidation. The grant of a warrant may be a purchase, a conversion may also be a purchase of the conversion securities, and so forth. The test is not a dictionary one; rather the definition that is usually stated is that a transaction will be considered a "purchase" or a "sale" for purposes of section 16(b) if it is of a kind that can possibly lend itself to the speculation encompassed by section 16(b). Under this test, commentators and lower courts have struggled with whether all sorts of transactions, such as recapitalizations, exchanges, conversions, mergers, puts, and calls should be considered "purchases" or "sales."

(5) Actual use of inside information is not a prerequisite for section 16(b) liability. Even a sale for entirely justifiable reasons—e.g. unexpected medical expenses— will trigger section 16(b) if there has been an offsetting transaction within the six-month period.

(6) Profits are payable to the corporation. However, if the corporation fails to take steps to recover the profit, any shareholder may bring suit. It is not necessary that the shareholder have owned shares when either of the transactions took place.

(7) Profits are computed by comparing the highest sale price with the lowest purchase price during any relevant six month period, the next highest sale price with the next lowest purchase price, and so forth. In this computation, all loss transactions are ignored and any individual transaction may be matched only once (though a single large purchase may be broken up and partially matched against two or more sales that occurred at different times). The purpose is to squeeze out all possible profits from the transaction. It is possible to have a substantial loss in a trading account and yet have an equally substantial section

16(b) profit under this method of computation. The United States Supreme Court has never passed on this rather draconian measure of recovery.

(8) All transactions by covered persons must be reported to the SEC and this information is published and is widely available. Certain attorneys regularly review all these filings in order to find section 16(b) violations. They are motivated by the attorneys' fees that may be awarded in a successful section 16(b) suit. Suits brought by these attorneys in the name of nominal shareholder plaintiffs (who need not be shareholders at the time either of the purchase or of the sale) may be champertous, but are the principal enforcement device of section 16(b). As a result, it is unlikely that a violation of section 16(b) will escape detection.

(9) Like rule 10b–5, the jurisdiction of section 16(b) suits is exclusively federal.

One basic fact about section 16(b) is that people do not knowingly violate it. Everyone subject to section 16(b) is aware of it. Corporations subject to this section distribute periodic warnings about the responsibility of officers and directors under the securities laws, particularly section 16(b). Substantial shareholders are sophisticated and also well aware of this arbitrary restriction on trading. Despite this general knowledge and these warnings, inadvertent violations of this section continue to occur. Most of the violations appear to be a result of ignorance rather than of actual misuse of inside information. Most inadvertent violations are a result of the failure to appreciate how broadly the words "purchase" and "sale" may be construed.

The Securities and Exchange Commission has authority to exempt classes of transactions from section 16(b). Historically, it has exercised this power sparingly, creating exemptions that tended to be narrowly drawn to cover specific situations. In 1991, however, the SEC issued regulations that are broader and more comprehensive, and designed to avoid the most arbitrary aspects of the section 16(b) jurisprudence. Of particular importance to corporate management are provisions relating to executive compensation, particularly stock options and incentive plans. In addition, these regulations attempt to rationalize the application of section 16(b) to derivative securities, such as puts and calls on publicly traded shares, as well as offsetting transactions in shares of different classes

In the 1970s, a significant area of section 16(b) jurisprudence was its application to takeover situations where an unsuccessful aggressor acquires over ten per cent of the target's shares and then sells. In Foremost–McKesson, Inc. v. Provident Securities Co. (S.Ct.1976), the Court finally "solved" the application of section 16(b) to the unsuccessful tender offeror by holding that the initial purchase that puts an aggressor over ten per cent was not a section 16(b) purchase. An earlier case, also of general interest, is Blau v. Lehman (S.Ct.1962), holding that a partnership not itself a ten per cent holder may violate section 16(b) if one of its partners is a director of the issuer and the partnership had "deputized" the partner to represent the partnership on the board.

In 1996 proposals have been seriously advanced that section 16(b) is obsolete in the modern era in which insider trading is regulated under rule 10b(5), ITSA, and ITSFEA, and should be repealed.

§ 14.27 Transfers of Control

For purposes of this section, a "controlling shareholder" is a person who owns either an outright majority of the shares of a corporation or a minority of the shares but the balance is so fragmented that he has working control and can deliver the management to a purchaser of the shares. The simplest method of "delivering" control in this sense is by the seriatim resignation of directors and their successive replacement by nominees of the purchaser, though the new controlling shareholder may wait until the next meeting and elect "his" directors at that meeting.

When a controlling shareholder sells his interest to third persons, something more than the property represented by the shares is being sold. The sale also involves transfer of control over a going business in which other persons— minority shareholders, senior security holders, and creditors—may have a substantial interest. Shares owned by a controlling shareholder command a premium over other shares simply because they represent not only a property interest in the shares but also the power to control the business, to designate the corporate officers, and so forth. This premium is usually referred to as the "control premium."

Generally a controlling shareholder may sell his or her shares for whatever price he can obtain in the same way as any other property. However, the courts recognize that the seller and buyer are not the only persons interested in this transaction and have imposed duties on the selling shareholder with respect to the purchaser. The "looting" cases are a clear illustration. Several cases have imposed liability on a controlling shareholder when, without investigation, he has sold his shares to unscrupulous third persons who thereafter "loot" the corporation by misappropriating or stealing corporate assets. If there is any indication or suspicion that a potential purchaser intends to loot the corporation, the controlling shareholder has a duty to make a reasonable investigation of that purchaser and not to transfer control to him if there is doubt as to his plans. Danger signs include, (1) an excessive price for the shares willingly paid, (2) excessive interest in the liquid and readily salable assets owned by the corporation, (3) insistence by the buyer on an immediate transfer of control, (4) insistence by the buyer that liquid assets be made available immediately, as by the delivery of certificates for negotiable securities endorsed in blank at the closing, (5) little interest being indicated by the purchaser in the detailed operation of the corporation's business, and (6) insistence by the purchaser that the transaction be handled with dispatch. Since the liability is based on negligence, the recovery may be based on the damage suffered, i.e., the amount looted, rather than on the purchase price paid or the amount of the control premium.

Outside of the looting cases, courts have not evolved consistent theories about the propriety of a controlling shareholder receiving a "control premium." Some cases in which the controlling shareholder has been compelled to share the control premium with minority shareholders contain broad statements to the effect that a director owes a fiduciary duty to the corporation and to the minority shareholders. E.g., Perlman v. Feldmann (2d Cir.1955). Such statements are little more than make-weight since they do not explain when the premium may be recovered and when it may not. Law review commentators have put forward theoretical arguments in both directions. Some have suggested that all control premiums in good conscience should be shared with all shareholders. These commentators essentially argue that since shares of stock are fungible, the control premium represents the pure power to control which should, if anything, be a corporate asset available to all shareholders. Cases, however, have rejected this position. Other commentators, particularly law and economics scholars, have argued that most sale of control transactions are beneficial from the standpoint of the buyer, the seller, the minority interests that remain, and by the economy in general, and that a mandatory sharing requirement would render impractical many desirable transfers of control. Most cases, including virtually all recent ones, have permitted the selling shareholder to keep the premium.

A form of control premium is also involved in cases such as Honigman v. Green Giant Co. (8th Cir.1962), where the holders of a class of voting shares agreed to share the voting power with the holders of a larger class of nonvoting common in exchange for a larger slice of the "equity." Such transactions have been approved where the premium is not excessive, or to put it a different way, where the transaction seems fair. On the other hand, the decision in Jones v. H. F. Ahmanson & Co. (Cal.1969), though involving unique facts, contains language that leans toward acceptance of the theory that control premiums are inherently improper, though the case may be viewed as a type of unfair freeze-out or squeeze-out. In this case, the majority shareholders of a savings and loan association created a holding company and exchanged their shares for holding company shares. Minority shareholders in the association were not permitted also to exchange their shares for holding company shares. The holding company then made a public offering and a public market was created for the holding company's shares from which the minority shareholders of the association were precluded while any market for the savings and loan shares dried up. The court held that this conduct violated the majority's fiduciary responsibility to the minority, and that recovery might be based either on the appraised value of the shares when the holding company was created or the value of a "derived block" of the holding company shares on the date litigation was commenced.

Some older cases have permitted the recovery of a control premium on a theory of "corporate action" or usurpation of corporate opportunity. If the purchaser first offers to buy the assets of the corporation, but the controlling shareholder suggests that the transaction be recast in the form of a purchase of the controlling shares, a reasonable argument may be made that the favorable sale opportunity was a corporate opportunity belonging to all the shareholders rather than an opportunity of the majority shareholder to sell controlling shares. The facts of Perlman v. Feldmann arguably present this pattern, though the opinion itself only partially articulates this theory. Other older cases adopt the theory that the control premium is for the sale of a corporate office rather than a sale of stock, and a sale of office is against public policy so that the excess payment may be recovered by the corporation for the benefit of the minority shareholders. The problem with this argument is that it proves too much—all sales of control stock at a premium accompanied by a transfer of control may be analyzed in this fashion. This argument is most likely to be accepted either where an additional payment is conditioned on the immediate transfer of offices or where the selling shareholders own a minuscule proportion of the outstanding shares and the sales agreement carefully provides for a seriatim resignation of directors. Petition of Caplan (App.Div.1964) is the leading case accepting this argument. In that case the selling shareholders owned only 3 per cent of the outstanding shares.

Liability for a control premium has also sometimes been based on a theory of nondisclosure or misrepresentation. In these cases a controlling shareholder contracts to sell more shares than he or she owns, planning to purchase the additional shares from other shareholders. If the controlling shareholder purchases the additional shares from other shareholders without disclosing the existence of the resale contract, the controlling shareholder may be liable under state or federal law (though an argument may also be made that the resale opportunity is not material since it was only made to the controlling shareholder). (See §§ 14.19, 14.23 of this Nutshell.) However, frontal attacks on sale of control premiums under rule 10b–5 have been unsuccessful because of the *Birnbaum* principle that the plaintiff must be a purchaser or seller of securities. (See § 14.23 of this Nutshell.)

Where a control premium is recoverable, courts have permitted either the corporation or the minority share-holders to recover, depending on the theory adopted. In a few cases, courts have required that a corporate recovery be paid over proportionally to the minority shareholders in order to avoid the recovery falling under the control of a wrongdoer.

[For unfamiliar terms see the Glossary]

CHAPTER FIFTEEN

INDEMNIFICATION AND INSURANCE

§ 15.1 Definitions of Terms

"Indemnification" by the corporation simply means the corporation reimburses a defendant who is a corporate officer or director for (a) expenses incurred in defending against a claim or prosecution, particularly legal fees but including other expenses as well, and (b) amounts paid in settlement of suits or to satisfy a judgment entered against (or fines imposed upon a conviction of) the defendant officer or director. Indemnification is specifically discussed in sections 15.3 and 15.4 of this Nutshell.

"Advances for expenses" are payments by the corporation to officers or directors who are named as defendants in a lawsuit to cover their expenses as they arise. Advances for expenses are discussed in section 15.5 of this Nutshell. They are governed by many of the same principles that govern indemnification by the corporation.

"Directors and officers liability insurance" (usually called "D & O insurance") is third party insurance written by many insurance companies that insures the corporation and individual officers and directors against expenses incurred in connection with litigation. D & O insurance may also cover amounts paid in settlement of suits or to satisfy a judgment against insured parties. D & O insurance is discussed in section 15.5 of this Nutshell.

§ 15.2 The Need for Protection of Directors and Officers

There are persuasive policy justifications in modern society for limiting the exposure of officers and directors to the risks and costs of litigation: (1) it encourages innocent directors to resist unjust charges, (2) it encourages responsible persons to accept the position of director, and (3) it discourages groundless shareholder litigation. However, the most important justification for indemnification protection for directors and officers today unquestionably is that it is essential in order to attract desirable persons to serve in these positions. The possibility of derivative or direct litigation which is groundless or of doubtful validity is great and the costs of successfully defending such suits are high. Concern about being ensnared in litigation is so great today that most persons of any wealth or property will refuse to even consider serving as a director or officer of a publicly held corporation unless they are guaranteed the maximum possible protection against such litigation.

Maximum protection today for directors typically involves three levels or layers of protection: (1) provisions in articles of incorporation and bylaws that minimize the exposure of the director to personal liability (see § 14.6 of this Nutshell), (2) broad indemnification protection provided by the corporation, and (3) D & O insurance in substantial amounts provided by and paid for by the corporation.

While corporations today generally seek to provide the maximum possible protection to its directors and officers, not all corporations may desire to provide this protection. A corporation with minimal capitalization may prefer to husband its resources for business purposes even though it thereby leaves its directors and officers exposed to some extent to liability claims. The Model Business Corporation

Act therefore also authorizes a corporation to limit or exclude all indemnification obligations if it expressly does so in its articles of incorporation [MBCA (1984) § 8.58(c)]. Most publicly held corporations do not elect to limit indemnification.

§ 15.3 Public Policy Limitations on Indemnification

Indemnification may violate basic tenets of public policy if it permits management to use corporate funds to avoid the consequences of improper conduct. Directors who intentionally inflict harm on the corporation or seek to line their own pockets by the misappropriation of corporate assets should not be able to receive corporate funds to assist them in avoiding the consequences of their own conduct. Indemnification of expenses incurred by such directors in defending unsuccessfully against valid claims also seems clearly to be against public policy. The director or officer engaged in significant misconduct should be required to pay both for judgments entered against him and for the costs of his defense out of his own pocket.

Equally strong policy considerations may apply in criminal prosecutions or agency investigations or administrative proceedings. Indemnification by the corporation may frustrate basic societal policies in these situations.

On the other hand, there is no policy objection if a corporation indemnifies a director or officer who is cleared of wrongdoing on the merits. In fact, indemnification in that situation strongly encourages persons to serve as a director or officer. Doubt may arise about the propriety of indemnification in certain other situations. For example, what if the director is absolved of liability on the basis of a defense, such as the statute of limitations, which is not on the merits? What about amounts paid or expenses incurred in connection with the settlement of a dispute? A settlement is fundamentally ambiguous. It may reflect a small payment to settle a nuisance suit which is without merit or it may be the result of the fact that the defendant recognizes that there is a high probability that he may lose on the merits. Finally, indemnification of judgments or settlements of derivative suits brought on behalf of the corporation creates obvious problems of circularity as indemnification payments are made by the corporation to the defendant who pays the funds back to the corporation to resolve the claim.

As phrased by one commentator, the goal of indemnification statutes is to "seek the middle ground between encouraging fiduciaries to violate their trust, and discouraging them from serving at all."

State statutes attempt to work out a compromise of these various competing considerations. A number of states have only very general statutes authorizing indemnification which give little indication of the outer limits, so that courts must address the outer limits of public policy. The indemnification provisions of Chapter 8 of the Model Business Corporation Act (1984) (which were substantially modified in 1994) have been particularly influential. The discussion below is based on the MBCA (1984) provisions as amended in 1994.

§ 15.4 Statutory Treatment of Indemnification

Indemnification statutes may be either "exclusive" or "non-exclusive." An exclusive statute defines the outer limits of the power to indemnify in the statute itself. Non-exclusive statutes define certain areas in which indemnification is required or is authorized, but corporations are permitted to increase the scope of indemnification by provisions in articles of incorporation or, more commonly, in bylaws or resolutions of the board of directors or shareholders. The New York BCL, § 721, is a typical non-exclusive statute: "The indemnification and advancement of expenses granted pursuant to ... this article shall not be deemed exclusive of any other rights to which a director or officer ... may be entitled to" by other corporate action. The outer limits of non-exclusive indemnification are set by broad principles of public policy, sometimes summarized in the statutes themselves. The New York statute, for example, prohibits indemnification to a director or officer "if a final adjudication adverse to the director or officer establishes that his acts were committed in bad faith or were the result of active and deliberate dishonesty ... or that he personally gained in fact a financial profit or other advantage to which we has not legally entitled."

The following discussion deals with statutes of both the exclusive and non-exclusive types.

Indemnification may be either "mandatory" or "discretionary." Mandatory indemnification is as a matter of statutory right. The basic test is that the defendant must have been "successful on the merits or otherwise." [MBCA (1984) § 8.52.] Under this provision, a defendant who prevails because of the statute of limitations or because of pleading defects is as entitled to indemnification as the defendant who prevails on the merits. This result has been justified on the theory that otherwise a defendant with a valid procedural defense would have to go to the expense of litigating the merits of the claim in order to establish a right of indemnification; it may also be based on the implicit premise that a defendant with a valid procedural defense has a high probability of winning on the merits as well.

Section 8.51 of MBCA (1984) deals with permissive indemnification, i.e., as a matter of discretion, not as a matter of right. The general test set forth in § 8.51(a) is that indemnification is permitted only if the following requirements are satisfied: the defendant director must have "(1) conducted himself in good faith and (2) reasonably believed: (i) in the case of conduct in his official capacity with the corporation, that his conduct was in the best interests of the corporation; and (ii) in all other cases, that his conduct was at least not opposed to the best interests of the corporation." [MBCA (1984) § 8.51(a)(1)(i) and (ii).] Further, indemnification may be permitted against criminal fines if the defendant "had no reasonable cause to believe his conduct was unlawful." [MBCA (1984) § 8.51(a)(2)]

These broad grants of authority to make discretionary indemnification are limited by MBCA (1984) § 8.51(d), which prohibits indemnification in two situations:

(a) in suits brought by or in the right of the corporation (except that expenses of such litigation may be indemnified if it is determined that the director met the relevant standards of conduct set forth in § 8.51(a)), and

(b) in any proceeding in which the director was adjudged liable "on the basis that personal benefit was improperly received." However, as a further qualification to this qualification, any director denied indemnification at any time may seek a court order that "in view of all the relevant circumstances, that it is fair and reasonable." [MBCA (1984) § 8.54(a)(3).]

No presumption that a person acted in bad faith is made merely because litigation is settled or a plea of *nolo contendere* is entered. Even a judgment or a criminal conviction entered against a director is not conclusive that the defendant is ineligible for permissive indemnification. [MBCA (1984) § 8.51(c)] Of course, a criminal conviction or civil judgment will usually involve a determination of bad faith and prevent indemnification.

Determinations as to entitlement to permissive indemnification under these standards may be made (a) by disinterested directors either as a board or as a committee, (b) by the shareholders, or (c) by special legal counsel.

[MBCA (1984) § 8.55.] Precise rules as to how these decisions are to be made and who may select a committee of the board or the independent legal counsel are set forth in this section. The Model Act also recognizes a distinction between decisions *determining* that a director has met the standards for discretionary indemnification (a quasi-judicial determination of good faith, etc.) and decisions *authorizing* such indemnification (a business determination that limited corporate resources should be expended for indemnification rather than for other purposes). [MBCA (1984) § 8.55.]

The Model Business Corporation Act (1984) also deals with technical questions about the scope of indemnification of officers and agents, and the peculiar problem of the rights of a director who is also an officer or agent. [MBCA (1984) § 8.56.]

Another important provision of the Model Act is that a corporation may commit itself in advance to provide indemnification "to the fullest extent permitted by law" [MBCA (1984), § 8.58], and authorizes courts to enforce that obligation at the request of a director or officer. [MBCA (1984) § 8.58] This provision ensures that indemnification will be available in situations where a change in corporate control may have occurred or the defendants have had a falling out with the persons in control of the corporation. This election ensures that all defendants who may be indemnified consistently with public policy under the statute are automatically entitled to mandatory indemnification.

Section 16.22(b) requires that discretionary indemnification of directors and officers be reported to shareholders.

§ 15.5 Advances for Expenses

Section 8.53 of the Model Business Corporation Act (1984), and the statutes of most states, authorize (but do not require) a corporation to advance funds to pay expenses of directors and officers prior to the final termination of a legal proceeding. As a practical matter, the right to make advances may be as vitally important as the grant of indemnification itself, since many directors would find it difficult or impossible to advance sizable sums out of their own pockets for their own defense for an extended period. Further, an effective defense may require employment of skilled counsel at the commencement of the proceeding. To deny all advances might therefore create an invidious discrimination against less wealthy directors.

The basic problem with advances is that they are made early in the proceeding before very much is known about the merits of the litigation. The persons authorizing an advance will usually have little information about whether or not the persons seeking advances will ultimately be eligible for or entitled to indemnification.

If the director is ultimately found not to be entitled to indemnification, he must of course repay the amounts advanced. MBCA (1984) § 8.53(a) requires a director, before any advance is made, to give a written affirmation of his good faith belief that he is eligible for indemnification. He must also file a written undertaking to repay the funds advanced if it is ultimately determined that he is not entitled to indemnification. However, this undertaking need not be secured and may be accepted without reference to the financial ability of the director to make repayment. The theory behind these provisions is to avoid unintentional discrimination between affluent and poorer directors (who may not be able to post security or establish financial ability to repay amounts advanced). However, the lack of security makes it less likely that repayment will actually be made. In any event, there does not appear to be a recent litigated example of repayment actually occurring or of a corporation actively seeking to recover advances for expenses.

Corporations may make advances for expenses mandatory on the corporation by an appropriate provision in the corporate articles or bylaws or by action by the directors or shareholders. Many corporations have done so in an effort to give the maximum protection possible to prospective directors and officers. These provisions, however, have sometimes had unexpected and undesirable consequences. In one case, a corporation conducted an investigation of certain transactions on its own and concluded that two officers had enriched themselves improperly in connection with transactions with the corporation, a charge that the officers denied. Because of the mandatory advance for expenses provision, the corporation found itself in the position of having to pay for the expenses of both the plaintiff and the defendants in a complex trial. In another case, two officers charged with racketeering and theft from the corporation requested advances for expenses before any determination of liability. Even though they clearly appeared to be entitled to advances, a court refused to order advances, relying on broad public policy and fiduciary duties of the remaining directors. Fidelity Fed. S & L Ass'n v. Felicetti (E.D.Pa.1993). A later court of appeals opinion in a similar case, refused to follow this decision, stating that "it is not the province of judges to second-guess" the policy determinations made by the corporation in approving mandatory advances for expenses provisions. Ridder v. Citifed Financial Corp. (3d Cir.1995).

Section 16.22(b) of MBCA (1984) requires decisions granting advances for expenses be reported to shareholders.

§ 15.6 D & O Insurance

Insurance against directors' and officers' liabilities (usually called "D & O" insurance) is of increasing importance in providing meaningful protection to corporate directors. First of all, it provides a third party source for payments; a director or officer entitled to indemnification is therefore assured of a solvent payer even if the corporation is in financial difficulty or is in reorganization. It may also cover claims which the corporation elects not to indemnify. Insurance is also important to the corporation because it covers amounts that the corporation may be obligated to pay to directors under the indemnification statutes and provisions in articles of incorporation or bylaws.

Companies writing D & O liability insurance are not eleemosynary institutions; they cover only insurable risks and establish premiums in light of the magnitude of the contemplated risks. They cover claims based on negligence, misconduct not involving dishonesty or knowing bad faith, and false or misleading statements in disclosure documents Wrongful misconduct, dishonest acts, acts in bad faith with knowledge thereof, or violations of statutes such as section 16(b) are not insurable events. Also excluded are actions entered into for personal profit or gain and suits based on claims of libel or slander. There are numerous express exceptions and exclusions in D & O policies, which may vary significantly from one policy to the next. D & O insurance is not cheap: In 1993, the median premium was $228,000 per year for an average liability limit of $30.7 million.

Unlike many types of insurance, the language of D & O policies varies considerably from issuer to issuer. There is no standard-form policy for D & O insurance. Competition among insurers may be in terms of improving policy language or enhancing coverage rather than by shaving of premiums. Changes or enhancement of policy language or coverage typically must be requested by the insured and negotiated; they do not occur automatically.

During the middle 1980s there was a "D & O insurance crisis" as payments to insureds increased dramatically.

Premiums skyrocketed while maximum limits of coverage were simultaneously being reduced. Many companies declined to write or renew D & O policies at all. During this period, policy language was revised to narrow provisions that proved open-ended or which permitted claims to be made that were not contemplated by the insurer. One example is the "insured against insured" exception, that excludes coverage for claims asserted voluntarily by the corporation against an insured officer or director. This was viewed as being the equivalent of "found money" by the corporation in effect suing itself. While the crisis of the 1980s ended a few years later, many of the exclusions and exceptions in current policies were developed during this period.

D & O policies are written on a "claims made" basis so that each year's policy only covers claims actually asserted during the year in question (though extensions for the period of reporting claims arising in a year that has ended may be negotiated). Policy applications require extensive disclosure of contingent or possible claims and a failure to disclose may permit the insurer to void the entire policy.

Many state statutes specifically permit corporations to purchase D & O insurance. [MBCA (1984) § 8.57.] Where there is no statutory authorization, the power to purchase insurance is probably implicit in the corporate power to provide executive compensation. During the 1980s "crisis" some states enacted legislation to enable marginal corporations to provide protection to outside directors independently of the traditional D & O insurance policy—"captive" insurance companies, for example, that insure only a single company, or escrow or trust arrangements for the benefit of officers and directors. Energy companies, in particular, had difficulties in obtaining D & O insurance during this period.

[For unfamiliar terms, see the Glossary]

CHAPTER SIXTEEN

SHAREHOLDER'S SUITS

§ 16.1 Direct and Derivative Suits In General

Litigation brought by shareholders against the corporation may be divided into two basic categories: direct and derivative.

A *direct* suit involves the enforcement by a shareholder of a claim belonging to the shareholder on the basis of being an owner of shares. These are suits involving contractual or statutory rights of the shareholder, the shares themselves, or rights relating to the ownership of shares. Classic examples of direct suits are suits to recover dividends, to examine corporate books and records, and to compel the registration of a securities transfer. The most controversial type of direct suit today are class actions brought by shareholders under rule 10b–5 described in Chapter 17 of this Nutshell. A *class* action is a direct suit in which one or more shareholder plaintiffs purport to act as a representative of a larger class or classes of shareholders for injuries to the interests of the class.

A *derivative* suit is an action brought by one or more shareholders to remedy or prevent a wrong to the corporation. In a derivative suit, the plaintiff shareholders do not sue on a cause of action belonging to themselves as individuals. Rather, they sue in a representative capacity on a cause of action that belongs to the corporation but which for some reason the corporation is unwilling to pursue; the real party in interest is the corporation. In effect, the shareholder is suing as a champion of the corporation. The derivative suit itself is controversial and raises a number of procedural and substantive questions that are the topic of this chapter.

A derivative suit usually has a class aspect, and is subject to the same potential abuses as a class action. In a derivative suit the plaintiff shareholder is in effect representing the interest of a class consisting of some or all of the other shareholders in the corporation.

Derivative suits are equitable in nature, a categorization that may be significant in resolving procedural questions. In Ross v. Bernhard (S.Ct.1970), the United States Supreme Court held that a right to jury trial may exist in derivative suits brought in federal courts where the issue is of a "legal" (as contrasted with an "equitable") nature.

The principal justification for permitting derivative suits is that it provides a device by which shareholders may enforce claims of the corporation against managing officers and directors of the corporation. Persons who are in control of the corporation are unlikely to authorize it to bring suit against themselves personally. The derivative suit permits a shareholder to prosecute these claims in the name of the corporation.

Derivative suits involve shareholder enforcement of corporate obligations and as a result may intrude on the traditional management powers of the board of directors. In recent years, there have been significant efforts by the board of directors to reassert control over derivative litigation, and these efforts, described in § 16.10 of this Nutshell, have had considerable success.

§ 16.2 Derivative and Direct Claims Distinguished

Different procedural and substantive rules are applicable to direct and derivative claims. As a result, there is a fair amount of litigation over whether a specific claim may be pursued as a direct or as a derivative suit. Unfortunately the line between the two types of injury is sometimes hazy. In one sense anything that harms the corporation also harms shareholders by reducing the value of their shares. However, a shareholder may not automatically transmute a derivative claim into a direct one simply by alleging a direct reduction in value of his shares because of injury to the property or business of a corporation. The justifications for requiring that injury to the corporation be remedied through derivative litigation are (1) it avoids multiplicity of suits, (2) it insures that all injured shareholders benefit proportionally from the recovery, and (3) it protects creditors and preferred shareholders against diversion of corporate assets directly to shareholders.

Many cases have considered whether a claim is derivative or direct. A few examples: A suit charging officers and directors with misapplication of corporate assets or other breaches of duty is derivative in character. Suits to recover improper dividends or to require a controlling shareholder to account for a premium received on the sale of his shares are also derivative in nature since the benefit inures to the corporation.

Cases recognize that claims are direct if they (1) violate a special duty (e.g. a contractual duty) owed to the shareholder (even though the action complained of may also significantly injure the corporation), or (2) cause an injury to the shareholder that is separate and distinct from the injury suffered by other shareholders. Thus, a suit claiming that it was improper for a controlling shareholder to vote on a resolution authorizing the corporation to issue additional shares to that shareholder is direct in character since it prevents the dilution of the voting power of the complaining shareholder's shares. A suit alleging a conspiracy by the directors to use their powers to depress the market price of the shares so that minority shares may be bought at less than fair value also states a direct claim.

As these examples indicate, not only is the line sometimes hazy, but careful pleading may affect the categorization. A suit claiming a denial of preemptive rights seems
direct; however, it may also be considered derivative if it
is alleged that the corporation was induced to issue the
shares for inadequate consideration through fraud or a
violation of federal securities law. In some situations a
single injury may give rise to both a direct and a derivative
claim; in these situations the plaintiff may be able to
proceed with two suits simultaneously.

The American Law Institute's Corporate Governance
Project includes a sensible provision that authorizes courts
to treat derivative claims as direct claims in cases involving
closely held corporations if it determines that to do so
would not unfairly expose the defendants to multiple
actions, prejudice the interests of creditors, or interfere
with the fair distribution of the recovery among all interested persons. Typically, this is sensible if all shareholders
are party to a direct suit and creditors will not be affected
by the outcome.

§ 16.3   Alignment of Parties in a Derivative Suit

In derivative suits, the shareholder is aligned as a nominal plaintiff and the corporation is aligned as a nominal
defendant even though recovery usually runs exclusively
in favor of the corporation. The corporation in a sense is
an involuntary plaintiff, and a necessary party in a derivative suit; without it, the action cannot proceed. The
plaintiff shareholder brings suit on behalf of and as champion for the defendant corporation and not as an individual. As a result, the plaintiff shareholder usually may not
combine individual or direct claims with a derivative action in the same suit. Similarly, the traditional view is that
counterclaims against the plaintiff shareholder individually
may not be asserted by the corporation or the individual

defendants in a derivative suit. See § 16.11 of this Nutshell.

Derivative litigation is essentially three-sided: In addition to the plaintiff shareholder and the corporation, the defendants include the persons who are alleged to have caused harm to the corporation or who have personally profited from corporate action. The claim of wrongdoing by these defendants is of course the central core of the derivative suit and the interest of the corporation in the litigation is usually directly adverse to the interest of these other defendants. Therefore, it is customary today for the individual defendants to be represented by attorneys other than the attorneys for the corporation. The corporation is usually an active party in the litigation though it may be entirely passive or it may side with the individual defendants and argue that their conduct did not harm the corporation.

In rare instances a recovery in a derivative suit may be paid directly to the injured shareholder rather than the corporation. See § 16.12 of this Nutshell.

§ 16.4   Role of the Plaintiff's Attorney

Typically, the plaintiff in a derivative suit is self-selected. If shares are widely held, thousands of potential plaintiff shareholders may exist. It is not infrequently alleged that an attorney is the principal mover in filing a derivative suit, that he locates a possible derivative claim and then finds himself an eligible shareholder to serve as plaintiff. Such conduct may be essentially champertous but is quite common in both derivative and class litigation. Also, there is no general requirement that the plaintiff shareholder have a large financial stake in the litigation. As a result, the plaintiff shareholder may be a purely nominal participant in the litigation, with his attorney having a much more direct and substantial financial interest in the case and its outcome.

Since a derivative suit has class as well as derivative aspects, multiple derivative suits may be filed by several different shareholders; in the absence of other considerations, the suit first filed is generally permitted to proceed while later actions may be stayed, dismissed, or consolidated with the initial suit. Intervention by other shareholders is permitted and indeed may be encouraged if for some reason the representation of the original plaintiff shareholder may be considered undesirable. The court has discretion to designate an attorney for another shareholder as the principal counsel for plaintiffs. In some circumstances, the corporation itself may be permitted to take over a law suit and prosecute it directly, though that is not very common in the modern era. The selection of lead counsel is of importance not only because of his control over litigation strategy but also because it may be critical in the apportionment of fees at a later date. In all such matters, the trial court has "great discretion."

Most derivative suits are settled and do not go through trial and appeal. The lead attorney for the plaintiff has the major voice in determining whether a proposed settlement is acceptable. Historically, the secret settlement of shareholders' suits was a serious evil. "Strike" suits were thereby encouraged, and the plaintiff shareholder sometimes received substantial sums which in fact were a payment to ignore a corporate wrong. Courts have held that where a secret settlement has led to a payment to the shareholder plaintiff, other shareholders may bring a derivative suit in the name of the corporation against the plaintiff shareholder to recover the amount of the secret settlement.

The fee to be paid the lead counsel for the plaintiff shareholder is usually negotiated as part of an overall settlement of a derivative suit. However, all aspects of the settlement is subject to judicial review and approval. The Federal Rules of Civil Procedure provide that derivative actions may "not be dismissed or compromised without the approval of the court, and notice of the proposed dismissal or compromise shall be given to shareholders or members in such manner as the court directs." A similar provision is applicable to class suits. Many state statutes (as well as section 7.45 of MBCA (1984)) contain similar requirements. In reviewing proposed settlements, courts consider several factors, including: (1) The size of the potential recovery and the size of the suggested settlement; (2) The probability of ultimate success; and (3) The financial position of the defendants. Shareholders may also appear at the hearing on a proposed settlement and object to its terms. However, if the attorneys for the plaintiff shareholder, the corporation, and the individual defendants all appear and support a proposed settlement, it may be difficult for a court to accurately evaluate the fairness of the settlement.

If the plaintiff is successful or the case is settled, the plaintiff may be awarded expenses, including attorneys' fees by the court, if they are not specified in the settlement agreement. Since most derivative suits are taken on a contingent or open fee basis, the plaintiff's attorney will receive compensation only on the successful prosecution of the suit or by its settlement. Such a recovery is justified on the theory that it encourages meritorious shareholder suits. The expenses and fees may be paid out of the funds obtained by the corporation as a result of the termination of the suit; however, expenses may be required to be paid by the corporation even where the corporation receives no money so long as the result of the suit "was of some benefit to the corporation." Thus, expenses and fees may be awarded in a suit which results only in an injunction against the officers and directors of a corporation from engaging in improper conduct. A settlement under which the corporation agrees to amend bylaws or make some procedural changes also may justify an award of expenses, including payment of a fee to the attorney. It should be noted that these rules may encourage the filing of marginal suits on a contingent fee basis as much as they encourage the filing of meritorious actions.

Theoretically, a payment of the plaintiffs' expenses by the corporation does not compel the "losing party" to pay the other's expenses since both the corporation and the plaintiff are winning parties.

The size of the attorneys' fee to be awarded depends on a variety of factors—the nature and character of the litigation, the skill required, the amount of work actually performed, the size of the recovery, the nature of the harm prevented, and other factors. The size of the fee is a question of fact. To choose one example more or less at random, a fee of $200,000 in a suit leading to a $1,025,-000 settlement was upheld. Of course, in cases that are settled, the fee is usually a matter of direct negotiation between the attorney and the corporation.

§ 16.5 Derivative Litigation as Strike Suits

There have been numerous complaints of long standing that derivative litigation is often abused. These complaints go back to before World War II, and have continued until this day. The principal complaint is that most derivative litigation is brought at the instigation of entrepreneurial attorneys who first find a potential violation and then find a plaintiff shareholder who is qualified to maintain the derivative suit. The objective of these suits is to obtain a settlement with the principal defendants and the corporation that provides the attorney with a generous attorney's fee. From the standpoint of the corporation and the individual defendants the benefit of a settlement of a marginal or unjustified claim is that the plaintiff "goes away," and the decision prevents the filing of other suits on the same claim. See § 16.13.

One consequence of the concern about strike suits is that states have established elaborate criteria to ensure that the plaintiff shareholder is an appropriate representative, and (in many states) that if he has a small financial interest in the outcome he be required to post security for expenses. These requirements are discussed in §§ 16.6–16.9 of this Nutshell. These devices, however, essentially have not prevented the filing of strike suits.

In the 1980s, a new device was created to handle perceived abuses of the derivative suit. This device, the litigation committee discussed in § 16.10 of this Nutshell, has provided for an expeditious disposition of many doubtful derivative claims, and possible some meritorious ones as well.

§ 16.6 Contemporary Ownership

Section 7.41(1) of the MBCA (1984) and most state statutes dealing with derivative litigation require the plaintiff to have been a shareholder when the cause of action arose and continuously since that time. A handful of states, most notably California, permits a shareholder to serve as a plaintiff even though not a shareholder when the cause of action arose if the shareholder acquired the shares in ignorance of the existence of the claim. This is usually called the "contemporaneous ownership" requirement.

The ostensible purpose of this requirement is to prevent the purchase of a lawsuit, or to put the matter somewhat differently, to prevent an attorney from creating an instant plaintiff simply by having someone purchase shares in the defendant corporation. Of course, if "buying a lawsuit" were the real concern, the contemporaneous ownership requirement might be safely liberalized to allow suit by plaintiffs who discover the facts giving rise to the lawsuit only after becoming a shareholder. Since most states do not permit such shareholders to act as plaintiff, this requirement in fact appears to be largely grounded on antipathy to derivative litigation.

The Federal Rules of Civil Procedure contain a contemporary ownership requirement primarily to prevent the collusive establishment of diversity citizenship. The state statutes described in the previous paragraph appear to be based primarily on notions of preventing "the buying of a lawsuit."

§ 16.7 Demand on Shareholders

A minority of states require either that a demand be made on shareholders before a derivative suit is filed or the showing of an "adequate reason" for not making the effort. MBCA (1984) does not contain this requirement.

Because making a demand on shareholders is expensive when the number of shareholders is large, most attention has been paid to acceptable reasons not to make this demand. Adequate reasons for omitting a demand on shareholders include the following: (1) The wrongdoers own a majority of the shares and hence favorable shareholder action is impossible, (2) The number of shareholders is so large that it is unreasonable to require the plaintiff to incur the expense of what is essentially a proxy solicitation when there is little chance of success, or (3) The acts complained of cannot be ratified by the shareholders, so that action by the shareholders is useless. While some cases have required a demand on shareholders even when the cost would be substantial, many cases have held that a demand on shareholders may be omitted when the number of shareholders make the cost prohibitive. Massachusetts appears to have adopted a stringent rule, requiring a demand in every case where a majority of shareholders are not wrongdoers without regard to the cost. Other state courts have proceeded on a case-by-case basis, not requiring a demand when there are thousands of shareholders, and apparently taking into account the motives of the plaintiff, the number of shareholders joining in the action, and the proximity to the next shareholders meeting.

§ 16.8   Security–For–Expenses Statutes

Some nineteen states require certain plaintiff shareholders in derivative suits to give to the corporation "security for the reasonable expenses, including attorneys' fees" which the corporation or other defendants may incur in connection with a derivative suit. The 1969 version of the Model Act included such a provision but it was omitted from MBCA (1984) because of increasing doubts about its efficacy and fairness.

Security-for expenses statutes apply only to plaintiffs. Shareholders required to post security are usually defined in terms of the size of their holdings: the 1969 Model Act provision, for example, required security from plaintiffs whose ownership was less than one per cent of the outstanding shares or the value of the shares was less than $25,000. Virtually all plaintiff shareholders seek exemption under the dollar requirement. Other states had similar provisions though the dollar and percentage limits varied from state to state. In a few states, a security-for-expenses filing is required only upon a judicial finding that the suit was apparently brought without reasonable cause or seems patently without merit.

Where security has to be posted, it is usually in the form of a bond with sureties, though it also may be in the form of cash or marketable securities. The size of the bond required depends on the estimated expenses of the corporation. Since they may include not only the direct expenses of the corporation, but also the expenses of other defendants for which the corporation may become liable by indemnification or otherwise, it is relatively easy for a substantial corporation to justify security running into the hundreds of thousands of dollars. The requirement of posting security of this magnitude obviously creates a major obstacle to the successful prosecution of a derivative suit, and a decision that the securities-for-expenses statute is applicable may well result in the litigation being abandoned.

Security-for-expenses statutes usually do not define when the corporation may actually look to the security for reimbursement; rather they usually state in effect that "[t]he corporation shall have recourse to such security in such amount as the court having jurisdiction shall determine upon the termination of such action." (This quotation is taken from the 1969 Model Act, § 49, last par.) Thus security-for-expenses statutes have a secondary effect of also creating a right of reimbursement in favor of the defendant against the plaintiff where none existed before. As a further consequence, an unsuccessful shareholder-plaintiff who actually posts security-for-expenses may easily end up paying the expenses of both sides of unsuccessful litigation.

The dollar limits on the security-for-expenses requirement has given rise to a considerable amount of litigation. Generally, it is held that intervening shareholder plaintiffs may have their shares counted toward meeting the statutory minimum. Another issue is whether the plaintiff must post additional security if the value of his holdings decline during the litigation below the statutory minimum. Yet another issue is whether the plaintiff may purchase additional shares after the cause of action arose in order to avoid the security of expenses requirement. The general answers are "no" to the first question and "yes" to the second.

Security-for-expenses statutes are applicable under the *Erie* principle to suits in federal court based on state-created causes of action. In other words, if a state has a security-for-expenses statute, the federal courts in that state must require security in cases arising under state law. Federal jurisdiction over state claims may be based on diversity of citizenship or on the doctrine of pendent jurisdiction. However, security-for-expenses statutes are not applicable to suits in federal court based on federal law. Nor are they applicable to direct class actions brought either in the federal or state courts since such statutes are only applicable to derivative suits. Such statutes therefore also probably have the incidental effect of encouraging suits to be brought under the federal securities acts rather than under state law.

One purpose of security-for-expenses statutes undoubtedly is to deter "strike" suits brought in the hope of securing a settlement profitable to the plaintiff shareholders and their attorneys. However, the older statutes do not distinguish between "strike" suits and bona fide shareholder suits. Rather, they are applicable to all shareholder suits, and thus have the effect of making all such suits more difficult.

Security-for expenses statutes were held to be constitutional, despite the arbitrary numerical limit, in Cohen v. Beneficial Industrial Loan Corp. (S.Ct.1949).

Section 7.46 of MBCA (1984) authorizes a court to assess costs, including attorneys' fees, against a plaintiff or defendant if the court determined that the suit was brought without just cause. Many states have similar rules.

§ 16.9 Verification of the Complaint

Many state statutes, as well as rule 23.1 of the Federal Rules of Civil Procedure, require that complaints in derivative suits be verified, i.e., sworn to. The purpose of this requirement is to provide some protection against groundless litigation without deterring suits brought in good faith. The leading case involving this requirement is Surowitz v. Hilton Hotels Corp. (S.Ct.1966), which holds that a complaint in a derivative suit verified by the plaintiff should not be dismissed merely because the plaintiff did not understand the specific allegations in the complaint.

A verification requirement appeared in the 1984 MBCA (1984) but was eliminated by the 1990 amendments to that Act after doubt was expressed that a verification requirement was a meaningful check against unjustified litigation.

§ 16.10 Demand on Directors and Litigation Committees

Virtually all states require that the plaintiff allege and prove that she first made a good faith effort to obtain action by the corporation before filing a derivative suit. Thus a good faith demand on the board of directors is usually a prerequisite to derivative suits. The demand requirements may appear in the corporation statutes, or, as in Delaware, in rules of court. A typical provision is rule 23.1 of the Federal Rules of Civil Procedure: "the complaint shall also allege with particularity the efforts, if any, made by the plaintiff to obtain the action he or she desires from the directors or comparable authority and the reasons for his or her failure to obtain the action or for not making the effort."

Under these provisions, a demand is not required in every case; in the alternative, the plaintiff may allege and prove a state of facts that makes it clear that an appeal to the directors would have been useless. One such example might be where "the wrongdoers are in complete control of the management of the corporation." Cases in which demand is excused on such a ground are referred to as "demand futile" or "demand unnecessary" cases; other cases are usually called "demand required" or "demand necessary" cases.

For many years, the requirement of a demand on directors was viewed as a minor procedural obstacle. Many suits were brought directly, based on the allegation that demand would have been futile; if the court disagreed, a formal demand could then usually be made, and the suit continued. This rather simple view of the demand requirement disappeared when the Supreme Court of Delaware held that an independent litigation committee could authoritatively dispose of a demand required case by a decision protected by the business judgment rule in some suits involving claims against other officers or directors of the corporation. See § 14.8 of this Nutshell for a discussion of the application of the business judgment rule in this context.

Early cases had established that the board of directors could dismiss a derivative suit seeking enforcement of a claim against an unrelated third party. Such a decision appears to be purely a matter of business judgment since presumably no director had a conflicting interest and the question whether a law suit should be filed against a third party involves issues of business relationship as much as the desire to recover on a claim. The novel development was to extend the same power to derivative suits in which the true defendants are directors or officers of the corporation itself. The first case that granted the board of directors (or an independent committee of the board) some authority to resolve such claims was Gall v. Exxon Corp. (S.D.N.Y.1976). (Prior to that decision it was generally assumed that a derivative action against corporate directors or officers could be automatically maintained assuming that the plaintiff qualified as an eligible plaintiff.) This principle was quickly accepted by other state and federal courts; broad arguments that even disinterested directors should not be trusted to make business judgments because of "structural bias" have been uniformly rejected.

Because of the importance of Delaware as the principal state of incorporation for publicly held corporations, most of the litigation involving dismissal of derivative suits has arisen in that state. In all cases, the litigation committee in Delaware must consist only of disinterested and independent directors not involved in the questioned transactions. The Delaware courts have tied the power of litigation committees to dismiss derivative litigation to the initial decision whether a case was a demand necessary case or a demand futile case:

(1) If the case is a demand futile case, it was properly brought without making a demand on the board of directors. However, the corporation may thereafter impanel a litigation committee to consider the merits of the claim. Assuming the committee recommends that the litigation not be continued, a reviewing court should first ascertain that the litigation committee was independent and free from conflict of interest, second, whether the decision appears to meet the requirements of the business judgment rule, and third, whether in the court's own "independent business judgment" the dismissal recommendation should be accepted. The last inquiry is not mandatory and may be dispensed with by the court under proper circumstances.

(2) If the case is a demand required case, the rules are quite different. In these cases, the board of directors retains its power to act, and may delegate that decision to a litigation committee. Hence, if the committee decides that the suit should not be pursued, and that decision is protected by the business judgment rule, the court must accept the committee's decision and dismiss the case. The court may not apply its "independent business judgment" or a standard of "intrinsic fairness" in reviewing the decision by the committee.

The difference in treatment of demand required and demand futile cases puts great stress on the preliminary decision whether demand is required. Subsequent Delaware cases establish the following principles: (i) if the shareholder makes a demand, that is an admission that the case is a demand required case, (ii) if the shareholder files suit without making a demand and the court subsequently determines that a demand is required, the case must be dismissed for failing to make the demand, (iii) that a demand is required unless the plaintiff pleads "particularized facts" that indicates that a demand would probably be futile, (iv) that the plaintiff is not entitled to discovery prior to the classification of the case as demand required or demand futile, and (v) if a demand is made and rejected, the shareholder may seek judicial review of the decision on the demand only by alleging particularized facts (without the benefit of discovery) that indicates the decision rejecting the demand was not proper.

There is no question but that the development of these rules in Delaware has dramatically changed the handling of derivative litigation. Plaintiffs generally do not make demands; to do so is to virtually concede control over the plaintiff's case to a litigation committee. Rather they file without making a demand, attempting to meet the particularized pleading requirement to excuse demand. The corporation then moves to dismiss the case for failing to make a demand. The court of chancery resolves this preliminary issue one way or the other, and the losing party appeals that resolution to the Delaware Supreme Court. If the Supreme Court decides that the case is a demand required case, the plaintiff has lost and the case disappears. If the Supreme Court decides that the case is a demand futile case and the plaintiff's case survives, the parties thereafter settle. In effect, derivative litigation under these rules is handled in a summary fashion with few trials on the merits. Since the general trend of this litigation has been in the direction of requiring a demand in close cases, the power of a committee of the board of directors to summarily dispose of undesired derivative litigation in Delaware has increased. What is surprising is that virtually every decision by a litigation committee in Delaware has been that the suit is without merit and should not be pursued.

The litigation committee experience in Delaware has caused a rethinking of the desirability of the "demand futile" exception. Why not require a demand in every case? It is relatively simple to make a demand. Should not the board or directors or a litigation committee be required in every case to respond to the claim before suit is filed? The problem with the Delaware rules is that the critical decision that largely resolves the merits of the litigation must be made solely on the pleadings and without the benefit of any discovery. It would be sensible to defer the decision on the merits to a later stage after the board has responded to the demand. In 1989 the Model Business Corporation Act (1984) was amended to make a demand a universal prerequisite for all derivative suits (MBCA (1984) § 7.42); the American Law Institute's Corporate Governance Project takes essentially the same position. In both of these codifications, the issue of the standard of review of dismissal recommendations is divorced from the demand requirement itself though the Model Act appears to accept a pure business judgment rule standard while the Corporate Governance Project assumes some level of review of the substance of the committee's decision.

Several state courts have also had occasion to consider the litigation committee approach to terminating derivative suits. Most of these cases accept the basic principle that independent litigation committees may resolve derivative suits involving officers and directors of the corporation. These opinions, however, appear to contemplate greater review of the reasonableness of the decision of the litigation committee than is contemplated by the Delaware cases.

§ 16.11 Defenses in a Derivative Suit

Defenses in derivative suits may be grouped into three broad categories. One category involves alleged failure to comply with requirements peculiar to such suits. A failure to make a demand on the directors, or a failure to post security when required to do so under the applicable security-for-expenses statute, for example, will result in the dismissal of the suit. A second category of defenses are those that would be available to the third party defendants if the corporation had sued directly on the claim that is the underlying basis of the derivative suit. If the action is barred by the statute of limitations or statute of frauds, for example, the derivative suit based on the same claim is also barred. Presumably, such defenses may only be raised by the third party defendants, not the corporate defendant. Somewhat similarly, a defense based on ratification of the transaction by directors or shareholders may be available if the transaction is voidable rather than void, or if it arguably falls within the ordinary business judgment of the directors. Such defenses may arise from director or shareholder action after the claim is presented by the plaintiff shareholder, and presumably may be raised by the corporate defendant. A third category of defenses are those available against the specific plaintiff shareholder but not against other shareholders.

Derivative suits basically involve two separate claims: the substantive claim by the corporation against a third person and the claim by the shareholder that he or she should be permitted to represent or champion the corporation. The particular category of defense may go to one claim or the other with quite different consequences.

Laches, for example, may bar some shareholders but not others from acting as plaintiff. If the plaintiff shareholder actually participated in the wrongful transaction, or assented to it, she may be estopped from questioning the transaction. Shares owned by that person may be considered "tainted shares" or "dirty stock" and innocent transferees of such shares may be estopped from questioning the transaction. (Such a transferee may also be barred under the contemporaneous ownership requirement.)

§ 16.12   Private Settlement of Derivative Suits

A recovery in a derivative suit is usually payable to the corporation rather than to individual shareholders on a pro rata basis. This principle normally protects fully the interests of shareholders and creditors alike, and does not involve the court in making a business judgment as to whether corporate funds should be distributed to some or all of the shareholders, or reserved for creditors.

If an individual wrongdoer is also a shareholder, a corporate recovery permits that wrongdoer to share indirectly in the recovery. In a few instances, courts have been persuaded to grant some shareholders a pro rata recovery in order to limit the recovery to "innocent" shareholders. For example, in Perlman v. Feldmann (2d Cir.1955), a control premium paid to a former controlling shareholder was held to be recoverable in the derivative suit but it was made payable to the non-selling shareholders pro rata on the theory that it was improper for the persons presently in control (who had paid the control premium to the defendants) to share in the recovery. Similarly, if the corporation is controlled by the wrongdoers, the court may order a pro rata recovery by the innocent shareholders on the theory that it is improper to permit the funds recovered to revert immediately to the control of the wrongdoers. Such situations, however, are uncommon, and a pro rata recovery is therefore the exception rather than the rule. Such a recovery may give rise to serious logical and practical problems. In the Perlman case, for example, the pro rata recovery by non-selling shareholders creates the possibility that the persons presently in control may themselves resell at a premium and then argue that the remaining shareholders have already been compensated for the loss of the control premium and should not be permitted to question the propriety of the second sale.

§ 16.13   Res Judicata Effect of Derivative Suits

A determination of a derivative suit on the merits is *res judicata* and precludes other derivative suits on the same claim on the theory that the suit is brought on behalf of the corporation. In this respect, derivative litigation differs from other types of class litigation in which potential plaintiffs may opt out. *Res judicata* prevents relitigation of the issues by shareholders who were original parties to the suit but thereafter withdrew. This assumes that the plaintiff shareholder was an adequate representative of the class of shareholders. A court-approved settlement ordinarily has the same effect as a final judgment on the merits, though problems may arise as to whether shareholders are bound if they were not notified of the proposed settlement.

The *res judicata* effect of a dismissal of a derivative suit depends on the reason for the dismissal. A voluntary dismissal, or a dismissal because the plaintiff shareholder is not a proper plaintiff (e.g., for not being a contemporaneous owner or for not posting security-for-expenses), is "without prejudice" and does not bind the remaining shareholders. On the other hand, a dismissal on the merits may be given full *res judicata* effect. In some situations, the court may order that notice be given to all other shareholders before a derivative action is dismissed voluntarily. Such action may then be continued by intervening shareholders, or if none appear, the action may be dismissed "with prejudice."

[For unfamiliar terms see the Glossary]

CHAPTER SEVENTEEN

CLASS ACTION SUITS

§ 17.1 Securities Class Action Suits In General

This chapter deals with direct class actions brought by shareholders against the corporation, its officers, directors, auditors or attorneys. Chapter 16 deals with derivative litigation in which the shareholder sues on behalf of a corporation on a corporate claim. This chapter deals with direct suits by shareholders, on behalf of a class of shareholders similarly situated, for an alleged wrong committed by the corporation. Many of the problems discussed in chapter 16 with respect to entrepreneurial attorneys and the possibility of "strike suits" are also common in securities class actions.

The most common type of modern securities class action involves a claim that the corporation in one or more of its public statements knowingly made false or misleading statements that had an adverse effect on the price of the corporation's securities. As a result all shareholders who bought or sold shares in reliance on the price influenced by the false or misleading statements were injured by the false or misleading statements. These class action suits are usually brought under rule 10b–5, promulgated under the Securities Exchange Act of 1934. See §§ 14.21–14.25 of this Nutshell. They may also claim a violation of rule 14a–9 promulgated under the same statute if the false or misleading statements appear in proxy solicitation documents. See § 13.21 of this Nutshell.

There is a widespread belief that securities class actions of the type described above are primarily brought by entrepreneurial attorneys in order to obtain a fee through a negotiated settlement. The Republican "Contract with America" in 1994 included a proposal to enact a "Common Sense Legal Reforms Act" addressed specifically to the perceived abuses of this type of litigation. In late 1995, a revised version of this bill, entitled "Private Securities Litigation Reform Act of 1995," was enacted by Congress which subsequently overrode President Clinton's veto. This statute is referred to hereafter as "PSLRA." This chapter specifically addresses this development which is certainly a major, if not a radical, change in securities litigation rules.

§ 17.2   SEC Disclosure Requirements

The SEC has long required corporations registered under section 12 of the Securities Exchange Act routinely to make public financial and other information about their activities. Periodic quarterly and annual disclosure is required as well as immediate disclosure of significant events affecting the issuer. These disclosure requirements are often referred to as creating a "goldfish bowl" atmosphere for publicly held corporations.

Prior to 1979, the SEC's general policy was to restrict disclosure to "hard" factual information of a historical character. However, it should be apparent that from the standpoint of investors forward looking information and projections are much more useful than purely historical data. In 1979, the SEC amended its disclosure policy to encourage dissemination of "soft" data, including projections of financial data, discussion of management objectives and goals for future performance, discussion of economic trends affecting the business, and information about the assumptions underlying the projections. Because there is an obvious risk that projections and the like might not in fact be borne out by events, the SEC at the same time adopted a "safe harbor" provision protecting issuers for liability for projections except those that were "made or reaffirmed without a reasonable basis or disclosed other than in good faith." Nevertheless, corporations cautiously made use of this freedom. Shortly thereafter, the SEC imposed a new requirement on issuers annually to prepare a "Management's Discussion and Analysis of Financial Condition and Results of Operations" (usually abbreviated as the "MD&A"), which requires management to make a frank assessment of its expectations for the short-term future and the factors that affect the ability of the business to meet those expectations.

As a result there is a flow of forward-looking information from publicly held corporations that is publicly available and widely disseminated through financial services, newsletters, newspapers, brokers, analysts, and advisers.

An important additional factor is that in the 1980s and 1990s many high technology companies have registered and sold their securities to the investing public. The shares of these companies have tended to be very volatile and sharp fluctuations in price occur regularly. Companies in these developing industries have particularly complained about class actions being filed following a substantial unexpected variation in the price of its securities. It is in this environment that the class action litigation "crisis" was viewed, and which gave rise to legislative correction.

§ 17.3 The Growth of Class Action Securities Litigation

The basic elements of a securities fraud claim under rule 10b–5 are (1) a misstatement or omission, (2) which is material in that a reasonable person would attach significance to it in deciding whether to make or dispose of an investment, (3) made with scienter, (3) which causes injury to a plaintiff, (4) who relied upon the misstatement or omission.

Class action proceedings became practical on a broad scale for rule 10b–5 cases because it is not necessary to establish that each plaintiff specifically or individually relied on a specific misrepresentation, or even that she was aware of the statement when she entered into a securities transaction. This is a result of the doctrine, called, the "fraud on the market" rule, that is based on the premise that an investor trading in an "efficient market" may rely on the price established in the market as being set by free market forces unaffected by fraud or misstatements. In Basic Inc. v. Levinson (S.Ct.1988), a sharply divided Court upheld by a plurality vote the view that the efficient market theory establishes a rebuttable presumption that each investor relies on the accuracy of the going market price in deciding whether to buy or sell, and if that price is affected by false statements, the investor necessarily has relied on the underlying misrepresentation.

According to the House Committee Report proposing the 1995 legislation, a typical modern securities class action proceeding involves "a high-growth, high-tech company that has performed well for many quarters, but ultimately misses analysts' expectations." Whenever an announcement is made that causes an unexpected change in stock prices, securities class actions are filed "immediately" complaining that some group of defendants " 'knew or should have known' " about the negative information, and which should have been disclosed earlier. The individual defendants that are named are "deep pockets" and the damages sought amount to hundreds of millions of dollars based on estimates of the aggregate market loss suffered by all shareholders who traded during the period. The plaintiff shareholders themselves own only a few shares and many of them are " 'professional plaintiffs' " who work with the same law firm and file many complaints each year. The leading plaintiff law firms keep a "stable of professional plaintiffs" that permit suits to be filed within hours after the news of a stock price decline and with no evidence of actual wrongdoing, using complaints that allege fraud, "while citing a laundry list of cookie-cutter complaints."

The House Report continues by stating that in "the typical case" the court refuses to dismiss the complaint, "triggering the costly discovery process, and imposing massive costs on the defendant who possesses the bulk of the relevant information." The costs of prosecuting the suit are advanced by the plaintiff's law firm. As the costs of discovery rise, the pressure to settle "becomes enormous," and as a result of the settlement, "the plaintiffs' lawyers take one third of the settlement, and the rest is distributed to the members of the class, resulting in pennies of return for each individual plaintiff. There is no adjudication of the merits of the case."

While this picture may be overdrawn, it was the picture presented to the Congress and which led to the enactment of PSLRA.

§ 17.4   Judicial Response to the Increased Litigation

Rule 10b–5 litigation is within the exclusive jurisdiction of the federal courts. As class action securities litigation grew, the federal courts exhibited increased impatience with suits that appeared to involve "cookie cutter" allegations and were filed within minutes after the facts were made public. This led to three developments:

First, both District Courts and Courts of Appeals appeared to be more willing to dismiss hastily filed complaints on motions to dismiss.

Second, rule 9(b) of the Federal Rules requires allegations of fraud to be plead "with particularity." Case law in the Second Circuit required not only that the plaintiff state facts with particularity but also these facts must give rise to a "strong inference" that the defendant's intent was fraudulent. See § 17.13 of this Nutshell.

Third, ten circuits have adopted a "bespeaks caution" principle that prevents reliance on forward looking statements (such as a forecast, projection, or statement regarding expectations of future performance) if the document includes sufficient cautionary warning statements that the investment was risky and results not guaranteed.

§ 17.5 The Private Securities Litigation Reform Act of 1995

Serious efforts to curb private securities litigation began in about 1992, pushed primarily by the major accounting firms and then joined by dozens of other business corporations. However, these bills went nowhere until the Republican victories in the 1994 off-year election.

The PSLRA makes numerous substantive amendments to the Federal securities laws and includes a number of innovative provisions. The following sections summarize only the most important provisions of this complex litigation. A special provision relating to the liability of issuers under the Securities Act of 1933 and a RICO provision are omitted.

§ 17.6 Class Action Provisions

The PSLRA contains a number of provisions relating to "professional" and "lead" plaintiffs. Every lead plaintiff must file a sworn and certified statement that he has reviewed and authorized the filing and that he did not purchase securities at the direction of counsel or to qualify him to act as a plaintiff. Generally, a lead plaintiff may not serve as such more than three times in the previous five years. Restrictions are also placed on the compensation that a lead plaintiff may receive: it generally may not exceed his proportionate share of any recovery, but he may be compensated for additional work and effort.

The general practice of allowing the first to file to serve as the lead plaintiff is discouraged. Within 20 days after filing, the plaintiff must give notice to all members of the class, identify the principal claims, and inform class members that they may move to serve as the lead plaintiff. In addition, courts are directed to select the lead plaintiff based on a presumption that the plaintiff with the "largest financial stake" should be selected. The intention was to encourage institutional investors to serve as lead plaintiff, though it is questionable whether these investors will desire to serve in that capacity.

Class counsel is to be selected by the lead plaintiff. Attorneys who own shares of the class may be disqualified from serving as class counsel. A cap is also placed on attorney's fees that may be paid to class counsel. The amount is to be based on a reasonable percentage of the amount of damages and pre-judgment interest recovered, and amounts paid to the corporation pursuant to disgorgement proceedings brought by the SEC may not be "dipped into" to pay or calculate the fee to be paid the class counsel.

§ 17.7 Safe Harbor Provisions

The law prior to PSLRA contained two safe harbor provisions for forward looking statements: the SEC's rule adopted in 1979 that protected statements made on a reasonable basis and in good faith and the "bespeaks caution" principle, some form of which had been adopted by most courts of appeals. The legislative history of PSLRA suggests that Congress believed that these protections were not sufficient and that issuers tended to say as little as possible about future predictions and forecasts. As a result PSLRA crafts a new statutory safe harbor provision that is based to some extent on the preexisting doctrines but broadens them. This provision is perhaps the most controversial single aspect of PSLRA.

The statutory safe harbor is a bifurcated test. Branch one protects persons from liability for misrepresentations or omissions in forward-looking statements if they are (i) identified as forward-looking, and (ii) accompanied by "meaningful cautionary statements" identifying important factors that could cause results to differ materially from those protected in the statement. The cautionary statements must convey substantive information about factors that realistically could cause operating results to differ materially from projected results. "Important" factors are those which are relevant to the forward-looking statement and could actually affect the ability of the issuer to achieve the results predicted. The legislative history suggests that safe harbor protection is available even though *all* important factors are not listed or even though the list does not include the factor that actually caused the results not to be realized. An *oral* forward-looking statement is protected by the safe harbor if it is identified as a forward-looking statement and it is stated that results may differ materially from the statement; it is not necessary to also identify orally "important factors" if they are described in a readily available document which is referred to.

Branch two of the statutory safe harbor test looks at the mind-set of the person making the forward-looking statement rather than the statement itself. A person is protected by the statutory safe harbor unless the plaintiff can show that the person made the statement with actual knowledge that it was false or misleading.

Several legislators voiced concern that the inter-relationship between these two branches might confer immunity from liability even for intentionally fraudulent forward-looking statements. The literal language of the section does not exclude this possibility, though one leading legislator supporting the bill stated that it does not give a "license to lie." Whether or not these concerns are born out can only be determined by future events.

Several classes of securities transactions are entirely exempted from the safe harbor provisions, including going private transactions, partnership roll-ups, and other types of transactions which the Securities and Exchange Commission had found to involve numerous violations of the securities laws.

§ 17.8   Discovery Provisions

As described above, excessive discovery costs were viewed as an important reason that compels defendant corporations to accept settlements even though the complaint may be without merit or frivolous. PSLRA addresses this concern by providing that courts must stay all discovery pending a ruling on a motion to dismiss except in exceptional situations where particularized discovery is necessary to preserve evidence that might otherwise be lost. At the same time, PSLRA makes it unlawful for any person named as a defendant to willfully destroy relevant evidence.

If the issue whether a forward-looking statement is protected by the statutory safe harbor provision (see § 17.7 of this Nutshell), a court must stay discovery (other than discovery directly related to the application of the safe harbor provision) until the issue of safe harbor protection is resolved.

§ 17.9   Proportionate Liability Provisions

Most securities class actions involve multiple defendants. The current rule is that defendants are jointly and severally liable, so that each defendant who is found liable is automatically fully responsible for the entire judgment even though his conduct may have made only a minor contribution to the total loss. Congress believed this rule contributed to the negative aspects of securities class actions: First, it encouraged plaintiffs to name as defendants as many persons with "deep pockets" as possible, including attorneys, auditors, underwriters, and directors, second, it was wildly unfair because a if a single defendant was found to be 1% liable he could be forced to pay 100% of the damages, and third, it contributed to settlements of marginal or groundless class actions because of the risk to deep pocket defendants of being exposed to liability for grossly disproportionate damages. Concern was also expressed that unlimited exposure had a chilling effect on the willingness of capable people to serve as directors of publicly held corporations.

PSLRA adopts several highly innovative provisions ameliorating the rules of traditional joint and several liability. First of all, it created a distinction between "knowing violations" and all other violations. A person who committed a knowing violation has full joint and several liability while all other persons are subject to a new regime of "proportionate liability" discussed in the following paragraphs. A "knowing violation" consists of making a material misrepresentation with actual knowledge that the statement is false and that persons are likely to rely on the information. Recklessness is not "knowing" behavior.

Defendants who are found liable but have not engaged in knowing violations are liable only for the portion of damages that are attributable to their conduct. The jury is to be instructed to decide what each defendant's percentage of responsibility is, considering the nature of that person's conduct and its causal relationship to the damages caused. There are, however, two qualifications:

First, all defendants continue to be jointly and severally liable to plaintiffs whose damages are in excess of 10% of their net worth and that net worth is less than $200,000. Investors who may benefit from this exception are viewed as small, unsophisticated, and in need of special protection under the securities law. The legislative history indicates that $200,000 was chosen to ensure that the majority of investors would not be affected by the proportionate liability principal.

Second, defendants who have not engaged in knowing violations may also be called upon to pay an additional amount up to 50% of their personal liability to make up any shortfall in the plaintiff's recovery due to insolvency of other defendants. Defendants who settle before the verdict or judgment are not subject to this additional "anteing up" requirement to cover claims against insolvent defendants.

§ 17.10   Settlement Provisions

Before a settlement agreement can be finalized, notice of the terms of the settlement must be given to all members of the class. The basic terms and other critical information about the settlement must appear in summary form on the cover page of the notice.

PSLRA provides that settlement agreements may not be filed under seal unless a party shows that "direct and substantial" harm, including reputational harm, would result from the open filing of the agreement.

§ 17.11   Fee Shifting Provisions

Congress actively debated the desirability of adopting a "loser pays" structure in PSLRA as a device to discourage the filing of ungrounded on frivolous securities class action suits. In the end, Congress strengthened the application of Rule 11 of the Federal Rules of Civil Procedure, but did not impose a general fee shifting requirement.

PSLRA requires the court at the conclusion of a case to make specific findings as to whether counsel for both sides complied with all aspects of rule 11(c). If not, there is a presumption that sanctions should be imposed unless the violation is *de minimis*. However, the sanctions imposed on the plaintiff and the defendant for violations of rule 11 are not the same. The sanctions to be imposed on the plaintiff should be all attorneys fees and costs incurred by the defendants. The sanctions to be imposed on the defendant are those specified by rule 11(b), which typically is limited to reasonable attorneys' fees incurred as a direct result of the violation. This disparate treatment appears to have been intended specifically to deter filings by plaintiffs in doubtful cases.

The court may require any party or attorney representing a party to post a bond to ensure that the person will be able to respond to a sanction that is imposed. The legislative history suggests that the bond requirement should usually be imposed on the plaintiff's counsel rather than on the plaintiff himself. Again this appears to have been intended specifically to deter filings by plaintiffs in doubtful cases.

§ 17.13   Pleading Provisions

Rule 9(b) of the Federal Rules of Civil Procedure requires allegations of fraud be made "with particularity." In the context of securities class actions, courts of appeals adopted varying standards as to how this requirement should be construed. The Second Circuit adopted the strongest standard, requiring allegations of fact "giving rise to a strong inference of fraudulent intent" on the part of the defendant. The First Circuit adopted a less stringent test, requiring the complaint to set forth specific facts making "it reasonable to believe" that the defendant knew that the statement was materially false or misleading. The test set forth by the Second Circuit is usually referred to as the "strong inference" test while the test of the First Circuit is described as a "some inference" test. The Ninth Circuit stated that the "with particularity" requirement was satisfied merely by alleging specifically that scienter existed, arguing that the rule only requires particularity in the ultimate allegation and no where requires allegations to support inferences.

PSLRA apparently adopts the most stringent Second Circuit standard. Under this statute, a plaintiff must allege facts that creates a "strong inference" that fraud occurred. The plaintiff must specify each statement alleged to be misleading and the reason or reasons why the statement is misleading. If the allegation is made on information and belief, all information on which the belief is formed must be pleaded. However, rather surprisingly, the legislative history states that "[b]ecause the Conference Committee intends to strengthen existing pleading requirements, it does not intend to codify the Second Circuit's case law interpreting this pleading standard." A footnote appended to this statement adds that "[f]or this reason, the Conference Report chose not to include in the pleading standard certain language relating to motive, opportunity, or recklessness."

A plaintiff must also allege and prove that the misstatement "actually caused" the loss incurred by the plaintiff, though this may be shown if the plaintiff can prove the price at which he bought the stock was artificially inflated as a result of the misstatement.

§ 17.14 Damage Provisions

Estimates of damages in securities fraud class action are usually based on the difference between the purchase price and the price of the security on the date the corrective information is disseminated to the market. The legislative history suggests that this method of calculation often overstates the actual damages caused by the misstatement.

PSLRA provides that damages should be calculated as the difference between the purchase price and the mean trading price of the security during the 90–day period after dissemination of the information correcting the misstatement, except that if the plaintiff sells the security during that 90–day period the price that should be used is the actual selling price.

The mean trading price is defined as the average of the closing prices of the security during the 90–day period.

§ 17.15   Aiding and Abetting Provisions

In Central Bank of Denver v. First Interstate Bank (S.Ct.1994), the Supreme Court held that rule 10b–5 did not authorize private suits against aiders and abettors. This ruling was surprising in that the Court on its motion directed that this issue be argued, and the decision was inconsistent with literally hundreds of decisions by the lower federal courts.

PSLRA reinstates aiding and abetting liability in suits brought by the Securities and Exchange Commission but does not reinstate it on behalf of private parties.

§ 17.16   Auditor Disclosure of Corporate Fraud Provisions

An innovative provision of PSLRA imposes new duties on independent public auditors. The general position of the auditing profession is that the discovery of fraud is not the central goal of outside auditors; rather, fraud should be detected by internal controls and internal audits. The role of outside auditors is to assure fidelity to generally accepted accounting principles and generally accepted auditing standards in the development of financial reports and financial statements.

PSLRA mandates a role for outside auditors in the detection of fraud. Audits by independent public accountants must include procedures designed to provide reasonable assurance of detecting illegal acts that would have a direct impact on the determination of financial statement amounts. In addition, procedures must be adopted that permit the identification of transactions with related parties that are material. Finally, procedures must be established that permit an evaluation of the issuer's ability to continue as a going concern. The power of the SEC to modify generally accepting auditing standards where necessary to effectuate these procedures is expressly confirmed.

The new statute also imposes a series of reporting requirements on the auditor who discovers fraud or an illegal action. If an auditor detects or becomes aware of conduct that may be illegal (whether or not it is believed to be material), he must report that information to the appropriate level of management of the issuer and assure that the board of directors or the audit committee is provided with adequate information about the conduct (unless the act is "clearly" inconsequential). If the effect of the action is material, or if the senior management does not take timely remedial action when the failure to take such action would warrant action, the auditor must report its conclusions to the board of directors.

The board of directors upon receiving a report of illegal action must notify the SEC within one business day. A copy of this notice must also be given to the auditor; if the auditor does not receive this notice he must either resign or directly notify the SEC of the apparent failure of the board to take action. If he resigns, he must notify the SEC of that action and the reason therefor.

Auditors have no personal liability in private suits for failing to comply with these requirements. However, the SEC is specifically authorized to impose civil penalties on auditors who willfully fail to comply with these reporting requirements.

§ 17.17 What the Future Holds as a Result of PSLRA

Only experience will be able to determine whether this legislation will have the desired effect of reducing entrepreneurial litigation in the federal courts. However, it is clear that since the effective date of this statute plaintiff's attorneys have halted the filing of new suits while evaluating the standards imposed by this legislation. It is possible that one or more test cases may be filed to evaluate the standards actually being applied by courts under this statute.

Two further possibilities exist that may affect the impact of this statute. The first is that the SEC may exercise its broad rule making authority to clarify the application of some of these new provisions. The second is the possibility that class action securities litigation may be brought in state courts under state securities laws rather than under Rule 10b–5. Legislation has been proposed in California to make that state's antifraud statute of more general application. Many states currently have broad antifraud provisions in their state blue sky laws; these statutes may permit recovery for reckless or negligent conduct by the issuer and liability may be imposed on underwriters and accountants for aiding and abetting. There are limitations to state actions, however. The first is that there may be no way to create a nation-wide class, and the class available within a state may be relatively small. The second is that state actions may not permit use of the fraud on the market theory to establish reliance by individual members of the class. However, it is likely that the feasibility of state law suits will be carefully investigated as an alternative to the traditional federal class action securities law suit.

[For unfamiliar terms see the Glossary]

CHAPTER EIGHTEEN

DIVIDENDS, DISTRIBUTIONS, AND REDEMPTIONS

§ 18.1 Cash or Property Dividends and Distributions

The profits of a business corporation—its purpose or goal—may be accumulated by the corporation or paid out, in whole or in part, in the form of dividends. The decision whether or not to pay dividends generally rests in the discretion of the board of directors of the corporation.

The dividend policy of a corporation depends in part on whether the corporation is publicly or closely held. In the large publicly held corporation, dividends are usually paid on a periodic basis, in amounts that remain stable from period to period. Stability of dividend policy is maintained by such corporations because frequent changes—and certainly any downward change—is interpreted by investors as indicating that the corporation has financial difficulties. Unpleasant surprises should be avoided. Many corporations will maintain a stable dividend even though current earnings are not sufficient to support the dividend in the hope that operations will improve in the future. Public shareholders, without effective voice in the management of the business, may look in part to the history of dividends by the corporation to determine whether to purchase shares of the corporation. Probably greater attention, however, is paid to the prospects of dividends in the future and to the hope that the market price of the shares will rise (which itself may be a function of the business prospects of the corporation).

In a closely held corporation that is taxed as a C corporation, on the other hand, the principal owners of the business usually prefer, for tax reasons, to distribute earnings in the form of salaries, interest, or rent to the principal shareholders rather than distribute them as dividends. See § 2.5 of this Nutshell.

The term "dividend" refers to distributions of earnings; where a distribution of capital (which may be in partial liquidation of the business of the corporation or simply a distribution of excess capital not needed in current operations) is made, the term "distribution" is more accurate than "dividend," though this usage is not uniform—e.g. it is not uncommon to refer to a "liquidating dividend" rather than a "liquidating distribution." The Model Business Corporation Act (1984) does not use the word "dividend"; section 1.40(6) defines the term "distribution" to include all distributions of assets or debt by corporations to their shareholders on account of their shares without regard to their source, and, as described below (see § 18.6 of this Nutshell), provides a single test for the validity of all distributions. Statutes of many states, however, do establish different legal tests for distributions of current or retained earnings on the one hand, and distributions of capital on the other.

Most discussions of dividends classify them into three categories: cash dividends, dividends-in-kind or property dividends, and share dividends (discussed in the following section). Cash and property dividends are true distributions by the corporation of assets or property whereas a share dividend is not. A cash dividend—the most common—as the name implies, pays cash (from legally available funds) among the shareholders in proportion to their holdings. The amount may be expressed either as so many cents or dollars per share or as a percentage of the par or stated value of the shares. A property dividend is a division of assets other than cash of the declaring corporation among the shareholders. For obvious reasons, the property so divided is usually fungible; it may consist, for example, of shares of a subsidiary corporation or of a corporation in which the declaring corporation has an investment, or undivided fractional interests in an asset or a fund.

Most publicly held corporations that pay cash dividends do so on a quarterly or semi-annual basis. Such dividends are referred to as "regular" dividends. A "special" dividend is a one-shot, non-recurring payment that cannot be counted on to be paid again in a following year. Most property dividends are special dividends. A special dividend that accompanies the payment of a regular dividend is sometimes referred to as an "extra."

An informal or irregular payment may be a "dividend" for some purposes. For example, excessive payments in the form of salary, rent, or interest may be treated as a dividend for tax purposes. Such payments, of course, usually will not be proportional to share holdings.

§ 18.2 Share Dividends

A share dividend distributes additional shares of the declaring corporation among the shareholders. A share dividend is not a true dividend since no cash or property leaves the corporation; a distribution of additional shares does not reduce the real worth of the corporation or increase the real worth of the shareholder. Rather, a share dividend increases the number of ownership units outstanding without decreasing the corporation's assets. Share dividends, however, may adversely affect the rights of other classes of shares. A distribution of common shares to common shareholders does not affect the interest of any senior class of shares: the residual ownership is simply divided up into a larger number of units. The same may not be true of distributions of senior securities, since the increased number of shares may lead to a larger preferential right to cash or property dividends or a larger preference on liquidation, thereby adversely affecting the interests of holders of more junior securities.

Share dividends are usually declared on the same class of shares: additional common shares may be distributed to the common shareholders and, less commonly, additional preferred shares may be distributed to the preferred shareholders. However, this is not necessarily so; holders of common shares may receive a dividend in the form of preferred shares, or vice versa. Such interclass distributions will almost always affect the interests of holders of both classes of shares.

Consider the practice of many publicly held corporations of declaring annual share dividends rather than paying cash dividends. As described above, such dividends do not reduce the aggregate assets of the corporation. If a shareholder receiving such a dividend sells the additional shares, he or she may view the transaction as involving essentially the same thing as a cash dividend, since the same number of shares are owned as before and the shareholder has, in addition, the cash received from the sale of the dividend shares. However, the shareholder who sells the dividend shares thereafter owns a slightly smaller percentage of the enterprise than he or she owned before the dividend (since the number of outstanding shares has increased by the number of dividend shares distributed). The dilution in such situations may be so slight as to be unimportant. But it is nevertheless a dilution. It is surprising that many people apparently are unaware that a share dividend is unlike property or cash dividends in this regard.

Where shares are publicly traded, a share dividend, other things being equal, will reduce the market price for each share proportionately; however, other things usually are not equal, and other factors may cause a price change which masks the decline attributable to the dividend. If no decline occurs, a small shareholder may sell his or her dividend shares for cash and yet have a diluted investment with undiminished market value.

A share dividend is often expressed as a ratio. Thus, a 20 percent dividend means that a shareholder receives a 20 percent increase—one additional share for each five shares held; a shareholder who owns less than five shares or a number of shares not divisible by five, will receive either a fractional share or "scrip," or at the election of the directors the fair value of the fractional share in cash. See MBCA (1984) § 6.04. "Scrip" differs from fractional shares in that it grants no voting or dividend rights; it represents merely the right to a fraction of a full share which may be bought or sold so that a full share may be assembled from the rights to fractional shares. Fractional shares may also be created in other ways as well.

A share "dividend" and a share "split" are closely related. Indeed, a dividend can be readily envisioned as a small split. In states with par value statutes, however, these transactions are accounted for differently in the capital accounts of the corporation. A share dividend results in the transfer of an amount equal to the par value of the dividend shares being transferred from earned surplus (or some other surplus) to stated capital and increases that account by the par value of the new shares, while a "split" simply divides the shares into a greater number of shares and reduces proportionally the par value of those shares so that there is no change in the aggregate stated capital of the corporation. The Model Business Corporation Act (1984) and states that have eliminated the concept of par value generally do not distinguish between share dividends and splits. However, this distinction is recognized by the New York Stock Exchange in its *Listed Company Manual* which requires more realistic accounting treatment than provided in the corporation statutes. The *Manual* defines a "stock dividend" as the distribution of less than 25 per cent of the outstanding shares (calculated before the distribution) while a "stock split" is a distribution of 100 per cent or more of the outstanding shares. Distributions of between 25 per cent and 100 per cent are called "partial stock splits." The *Manual* also requires the capitalization of the full market value of share dividends (rather than merely the par value) but no capitalization of stock splits and warns against the use of the word "dividend" in connection with splits or partial stock splits.

A practical difference between share dividends and share splits may also exist in connection with the adjustment of dividend rates on shares on which a dividend or split has been announced. Since cash dividend rates are usually not adjusted for a share dividend, such a dividend may increase slightly the effective rate of dividend payouts. In other words, the dividend rate remains the same but the total number of shares against which that rate is applied has been increased. The dividend rate is usually adjusted in a share split; for example, if a share of a corporation which regularly pays dividends of $1.00 per share is split two-for-one (i.e. each holder of 100 shares receives a certificate for another 100 shares and now owns 200 shares in all), the dividend on the split shares may be set at $0.55 cents per share, or an effective rate on the old shares of $1.10.

Shares may be split by publicly held corporations in order to keep the trading price within its historical range, or to broaden the market for the shares by decreasing the cost of a round lot for trading purposes. The New York Stock Exchange *Listed Company Manual* lists these as among the justifiable reasons for a corporation to split its shares.

§ 18.3   Distributions of Rights or Warrants

"Rights" or "warrants" are simply options to purchase additional shares at a price usually (through not invariably) below the current market price of the shares. Most rights are short lived (usually a period of weeks at the most); where they remain in effect for longer periods they are usually called warrants. Rights or warrants when distributed to shareholders are also not true dividends, though they may be so regarded by recipients. The effect of a distribution of rights or warrants in proportion to existing shareholdings is that a shareholder must add new capital to the enterprise in order to retain his or her relative ownership interest in the corporation. Rights or warrants issued by publicly held corporations are themselves traded and often listed on securities exchanges, the price fluctuating with the price of the underlying shares. A shareholder who sells rights or warrants distributed as a "dividend" thereby dilutes his or her proportionate interest in the corporation.

The price at which rights or warrants may be exercised is sometimes called the strike price. The value of rights or warrants that are issued with a strike price below the current market price is based on two variables: the inherent value reflected by the difference between the market and strike price and the time value that reflects the possibility that the market price of the underlying shares will rise during the life of the right or warrant. Rights or warrants that are issued with a strike price above current market price may have a time value even though they have no inherent value.

§ 18.4   Share Reacquisitions as Distributions

The acquisition by a corporation of its own shares decreases the real worth of the corporation by the amount of the consideration paid for the shares. The shares so acquired are not assets of the issuing corporation any more than authorized but unissued shares are assets. As a result, a reacquisition of shares is a type of distribution, and is included within the Model Business Corporation Act (1984) definition of that term. If the corporation reacquires a proportional part of the shares owned by each shareholder, the result is clearly the equivalent of a dividend. If the reacquisition is not proportional (the normal case), the interest represented by each share in the corporation which is not reacquired is increased proportionally to the shares reacquired.

Only reacquisitions of a corporation's own shares constitute distributions. If a corporation purchases shares of another corporation, that is an investment. The difference can be readily envisioned by considering how the transactions are reflected on a balance sheet. A purchase of shares of another corporation affects only the asset side of the balance sheet; a corporation that purchases its own shares, however, must account for the transaction by reducing both the "asset" and "equity" sides of the balance sheet.

Under older state statutes, shares issued by a corporation that are reacquired by that corporation are called "treasury shares"; such shares are viewed as having an intermediate status. They are not issued shares for purposes of quorum or voting purposes or for the payment of dividends. But they are viewed as not having been canceled: they are in limbo, in an intermediate status of being neither issued nor canceled; they may be resold by the corporation without regard to the restrictions on original issue of shares described in an earlier Chapter (see § 7.8 of this Nutshell).

Obviously if treasury shares are reissued as a share dividend, the assets and relative positions of the common shareholders are unchanged; if they are resold to third persons, the assets of the corporation will be increased by the resale price and the relative voting interests of the other shareholders will be diluted. If the treasury shares are resold at a bargain price, the financial interest of the remaining shareholders will also be diluted.

The Model Business Corporation Act (1984) does not recognize the concept of treasury shares. Section 6.31(a) provides simply that reacquired shares have the status of authorized but unissued shares. This simplification was a byproduct of the elimination of the concepts of par value, stated capital, and eligible and ineligible consideration in the Model Act.

§ 18.5 Shareholders' Rights to a Dividend

A dividend is distributable to shareholders of record on a specific date. Record dates may be determined in the same ways as record dates are established to make determinations of eligibility to vote at meetings. (See § 9.4 of this Nutshell.) If no record date for a distribution is fixed, the record date is the date the directors authorize the distribution. MBCA (1984) § 6.40(b). Generally, when a dividend has been declared it becomes a debt of the corporation and cannot be rescinded or repealed by the directors.

Where shares are transferred shortly before or shortly after the record date but before the dividend is actually paid, the purchaser and seller may agree between themselves as to who is entitled to the dividend. Such an agreement, of course, is binding between the purchaser and seller but generally not binding on the corporation, which will simply pay the dividend to whoever is the record owner on the record date. The date on which payment is actually made is usually referred to as the "payable date," which in the case of a publicly held corporation may be set three weeks or so after the record date. Securities exchanges have promulgated conventions or rules dealing with whether the buyer or seller of publicly held shares is entitled to dividends. The "ex dividend" date is the first date the seller becomes entitled to keep the dividend, i.e., the date that a purchaser of the shares buys the shares without the dividend. Under the New York Stock Exchange rules, shares normally are traded ex dividend on and after the third business day before the record date for the dividend. For example, a dividend may be made payable on March 28 to shareholders of record on March 14. The stock goes ex dividend on March 11 according to the conventions of the New York Stock Exchange. A purchaser of the shares on March 10 is entitled to the dividend; a purchaser on March 11 is not. In either event the dividend will be paid on March 28 to whoever was the record owner on March 14. In contracts for the purchase and sale of shares after the ex dividend date, the seller retains the right to the dividend, and the amount of the dividend is not included in the contract price. Since most transactions in publicly held shares involve brokers, the purchaser or seller is not directly involved in the mechanics of transferring the amount of the dividend if it is received by a selling party to a transaction occurring before the ex dividend date.

The theory of the ex-dividend date is that it is tied to the traditional settlement date for transactions in publicly traded securities, which historically has been five business days after the trade (T + 5). In 1996, the SEC mandated a change in the settlement date to T + 3. The ex-dividend date changed at the same time.

The price of a stock usually declines when it goes ex dividend. It may or may not decline from the previous closing price by exactly the amount of the dividend; other factors may also affect the market price simultaneously and bring about a greater or lesser change than the adjustment due to the shares going ex-dividend. Where the corporation issues rights, shares go "ex rights" on the same basis as they go ex dividend.

§ 18.6 Statutory Restrictions on the Declaration of Dividends

Statutory restrictions on the distribution of dividends are basically designed to assure that payments to shareholders are made out of current or prior earnings and not out of corporate capital. These restrictions are rarely a problem in connection with publicly traded shares, but often must be taken into account when considering the legality of distributions by smaller, closely held corporations. The Model Business Corporation Act (1984) has developed a simpler set of rules that are discussed below after the discussion of statutory restrictions appearing in traditional par value statutes.

(1) *Traditional Statutes.* In these statutes restrictions are phrased in accounting terms applicable to the right hand side of the traditional balance sheet. (If this reference is unclear read § 7.4 of this Nutshell.) Unfortunately the language of traditional state statutes varies widely, and an examination of the specific statute is necessary to ascertain whether specific payments are prohibited. The principal state statutory provisions are as follows:

(a) *Solvency.* All states provide that the payment of a dividend is prohibited if the corporation is "insolvent" or the payment of the dividend will render the corporation insolvent. "Insolvency" is usually defined in the equity sense of being unable to meet corporate obligations as they mature, though a few states define insolvency in the bankruptcy sense of the corporate liabilities exceeding the corporate assets. A payment in violation of the bankruptcy test may also constitute an act of bankruptcy under the Federal Bankruptcy Act.

(b) *Surplus Test.* A number of states permit distributions to be paid from "surplus" as contrasted with "capital." Under statutes of this type, dividends usually may be paid from earned surplus and capital distributions from capital surplus without special designation of the source. The statutes of this type may be phrased in terms of prohibitions against impairment of "capital" or "capital stock," but the net effect is that the available assets may be reduced to the minimum core of "capital" that the corporation must maintain. California has a surplus test, but it is unusual in that it is not based on an irreducible minimum of capital; rather it requires assets to be maintained at least equal to one and one fourth times specified liabilities.

Randall v. Bailey (N.Y.1940) raised the question whether it was permissible for directors to write up the value of appreciated assets on the books of the corporation in order to increase the amount available for distribution as dividends. In holding that it was permissible to use asset write-ups to increase the dividend paying capacity of the corporation, the court relied in part on the language of the New York statute that only prohibited dividends that "impaired capital stock."

(c) *Earned Surplus Test.* This test permits dividends to be paid only from "earned surplus." (As described in the following section, however, these statutes also usually permit distributions from capital accounts such as capital surplus but they are not "dividends" in the strict sense.) In these statutes earned surplus is defined to be a composite income item determined by adding together all net profits, income, gain and losses during each accounting period going back to the original creation of the corporation with reductions for prior dividends or transfers to other accounts. It is questionable whether write-ups of the *Randall v. Bailey* type are permissible to increase earned surplus available for dividends in Model Act states, and if written up, it is also questionable whether they may thereafter have to be written down.

(d) *Distributions From Capital.* State statutes with an "earned surplus" test often permit distributions to be made from capital accounts when there is no earned surplus. They typically permitted distributions of capital surplus to common shareholders if the articles of incorporation so provided or with the approval of the holders of a majority of the common shares. Distributions of capital surplus to holders of cumulative preferred shares in discharge of cumulative dividend rights are generally permitted in any event. The justification for permitting cumulative dividends to be paid from capital surplus was that it permitted a corporation to avoid building up preferred arrearages during the early years of operation when there was no earned surplus. As a result, dividends may be paid to common shareholders at an earlier time and in a greater amount.

Distributions from capital surplus cannot be made if the corporation is insolvent or the distribution renders the corporation insolvent. Further, a distribution to common shareholders is permitted only if all preferential cumulative dividends have been paid, and the capital remaining in the corporation is sufficient to cover all preferential rights on liquidation.

Most statutes following this approach require that payments made from capital surplus be identified as such when made to shareholders.

(e) *Net Profits Test.* A number of states permit distributions from current profits even if there is an earnings deficit from operations for prior periods. These dividends are sometimes called "nimble dividends." The leading case holding that current earnings may be distributed without being used to eliminate prior deficits is Goodnow

v. American Writing Paper Co. (N.J.1908). Some states do not permit nimble dividends.

(f) *Restrictions on Surplus.* Many statutes permit dividends to be paid only from "unrestricted" earned surplus and distributions of various kinds only from "unrestricted" capital surplus. Restrictions on surplus arose from the acquisition of treasury shares by the corporation. When treasury shares were acquired, the earned or capital surplus used for their acquisition is restricted so that the same surplus cannot be used again for distributions or dividends. Restrictions on surplus rather than reductions of surplus are used in this situation because the treasury shares may later be reissued, in which event the restrictions are removed *pro tanto* to the extent of the consideration received for the treasury shares. If the treasury shares are instead canceled, the restrictions were changed to permanent reductions in the appropriate surplus accounts.

(g) *Reduction of Stated Capital.* State statutes generally permit a corporation to reduce its stated capital simply by amending the articles of incorporation to reduce the par value of outstanding shares. Stated capital represented by no par shares or by amounts previously transferred from other accounts to stated capital may be reduced by a simple procedure involving approval of the shareholders and directors.

These provisions relating to the reduction of stated capital made it clear that the par value capital structure in fact provides no protection to creditors, since it is possible for the shareholders acting alone to eliminate the "cushion" reflected by stated capital without the approval of creditors.

(h) *Restrictions on Distributions by Repurchase or Redemption of Shares.* Statutory restrictions on the power of a corporation to repurchase its own shares are generally analogous to statutory restrictions on the payment of dividends. For example, they are also phrased in accounting terms applicable to the right hand side of the traditional balance sheet and are subject to insolvency prohibitions, or, in some states, the requirement that after such purchase, the fair value of the corporation's total assets will be less than the total amount of its debts. These restrictions may create serious problems for closely held corporations desiring to repurchase a substantial fraction of their common shares.

Statutes dealing with share repurchases often permit repurchases out of earned surplus, or out of capital surplus if authorized by the articles of incorporation or a vote of shareholders. They also permit shares to be purchased out of stated capital (or any other capital account) for certain limited purposes, namely:

(i) To eliminate fractional shares;

(ii) To collect or compromise indebtedness owed by or to the corporation;

(iii) To pay dissenting shareholders entitled to payment for their shares under the act; and

(iv) To effect the purchase or redemption of its redeemable shares in accordance with the provisions of the act.

(2) *The Model Business Corporation Act (1984).* The 1984 Model Business Corporation Act drastically revises the financial provisions described above. The provisions relating to distributions in section 6.40 apply the same tests to all types of distributions: to distributions of cash or property, to corporate reacquisitions of shares, and to less common types of distributions, such as creating evidences of indebtedness and distributing them to shareholders. No distinction is made between distributions of capital or of earnings; all distributions are subject to the same tests. Section 6.40 also provides firm answers for a

number of technical questions about the lawfulness of distributions that are not covered in most existing statutes.

Section 6.40(c) sets forth a dual test for the legality of distributions of all types: after giving effect to the distribution, (a) the corporation must be "able to pay its debts as they become due in the usual course of business," and (b) the corporation's assets must exceed its total liabilities after making provision for the liquidation preferences of senior securities. The first test is usually referred to as the "insolvency" test (since it in effect defines equity insolvency) and the second "the balance sheet" test. Both must be satisfied if the distribution is to be lawful.

The balance sheet test presupposes the use of some kind of accounting conventions to determine "assets" and "liabilities." Section 6.40(d) permits the board of directors to base a determination either on "accounting practices and principles that are reasonable in the circumstances" or on a "fair valuation or other method that is reasonable in the circumstances." Because section 6.40 is applicable to all corporations, large and small, it was not thought appropriate to require all corporations to use generally accepted accounting principles or some other accounting standard that might require the employment of an accountant. The Official Comment describes in some detail what the determination of solvency requires and also points out that in making all decisions under this section, the directors are liable for an unlawful distribution only if the directors fail to meet their duty of care under section 8.30. MBCA (1984) § 8.33.

Section 6.40(e) also describes at what time the insolvency and balance sheet tests are to be applied. To some extent, the time is determined by the nature of the distribution, and to a lesser extent, the time of declaration in relation to the time of payment.

§ 18.7 Contractual Provisions Relating to Declarations of Dividends

Because of the great liberality of modern business corporation statutes in permitting distributions to shareholders of earnings and capital, much of the modern law of dividends is contractual in nature. Creditors of a corporation are naturally anxious that the assets of the corporation not be dissipated through unwise distributions. Provisions are therefore routinely inserted in loan agreements and similar contracts to prohibit or restrict the power of the corporation to make distributions to shareholders. The nature of such restrictions varies widely. If the debtor is a publicly held corporation with an established history of regular dividend payments, the agreement may permit dividends of specified amounts provided that certain ratios are maintained between assets and liabilities, or between current assets and current liabilities. Other restrictions may permit any distribution so long as a minimum net worth and minimum cash balance are maintained. Similar agreements with closely held corporations may prohibit all dividends, and may even impose restrictions on salary payments, bonuses, and other distributions having the effect of a dividend.

Contractual provisions relating to dividends also may appear in articles of incorporation. Where classes of preferred are authorized, complex provisions relating to dividends may be negotiated. Not only must the preference rights of the senior security be defined (e.g., cumulative, non-cumulative, or cumulative to the extent earned), but provisions may be inserted as part of the preferred shareholders' rights restricting the amount of common dividends that may be paid, requiring a portion of earnings to be set aside as a sinking fund to be used to retire a portion of the preferred each year, limiting senior indebtedness that may be created, and so forth. The preferred shareholder otherwise receives scant protection under most business corporation acts since claims to preferential dividends, even if cumulative, are not corporate debts but a mere priority to possible future distributions.

§ 18.8 Liability of Directors and Shareholders for Illegal Dividends

Directors who vote for or assent to a declaration of dividends or the distribution of assets to shareholders which is wholly or partially in violation of statutory limitations or a provision in the corporation's articles of incorporation, are jointly and severally liable to the corporation for the illegal portion of the dividend or distribution. This statutory liability is ameliorated in many states by possible defenses discussed earlier. See § 14.18 of this Nutshell.

Shareholders "who accepted [a distribution] knowing the distribution was made in violation of this Act or the articles of incorporation" may be liable to return or restore the unlawful payment received. This qualified provision in effect protects the probable reliance of an innocent shareholder upon receipt of a distribution; the directors authorizing the illegal dividend of course remain responsible to restore the unlawful payment. If the shareholder knows the payment was unlawful, she may be required to restore it to the corporation, and the liability of the directors will be reduced accordingly. Not all states extend similar protection to innocent shareholders.

§ 18.9 Shareholders' Right to Compel a Dividend

Minority shareholders in closely held corporations are likely to be unhappy about the dividend policy established by the corporation. In a C corporation the shareholders in control of the corporation usually prefer to pay salaries to themselves or make other tax-deductible payments rather than pay the same funds in the form of dividends to all the shareholders. In an S corporation, shareholders must include their pro rata share of corporate earnings in their own tax returns whether or not anything is distributed to them. A no-dividend policy in such a corporation may cause serious cash flow problems to minority shareholders who may lack the funds to pay the additional tax due to the allocation of S corporation income to them. Distributions in the form of salaries to controlling shareholders in an S corporation also have the effect of diverting corporate income to the controlling shareholders at the expense of the minority. What, if anything, can the minority shareholder do to secure a more favorable dividend policy? The two most likely approaches involve litigation either (1) to compel the controlling shareholders to return part of the amounts distributed to them as being irregular dividends or amounts paid in violation of fiduciary duties, or (2) to compel the declaration of a dividend to all shareholders.

A common provision in S corporation bylaws requires the corporation, if it has eligible earnings, to pay a dividend at least equal to the amount of additional taxes incurred by each shareholder as a result of the allocation of S corporation income to them. These distributions are usually called "tax distributions."

In light of the business judgment rule and the principle of fairness applicable to self dealing transactions, attempts to pare back salaries face formidable hurdles though some cases have been successful. This approach is often less attractive than suits to compel a dividend, since success in causing the return of excess salary to the corporation does not necessarily lead to a greater distribution to the plaintiffs.

Historically, suits to compel the declaration of a dividend also faced serious obstacles. The discretion of the board of directors with respect to business decisions was so broad that a strong showing of fraud, bad faith, or abuse of discretion was necessary. In short, an abuse of power or a clear failure to exercise it honestly for the corporation and all its shareholders must be shown. Dodge v. Ford Motor Co. (Mich.1919) is a classic case in which minority shareholders were successful in compelling the declaration of a dividend, though the court there appeared to rely heavily on the unusual frankness of the majority shareholder and the court's own view of desirable social policy. Other cases have also compelled the declaration of a dividend particularly where the defendant was outspoken as to his strategy of freezing out the minority, though in a "head count" of such cases, plaintiffs come off as net losers. A major concern of courts in ordering a dividend to be paid is that there appears to be no standard to guide the court as to how much may safely be paid out and how much should be retained by the corporation for contingencies and future growth. Judges are usually not businessmen and in any event have little knowledge or familiarity with the specific business before them. Hence even where a finding of bad faith may be made in connection with refusing to declare a dividend, a court is likely to be conservative in establishing the amount of any judicially-declared dividend.

§ 18.10   Tax Consequences of Failure to Pay Dividends in Closely Held Corporations

Section 531 of the Internal Revenue Code imposes a special penalty tax on C corporations "formed or availed of for the purpose of avoiding the income tax with respect to its shareholders" by the expedient of permitting earnings and profits to accumulate rather than distributing them in the form of taxable dividends. A tax is imposed on that portion of current earnings which is retained in excess of the "reasonably anticipated" needs of the business. The tax is at a rate of $27\frac{1}{2}$ per cent on the first $100,000 and $38\frac{1}{2}$ per cent on the balance of the excess retained income, and is in addition to the regular federal income taxes applicable to corporations. However, a deduction may be taken for dividends paid shortly after the close of the taxable year, and an aggregate of $150,000 may be accumulated without any justification. A test based on the "reasonably anticipated" needs of a business is obviously very imprecise, and in fact has given rise to a substantial amount of litigation. Guidelines for the proper application of this test appear in IRS regulations.

Section 531 is often administered informally. An internal revenue agent auditing a closely held corporation may raise an issue about paying a dividend without actually seeking the imposition of the section 531 penalty tax. The corporation may take the hint and declare a dividend in the immediate future.

§ 18.11   Corporate Repurchase of Its Own Shares

The distributional aspect of repurchases by corporations of their own shares has previously been commented upon (see § 18.4 of this Nutshell). Such transactions create several additional problems that are not present in the dividend area that deserve additional consideration.

Since redemptions are almost never proportional to shareholdings, the shareholders' relative positions among themselves are affected by the corporate repurchase, and it is often possible for managing shareholders in a closely held corporation to utilize a share repurchase for personal reasons. For example, a leading Massachusetts case has held that it is a breach of fiduciary duty for the majority shareholder to cause the corporation to purchase a portion of a family member's shares at inflated prices while offering to purchase the shares owned by a non-family member at significantly lower prices. Donahue v. Rodd Electrotype Co. of New England, Inc. (Mass.1975). In this case, the family member whose shares were redeemed was elderly and the effect of the redemption was to further the goals of an estate plan set up by him some time earlier. The court articulated the view that shareholders in a closely held corporation have fiduciary duties to each other that rival those that exist in a partnership; at a narrower level this case in effect recognized a reverse preemptive right on the purchase of shares in some situations. While later Massachusetts cases have retreated to some extent from the broad fiduciary duty language in the opinion and not all cases from other jurisdictions involving disproportionate redemptions have followed the reasoning of this decision, it nevertheless is an important case describing duties that exist among shareholders in closely held corporations in connection with transactions that favor some shareholders but not others without any apparent business justification.

In a closely held corporation, the usual reason to reacquire shares is to eliminate the interest of one or more shareholders in the enterprise who desire to leave. The reason for the elimination may be a death or desired retirement, or a negotiated withdrawal following disagreements as to business policies. Usually, the remaining shareholders do not wish to increase their investment in the business by purchasing the shares personally (and they may lack the liquid assets to do so). A repurchase by the corporation also does not affect the relative voting power of the remaining shareholders. Hence acquisition by the corporation is a logical choice to purchase the shares. If the corporation has not been in existence for a long time or has suffered losses in the past, the legal restrictions on repurchase of shares discussed in a preceding section may create serious problems in effectuating the corporate repurchase.

The corporation may deliver promissory notes to the selling shareholder representing the future payments of principal. Usually, an installment sale occurs because the corporation lacks the assets to buy the shares outright and it is contemplated that future payments will be made in whole or in part out of (hoped for) future earnings. Where an installment sale is made the question arises whether the insolvency and availability of surplus requirements applicable to dividends should be applied only when shares are reacquired and the notes issued, or whether those requirements should be repetitively applied to determine the validity of each payment when it is made. The limited case law tends to apply the tests to each payment but section 6.40(e)(1) of the Model Business Corporation Act (1984) provides that the test should be applied only when the shares are acquired and the notes issued. The argument for this position is that the transaction should be treated no differently than if the corporation borrowed the purchase price from a bank in order to acquire the shares for cash. The alternative view would require at least the insolvency test to be applied at the time of each payment. A further question may arise as to whether the promissory notes issued by the corporation for the balance of the purchase price should be viewed as on a parity with general trade creditors or as subordinate to them. Section 6.40(f) provides that such notes should be on a parity with general unsecured creditors if the notes were validly issued to begin with; the theory is that the corporation could have used cash to buy the shares, borrowing if necessary from a third party, and there is no reason to treat the shareholder who accepts promissory notes from the corporation any differently from any third party lender.

In a public corporation, shares may be reacquired in order to have them available for stock options or other compensation plans, or for acquisitions of other corporations. Many corporations purchase their own shares for these purposes. Of more importance, publicly held corporations repurchase their own shares for financial reasons, planning to retire them. In these situations the corporation has made the judgment that the market has in some way under-priced the corporation's securities. Retirement of shares may have the effect of increasing the price and earnings per share of the remaining outstanding shares; this assumes, of course, that the corporation has idle cash that is surplus to its reasonably anticipated business needs and its use to retire shares does not significantly reduce overall earnings.

A corporation may desire to purchase its own shares for improper considerations as well as for proper ones. Corporate management faced with the threat of a takeover by an outside corporation may cause the corporation to purchase its own shares as a defensive measure to entrench incumbent management. Purchases on the open market may drive up the price of the shares, thereby tending to defeat a cash tender offer or public exchange offer. A filing under the Williams Act may be required before such transactions are undertaken. Or the insurgent group may be willing to accept "green mail," i.e., to sell its block of shares (at a premium over what it paid for them) back to the corporation, thereby eliminating a threat to control. The appropriate test in such a case, according to the Delaware Supreme Court, is the *Unocal* test, whether the repurchase is reasonable in relation to the threat posed to the corporation. See § 13.25 of this Nutshell.

§ 18.12   Redeemable Securities

Corporations may, when permitted by their articles of incorporation, issue shares that are redeemable at the option of the corporation. See MBCA (1984) § 6.01(c)(2). The statutes of many states permit redeemable *preferred* shares but not redeemable *common* shares, but the MBCA (1984) does not contain such a limitation. The concern with redeemable common shares is that management may use the redemption device to discipline or eliminate antagonistic shareholders. One commentator has stated that even the suggestion of redeemable common shares is "corporate heresy." Such concerns, however, do not appear to be borne out in practice.

In modern financing practice within publicly held corporations, preferred shares are usually cumulative and redeemable, and in addition are often convertible into publicly traded common shares (the "conversion shares") on a predetermined ratio. Typically, the conversion ratio is established at a level that requires a significant increase in price of the conversion shares before conversion becomes economic. Thereafter, if the market price of the conversion shares does in fact rise to the point that the conversion shares are worth more than the preferred shares (priced without the conversion feature), the preferred will fluctuate in price in tandem with the common. If these securities are thereafter called for redemption, preferred shareholders should rationally elect to convert rather than permit the shares to be redeemed. Such conversions are described as "forced." The economic justification for a forced conversion is that usually the dividend payable on the conversion security is significantly lower than the dividend on the convertible security.

In modern financing practice, shares may also be made redeemable at the option of the holder or upon the occurrence of some event (such as an increase in interest rates). Earlier statutes contemplated redemption only at the option of the corporation, but section 6.01(c)(2) of MBCA (1984) authorizes redemptions to be triggered by other events as well. Shares redeemable at the option of the holder have some of the same characteristics of a demand note.

See generally §§ 7.10–7.13 of this Nutshell.

[For unfamiliar terms see the Glossary]

CHAPTER NINETEEN

INSPECTION OF BOOKS AND RECORDS

§ 19.1 Inspection by Directors and Shareholders Compared

Both shareholders and directors have the right to inspect corporate books and records in certain circumstances. However, the inspection right of a director is considerably broader than the right of a shareholder and rests on an entirely different theoretical base.

A director is a manager of the corporation and owes certain duties to it and to all the shareholders. Indeed, a director may be liable for negligent mismanagement if he or she does not adequately acquaint himself or herself with the business and affairs of the corporation. For this reason, some cases state that the directors' right to inspect books and records is absolute and unqualified. However, as with many supposedly absolute principles, there are exceptions. Courts have sometimes denied inspection rights to directors where it was clear that the director was acting with manifestly improper motives and adequate information prepared by unbiased persons was otherwise available to the director. Such cases, however, are exceptional and unusual.

The right of a shareholder to inspect books and records, on the other hand, is considerably narrower. A shareholder has a financial interest in the corporation, and the common law recognizes a right to inspect books and records to protect this interest. However, because the shareholder is not charged with management responsibility and is not subject to broad duties, the right to inspect is available only for a "proper purpose," and is otherwise hedged with restrictions. The balance of this chapter deals exclusively with the "proper purpose" test and the more limited inspection rights of shareholders.

§ 19.2 Common Law and Statutory Rights of Inspection by Shareholders

A right of shareholders to inspect books and records of the corporation may arise from several different sources. Corporation statutes grant a right of inspection in some circumstances and these statutes form the bulk of the discussion in the balance of this chapter. In addition, a shareholder who is in litigation against the corporation may have the same rights of discovery as any other litigant. Some state statutes require corporations to make reports or submit tax statements that are then available for inspection by shareholders. And, of course, if information must be made publicly available, any shareholder may examine it. Finally, in some states there may exist a residual common law right of inspection that has not been superseded by the statutory right of inspection.

From the standpoint of the corporation, a shareholder's demand to inspect books and records is almost always viewed as a hostile and threatening act. Before the statutory right of inspection was created, the practice developed of denying all inspection requests out-of-hand and compelling the shareholder to litigate, relying on whatever pretext may be available for the denial. The first statutes defining a statutory right of inspection were enacted in an effort to combat this attitude. The most notable feature of these statutes was that they combined a restatement of the common law right of inspection with penalties imposed on corporate officers with custody of the books and records who arbitrarily refuse to permit proper examination of books and records. These statutes retain the "proper purpose" standard of the common law.

The statutory right of inspection in many states is available to persons whose shareholdings meet certain objective criteria; a typical provision extends the statutory right to persons (1) who have been shareholders of record for at least six months prior to the demand or (2) who own at least five per cent of the outstanding shares of the corporation. As indicated above, a person who meets these objective criteria must also state a "proper purpose" for the inspection in a written demand. However, under many statutes, the burden of proof as to proper purpose shifts if the shareholder meets the objective criteria and alleges a proper purpose, so that the corporation then has the burden of showing the plaintiff did not in fact have a proper purpose; shareholders who do not meet these objective criteria continue to have the common law burden of establishing that their purpose is a proper one.

A corporate officer who improperly refuses to grant a statutory right of inspection is liable for a penalty that may be defined in various ways. Several states made the penalty one or two per cent of the value of the plaintiff's shares, others imposed a maximum penalty of $500; still others imposed a per diem penalty of $25 or some other amount. Some states required the officer to pay the litigation expenses, including attorneys' fees, of the shareholder who was forced to sue in order to vindicate his or her right to inspect. As a practical matter, these provisions were not widely invoked, though there are a handful of instances in which penalties of fairly substantial amounts were actually imposed on recalcitrant officers. Of course, the number of litigated cases may not describe the informal impact that these penal provisions had, since the potential of a substantial penalty may have caused some corporate officers to grant inspection rights they might otherwise have resisted for fear of the consequences.

The Model Business Corporation Act (1984) rejects the penalty approach, though it does contain provisions designed to assure that the right to inspect is made available on a timely basis. First, like the statutes of several states, section 16.02(a) requires a shareholder desiring to inspect books and records to give five days written demand in advance. Second, section 16.02(b) describes in considerable detail the types of records a shareholder may examine. Third, in an effort to reduce "fishing expeditions," section 16.02(c) requires the demand to be in "good faith" and for a "proper purpose" and that the shareholder define with reasonable particularity his or her purpose and establish that the records sought are "directly connected" with that purpose. Section 16.04(b) provides for direct judicial action to enforce a right of inspection under section 16.02; the court is directed to dispose of such a case on an "expedited basis." Further, if the court orders inspection, under section 6.04(c), it must order the corporation to pay the shareholders' costs of the proceeding, including reasonable attorney's fees unless the corporation can prove "that it refused inspection in good faith because it had a reasonable basis for doubt about the right of the shareholder to inspect the records demanded." This is a corporate obligation, not an obligation of the officer with custody of the books and records, as was the case under older inspection statutes.

§ 19.3 Corporate Records: What May Be Examined?

Business corporation acts require each corporation to keep minutes of meetings, books and records of account, and information about record shareholders so that an appropriate voting list of shareholders may be created. The language of these statutes varies widely from state to state. Section 16.01 of the Model Business Corporation Act (1984) is a carefully drafted provision that is designed not to impose unreasonable record-keeping requirements on corporations. In addition to a record of shareholders [section 16.01(c)], it generally requires keeping of "records" of actions taken at meetings rather than "minutes" of meetings; it also requires only "appropriate accounting records" to be maintained rather than the older language of "books and records of account." MBCA (1984) §§ 16.01(a), (b). Of course, many corporations may find it necessary to keep much more detailed and elaborate records: section 16.01 sets forth the irreducible minimum. In a bow to the computer age, section 16.01(d) and the statutes of many states permit these records to be kept on tape or in machine-readable form capable of being converted into written form in a reasonable time.

Under most state statutes, the shareholder's right to inspect extends not only to enumerated records but to corporate records in general. Case law has tended to be expansive in this regard. One case authorized the examination of "records, books of account, receipts, vouchers, bills and all other documents evidencing the financial condition of the corporation." Another case authorized the examination of the books of a subsidiary controlled by the corporation. Corporate contracts and even the correspondence of the chief executive officer have been held to be subject to inspection in appropriate cases. The right generally extends to all relevant records necessary to inform the shareholder about corporate matters in which he or she has a legitimate interest. The corporation cannot defeat this right by offering summaries, substitute papers, or financial statements prepared by the corporation's auditors.

Section 16.02(b) of the Model Business Corporation Act (1984) is considerably more restrictive than most statutes, since it contains an exclusive enumeration of what records may be examined. Shareholders may inspect only excerpts of minutes, the accounting records, and the record of shareholders under this section. This does not mean, however, that all records not described in that section are immune from inspection. Rather the shareholder seeking such information must persuade the court that he or she has a non-statutory right to the documents under section 16.02(e)(2) which preserves "the power of a court, independently of this Act, to compel the production of corporate records for examination."

§ 19.4   What Is a "Proper Purpose"?

The basic test of inspection by shareholders is a "proper purpose." A "proper purpose" means a purpose that is reasonably relevant to the shareholder's interest as a shareholder. A purpose is proper under this definition if it is directed toward obtaining information bearing upon or seeking to protect the shareholder's interest and that of other shareholders of the corporation. A purpose to determine the worth of the shareholder's holdings is a proper purpose. So is a purpose of seeking reasons for a decline in profits. So is a purpose of ascertaining whether there has been mismanagement or alarming transactions.

A corporation cannot deny the right to inspect by arguing that the shareholder has an improper purpose simply because he or she is unfriendly to management. An improper purpose is one with ulterior or vindictive motives. Obvious examples are general harassment of management or a desire to obtain trade secrets for a competitor. Probably mere idle curiosity is not a proper purpose, though it is a rare shareholder who cannot allege a more specific purpose. Some courts appear to be more willing than others to countenance "fishing expeditions."

Obviously, substantial and difficult factual issues arise as to the shareholder's true purpose. The issue may come down to predominant motive and intent. The burden of proof, discussed earlier, may be significant. It is probably fair to conclude that it is always easy to couch an inspection demand in the form of a purpose that is proper, and that careful coaching of testimony may lead to the conclusion that the purpose for inspection is proper, while an outspoken or unusually forthright witness may run into difficulty. The mere fact that a shareholder making a demand to inspect books or records is a competitor of the corporation does not necessarily make the demand improper, though it may raise suspicions. In this type of situation, some courts have imposed restrictions on the use or distribution of the information being produced, apparently without express statutory authority to do so. Section 16.04(d) of the Model Business Corporation expressly endorses this practice.

§ 19.5   Who Is Entitled to Inspect?

A person who is a beneficial owner of shares but is not the record owner has a common law right of inspection, and depending on the wording of the specific statute, may have a statutory right as well. See MBCA (1984) § 16.02(f). Pledgees, judgment creditors, and holders of voting trust certificates also have a statutory right to inspect under the statutes of many states.

Section 16.03 of the 1984 Model Act makes clear that an inspecting shareholder may be accompanied by an attorney or agent. Further, the right to inspect entails, if reasonable, the right to obtain copies of the inspected documents; the corporation may impose a reasonable charge for providing those copies. While many courts doubtless would require corporations to provide copies as a matter of common sense, express provisions covering these commonly recurring issues seem desirable.

§ 19.6 Inspection of Shareholders Lists

Every corporation must maintain "a record of its shareholders, in a form that permits preparation of a list of the names and addresses of all shareholders in alphabetical order by class of shares showing the number and class of shares held by each." [MBCA (1984) § 16.01(c)] This is a list of record owners, not beneficial owners. This record is subject to the statutory or common law right of inspection possessed by every shareholder. In contrast, the voting list compiled immediately before the meeting (see § 9.5 of this Nutshell) is automatically open to inspection by any shareholder without any proof of proper purpose before and during the shareholders meeting. There has been a substantial volume of litigation over shareholders' lists in publicly held corporations since such lists have historically been, to quote a colorful phrase, "the line of scrimmage for contests involving incumbent management, dissident shareholders, acquisition-minded corporations, and those who have been described in current fiction as 'corporate raiders'." Of course, the widespread use of nominees, street names, and the book entry system for recording ownership (see § 13.9 of this Nutshell) all greatly reduce the value of such a list from the standpoint of a potential aggressor seeking to take over a publicly held corporation. On the other hand, many institutional investors regularly disclose their entire portfolios, so that considerable information about holdings of securities in specific companies by specific institutional investors is publicly available for anyone who is willing to collect the data.

A list of names and addresses of numerous well-to-do persons is itself valuable, and at least theoretically may be sought in order to sell it to mail solicitation firms. New York and several other states specifically provide that a shareholders' list need not be produced if the applicant has offered to sell or assisted another person in the sale or offering for sale of a shareholders' list within the preceding five years. The modern use of nominees, street names, and the book entry system in publicly held corporations largely deprive this list of commercial value and there appears to have been no recent case involving sales of lists of record shareholders.

Much of the litigation dealing with shareholders' lists involves closely held corporations and the "proper purpose" test. Generally it has been held that it is a proper purpose to desire to communicate with other shareholders about matters of corporate concern: to solicit proxies, to initiate a proxy contest, to publicize mismanagement, to discuss a derivative suit, to discuss proposals of management, to form a protective committee, and the like. It has also been held to be a proper purpose to communicate to other shareholders an offer to purchase the shares of the corporation. Courts probably tend to be more lenient in granting access to shareholders' lists than to other books and records. However, it has been held that it is not a proper purpose to seek the list in order to sell to the shareholders securities of unrelated corporations

In a Viet Nam war era case, it was held that a purpose to seek the list in order to communicate one's own social or political views to shareholders of a publicly held corporation was not a proper purpose. Where a corporation is large enough to be registered under section 12 of the Securities Exchange Act of 1934 (500 shareholders of record of any class and $5,000,000 of assets), the federal proxy regulations provide an alternative basis for an inspection of the shareholders' list. Rule 14a–7 requires a corporation either to supply a shareholders' list or to mail solicitations to shareholders on behalf of a shareholder upon payment of the postage by that shareholder. The corporation will usually elect the latter alternative.

One case that predates the creation of the book entry system for holding shares of publicly held corporations holds that a solicitation of shareholders asking them to join in a request for a shareholders' list (in order to meet the 5 per cent requirement of state law) is itself a solicitation under the proxy rules, and requires filing with the Securities and Exchange Commission if more than ten such solicitations are made. Studebaker Corp. v. Gittlin (2d Cir.1966).

§ 19.7   Financial Reports for Shareholders

Corporations that have a class of securities registered under section 12 of the Securities Exchange Act of 1934 must provide shareholders with annual reports that contain audited financial statements. Such corporations also must file data with the SEC on a quarterly and annual basis that is immediately made publicly available, and is widely disseminated.

In many states, there is no requirement that corporations provide any financial information at all to shareholders, though some states provide that tax returns or annual reports filed with state officials may be inspected by shareholders.

Section 16.20 of the 1984 Model Act requires all corporations to provide at least some financial data to shareholders. Because many small corporations do not have auditors or accountants, the requirement is carefully phrased so as not to impose unreasonable burdens on small corporations. However, section 16.20(a) requires a corporation that prepares financial statements on the basis of generally accepted accounting principles to prepare annual financial reports to shareholders on the same basis.

[For unfamiliar terms see the Glossary]

CHAPTER TWENTY

ORGANIC CHANGES: AMENDMENTS, MERGERS, AND DISSOLUTION

§ 20.1 Amendments to Articles of Incorporation In General

Articles of incorporation may be freely amended subject only to the broad requirement that the amended articles of incorporation may contain only provisions that may be lawfully contained in original articles of incorporation at the time of the amendment. MBCA (1984) § 10.01(a). Additionally, if a change in shares or rights of shareholders, or an exchange, reclassification or cancellation of shares or rights is to be made in connection with the amendment, either the articles of amendment, or the amendments themselves, must set forth the provisions necessary to effectuate the change, exchange, reclassification, or cancellation. MBCA (1984) § 10.06(3).

Under the Model Business Corporation Act (1984) and most state statutes, the board of directors must first recommend that an amendment be adopted before it can be considered by the shareholders. The board has a "gate keeper" function in this regard; its favorable recommendation is necessary before the shareholders may even consider a proposed amendment. The board of directors has a similar function in connection with mergers, sales of assets requiring approval of the shareholders, and other organic changes discussed in this chapter. Shareholders may be able to act by unanimous or majority written consent without prior recommendation of the board of directors pursuant to specific statutory provision.

States require amendments to articles of incorporation to be approved by a super-majority vote. Older statutes generally require a two-thirds vote of approval by all outstanding shares, voting and non-voting. Most states today, however, follow the less restrictive requirement of MBCA (1984) and require amendments to be approved by only an absolute majority of the voting shares. The Model Business Corporation Act even reduces this requirement in certain situations. See MBCA (1984) § 10.03(e).

A final set of principles with respect to fundamental changes generally is that there is a broad equitable principle that directors and majority shareholders must act in a fair way toward the corporation and minority shareholders. This principle may provide entry into the courtroom for minority shareholders who claim that an amendment serves no purpose other than injuring minority shareholders. In other words, vindictive amendments that seem to serve no purpose other than to enrich the majority at the expense of the minority may be subject to attack on fiduciary principles. The test may be phrased as "good faith" or "reasonableness" or "conflict of interest." (See §§ 14.9, 14.14 of this Nutshell.) An obligation of full disclosure may also exist under the federal securities laws if a proxy is being solicited.

§ 20.2 Vested Rights

Under modern statutes no shareholder has a vested right in any specific provision in articles of incorporation. MBCA (1984) § 10.01(b). It is therefore possible for the majority of the shareholders to adopt amendments that dramatically change or eliminate the rights of minority shareholders or the rights of holders of classes of nonvoting or senior securities. Shareholders may mistakenly believe that provisions of articles of incorporation that are significant to them can be changed only with their consent. That position is erroneous in most states: while it is possible that a court might give shareholders protection not found in the statute, on the basis of self dealing or fiduciary principles in connection with an amendment, one can hardly count on it. As a result, careful attention must be given to the procedural protections provided in the corporation statutes, and if the statutory protections are not adequate, special voting requirements should be insisted on if a veto power is to be assured.

Some early judicial decisions evolved the theory that certain rights, such as accrued cumulative dividend rights of preferred shares, are "contractual" or "vested" rights and cannot be eliminated over the objection of the shareholder by an amendment to the articles of incorporation. In order to reverse these decisions decisively and unambiguously the statutes of many states contain a nonexclusive "laundry list" of permissible amendments. In the Revised Model Business Corporation Act this "laundry list" appears in the Official Comment rather than in the statute itself. Among the powers referred to in this list are the following:

Amendments increasing or decreasing the number of shares a corporation is authorized to issue;

Amendments exchanging, classifying, reclassifying, or canceling any part of a corporation's shares, whether or not previously issued;

Amendments limiting or canceling the right of holders of a class of shares to receive dividends, whether or not the dividends or rights to receive the dividends had accumulated in the past;

Amendments creating new classes of shares whether superior or inferior to shares already outstanding, or changing the designations of shares or the preferences, limitations, or rights of classes of shares, whether or not previously issued; and

Amendments changing the voting rights of outstanding shares, including elimination of the power to vote cumulatively or assigning multiple or fractional votes per share, or denying the power to vote entirely to classes of shares, whether or not previously issued.

In the Model Business Corporation Act (1984) and the statutes of most states there are two basic protections against abuse of the majority's power of amendment: first, the right to vote by classes on specified kinds of amendments discussed immediately below[in the MBCA (1984) this right is described as the right to vote by "voting groups," but the concept is the same]; and second, the statutory right of dissent and appraisal described in § 20.8 of this Nutshell.

It should be added parenthetically that not all statutes contain all of these broad provisions; in some states there may be limitations on the power of amendment, though there is not in most states.

§ 20.3 Voting by Classes

One major protection of shareholders against unacceptable amendments imposed by other classes of shares is the right to vote by class (or "by voting groups") on specific amendments. The scope of this right depends on the specific statute, but generally, the objective is to require class voting on all amendments that are burdensome to a single class as such and beneficial to other classes. See MBCA (1984) § 10.04. Class voting may also be negotiated and be included and be placed in the articles of incorporation as part of that class's "contract" with the corporation. The discussion below is limited to the statutory protection of class voting.

The concept of class voting is quite simple. A class of shares are entitled to vote as a class if *the class* is affected in one of the ways specified by the statute. In most states amendments that require class voting must be approved by the required percentage (either an absolute majority or two-thirds) of each class voting as a separate class, and in addition, by the required percentage of all voting shares in the aggregate entitled to vote on the amendment. Classes of shares that are specifically designated as nonvoting are nevertheless entitled to vote as a class if they are affected in one of the ways specified in the statute. See MBCA (1984) § 10.04(d). This is class veto not individual shareholder veto. The basic idea is that if the specified percentage of a class of shares is willing to accept a real or potentially burdensome amendment, the balance of the class may not block it (though dissenting members may have the statutory right of dissent and appraisal.)

In some situations, one class of shares may be entitled to be counted in two separate elections: the class election and the general vote on the amendment by shares entitled to vote generally. More typically, however, the class of shares that is entitled to vote as a class will not have been given the right to vote generally, and therefore they participate only in the class vote.

The concept of "voting groups" in the Revised Model Business Corporation Act is identical to the traditional class voting. Because the MBCA (1984) permits some series of shares to vote as separate classes in some circumstances [see MBCA (1984) §§ 10.04(b) and (c)], and requires two or more series in some situations to be combined into a single voting group, a new linguistic convention was necessary to distinguish between voting units and classes as set forth in the articles of incorporation. See MBCA (1984) §§ 1.40(26), 7.25, 7.26. The term "voting groups" is also less confusing linguistically and is used hereafter to describe the basic class voting concept.

Section 10.04(a) of the MBCA (1984) lists nine types of proposed amendments that trigger the right of a class of shares to vote as a separate voting group on an amendment: amendments that would increase or decrease the number of authorized shares of that class; that would effect an exchange or reclassification (or create a right to exchange or reclassify) of shares of that class into shares of another class; that would permit shares of some other class to be exchanged or reclassified into shares of the class; that would change the designations, rights, preferences or limitations of all or part of the class; that would change some or all of the shares of that class into a different number of shares of the same class; that would create a new class of shares having rights or preferences prior to, superior to, or substantially equal with the class; change the rights of some other class so that they will then have rights or preferences prior to, superior to, or substantially equal with the class; that would limit or deny an existing preemptive right of the class; and that would cancel or affect cumulative dividends to which the class is entitled. Each of these types of amendments that trigger the right to vote as a separate voting group has the characteristic of harming the class as such.

§ 20.4 Mergers and Consolidations

Business corporation acts specifically authorize several types or kinds of corporate amalgamations:

(1) The merger of one domestic corporation into another domestic corporation;

(2) The consolidation of two domestic corporations into a new domestic corporation;

(3) The merger or consolidation of a domestic corporation and a foreign corporation, with the surviving or new corporation being either a domestic or a foreign corporation.

(4) In about a dozen states, the mandatory exchange of shares of one corporation for shares, cash, or other consideration provided by another corporation.

(5) In a handful of states, a corporation may be able to "convert" itself into another business form, such as a

limited liability company or limited partnership, without undergoing a formal dissolution and reconstitution in the new business form.

Technically a "merger" of corporation A into corporation B means that corporation B survives and corporation A disappears, while in a "consolidation" of corporation A and corporation B, both corporations disappear and a new corporation C is created. The Model Business Corporation Act (1984) does not recognize the consolidation as a separate amalgamation device; the Official Comment states that such a device is obsolete since it almost always is advantageous for one entity or the other to survive, and if it is not, it is always possible to create a new entity and merge the other corporations into it.

These statutory methods of amalgamations are often simply described as "statutory mergers" to distinguish them from the asset-purchase and stock-purchase transactions described immediately below. Upon a statutory merger, the surviving or new corporation automatically has title to all assets of the disappearing corporations, and assumes all the liabilities of those corporations. Shareholders in all the corporations involved are entitled to receive whatever consideration is specified in the plan of merger.

A statutory merger or consolidation is only one of several possible ways of effecting a corporate acquisition or creating an amalgamated corporation out of formerly independent operations. The Internal Revenue Code has its own set of definitions that provide a useful summary of non-statutory amalgamation techniques. It describes a statutory merger or consolidation as a class "A" reorganization, and the most important alternative types are class "B" and "C" reorganizations.

A class "B" reorganization occurs when one corporation exchanges its voting shares for all or most of the outstanding shares of the other corporation, if the acquiring corporation has control of the other corporation immediately after the transaction. The distinguishing feature of a class B reorganization is that it involves an acquisition of stock. Two possible disadvantages of a stock acquisition are that the acquiring corporation may have to deal with a fairly large number of sellers, and the acquired business remains liable for all undisclosed or unknown liabilities, such as income tax deficiencies of prior years. This transaction often is referred to as a "stock purchase" or "stock acquisition" transaction.

A class "C" reorganization occurs when one corporation exchanges its voting shares for the assets of another corporation. The purchase may include all or most of the assets of the acquired corporation, or may include only the assets used in one line of business. After the transaction is completed, the acquired corporation remains in existence with assets consisting primarily of the proceeds of the sale. It also remains liable for liabilities not expressly assumed by the purchaser. Usually such a corporation will thereafter liquidate after making provision for liabilities not assumed by the purchaser, distributing the remaining proceeds to its shareholders. However, such a corporation may continue in existence operating as a holding or investment corporation. This transaction is often referred to as an "asset purchase" or "asset acquisition" transaction.

Another alternative, of course, is to structure an acquisition as a stock for cash or assets for cash transaction. Those transactions are taxable events, involving the recognition of gain or loss, and the establishment of a new tax basis for the assets or stock acquired. The statutory mergers and reorganizations described above involve transactions that do not give rise to taxable gain or loss.

Clearly, the same basic economic result can be reached by casting a transaction in the form of a statutory merger, a Class B or C reorganization, a stock purchase, or an asset purchase. The question as to which form a particular transaction should take is a complex one, involving a variety of tax and non-tax considerations. Often the parties to a specific transaction will have different views on which form of transaction is most desirable.

Because of the similar economic effect no matter which form is followed, there is a possibility that the selection of a particular form to achieve some goal, such as not assuming certain types of liabilities, will not be successful. A court may reject form, "look at substance," and recast the transaction into a different form. This is the "de facto merger" notion, adopted in Farris v. Glen Alden Corp. (Pa.1958). The court held in that case that dissenting shareholders had the appraisal rights of a statutory merger despite the fact that the transaction was cast as an asset acquisition transaction. In this transaction the "selling" corporation sold assets for shares of the acquiring corporation and was required to dissolve and distribute the shares to its shareholders after the completion of the transaction. Because the "selling" corporation was much larger than the "acquiring" corporation, the latter dominated the former after the transaction in all material respects. The court referred to this transaction as a "hybrid form of corporate amalgamation" and said:

[I]t is no longer helpful to consider an individual transaction in the abstract and solely by reference to the various elements there in determining whether it is a "merger" or a "sale." Instead, to determine properly the nature of a corporate transaction, we must refer not only to all the provisions of the agreement, but also to the consequences of the transaction and to the purposes of the provisions of the corporation law said to be applicable.

Several cases are contra to *Farris,* and most academic writing has been highly critical of the de facto merger

doctrine, since it makes rational corporate planning difficult if not impossible in many situations.

§ 20.5 Triangular Mergers, Cash Mergers, Short Form Mergers, and Related Developments

Until about 1960, statutory mergers and consolidations
contemplated that mergers involved the amalgamation of
two independent businesses into a single entity, and that
all shareholders in a disappearing corporation would receive shares in the surviving corporation in exchange for
their shares in the disappearing corporation. These notions are now obsolete; today the consideration in a
statutory merger may consist in whole or in part of cash or
property other than shares, and most mergers do not
involve the amalgamation of corporations of approximately the same size with both sets of shareholders being
involved in the combined enterprise. Rather, they usually
involve acquisition-type transactions, the elimination of
minority interests in corporations for cash, the change in
the state of incorporation of a corporation, or some other
unexpected kind of transaction that at first blush has
nothing to do with the traditional concept of a merger,
but which can be effectuated through a statutory merger.
These transactions are possible because modern merger
statutes permit a merger agreement to be extremely flexible. The merger statutes of most states now provide
expressly that one or more parties to the merger may have
their shares converted by the merger into "shares, obligations or other securities of the surviving corporation or
any other corporation, or into cash or other property in
whole or part." [MBCA (1984) § 11.01(a)(3)]

Many mergers today are triangular or reverse-triangular
mergers, or some variation of them. In a triangular merger
the acquiring corporation forms a wholly owned subsidiary, "drops" cash or its own shares into that subsidiary,

and then merges the corporation being acquired into the subsidiary. The shareholders of the acquired corporation may receive the cash or shares of the acquiring corporation (not, it should be noted, shares of the subsidiary into which the acquired corporation is merged). In this way, the acquiring corporation acquires all of the shares of the acquired corporation; the shareholders of the acquired corporation receive cash or marketable shares of the acquiring corporation, and that corporation does not become individually responsible for liabilities of the acquired corporation.

A reverse-triangular merger is a more complex transaction in which a new wholly-owned subsidiary is merged *into* the acquired corporation (which therefore ends up being a wholly-owned subsidiary of the acquiring corporation). The shares of the subsidiary momentarily held by the acquiring corporation are exchanged for newly issued shares of the acquired corporation and the shareholders of the acquired corporation receive cash or shares of the acquiring corporation in exchange for their shares of the acquired corporation. As a result, the acquired corporation becomes a wholly-owned subsidiary of the acquiring corporation and unassignable government contracts or non-transferable tax characteristics will be (hopefully) unaffected. The critical point here is not the detail of the transactions: indeed, one commentator has stated that the "procedure is a magical one" and those who claim to understand it fully "are under an illusion." Rather, the critical point is that in both instances a three-way merger is used as an acquisition device and the acquired corporation's shareholders receive cash or shares of the parent corporation even though the merger is with a subsidiary of the parent corporation. (In these situations, the parent corporation is usually a publicly held corporation and a market exists for its shares; the subsidiary is created solely for the purpose of the particular transaction and obviously there is no market for its shares.)

Section 11.02 of the Model Business Corporation Act (1984) creates a mandatory "share exchange" procedure as a substitute for a reverse triangular merger. This transaction is misnamed; it is not so much an exchange of shares as it is a device to compel a mandatory sale of shares. Under this procedure, a corporation may adopt a plan by which all of its shares are sold upon approval by a majority of the shareholders. Shareholders who object to the sale are nevertheless bound by it but have a statutory right of dissent and appraisal.

§ 20.6 Cash-Out Mergers

These modern merger statutes permit another type of transaction, the "cash merger" (or "freeze out" or "squeeze out" merger, as they sometimes are called). In these transactions, certain shareholders are compelled to accept cash or property for their shares. Such a merger is in effect a device to force out or chase out unwanted shareholders.

For example, a corporation might merge into its own subsidiary with the majority shareholders receiving stock in the subsidiary and the minority shareholders being compelled to accept a specified amount of cash for their shares. This procedure may be used not only to force out unwanted minority shareholders, but also to eliminate all public shareholders in a "going private" transaction or to "mop up" the non-selling shareholders following a successful tender offer. It also permits a majority shareholder in a corporate subsidiary to eliminate unwanted minority shareholders in that subsidiary.

Transactions of this nature raise two basic questions to be addressed in §§ 20.9 and 20.11 of this Nutshell: (1) may such transactions be attacked on the ground that they lack any business purpose other than freezing or squeezing out a minority, or are unfair to the minority, and (2) are statutory appraisal rights an adequate protection for the frozen- or squeezed-out shareholder?

§ 20.7   "Upstream" and "Downstream" Mergers

A somewhat parallel development to cash-out mergers has occurred in a related area: mergers between parent corporations and their subsidiaries. Such a merger is referred to as an "up stream" merger if the surviving corporation is the parent corporation and a "down stream" merger if the surviving corporation is the subsidiary.

A good example of a downstream merger occurs when a publicly held corporation wishes to change its state of incorporation. It creates a wholly-owned subsidiary in the new state of incorporation, and then merges itself into its subsidiary in a downstream merger with all shares and financial interests of the parent being mirrored in the subsidiary. When the merger occurs, each shareholder and creditor of the old publicly held corporation incorporated in State A automatically becomes a shareholder in a corporation incorporated in State B.

§ 20.8   Short Form Mergers

Many states have adopted statutes that provide a special summary merger procedure for upstream mergers by which a parent corporation, owning a large majority but less than all (e.g., 90 or 95 per cent) of the subsidiary's shares, may merge the subsidiary into the parent without a shareholders' vote of either corporation. [MBCA (1984) § 11.04] This procedure is called a "short form merger." The theoretical basis of omitting both votes is that (1) a vote of the subsidiary's shareholders is unnecessary because the minority shareholders are, in any event, unable to block the merger, and (2) a vote of the parent's shareholders is unnecessary because the merger will not materially affect their rights which already include a 90 or 95 per cent interest in the subsidiary. The latter conclusion is based on the relatively slight increase in the parent's interest in the subsidiary resulting from the merger.

The major practical justification for the short form merger statute is that it effectuates a saving of the cost of proxy solicitations and meetings where the parent corporation is publicly held. The short form merger procedure creates no appraisal rights on the part of dissenting shareholders of the parent though it does for minority shareholders of the subsidiary who are "cashed out."

Short form merger statutes are applicable only to upstream mergers; they are not applicable to downstream mergers of the type used, for example, in changing the state of incorporation.

The most difficult theoretical problem with the short form merger statute lies in its treatment of the minority shareholders of the subsidiary. In a merger between independent corporations, it is unlikely that the shareholders of a corporation will approve a merger that is unfair to them if there has been full and accurate disclosure. However, in the merger of a subsidiary into its parent, no such automatic protection exists against terms unfair to the subsidiary's minority shareholders; indeed, terms that are unfair to the minority shareholders are advantageous from the standpoint of the majority shareholder who is the parent. The short form merger statute attempts to avoid this problem by creating appraisal rights. (See § 20.11 of this Nutshell.)

§ 20.9   Fiduciary Duties in Mergers

The developments discussed above—cash mergers, going private transactions, short form mergers, and related practices—raise the question whether courts should have any role in judging or evaluating these transactions so long as the formal statutory procedural requirements have been complied with. Despite some academic argument that (1) courts should not judge motive or subjective fairness, and (2) judicial review should be limited to assuring that the minority protection devices granted by statute are made available, the case law has developed in the opposite direction.

Cases recognize that cash mergers and related practices are self-dealing transactions that must be judged by fiduciary principles applicable to those transactions. See § 14.10 of this Nutshell. The reason for this should be obvious when it is recognized that the price being offered minority shareholders in these types of transactions is in effect being set by the majority. The first case clearly accepting this principle was Singer v. Magnavox Co. (Del. 1977) which established a dual test: the transaction must have a "business purpose" and the transaction must meet a standard of "intrinsic" or "entire" fairness. Other states quickly followed the lead of Delaware in this regard. However, in Delaware the court, after struggling in several cases with the meaning of "business purpose," concluded in Weinberger v. UOP, Inc. (Del.1983) that the "business purpose" test provided little or no protection to shareholders and eliminated it; the court continued to apply a strict "intrinsic fairness" test that includes a requirement of full and meaningful disclosure. These cases are analyzed in § 14.15 of this Nutshell. The court also concluded that in the future the remedy in the event of a claim of inadequate price should be limited to a more generous appraisal remedy (see § 20.11 of this Nutshell) than was available in Delaware previously.

Some courts in other states continue to apply a "business purpose" test in evaluating cash out transactions. Both New York and Massachusetts, for example, apparently still impose the dual test derived from *Singer*.

These fiduciary duty tests for cash merger and similar transactions were developed by state courts as a matter of state law. An attempt to find a "fairness" standard in rule 10b–5 to evaluate such transactions was rejected by the United States Supreme Court in Santa Fe Industries, Inc. v. Green (S.Ct.1977), holding that the essence of a rule 10b–5 violation was nondisclosure or misrepresentation of material facts. As a result of this holding, judicial controls over the transactions described in this section are solely within the province of state courts.

§ 20.10   Sales of All or Substantially All the Assets of a Corporation

A sale, lease, exchange, or other disposition of all, or substantially all, the property and assets of a corporation, not in the usual and regular course of business, must, under the statutes of most states, be approved by the shareholders as an organic change in the corporation. MBCA (1984) § 12.02. If the transaction is in the ordinary course of business (as may be the case with a corporation that is in the business of buying and selling real estate), shareholder approval is not usually required. MBCA (1984) § 12.01. Most states specifically consider a pledge, mortgage, or deed of trust covering all the assets of the corporation to be within the ordinary course of business and therefore shareholder approval is not required. Section 12.01 also includes deployment of assets through a wholly-owned subsidiary as a transaction not requiring shareholder approval.

The phrase "all or substantially all" has received varied judicial treatment. Most courts have construed this language flexibly, and required shareholder approval when significant components of a corporation are sold even though other significant components are retained. The Official Comment to section 12.01 of the Model Business Corporation Act (1984) suggests that this phrase is synonymous with "all or nearly all" and "was added merely to make clear that the statutory requirements could not be avoided by retention of some minimal or nominal residue of the original assets." Most decisions have not adopted this stricter approach.

In most states, shareholders have a statutory right of dissent and appraisal in connection with transactions involving the disposition of substantially all the assets of the corporation not in the ordinary course of business. MBCA (1984) § 13.02(a)(3).

When a corporation sells substantially all its assets, the business is normally continued by the purchaser of the assets, though it may be broadened or narrowed in scope, and the selling corporation thereafter dissolves and distributes the proceeds of the sale to its shareholders. In such a transaction, the purchaser may assume specified liabilities arising in the ordinary course of business, but typically will expressly not assume any other liabilities of the enterprise, known or unknown. Following the sale, the selling corporation will discharge unassumed obligations of which it is aware before it distributes the remaining assets to its shareholders. However, provision will usually not be made for unknown liabilities or liabilities that may arise in the future. A major problem is created if persons are thereafter injured by products manufactured by the selling corporation. The injuries may occur many years after the transaction in question was closed and many years after the dissolution of the selling corporation. The purchaser of the assets (that is continuing the business) is invariably sued in this situation, and typically argues that it is not liable because it did not expressly or impliedly assume products liabilities in connection with the asset purchase. In recent years, many courts have evolved theories of de facto merger, continuity of business, or product line liability by which the purchaser may be held liable for such claims despite the absence of an express assumption of liability (or, indeed, despite an express negation of any such assumption). A number of courts, however, have also declined to impose liability on the purchaser in this situation, either because of the specific facts of the transaction or by rejecting broad theories by which liability might be imposed.

A corporation that sells substantially all of its assets may not dissolve. It may thereafter deploy its assets by purchasing or creating another business. Arguably, shareholder approval should be required before such a radical change in the nature of the corporation's business is made. Or it may simply invest the proceeds in marketable securities and continue in business. Such a corporation is taxed as a personal holding company if the number of shareholders is small.

§ 20.11 The Right of Dissent and Appraisal

State statutes give shareholders the right to dissent from certain types of transactions and to obtain the appraised value of their shares through a judicial proceeding. MBCA (1984) ch. 13. Since this right is entirely the creature of statute, it is generally thought to be available only when the statute expressly provides that it is available. In a handful of cases, however, innovative courts have created appraisal-type remedies in non-statutory situations.

The remedy of dissent and appraisal was originally created as part of the decision to liberalize the rules relating to shareholder approval of fundamental transactions at the beginning of this Century; statutes in the Nineteenth Century usually required unanimous consent, a rule that permitted a small minority to block a decision desired by the large majority. In exchange for eliminating this individual shareholder veto, shareholders who objected to the transaction were given the right to be bought out at an appraised price. Today, this remedy serves the quite different purpose of assuring that controlling shareholders offer a fair price in cash out and related transactions in which minority shareholders are compelled to accept cash for their shares.

The statutory appraisal remedy is surrounded by elaborate statutory procedures and the right may be lost if these procedures are not precisely followed. If the right is lost, the dissenting shareholder must go along with the objectionable transaction. These procedures, which are designed to indicate to the corporation the number of dissenting shareholders, may have made sense in the original conception of the right of dissent and appraisal. Today, however, they tend to be a trap for the unwary frozen-out shareholder, who may well lose his right of dissent if mandatory notice and other requirements are not complied with.

Under section 13.02 of the Model Business Corporation Act the appraisal right is extended to regular mergers, short form mergers (shareholders of the subsidiary only), compulsory share exchanges, sales of substantially all corporate assets not in the ordinary course of business, and specific types of adverse amendments to articles of incorporation. The standards for determining when the right of dissent and appraisal exists in section 13.02 differ to some extent from the standards (described in § 20.3 of this Nutshell) for determining when shares are entitled to vote by classes (or by voting groups) in section 10.04. The MBCA (1984) limits the right of dissent and appraisal basically to shares that are entitled to vote on the transaction, but many states do not impose this limitation and may permit nonvoting shares to elect to dissent from specific transactions.

The statutes of many states purport to make the statutory appraisal remedy exclusive in the absence of fraud, though some states purport to make it exclusive without exception, and some make it nonexclusive in all cases. Section 13.02(b) of the Model Business Corporation Act (1984) follows the New York statute and makes that remedy exclusive "unless the action is unlawful or fraudulent with respect to the shareholder or the corporation."

The Delaware Supreme Court in Weinberger v. UOP, Inc. (Del.1983) indicated that in the future, shareholders objecting to cash mergers solely on the basis of inadequate price must rely on the appraisal remedy rather than seek recissory damages or an order setting aside the transaction. (See § 20.5 of this Nutshell.) The court also relaxed the principles previously applicable in Delaware to determine the value of shares in appraisal proceedings, which should also make that remedy more attractive. Cede & Co. v. Technicolor, Inc. (Del.1988) permits the plaintiff in an appraisal proceeding to maintain simultaneously a suit for recissory damages based on a breach of fiduciary duty discovered after the appraisal proceeding was commenced.

Because appraisal claims may constitute serious cash drains, it is not uncommon in merger and other agreements to provide an "out" for the parties if an excessive number of dissents are filed. Following the affirmative vote on the proposal, the dissenting shareholder automatically has the status of creditor rather than shareholder. The MBCA (1984) sets forth an elaborate procedure by which the shareholder must designate in writing a price at which he or she is willing to sell, the corporation must respond by setting a written price at which it is willing to buy; if negotiation fails, a court proceeding to establish the appraised price follows. This appraised price is to be fixed as of a time immediately before the transaction in question is to occur, but no account is to be taken of the potential impact of the transaction on the value of the shares.

The traditional appraisal remedy has a superficial appeal and plausibility. However, from the dissenting shareholder's point of view it is usually not an attractive remedy, and there has been considerable litigation by parties seeking to avoid appraisal proceedings and suing on breach of fiduciary duties or other theories. Not only does the process involve potentially long delays while the price is established, but litigation over the value of shares is likely to be expensive and unrewarding. Since the corporation is an active participant in the judicial proceeding seeking to establish the lowest possible valuation, the cards are to some extent stacked against the dissenting shareholders. They must accept the judicially determined price which may be based primarily on the evidence and materials presented by the corporation with its extensive knowledge about its own affairs and virtually unlimited resources. Finally, the corporation in many states may pay nothing until the proceeding is completed years later, and many corporations have apparently decided to litigate at leisure in an effort to wear down the dissenting shareholders. Further, some states calculate interest on a simple interest basis, which further reduces the attractiveness of this remedy.

Chapter 13 of the Revised Model Business Corporation Act was designed to make the appraisal remedy more attractive and useful. On the one hand, provisions were included requiring potential dissenters to identify themselves as early as possible so that corporations would know the extent of the potential liability. Further, when the corporation estimates the value of the dissenters' shares, it must pay that amount immediately without waiting for a final disposition of the proceeding. Procedures are also established that are designed to encourage a negotiated price rather than a litigated price; if a judicial appraisal is necessary, the court has authority to award costs, including attorneys' fees, either for or against the corporation depending on the court's estimate as to whether valuations were made in good faith.

The statutes of many states contain a "market exception" to the appraisal remedy. Under these statutes, the right to dissent does not exist if there is a market for the shares in question. Earlier versions of the Model Business Corporation Act contained such a provision, but it is not included in the Model Business Corporation Act. The theory behind the market exception is that the dissent remedy is appropriate only for minority shareholders locked into the corporation, and that there is no need for a statutory appraisal if an established market exists for the dissenters' shares. The argument against such a restriction basically is that the modern purpose of the appraisal remedy is to protect shareholders against unattractive cash-out transactions.

§ 20.12 Voluntary Dissolution

Most state statutes contain a variety of dissolution provisions. These include streamlined provisions for dissolution before commencement of business by the incorporators or initial directors and dissolution at any time with the unanimous consent of the shareholders. The regular dissolution process involves adoption of a resolution to dissolve by the board of directors and approval of it by a majority or some other specified percentage of the shareholders. In this regard, dissolution is similar to other organic changes by the corporation in which the board of directors serves a gate keeping function.

Some older states require the filing of a notice of intent to dissolve, followed by a period in which the business and affairs of the corporation are wound up, followed by the filing of final articles of dissolution. In other states, only articles of dissolution are filed when the corporate affairs are wound up. Irrespective of the type of statute involved, notice to creditors must be given, and final dissolution is permitted only after all franchise and other tax obligations have been fully satisfied. Directors are under a fiduciary duty to pay, discharge, or make provision for all known liabilities of the corporation before making final liquidating distributions to shareholders.

State statutes provide that the existence of a corporation continues after dissolution for a stated period so that the corporation may be sued on claims. A major problem in post-dissolution litigation is the status of tort claimants who are injured by products manufactured by the corporation after the corporation has dissolved. The stated period in which suit must be brought may also have expired before the injury occurred. If the corporation sold its operating assets before dissolving, suits by such claimants may be brought against the purchaser of the assets on theories of de facto merger, continuity of enterprise, or similar theories.

For obvious reasons, there is no statutory right of appraisal in connection with a voluntary dissolution. There may be, however, some equitable limitations on the power to dissolve. These involve situations where a voluntary dissolution is arguably unfair to minority shareholders or which may constitute a "freeze out" of such shareholders. Cases have arisen where the objective of dissolution was apparently to eliminate some shareholders from sharing in the profits of a desirable business, or where the proposal was not to discontinue the business, but to turn it over to a new corporation owned by some but not all of the original owners. Were such behavior sanctioned, a minority could be ejected from a successful venture through the process of dissolution as readily as through a cash merger. If so, the test of "entire fairness" developed in the merger cases should logically apply to at least some statutory dissolutions as well.

[For unfamiliar terms see the Glossary]

GLOSSARY

ADOPTION is a contract principle by which a person agrees to assume a contract previously made for his or her benefit. An adoption speaks only from the time such person agrees, in contrast to a "ratification" which relates back to the time the original contract was made. In corporation law, the concept is applied when a newly formed corporation accepts a preincorporation contract made for its benefit by a promoter.

ADVANCES FOR EXPENSES refers to the payment of litigation expenses of a director or officer prior to the determination whether the director or officer has violated a duty to the corporation. See *indemnification.*

AFFILIATE is a corporation that is related to another corporation by shareholdings or other means of control. It includes not only a parent or a subsidiary but also corporations that are under common control.

AGGRESSOR CORPORATION is a corporation that attempts to obtain control of a publicly held corporation, often by a direct cash tender or public exchange offer to shareholders, but also possibly by way of merger, which requires agreement or assent of the target's management.

ALL HOLDERS' RULE is a rule adopted by SEC that prohibits a public offer by the issuer of shares to all but certain designated shareholders.

ALTER EGO literally means "other self" and is a phrase used in piercing the corporate veil cases.

AMORTIZATION is an accounting procedure that gradually reduces the cost or value of a limited life or intangible asset through periodic charges against income. For fixed assets amortization is called "depreciation," and for wasting assets (natural resources) it is "depletion." The periodic charges are usually treated as current expenses for purposes of determining income.

AMOTION is the common law procedure by which a director may be removed for cause by the shareholders.

ANTI-DILUTION PROVISIONS appear in convertible securities to guarantee that the conversion privilege is not affected by share reclassifications, share splits, share dividends, or similar transactions that may increase the number of outstanding shares without increasing the corporate capital.

APPRAISAL in corporation law is a limited statutory right granted to minority shareholders who object to specified fundamental transactions, e.g. mergers. In an appraisal proceeding a court determines the value of their shares and the corporation pays that value to the dissenting shareholders in cash. The Model Business Corporation Act (1984) uses the term "dissenters' rights to obtain payment for their shares" to describe this right.

ARBITRAGEURS are market investors who take off-setting positions in the same or similar securities in order to profit from small price variations. An arbitrageur, for example, may buy shares on the Pacific Coast Exchange and simultaneously sell the same shares on the New York Stock Exchange if any price discrepancy occurs between the quotations in the two markets. By taking advantage of momentary disparities in prices between markets, arbitrageurs perform the economic function of making those markets more efficient.

ARBS is a slang term for arbitrageurs.

ARTICLES OF INCORPORATION is the name customarily given to the document that is filed in order to form a corporation. Under various state statutes, this document may be called the "certificate of incorporation," "charter," "articles of association," or other similar name.

AUTHORIZED SHARES are the shares described in the articles of incorporation which a corporation may issue. Modern corporate practice recommends authorization of more shares than it is currently planned to issue.

BENEFICIAL HOLDERS OF SECURITIES are persons who own shares but who have not registered the shares in their names on the records of the corporation. See also: record owner.

BLOCKAGE is a price phenomenon: a large block of shares may be more difficult to market than a smaller block, particularly if the market is thin. The discount at which a large block sells below the price of a smaller block is blockage. Blockage is generally a phenomenon of shares which do not represent the controlling interest in a corporation. Compare: control premium.

BLUE SKY LAWS are state statutes that regulate the sale of securities to the public within the state. Most blue sky laws require the registration of new issues of securities with a state agency that reviews selling documents for accuracy and completeness. Blue sky laws also often regulate securities brokers and salesmen.

BONDS are long term debt instruments secured by a lien on some or all the corporate property. Historically, a bond was payable to bearer and interest coupons representing annual or semi-annual payments of interest were attached (to be "clipped" periodically and submitted for payment). Today, most bonds are issued in registered or book entry form. Bondholders are creditors and not owners of the enterprise. The word bond is sometimes used more broadly to refer also to unsecured debt instruments, i.e., debentures.

BONUS SHARES are par value shares issued without consideration, usually in connection with the issuance of preferred or senior securities, or debt instruments. Bonus shares are considered a species of watered shares and may impose a liability on the recipient equal to the amount of par value.

BOOK ENTRY describes the method of reflecting ownership of publicly traded securities in which customers of brokerage firms receive confirmations of transactions and monthly statements but not certificates. Brokerage firms also may reflect their customers' ownership of securities by book entry in the records of a central clearing corporation, principally Depository Trust Company (DTC). DTC reflects transactions between brokerage firms primarily by book entry in its records rather than by the physical movement of securities. Shares held by DTC are recorded in the name of its nominee, Cede and Company.

BOOK VALUE is the value of shares determined on the basis of the books of the corporation. Using the corporation's latest balance sheet, the liabilities are subtracted from assets, an appropriate amount is deducted to reflect the interest of senior securities (preferred shares), and what remains is divided by the number of outstanding common shares to obtain the book value per share.

BROKER in a securities transaction, means a person who acts as an agent for a buyer or seller, or an intermediary between a buyer and seller, usually charging a commission. A broker who specializes in shares, bonds, commodities, or options must be registered with the exchange where the specific securities are traded. A broker should be distinguished from a dealer who, unlike a broker, buys or sells for his own account. Securities firms typically act as dealers and brokers, depending on the security involved.

BUYOUT is the purchase of a controlling percentage of a company's shares. A buyout often involves all of the company's outstanding shares. A buyout can be accomplished through negotiation, through a tender offer, or through a merger.

BYLAWS are the formal rules of internal governance adopted by a corporation. State corporation statutes contemplate that every corporation will adopt bylaws, though special close corporation statutes may make bylaws optional for qualifying close corporations.

C CORPORATION is a corporation that is subject to federal income tax at the corporate level. See S Corporation.

CALL FOR REDEMPTION. See: redemption.

CALLS are options to buy securities at a stated price for a stated period. Calls are written on a variety of indexes, foreign currencies, and other securities. The person who commits himself or herself to sell the security upon the request of the call holder is referred to as the call writer; the act of making the purchase of the securities pursuant to the call option is referred to as exercise of the option. The price at which the call is exercisable is the strike price. See also: puts.

CAPITAL STOCK is another phrase for common shares, often used when the corporation has only one class of shares outstanding.

CAPITAL SURPLUS, in the old Model Business Corporation Act nomenclature, is an equity or capital account which reflects the capital contributed for shares not allocated to stated capital: the excess of issuance price over the par value of issued shares or the consideration paid for no par shares allocated specifically to capital surplus.

CAPITALIZATION is an imprecise term that usually refers to the amounts received by a corporation for the issuance of its shares. However, it may also be used to refer to the proceeds of loans to a corporation made by its shareholders (which may be in lieu of capital contributions) or even to capital raised by the issuance of long term bonds to third persons. Depending on the context, it may also refer to accumulated earnings not withdrawn from the corporation.

CASH FLOW refers to an analysis of the movement of cash through a venture as contrasted with the earnings of the venture. For example, a mandatory debt repayment is taken into account in a cash flow analysis even though such a repayment does not reduce earnings. See: negative cash flow.

CASH MERGER is a merger transaction in which certain shareholders or interests in a corporation are required to accept cash for their shares.

CASH TENDER OFFER is a technique by which an aggressor corporation seeks to obtain control of a target corporation by making a public offer to purchase a specified fraction (usually a majority) of the target corporation's shares from persons who tender their shares.

C CORPORATION is a corporation that has not elected S corporation tax status. The taxable income of a C corporation is subject to tax at the corporate level while dividends continue to be taxed at the shareholder level.

CEDE & COMPANY is the nominee for Depository Trust Company, the principal central clearing corporation.

CEO stands for "chief executive officer" of a publicly held corporation. *CEO* is a preferred and useful designation because official titles of such persons vary widely from corporation to corporation.

CFO stands for "chief financial officer."

CLO stands for "chief legal officer."

COO stands for "chief operations officer."

CERTIFICATE OF INCORPORATION in most states is the document prepared by the Secretary of State that evidences the acceptance of articles of incorporation and the commencement of the corporate existence. In Delaware the certificate of incorporation is the name given to the document filed with the Secretary of State. The Model Business Corporation Act (1984) has eliminated certificates of incorporation, requiring only a fee receipt.

CHARTER may mean (i) the document filed with the Secretary of State, i.e., the articles of incorporation, or (ii) the grant by the State of the privilege of conducting business with limited liability. Charter is often used in a colloquial sense to refer to the basic constitutive documents of the corporation.

CLASS A SHARES. See participating preferred shares.

CLASS ACTION is a suit brought by a plaintiff in behalf of all members of a class of plaintiffs suffering a common wrong.

CLASS VOTING. See: voting group.

CLASSIFIED BOARD OF DIRECTORS may refer either (1) to a board of directors of which the individual members are elected by different classes of shares or (2) to a board of directors of which one-third or one-half are elected each year. See Staggered Board.

CLOSE CORPORATION or **CLOSELY HELD CORPORATION** is a corporation with relatively few shareholders and no regular markets for its shares. Close corporations usually have never made a public offering of shares and the shares themselves may be subject to restrictions on transfer. Close and closely held are synonymous.

COMMON SHAREHOLDERS are holders of common shares, the ultimate owners of the residual interest of a corporation.

COMMON SHARES represent the residual ownership interests in the corporation. Holders of common shares select directors to manage the enterprise, are entitled to dividends out of the earnings of the enterprise declared by the directors, and are entitled to a per share distribution of whatever assets remain upon dissolution after satisfying or making provisions for creditors and holders of senior securities.

CONSOLIDATION is an amalgamation of two corporations pursuant to statutory provision in which both of the corporations disappear and a new corporation is formed. The Model Business Corporation Act (1984) eliminates the consolidation as a distinct type of corporate amalgamation.

CONTROL OF A CORPORATION BY A PERSON normally means that the person has power to vote a majority of the outstanding shares. However, control may be reflected in a significantly smaller block if the remaining shares are scattered in small, disorganized holdings.

CONTROL PERSON in securities law is a person who is deemed to be in a control relationship with the issuer. Sales of securities by control persons are subject to many of the requirements applicable to the sale of securities directly by the issuer. In addition, controlling persons have a duty under ITSFEA to prevent insider trading by persons under their control.

CONTROL PREMIUM refers to the pricing phenomenon by which shares that carry the power to control a corporation are more valuable per share than the shares that do not carry a power of control. The control premium is often computed not on a per share basis but on the aggregate increase in value of the "control block" over the going market or other price of shares which are not part of the "control block."

CONVERSION SECURITIES are the securities into which convertible securities may be converted.

CONVERTIBLE SECURITIES are securities that include the right of exchanging the convertible securities, usually preferred shares or debentures, at the option of their holder, for a designated number of shares of another class, usually common shares, called the conversion securities. The ratio between the convertible and conversion securities is fixed at the time the convertible securities are issued, and is usually protected against dilution.

CO–PROMOTERS. See: promoters.

CORPORATE OPPORTUNITY is a fiduciary concept that limits the power of officers, directors, and employees to take personal advantage of opportunities that belong to the corporation.

CORPORATION BY ESTOPPEL is a doctrine which prevents a third person from holding an "officer," "director," or "shareholder" of a nonexistent corporation personally liable on an obligation entered into in the name of the nonexistent corporation on the theory that the third person relied on the existence of the corporation and is now "estopped" from denying that the corporation existed.

CUMULATIVE DIVIDENDS on preferred shares carry over from one year to the next if a preference dividend is omitted. An omitted cumulative dividend must be made up in a later year before any dividend may be paid on the common shares in that later year. However, cumulative dividends are not debts of the corporation but merely a right to priority in future discretionary distributions.

CUMULATIVE TO THE EXTENT EARNED DIVIDENDS on preferred shares are cumulative dividends that are limited in any one year to the available earnings of the corporation in that year.

CUMULATIVE VOTING is a method of voting that allows substantial minority shareholders to obtain representation on the board of directors. When voting cumulatively, a shareholder may cast all of his or her available votes in an election in favor of a single candidate.

D & O INSURANCE refers to directors' and officers' liability insurance. Such insurance, which is widely available commercially, insures persons against claims based on negligence, failure to disclose, and to a limited extent, other defalcations. D & O insurance provides coverage against expenses and to a limited extent fines, judgments, and amounts paid in settlement.

DEADLOCK in a closely held corporation arises when a control structure permits one or more factions of shareholders to block corporate action if they disagree with some aspect of corporate policy. A deadlock often arises with respect to the election of directors, e.g., by an equal division of shares between two factions, but may also arise at the level of the board of directors itself.

DEBENTURES are long term unsecured debt instruments. See: bonds.

DEEP ROCK DOCTRINE is a principle in bankruptcy law by which unfair or inequitable claims presented by controlling shareholders of bankrupt corporations may be subordinated to claims of general or trade creditors. The doctrine received its name from the corporate name of the subsidiary involved in the leading case articulating the doctrine.

DE FACTO CORPORATION at common law is a partially formed corporation that provides a shield against personal liability of shareholders for corporate obligations; such a corporation may be attacked only by the state.

DE FACTO MERGER is a transaction that has the economic effect of a statutory merger but is cast in the form of an acquisition of assets or an acquisition of voting stock and is treated by a court as if it were a statutory merger.

DE JURE CORPORATION at common law is a corporation that is sufficiently formed to be recognized as a corporation for all purposes. A de jure corporation may exist even though some minor statutory requirements have not been fully complied with.

DELECTUS PERSONAE is a Latin phrase used in partnership law to describe the power each partner possesses to accept or reject proposed new members of the firm.

DEPOSITORY TRUST CORPORATION is the principal central clearing agency for securities trades. See: book entry.

DEREGISTRATION of an issuer occurs when the number of securities holders of an issuer registered under section 12 of the Securities Exchange Act of 1934 has declined to the point where registration is no longer required. See: registered corporation.

DERIVATIVE SUIT is a suit brought by a shareholder in the name of a corporation to correct a wrong done to the corporation.

DILUTION of outstanding shares results from the issuance of additional shares. The dilution may be of voting power if shares are not issued proportionately to the holdings of existing shareholders, or it may be financial, if shares are issued disproportionately and the price at which the new shares are issued is less than the value of the outstanding shares prior to the issuance of the new shares.

DIRECTORY REQUIREMENTS are minor statutory requirements. At common law, a de jure corporation may be created despite the failure to comply with directory requirements relating to its formation.

DISCOUNT SHARES are par value shares issued for cash less than par value. Discount shares are a species of watered shares or watered stock.

DISSENSION in a closely held corporation refers to personal quarrels or disputes between shareholders that may make business relations unpleasant and interfere with the successful operation of the business. Dissension may occur without constituting oppression or causing a deadlock or adversely affecting the corporation's business.

DISSENTERS' RIGHT. See: appraisal.

DISTRIBUTION is a payment to shareholders by a corporation. If out of present or past earnings it is a dividend. The word distribution is sometimes accompanied by a word describing the source or purpose of the payment, e.g., Distribution of Capital Surplus, or Liquidating Distribution.

DIVIDEND is a payment to shareholders from or out of current or past earnings.

DOUBLE TAXATION refers to the structure of taxation under the Internal Revenue Code of 1954 which subjects income earned by a C corporation to an income tax at the corporate level and a second tax at the shareholder level if the previously taxed income is distributed to shareholders in the form of dividends.

DOWN STREAM MERGER is the merger of a parent corporation into its subsidiary.

EARNINGS PER SHARE equals a firm's net income divided by the number of shares held by shareholders.

EQUITY or **EQUITY INTEREST** are financial terms that refer in general to the extent of an ownership interest in a venture. In this context, equity refers not to a legal concept but to the financial definition that an owner's equity in a business is equal to the business's assets minus its liabilities.

EQUITY FINANCING is raising money by the sale of common shares or preferred shares.

EQUITY SECURITY is a security that represents an ownership interest in the business, i.e., common or preferred shares.

EX DIVIDEND refers to the date on which a purchaser of publicly traded shares is not entitled to receive a dividend that has been declared and the seller of such shares is entitled to retain the dividend. The ex dividend date is a matter of agreement or of convention to be established by the securities exchange.

EX RIGHTS refers to the date on which a purchaser of publicly traded shares is not entitled to receive rights that have been declared on the shares.

FACE VALUE is the value of a bond, note, mortgage, or other security, as stated on the certificate or instrument, payable upon maturity of the instrument. Face value is also often referred to as the par value or nominal value of the instrument.

FORCED CONVERSION refers to a conversion of a convertible security that follows a call for redemption at a time when the value of the conversion security is greater than the amount that will be received if the holder permits the security to be redeemed.

FORWARD LOOKING STATEMENT is a public statement by a corporation that makes projections of financial data, estimates of future sales or profitability, discussion of management objectives and goals, or discussion of economic trends affecting the business.

FREEZE–OUT refers to a process, usually in a closely held corporation, by which minority shareholders are prevented from receiving financial return from the corporation in an effort to persuade them to liquidate their investment in the corporation on terms favorable to the controlling shareholders.

FREEZE–OUT MERGER. See: cash merger.

GENERAL PARTNERS are partners that participate in management of the business. General partner is traditionally used in contrast with limited partner in a limited partnership, but general partner is also sometimes used to refer to any partner in a general partnership. A general partner is liable for the obligations of the business if the partnership has not elected to be a limited liability partnership.

GOING PRIVATE refers to a transaction in which shareholders of a publicly held corporation are compelled to accept cash for their shares while the business continues to be owned by officers, directors, or large shareholders. A going private transaction may involve a merger of the publicly held corporation into a subsidiary in a cash merger.

GOLDEN PARACHUTE is a slang term for a lucrative contract given to a top executive of a corporation which provides additional benefits in case the company is taken over and the executive is either forced to leave the target company or voluntarily leaves it. A golden parachute may include severance pay, stock options, or a bonus payable when the executive's employment at the company ends.

GREENMAIL is a slang term that refers to a payment by the target to a potential aggressor to purchase at a premium over market shares that have been acquired by the aggressor. The acquirer in exchange agrees not to pursue its takeover bid.

HOLDING COMPANY is a corporation that owns a majority of the shares of one or more other corporations. A holding company is not engaged in any business other than the ownership of shares. See: investment companies.

HYBRID SECURITIES are securities that have some of the attributes of both debt securities and equity securities.

INCORPORATORS are the person or persons who execute the articles of incorporation. Historic restrictions on who may serve as incorporators have largely been eliminated.

INDEMNIFICATION refers to the practice by which corporations pay expenses of officers or directors who are named as defendants in litigation relating to corporate affairs. In some instances, indemnification of judgments or settlements may also be proper.

INDENTURE is the contract which defines the rights of holders of bonds or debentures as against the corporation. Typically, the contract is entered into between the corporation and an indenture trustee whose responsibility is to protect the bondholders.

INDEPENDENT DIRECTORS are directors of a publicly held corporation who are not officers or executives of the corporation and have no substantial direct or indirect financial interest in transactions with the corporation.

IN PARI DELICTO is a common law principle also known as the "unclean hands" doctrine. The principle limits a person intending to engage in wrongful conduct from suing another wrongdoer when things do not work out as expected.

INSIDE DIRECTORS are directors of a publicly held corporation who hold executive positions with management.

INSIDER is a term of uncertain scope that refers to persons having some relationship to a corporation, and whose securities trading on the basis of nonpublic information may be a violation of law. Insider is broader than inside director.

INSIDER TRADING refers to transactions in shares of publicly held corporations by persons with inside or advance information on which the trading is based. Usually the trader himself is an insider with an employment or other relationship of trust and confidence with the corporation.

INSOLVENCY may refer to either equity insolvency or insolvency in the bankruptcy sense. Equity insolvency means that the business is unable to pay its debts as they mature while bankruptcy insolvency means that the aggregate liabilities of the business exceeds its assets. Since it is not uncommon for a business to be unable to meet its debts as they mature yet have assets that exceed in value its liabilities, or vice versa, it is important to specify in which sense the term insolvency is being used.

INSTITUTIONAL INVESTORS are large investors who largely invest other people's money, e.g. mutual funds, pension funds, insurance companies, and others.

INTERLOCKING DIRECTORS are persons who serve simultaneously on the boards of directors of two or more corporations that have dealings with each other.

INVESTMENT BANKERS are commercial organizations involved in the business of handling the distribution of new issues of securities.

INVESTMENT COMPANIES are corporations that are engaged in the business of investing in securities of other businesses. The most common kind of investment company is the mutual fund. An investment company differs from a holding company in that the latter seeks control of the ventures in which it invests while an investment company seeks the investment for its own sake and normally diversifies its investments.

ISSUED SHARES are shares a corporation has actually issued and has not canceled.

ITSA is the acronym for the Insider Trading Sanctions Act of 1984.

ITSFEA is the acronym for the Insider Trading and Securities Fraud Enforcement Act of 1988.

JOINT VENTURE is a limited purpose partnership largely governed by the rules applicable to partnerships. In an earlier day, many states permitted corporations to participate in joint ventures but treated as ultra vires an attempt by a corporation to become a partner in a general partnership.

JUNIOR SECURITIES are issues of debt or equity that are subordinate to other issues in terms of dividends, interest, principal, security, or payments upon dissolution.

LBO means leveraged buyout.

LEVERAGE refers to the advantages that may accrue to a business through the use of debt obtained from third persons in lieu of contributed capital. Third party debt improves the earnings allocable to contributed capital if the business earns more on each dollar invested than the interest cost of borrowing funds.

LEVERAGED BUYOUT (or "LBO") is a transaction by which an outside entity purchases all the shares of a public corporation primarily with borrowed funds. Ultimately the debt incurred to finance the takeover is assumed by the acquired business. If incumbent management has a financial and participatory interest in the outside entity, the transaction may be referred to as a management buyout or MBO.

LIMITED LIABILITY COMPANY (usually called an LLC) is an unincorporated business form that provides limited liability for its owners and may be taxed as a partnership. To create an LL. a certificate must be filed with a state official.

LIMITED LIABILITY PARTNERSHIP (usually called an LLP) is a general partnership that has elected to register under state statutes that provide some protection against liability for actions of co-partners. To create an LLP a certificate, renewable annually, must be filed with a state official.

LIMITED LIABILITY LIMITED PARTNERSHIP (usually called an LLLP) is a limited partnership that has elected to register under state statutes that provide some protection for general partners against liability for actions of other general partners. To create an LLLP a certificate, renewable annually, must be filed with a state official.

LIMITED PARTNERSHIP is a partnership consisting of one or more limited partners (whose liability for partnership debts is limited to the amount originally invested) and one or more general partners. To create a limited partnership a certificate must be filed with a state official.

LIQUIDATING DISTRIBUTION or **LIQUIDATING DIVIDEND** is a distribution of assets in the form of a dividend from a corporation that is reducing capital or going out of business. Such a payment may arise, for example, when management decides to sell off certain company assets and distribute the proceeds to the shareholders. Such a distribution may not be from current or retained earnings.

LIQUIDITY refers to the market characteristic of a security or commodity with enough units outstanding and traded to allow large transactions to occur without a substantial variation in price.

LOCKUP is a slang term that refers to a transaction designed to defeat one party in a contested takeover. A lockup usually involves the setting aside of securities for purchase by friendly interests in order to defeat or make more difficult the competitive takeover.

MANDATORY REQUIREMENTS are substantive statutory requirements that must be substantially complied with if a de jure corporation is to be formed.

MATURITY DATE is the date on which the principal amount of a note, draft, acceptance, bond, or other debt instrument becomes due and payable.

MD&A is an abbreviation for "Management's Discussion and Analysis of Financial Condition and Results of Operations."

MERGER is an amalgamation of two corporations pursuant to statutory provision in which one of the corporations survives and the other disappears.

MUTUAL FUND is a publicly held open end investment company that usually invests only in readily marketable securities. An "open end" investment company stands ready at all times to redeem its shares at net asset value. A mutual fund thus provides the advantages of complete liquidity, diversification of investment, and skilled investment advice for the small investor.

NASDAQ is an acronym for "National Association of Securities Dealers Automated Quotations" and is the principal recording device for transactions on the over-the-counter market.

NEGATIVE CASH FLOW refers to a situation where the cash needs of a business exceed its cash intake. Short periods of negative cash flow create no problem for most businesses; longer periods of negative cash flow may require additional capital investment if the business is to avoid insolvency in the equity sense.

NET WORTH is the amount by which assets exceed liabilities.

NEW ISSUE is a security being offered to the public for the first time. The distribution of new issues is usually subject to SEC rules. New issues may be initial public offerings by previously private companies or additional securities offered by public companies.

NIMBLE DIVIDENDS are dividends paid out of current earnings at a time when there is a deficit in earned surplus (or other financial account from which dividends may be paid). Some state statutes do not permit nimble dividends and the concept of nimble dividends has application only under traditional legal capital statutes.

NOMINEE REGISTRATION is a form of securities registration widely used by institutional investors to avoid onerous requirements of establishing the right of registration by a fiduciary.

NON-CALLABLE preferred shares or bonds are securities that cannot be redeemed at the option of the issuer.

NON-CUMULATIVE VOTING or **STRAIGHT VOTING** limits a shareholder to voting no more than the number of shares he or she owns for a single candidate.

NONVOTING COMMON SHARES are shares that expressly have no general power to vote for directors and for other issues coming before the shareholders. Nonvoting shares may be entitled to vote as a separate voting group on certain proposed changes adversely affecting that class as such.

NO PAR SHARES are shares issued under a traditional par value statute that are stated to have no par value. Such shares may be issued for the consideration designated by the board of directors. In many respects no par shares do not differ significantly from par value shares. In states that have abolished par value, the concept of no par shares is obsolete.

NOVATION is a contract principle by which a third person takes over the rights and duties of a party to a contract, such party thereby being released from obligations under the contract. A novation requires the consent of the other party to the contract, but that consent may be implied from the circumstances.

OPPRESSION in a close corporation involves conduct by the controlling shareholder that deprives a minority shareholder of legitimate expectations concerning roles in the corporation, including management and earnings.

ORGANIZATIONAL EXPENSES are the costs of organizing a corporation, including filing fees, attorneys' fees, and related expenses. Organizational expenses may also include the cost of raising the initial capital through the distribution of securities.

OUTSIDE DIRECTORS are directors of publicly held corporations who do not hold executive positions with management. Outside directors, however, may include investment bankers, attorneys, or others who provide advice or services to incumbent management and thus have financial ties with management.

OVER–THE–COUNTER refers to the NASDAQ securities market which consists of brokers who purchase or sell securities by computer hook-up or telephone rather than through the facilities of a securities exchange.

PAR VALUE or **STATED VALUE** of shares is an arbitrary or nominal value assigned to each such share. At one time par value represented the selling or issuance price of shares, but in modern corporate practice, par value has little or no significance. Shares issued for less than par value are usually referred to as watered shares. The Model Business Corporation Act (1984) and the statutes of many states have eliminated the concept of par value.

PARTICIPATING PREFERRED SHARES are preferred shares that, in addition to paying a stipulated dividend, give the holder the right to participate with the common shareholder in additional distributions of earnings, if declared, under specified conditions. Participatory preferred shares may be called class A common or given a similar designation to reflect their open-ended rights.

PAYABLE DATE is the date on which a dividend or distribution is actually paid to a shareholder.

PENDENT JURISDICTION is a principle applied in federal courts that allows state-created causes of action arising out of the same transaction to be joined with a federal cause of action even if diversity of citizenship is not present.

POISON PILL is an issue of shares by a corporation as a protection against an unwanted takeover. A poison pill creates rights in existing shareholders to acquire debt or stock of the target (or of the aggressor upon a subsequent merger) upon the occurrence of specified events, such as the announcement of a cash tender offer or the acquisition by an outsider of a specified percentage of the shares of the target. A poison pill raises the potential cost of an acquisition, usually thereby compelling the aggressor to negotiate with the target in order to persuade it to withdraw the pill.

POOLING AGREEMENT is a contractual arrangement among shareholders relating to the voting of their shares.

PREEMPTIVE RIGHTS give an existing shareholder the opportunity to purchase or subscribe for a proportionate part of a new issue of shares before it is offered to other persons. Its purpose is to protect shareholders from dilution of value and control when new shares are issued. In modern statutes, preemptive rights may be limited or denied.

PREFERRED SHARES are shares that have preferential rights to dividends or to amounts distributable on liquidation, or to both, ahead of common shareholders. Preferred shares are usually entitled only to receive specified limited amounts as dividends or on liquidation.

PREFERRED SHAREHOLDERS' CONTRACT refers to the provisions of the articles of incorporation, the bylaws, or the resolution of the board of directors, creating and defining the rights of holders of the preferred shares in question. Preferred shareholders have only limited statutory or common law rights outside of the preferred shareholders' contract. Provisions creating and defining the rights of holders of preferred shares may usually be amended without the consent of each individual holder of preferred shares if they are approved by the holders of the class of preferred shares.

PREINCORPORATION SUBSCRIPTION. See: subscription.

PRICE–EARNINGS RATIO is the ratio of earnings per share to current stock price.

PROMOTERS are persons who develop or take the initiative in founding or organizing a business venture. Where more than one promoter is involved in a venture, they are described as co-promoters.

PROSPECTUS is a document furnished to a prospective purchaser of a security that describes the security being purchased, the issuer, and the investment or risk characteristics of the security.

PROXY is a person authorized to vote someone else's shares. Depending on the context, proxy may also refer to the grant of authority itself [the appointment], or the document granting the authority [the appointment form].

PROXY SOLICITATION MACHINERY is a phrase commonly used to describe the process by which proxy documents are delivered to shareholders. Incumbent management of a publicly held corporation may produce large majorities of shareholder votes on many issues because of its ability to use corporate funds to communicate at will with the shareholders and its ability to represent their views as the views of "management."

PROXY STATEMENT is the document that must accompany a solicitation of proxy appointment under SEC regulations. The purpose of the proxy statement is to provide shareholders with the appropriate information to permit an intelligent decision.

PSLRA stands for the "Private Securities Litigation Reform Act of 1995."

PUBLIC OFFERING involves the sale of securities by an issuer or a person controlling the issuer to members of the public. Generally, any offering that is not exempt under Regulation D or the private offering exemption of the Securities Act of 1933 and/or similar exemptions under state blue sky laws is considered a public offering. Normally registration of a public offering under those statutes is required though in some instances other exemptions from registration may be available.

PUBLICLY HELD CORPORATION is a corporation with shares held by numerous persons. Shares of publicly held corporations are usually traded either on a securities exchange or over-the-counter.

PUTS are options to sell securities at a stated price for a stated period. If the price declines, a holder of a put may purchase the shares at the lower market price and "put" the shares to the put writer at the contract price.

QUO WARRANTO is a common law writ designed to test whether a person exercising power is legally entitled to do so. In the law of corporations, quo warranto may be used to test whether a corporation was validly organized or whether it has power to engage in the business in which it is involved.

RAIDER is a slang term for an aggressor, an individual or corporation who attempts to take control of a target corporation by buying a controlling interest in its stock.

RATIFICATION. See **ADOPTION.**

RECAPITALIZATION is a restructuring of the capital of the corporation through amendment of the articles of incorporation or a merger with a subsidiary or parent corporation. Recapitalizations may involve the elimination of unpaid cumulated preferred dividends, the reduction or elimination of par value, the creation of new classes of senior securities, or similar transactions. A leveraged recapitalization involves the substitution of debt for equity in the capital structure.

RECORD DATE is the date on which the identity of shareholders entitled to vote, to receive dividends, or to receive notice is ascertained.

RECORD OWNER of shares is the person in whose name shares are registered on the records of the corporation.

A record owner is treated as the owner of the shares by the corporation whether or not he is the beneficial owner of the shares.

REDEMPTION means the reacquisition of a security by the issuer pursuant to a provision in the security that specifies the terms on which the reacquisition may take place. Typically, a holder of a security that has been called for redemption will have a limited period thereafter to decide whether or not to exercise a conversion right, if one exists.

REDUCTION SURPLUS is a term used in a few states with par value statutes to refer to the surplus created by a reduction of stated capital. In many states, such surplus is treated simply as capital surplus.

REGISTERED CORPORATION is a publicly held corporation which has registered a publicly held class of securities under section 12 of the Securities Exchange Act of 1934. Section 12 may apply to issuers other than corporations. The registration of an outstanding issue under this section of the 1934 Act should be contrasted with the registration of a public distribution under the Securities Act of 1933.

REGISTRATION of an issue of securities under the Securities Act of 1933 permits the public sale of those securities in interstate commerce or with the use of the mails. That registration should be distinguished from the registration of already publicly held classes of securities under the Securities Exchange Act of 1934.

REGISTRATION STATEMENT is the document that must be filed to permit registration of an issue of securities under the Securities Act of 1933. A major component of the registration statement is the prospectus that is to be supplied prospective purchasers of the securities.

REORGANIZATION is a general term describing corporate amalgamations or readjustments. The classification of the Internal Revenue Code is widely used in general corporate literature. A Class A reorganization is a statutory merger or consolidation (i.e., pursuant to the business corporation act of a specific state). A Class B reorganization is a transaction by which one corporation exchanges its voting shares for the voting shares of another corporation. A Class C reorganization is a transaction in which one corporation exchanges its voting shares for the property and assets of another corporation. A Class D reorganization is a "spin off" of assets by one corporation to a new corporation. A Class E reorganization is a recapitalization. A Class F reorganization is a "mere change of identity, form, or place of organization, however effected." A Class G reorganization is a "transfer by a corporation of all or part of its assets to another corporation in a title 11 or similar case."

RESCISSORY DAMAGES are damages calculated on the basis of what an interest in a business would have been worth today if an invalid or voidable transaction that affected the value of that interest had never occurred.

RETAINED EARNINGS are net profits accumulated by a corporation after payment of dividends. Retained earnings are also called "undistributed profits" or "earned surplus."

REVERSE STOCK SPLIT is an amendment to the articles of incorporation that reduces the number of shares outstanding. Reverse stock splits may create fractional shares and may be used as a device to go private by reducing the number of shares to the point that no public shareholder owns a full share of stock, and then providing that all fractional shares are to be redeemed for cash.

REVERSE TRIANGULAR MERGER. See triangular merger.

RIGHTS are short term options to purchase shares from an issuer at a fixed price. Rights may be issued as a substitute for a dividend or as a "sweetener" in connection with the issuance of senior or debt securities. Rights are often publicly traded.

ROUND LOT is the standard trading unit of securities. On most securities exchanges a round lot is 100 shares.

S CORPORATION is a corporation that has elected to be taxed under Subchapter S. The taxable income of an S corporation is not subject to tax at the corporate level, but is allocated to the shareholders to be taxed at that level. S corporation taxation is similar but not identical to partnership taxation.

SCRIP is issued in lieu of fractional shares in connection with a stock dividend. Scrip merely represents the right to receive a portion of a share; scrip is readily transferable so that it is possible to acquire scrip from several sources and assemble the right to obtain the issuance of a full additional share.

SATURDAY NIGHT SPECIAL is a surprise tender offer which expires in one week. Designed to capitalize on panic and haste, such an offer may be made Friday afternoon to take advantage of the fact that markets and most offices are closed on Saturday and Sunday. Saturday night specials are prohibited by the Williams Act.

SECONDARY MARKET consists of the securities exchanges and over-the-counter markets where securities are bought and sold after their original issue (which took place in the primary market). Proceeds of secondary market sales accrue to selling investors, not to the company that originally issued the securities.

SECURITIES is a general term that covers not only traditional securities such as shares of stock, bonds, and debentures, but also a variety of interests that have the characteristics of securities, i.e., that involve an investment with the return primarily or exclusively dependent on the efforts of a person other than the investor.

SECURITIES EXCHANGES are markets for the purchase and sale of traditional securities at which brokers for purchasers and sellers may effect transactions. The best known and largest securities exchange is the New York Stock Exchange.

SECURITY–FOR–EXPENSES statutes require certain plaintiffs in a derivative suit to post a bond with sureties from which the corporation and the other defendants may be reimbursed for their expenses if they prevail. The Model Business Corporation Act (1984) does not impose a security-for-expenses requirement.

SENIOR SECURITY is a debt security or preferred share that has a claim prior to that of junior obligations or common shares on a corporation's assets and earnings.

SERIES OF PREFERRED SHARES are subclasses of preferred shares with differing dividend rates, redemption prices, rights on dissolution, conversion rights, or the like. The term of a series of preferred shares may be established by the directors so that a corporation periodically engaged in preferred shares financing may readily shape its preferred shares offering to market conditions through the use of series of preferred shares.

SHARE DIVIDEND is a proportional distribution of shares without payment of consideration to existing shareholders. A stock dividend is often viewed as a substitute for a cash dividend, and shareholders may sell a stock dividend without realizing that they are diluting their ownership interest in the corporation.

SHARE SPLIT is a proportional change in the number of shares owned by every shareholder. It differs from a stock dividend in degree; however, typically in a stock dividend no adjustment is made in the dividend rate per share while such an adjustment is usually made in a stock split. There are other technical differences in the handling of stock splits and stock dividends under the statutes of most states. Stock splits usually result in an increase in the number of outstanding shares.

SHAREHOLDERS or **STOCKHOLDERS** are the persons who own shares of either common or preferred stock. The Model Business Corporation Act (1984) and modern usage generally tends to prefer "shareholder" to "stockholder" but the latter word is deeply ingrained in common usage.

SHORT FORM MERGER is a merger of a largely or wholly owned subsidiary into a parent through a stream-lined procedure permitted under the Revised Model Business Corporation Act and statutes of many states.

SINKING FUND refers to an obligation sometimes imposed pursuant to the issuance of debt securities or preferred shares by which the issuer is required each year to devote a certain amount to the retirement of the securities when they mature. A sinking fund may be used each year either to redeem a portion of the outstanding securities or to purchase the securities on the open market and retire them.

SQUEEZE–OUTS are techniques by which a minority interest in a corporation is eliminated or reduced. Squeeze-outs may occur in a variety of contexts, e.g., in a "going private" transaction in which minority shareholders are compelled to accept cash for their shares, or the issuance of new shares to existing shareholders in which minority shareholders are given the choice of having their proportionate interest in the corporation reduced significantly or of investing a large amount of additional or new capital over which they have no control and for which they receive little or no return. Many squeeze-outs involve the use of cash mergers. Squeeze-out is used synonymously with freeze-out.

STAGGERED BOARD is a classified board of directors in which a fraction of the board is elected each year. In staggered boards, members serve two or three years, depending on whether the board is classified into two or three groups.

STATED CAPITAL in the old Model Business Corporation Act nomenclature represents the basic capital of the corporation. Technically, it consists of the sum of the par values of all issued shares plus the consideration for no par shares to the extent not transferred to capital surplus plus other amounts that may be transferred from other accounts.

STATED VALUE. See: par value.

STOCKHOLDERS. See: shareholders.

STRAIGHT VOTING. See: non-cumulative voting.

STREET NAME refers to the practice of registering publicly traded securities in the name of one or more brokerage firms with offices on Wall Street. Such certificates are endorsed in blank and are essentially bearer certificates transferred between brokerage firms. The use of street name shares has declined with the creation of a central clearing corporation and book entry registration of ownership.

STRIKE SUITS is a slang term for derivative or class litigation instituted for its nuisance value or to obtain a favorable settlement.

SUBCHAPTER S refers to the subchapter of the Internal Revenue Code of 1954 that regulates the S corporation. See S Corporation.

SUBORDINATED. See: junior security.

SUBSCRIBERS are persons who agree to invest in the corporation by purchasing shares of stock. Subscribers usually commit themselves to invest by entering into contracts defining the extent and terms of their commitment; at common law subscribers usually executed "subscriptions" or "subscription agreements."

SUBSCRIPTION is an offer to buy a specified number of theretofore unissued shares of a corporation. If the corporation is not yet in existence, a subscription is known as a preincorporation subscription, which is enforceable by the corporation after it has been formed and is irrevocable despite the absence of consideration or the usual elements of a contract.

SUBSIDIARY is a corporation that is at least majority owned, and may be wholly owned, by another corporation.

SURPLUS is a general term in corporate accounting that usually refers to either the excess of assets over liabilities or that amount further reduced by the stated capital represented by issued shares. Surplus has a more definite meaning when combined with a descriptive adjective from par value statutes, e.g., earned surplus, capital surplus, or reduction surplus.

TAINTED SHARES are shares owned by a person who is disqualified for some reason from serving as a plaintiff in a derivative action. The shares are "tainted" since for policy reasons a good faith transferee of such shares will also be disqualified from serving as a plaintiff.

TAKEOVER ATTEMPT or **TAKEOVER BID** are generic terms to describe an attempt by an outside corporation or group, usually called the aggressor or "insurgent," to wrest control away from incumbent management. A takeover attempt may involve purchase of shares, a tender offer, a sale of assets, or a proposal that the target merge voluntarily into the aggressor.

TARGET CORPORATION is a corporation the control of which is sought by an aggressor corporation.

TENDER OFFER is a public invitation by an aggressor to shareholders of a target corporation to tender their shares for purchase by the aggressor at a stated price.

THIN CORPORATION is a corporation with an excessive amount of debt in its capitalization. A thin corporation is primarily a tax concept.

TIP is information not available to the general public passed by one person (a "tipper") to another (a "tippee") as a basis for a decision to buy or sell a security. Trading by tippees in some circumstances violates federal law.

TRANSFER AGENT is an organization, usually a bank, that handles transfers of shares for a publicly held corporation. Generally, a transfer agent assures that certificates submitted for transfer are properly endorsed and that there is appropriate documentation of the right to transfer. The transfer agent issues new certificates and oversees the cancellation of the old ones. Transfer agents also usually maintain the record of shareholders for the corporation and arrange for the distribution of dividends.

TREASURY SHARES are shares that were once issued and outstanding but which have been reacquired by the corporation and "held in its treasury." Treasury shares are economically indistinguishable from authorized but unissued shares but historically have been treated as having an intermediate status. The Model Business Corporation Act (1984) and statutes of several states eliminate the concept of treasury shares. Under these statutes reacquired shares automatically have the status of authorized but unissued shares.

TRIANGULAR MERGER is a method of amalgamation of two corporations by which the disappearing corporation is merged into a subsidiary of the surviving corporation and the shareholders of the disappearing corporation receive shares of the surviving corporation. In a reverse triangular merger the subsidiary is merged into the disappearing corporation so that the corporation being acquired becomes a wholly owned subsidiary of the surviving corporation.

ULTRA VIRES is the common law doctrine relating to the effect of corporate acts that exceed the powers or the stated purposes of a corporation.

UNDERWRITERS are persons who buy shares with a view toward their further distribution. Used almost exclusively in connection with the public distribution of securities, an underwriter may be either a commercial enterprise engaged in the distribution of securities (an investment banker), or a person who simply buys securities without an investment intent and with a "view" toward further distribution.

UP STREAM MERGER is a merger of a subsidiary corporation into its parent.

VOTING GROUP is a term defined in the Model Business Corporation Act (1984) to describe the right of shares of different classes or series to vote separately on fundamental corporate changes that adversely affect the rights or privileges of that class or series. Most older state statutes use the terms "class voting" or "voting by class" to refer to essentially the same concept.

VOTING TRUST is a formal arrangement by which record title to shares is transferred to trustees who are entitled to exercise the power to vote the shares. Usually, all other incidents of ownership, such as the right to receive dividends, are retained by the beneficial owners of the shares.

VOTING TRUST CERTIFICATES are certificates issued by voting trustees to the beneficial holders of shares held by the voting trust. Such certificates may be readily transferable, carrying with them all the incidents of ownership of the underlying shares except the power to vote.

WARRANTS are a type of option to purchase shares issued by a corporation. Warrants are typically long period options, are freely transferable, and if the underlying shares are listed on a securities exchange, are also publicly traded.

WATERED SHARES are par value shares issued for property which has been overvalued and is not worth the aggregate par value of the issued shares. Watered shares is often used as a generic term to describe all shares issued for less than par value—including discount and bonus shares.

WHITE KNIGHT is a friendly suitor: a potential acquirer usually sought out by the target of an unfriendly takeover to rescue it from the unwanted bidder's takeover.

---

*

INDEX

References are to Pages

---

†